THE LION'S LAST ROAR

THE LION'S LAST ROAR

Suez, 1956

Chester L. Cooper

HARPER & ROW, PUBLISHERS

New York, Hagerstown, San Francisco, London

962

Grateful acknowledgment is made for permission to reprint:

Excerpts from *Riding the Storm 1956–1959* by Harold Macmillan. Copyright © 1971 by Thomson Newspapers Ltd. Reprinted by permission of Harper & Row, Publishers, Inc. and Macmillan, London and Basingstoke.

Excerpts from *Full Circle: The Memoirs of Anthony Eden* by Earl of Avon. Copyright © 1960 by The Times Publishing Co. Ltd. Reprinted by permission of Houghton Mifflin Company and Cassell & Co. Ltd.

Excerpts from *The White House Years, Waging Peace: 1956–1961* by Dwight D. Eisenhower. Copyright © 1965 by Dwight D. Eisenhower. Reprinted by permission of Doubleday & Company, Inc.

FIRST EDITION

Designed by C. Linda Dingler

Library of Congress Cataloging in Publication Data

Cooper, Chester L
  The lion's last roar.
  Bibliography: p.
  Includes index.
  1. Egypt—History—Intervention, 1956. I. Title.
DT107.83.C66 1978   962'.05   78-2121
ISBN 0-06-010858-4

---

78 79 80 81 82 10 9 8 7 6 5 4 3 2 1

For Hannah
1886–1976

CONTENTS

ACKNOWLEDGMENTS

There have been many accounts written of the Suez crisis of 1956; there will be many more. If this one adds to the reader's understanding of that complex and murky period of post-World War II history, it will largely be due to the efforts of those who helped reconstruct and relate the story of the lion's last roar.

Noëlle Beatty, assiduous and careful researcher with a discerning editorial eye, was both a willing assistant and a stern critic. She also prepared the bibliography. Rayola Dougher, who tactfully stopped counting the number of drafts of each page that went through her typewriter, cheerfully and intelligently produced the manuscript. Daniel Davidson brought his keen perception of international issues and an awesome knowledge of the literature to bear in reviewing the manuscript in its early incarnations. I can only hope that they realize how grateful I am.

Suzanne Gerson, Jane Freundel, and Eileen Harris helped immeasurably with research and other tasks and cheered me on when the spirit sagged. Marcella Jones' intimate knowledge of the Library of Congress brought forth elusive source material. Alan Teichrow and Thomas Duesterberg unearthed several important historical items. Robert Amory, William Clark, Jacques Billy, and Brigadier David Houston, together with a host of British, American, French, Israeli, and Egyptian friends who would prefer to remain anonymous, provided a wealth of firsthand information. Librarians at the Library of Congress, Chatham House, the Bibliothèque Nationale, and the American Embassy Library in Paris also deserve mention and thanks, as does Phyllis Hansen of the Carnegie Endowment, who facilitated progress by providing a hideaway office and other assistance.

Finally, and as always, there is my family—solicitous, encouraging, loving. Orah, Joan, Susan, and Ron make even the task of writing a book a pleasurable one.

I owe a special debt to the late Lord Avon (Anthony Eden). Desperately ill, in the winter of 1976, he nevertheless consented to a long interview on the painful subject of Suez, 1956.

But, in the last analysis, the book is mine, and I assume responsibility for all sins of omission or commission.

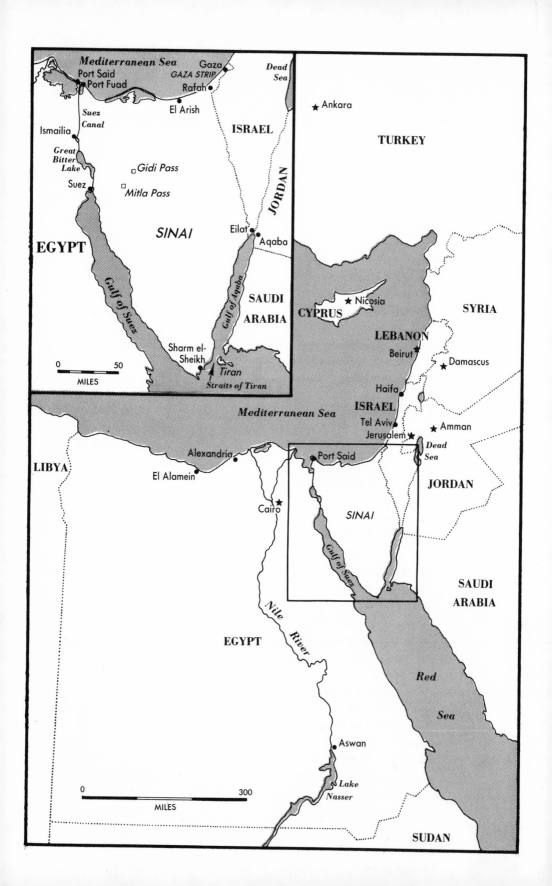

1

TURNING POINT

A narrow channel slices southward a hundred miles through Egypt's sands from Port Said to Suez. It is a man-made bridge of water between the continents of Europe and Asia. My first sight of the Suez Canal remains fresh in memory for I was on a consequential voyage. Virtually every day of the torpid journey from the Bay of Bengal to the Mediterranean and of the stormy North Atlantic crossing comes, still, easily to mind. That day in late 1945 when the crowded troopship inched its way through the Canal was the most memorable of them all. The USS *Patrick* had left India almost three weeks before. Except for the busy Ceylon harbor where we had made a brief fueling stop, there had been nothing to see beyond the bounds of the ship itself, nothing but vast stretches of water and sky.

Now, leaning over the rail, I could almost touch land—the driest land I had ever seen. But the moment was notable for more even than this—it was a sharp break in the dreary shipboard routine; even for those on board who had spent the war in the unfamiliar surroundings of India, Burma, and China, the sight of the Canal and of the town of Suez seemed strange, even romantic.

The queue of vessels awaiting the signal to inch their way north formed off the port on the Red Sea. The official start of the journey was marked by the appearance of a pink and bouncy British pilot who scampered briskly up the rope ladder in his natty cap, crisp white shirt, trim shorts, and knee-high socks. His arrival on deck was greeted by jeering hoots from thousands of grimy GIs. The pilot was soon joined by sullen platoons of ragged Egyptian Canal hands whose task it would be to handle the lines and the boat hooks as the *Patrick* was nursed through that thin gap in the desert. "Wogs are coming aboard!" some unseen authority warned over the ship's PA system as the Egyptians came over the side. "Secure anything valuable, everything movable."

The jeering and the warning sounded a discordant note coming, as they did, so soon after the lofty wartime oratory of Roosevelt and Churchill—the brotherhood of man and all that. I thought wryly of the shiny new world we were all—Yanks, Limeys, Frogs, and Wogs—about to enter. But this was quickly submerged in the fascination of the moment. The bustle

1

on board contrasted sharply with the lassitude on shore. Veiled women, pajama-clad men, fly-covered naked children, even a few moth-eaten donkeys and camels gazed solemnly up at the ship. Some scruffy shacks and a few ancient vehicles provided them with a bit of shade against a sun already scorching, although the morning was still young.

For me, at least, that November day was more than a sightseeing experience. I was weaned on a literary diet provided mostly by British writers—Dickens and Tennyson, Locke and Thackeray, Wordsworth and Browning, A. Conan Doyle and John Maynard Keynes. A groaning smorgasbord of poets, essayists, novelists, and—God help me—even economists formed kaleidoscopic impressions in my mind of an England I had never seen. And in the early 1940s my already strong case of Anglophilia had been consolidated by the retreat from Dunkerque, the Battle of Britain, and Churchill's ringing phrases.

But it was the British Empire rather than just England itself that, many years before, had stirred my imagination. A Union Jack drooping in the stagnant, hot air from a mast planted someplace in the cluster of buildings on the left bank of the Canal brought back memories of dreary schoolrooms ornamented only by a dusty picture of George Washington and a brightly colored map of the world. That map had given generations of schoolchildren an early, almost subliminal sense of the power of the British raj; except for Russia (green), the United States (also green), and China (yellow—racist?), nearly all the rest of the world—from the tiny British Isles to the vast Indian subcontinent—was salmon pink. The glue that held the geography of the Empire together, I was told by such authorities as Miss Donnelly, my third-grade teacher, and, much later, Winston Churchill, was the Suez Canal. The barely visible, limp British flag seemed a mute confirmation of their point.

At long last, our turn came to join the convoy of troop transports, freighters, and warships proceeding toward the Mediterranean. The ship moved slowly with but a few feet of water between its sides and the desert; we seemed to be gliding through the sand. The scenery on either side of the Canal was unchanging—a palm tree here and there, vast stretches of sand everywhere. The sleepy little town of Ismailia midpoint on the journey offered the only visual relief. The long passage was, in truth, a crashing bore. The air was still and the heat was oppressive—until the sun set, and then the temperature dropped so quickly and sharply that it became uncomfortably cold.

About fifteen hours later the ship finally reached Port Said. Dim electric lights and flickering oil lamps gave the town a mysterious, slightly threatening air. The pilot left us there without ceremony or notice. Ahead, in the blackness, lay the Mediterranean. In the darkness, looming over the town and the harbor, was the faint outline of a statue—a man. I learned years later that the towering figure memorialized neither an Egyptian nor an Englishman, but a Frenchman, Ferdinand de Lesseps, the builder of the Canal. Thanks to de Lesseps I was able to return home to America from the Far East weeks earlier than if the *Patrick* had been forced to make the long journey around the Cape of Good Hope.

A decade after that voyage much would change—the Canal, Egypt, England, the whole Middle East, the whole world. I wish I could say I sensed this on the deck of the USS *Patrick.* Such a chilly prescience would have lent a sense of drama to the occasion. But all I experienced as I looked out at the Mediterranean Sea was a sense of impatience to get home.

Soon after my return home I joined the Central Intelligence Agency, and several years later I became an assistant to Director Allen Dulles.* This involved working on matters coming before the National Security Council, the organization established by Congress in 1947 to marshal governmentwide advice to the President on international issues. Here I renewed my nodding acquaintance with the Suez Canal.

By the late 1940s it became virtually obligatory for every government agency involved in national security problems to take a periodic inventory of areas of the world that, for one reason or another, warranted special attention. Over the years, lists of "strategically important" territories, waterways, and communication crossroads were drawn up in the Departments of Defense and State and in the Central Intelligence Agency and were duly considered by the National Security Council. The lists were then filed away, sometimes to be referred to as the basis for major national security pronouncements (as in 1950 when Secretary of State Dean Acheson warned Moscow and Peking of the importance Washington attached to Asia's offshore island chain), sometimes to gather dust.

In every review, the Suez Canal ranked high. Occasionally, and especially in assessments emanating from the navy, Suez was ranked as of "critical" importance; presumably the United States would send military forces to the Canal area to protect it from falling into unfriendly hands. More often, and especially in assessments made by the army, air force, or State Department, the Canal was described as being merely of "great" strategic importance; presumably Washington would raise a hell of a ruckus in the UN if unimpeded international passage through the Canal

---

*I resigned from the CIA in the early 1960s when I was appointed to the National Security Council staff. A few years later I joined the Department of State as Special Assistant to Ambassador-at-Large W. Averell Harriman.

seemed threatened. But whether its importance was regarded as "critical" or "great," every reader who plowed through a long and dreary "Memorandum to the NSC" dealing with the strategic areas of the world had to conclude that American planners regarded the Suez Canal as a consequential piece of territory. This judgment was based on the world's growing reliance on Middle East oil, much of which passed through Suez, and on the vital role the Canal played in the strategic deployment of friendly military forces.

In retrospect, the whole process was probably taken too lightly. Even then, when Washington perceived itself as the world's policeman, American power, great as it was, could not possibly have been extended to shelter the Suez Canal, together with two score other areas, from Cuba to Thailand, on the "strategic importance" list.

In 1955, I was posted to the American Embassy in London to act as a liaison between the analytical intelligence services of the United States and Great Britain. It was in London I again met up with the Suez Canal. Only this time the confrontation was neither romantic nor intellectual; it was ugly and personal, and it would remain with me for the rest of my life. And it was there I found myself caught up in swift crosscurrents of a situation I did not fully understand and became involved in a series of American policies I intuitively felt were seriously flawed.

In the early summer of 1956 Gamal Abdel Nasser nationalized the Suez Canal, which since the nineteenth century had been under the ownership and control of France and Great Britain. Soon after, Britain, France, and Israel, too, went to war against Egypt. They comprised a strange alliance and acted out an elaborate but threadbare charade.

In late October, the Israelis invaded Sinai. The British and French intervened, ostensibly to insulate the Suez Canal from the fighting. But their unstated goal was to retrieve the Canal from Egyptian control. And their ultimate purpose was to overthrow Nasser himself. The first goal was contrived. The second and third were unfulfilled. In the end, Gamal Abdel Nasser carried the day.

In 1947 the British had, with a degree of fatalism if not enthusiasm, agreed to the independence of India. But a decade later London could not bring itself to accept the decline of British influence in the Middle East—despite the fact that no country in the area had ever been technically part of the Empire. Nasser was regarded as the evil influence behind every nationalist, anti-British movement in the region; to Britain, he was the Hitler of the 1950s. His seizure of the Suez Canal gave Prime Minister Anthony Eden the opportunity to strike back.

France had its own reasons for hating the new ruler of Egypt. It was fighting a desperate battle against a resolute and growing army of Egyptian-supported, left-leaning nationalists. At stake was the French "province" of Algeria. Nasser's nationalization of the Canal gave Premier Guy Mollet an excuse to eliminate Egypt as a source of aid to the Algerian independence movement.

As for Israel, it was hoping to free itself, at long last, of Arab terrorists, the fedayeen, who struck from across its borders. Israel was equally anxious to lift the crippling Egyptian blockade of the Gulf of Aqaba. Now, with clandestine but substantial support from Britain and France, David Ben-Gurion's armies could take over Gaza, the Sinai, and the Egyptian fortresses along the Gulf.

Great swings in the tide of history are frequently associated with single climactic events. Historians realize, of course, that these are but dramatic, visible culminations of forces and counterforces that extend back through time. Nonetheless, a particular incident can serve as a convenient peg on which to hang a complicated, untidy story: Sputnik as "the beginning of the Space Age"; the Cuban missile crisis as "a watershed in the Cold War"; Vietnam as "the end of America's innocence."

The Suez crisis was another such event, marking, as it did, a turning point in the post–World War II configuration of power in Europe and the Middle East. "Suez" cleared the way for a strong Soviet presence in the Middle East and thus changed the strategic balance there. It produced a major shift in Britain's perception of its international role. In part as a consequence of these developments, America began to play a dominant role in the Arab-Israeli struggle and in Middle Eastern affairs generally.

"Suez" eroded the Entente Cordiale; British-French relations have never since fully recovered. And "Suez" also placed the Anglo-American special relationship in grave jeopardy; two partners bound together by ties of culture and education dating back over a century, by intertwined threads of politics and economics, by close alliances in two bloody wars, by intimate friendships among their leaders, found in 1956 that their relations had plunged to the lowest point since the American Civil War.

Every major international crisis is a dramatic extravaganza—there is an all-star cast, high stakes are involved, the action takes place in circumstances of sustained tension. The Suez crisis was no exception. Indeed, it was a special example of the genre. Its plot called for brothers to become enemies, enemies to become partners; its denouement was marked by personal as well as national tragedy and triumph. Surely it had a star-studded cast: Edgy Eden, Dour Dulles, Nasty Nasser, Peripatetic Pineau, Bulganin the Bully, and Ben-Gurion the Bull Dog.

Each participant in the Suez affair can make a case for the role he played, but each case is truly not a little soiled and squalid. Stupidity and duplicity run deep throughout the course of the story. Intrigue and blackmail became the preoccupation of high councils. Pride, threat, and revenge became surrogates for cool and farsighted national policy. Each of the principals has attempted to rationalize what he did or failed to do. But in the cold, more objective light of history we see a stage crowded with dupes, naifs, bullies, and rascals. There were no heroes.

Tomorrow's scholars can carefully weigh the nuances and assess the barely observable influences that have colored and shaped the decades since World War II. But we must judge major events and those who have influenced them from ground level and in real time. More often than not, we ruefully conclude that our lives, and thus our era, appear to have been molded by the wrong men in the wrong places. What future historians from their lofty perches or we in the heat of the moment frequently ignore, however, is the role fortune or karma has had in influencing the acts of men, the turn of affairs. Chance or fate has frequently made the difference between triumph and disaster. The forces in play and the context in which contests are waged are at once so complex and fluid that even the most carefully planned campaigns have fallen victims to vagaries and accidents.

"Throughout the whole world," wrote Pliny the Elder two thousand years ago, "at every place and hour, by every voice Fortune is invoked and her name spoken: . . . She is worshiped with insults, counted as fickle and often as blind, wandering, inconsistent, elusive, changeful, and friend of the unworthy. . . . We are . . . at the mercy of Chance." At Suez in 1956 chance, too, was a member of the cast—a silent but important one.

"Suez," no less than other world crises, was unique. Confrontations in the Middle East since then have been very different—so different that reflections on what national leaders did do, did not do, or should have done in 1956 may be interesting, but seem hardly relevant. Yet history does not begin anew with every fresh generation of policymakers. To be sure, men and fortune influence the resolution of each major international event. And men vary, while fortune is capricious. But as busy officials themselves recognize in their more thoughtful moments, each crisis gives shape, texture, and color to those that follow. While "Suez" was sui generis, its shadow still hangs over much of today's world.

Thus John Foster Dulles, at the height of the crisis in 1956, took pains to distinguish between the Canal across Egypt and the one across Panama; he did not wish to see any arrangement for Suez that might prejudice continued American control over the Panama Canal. But twenty years later, America, too, would have to face up to this very issue.

There are, as we shall see, fundamental differences between Suez and Panama. But there are important similarities as well. They stem from the growing appeal and strength of nationalism—an appeal and strength that the Suez crisis did much to stimulate. The events of October 1956 should be heeded by those who continue to believe that even a major power can indefinitely thwart the nationalist aspirations of another, smaller one.

The great events that comprise the stuff of history are not encapsulated incidents with sharp beginnings, sudden endings. The Suez crisis did not emerge out of the blue in July 1956 when Gamal Nasser nationalized the Canal, did not melt into the night in January 1957 when Anthony Eden resigned as prime minister. And so, in what follows, I shall trace the saga back to the nineteenth century, where the roots lie deep, and follow it through to recent years, where the effects still remain. But mostly I shall address the crisis itself.

Much has been written about that sad, tense autumn more than twenty years ago. Some are self-serving accounts prepared by active participants who were anxious to put their own role in the best light. Others are polemical tracts written by outraged observers who were reflecting the frustrations and anger of that dark time.

This version of the tale of Suez takes into account memoirs, memories and, where possible, memoranda of several of the principals. But there were others—ambassadors, assistant secretaries, generals, and lesser officials—whose vantage point somewhat removed from the eye of the storm gave them a view of the crisis that adds perspective to the events of 1955–56. In the course of the telling, then, I shall bring in the views, concerns, and biases of many of my colleagues who were foreign service officers of the United States and diplomats and soldiers of Great Britain, France, and Israel. At its core, however, this is a somewhat personal story because I was a witness to this conflict of men and nations, this play of politics, this turning point in contemporary history, and feel bound to flesh out the story I saw unfold.

2

GENESIS

During the centuries that intervened between the Caesars of Rome and the Georges of England, Egypt lay all but forgotten by the European world beyond the Mediterranean. Europe was caught up in the flow of the Christian tide, the fortunes of local chieftains, the busyness of its political and cultural renaissance, and the excitement of overseas exploration and exploitation. There were momentary bursts of interest in Egypt, of course. News of Islam's triumph in Spain in the eighth century stirred Europe's religious and lay leaders. And the coast of Egypt even became a target for the Fifth and Seventh Crusades in the thirteenth century when the city of Damietta was captured and occupied. But by and large, to the Western world Egypt seemed far away and was out of mind.

As for the Egyptians, they enjoyed a period of intellectual and cultural brilliance under the early Fatimite dynasty in the tenth and eleventh centuries. But from that time on they spent virtually all their strength struggling against the cruel forces of nature and the hostile attacks of their neighbors.

By the end of the eighteenth century, the Egyptians, the Sphinx, and the River Nile were known to the West only as bit players, stage properties, or background scenery for Old Testament sagas and for Shakespeare's *Antony and Cleopatra.*

It was Napoleon Bonaparte who catapulted the land of the Pharaohs across two thousand years from ancient to modern history. Fresh from victories in Italy during the final days of the Directoire, he sought an even richer prize to consolidate his standing in Paris. France was now at war with England. What could be better than to deliver India, England's richest overseas possession, at the feet of Messieurs les Directeurs? And so it was that, on the eve of the nineteenth century, Napoleon instructed Paris in a lesson that London was soon to learn: The strategic importance of Egypt depended not on the resources to be found in its baked and barren land, but rather on its situation; it occupied a pivotal position between Europe and Asia.

Napoleon's dreams for Egypt were even grander than those of the Romans; by rearranging its geography, he would place French forces athwart England's sea lanes to India. With the Ottoman Empire (in whose domain Egypt lay) in a state of creeping decay, France might easily occupy this gateway to the Orient.

Perhaps the Directoire was convinced of the soundness of Napoleon's plans. Perhaps they felt more comfortable in the knowledge that he would be busily occupied far from Paris. In any event, within a year Napoleon received his marching orders: He was to take possession of Egypt, cut a canal through the Isthmus of Suez, and secure the Red Sea for the Navy of the French Republic.

Landing at Alexandria in 1798, Napoleon's forces quickly took over much of Egypt. His engineers were immediately dispatched to survey the Isthmus. For a few brief months it appeared that the French had outflanked their enemy. The British fleet controlled the Cape of Good Hope, which was the only sea route from Europe to the East. But if the French could hold Egypt until a shortcut could be constructed from the Mediterranean to the Red Sea, Napoleon could move quickly to his prime objective, the great subcontinent of India. On the way, Bonaparte planned to reduce, one by one, the British trading and military posts along the Red Sea. Victory must have seemed near to Napoleon during the early summer.

By the end of July he had marched from Alexandria to Cairo after defeating an army of elite Ottoman troops. He soon organized a modern administration and, with a formidable array of French scientists, engineers, and scholars, began a systematic study of Egyptian civilization. There was now only one obstacle in his path toward making Egypt a colony of France. It was the formidable Royal Navy. The French had permitted their own fleet to deteriorate after the Revolution; British ships of the line now outnumbered French more than three to one. But this was a matter of indifference to Napoleon. His métier was the overland movement and tactical deployment of troops, and he had a disdain, perhaps born of inexperience, for naval warfare. It was to cost him not only Egypt, but India.

In August 1798, during the Battle of the Nile, Nelson's fleet attacked and sank virtually every French ship anchored off the Egyptian coast. Napoleon's reach had exceeded his grasp; his grandiose plan and most of his forces were to be the first of many victims of England's sensitivity to any threat to India.

Napoleon and his army were now sealed off from France. They were left to fend for themselves in an inhospitable climate and an impoverished land. About a year later, however, Napoleon and a few members of his staff managed to slip the British blockade. He returned to Paris in triumph (bad news could be manipulated then, as now) and was soon elected (elections could also be manipulated then, as now) First Consul of the new French regime. His soldiers were abandoned to march and countermarch in the arid sands until a combined British and Turkish force landed in the winter of 1801 to finish off or kick out the survivors.

The British, too, left Egypt. They returned six years later, but now it was *their* fate to be thrown out; they met total defeat at the hands of the terrifying Mohammed Ali, who then ruled Egypt under the authority of the Ottoman Empire.

It would be fifty years before the French would mount another expedition to Egypt. This time, engineers rather than soldiers would comprise the force. It would be seventy before the British would return. And this time their warships and regiments would prevail.

The ancient Egyptians rivaled the Romans as history's most accomplished civil engineers. The pyramids of the Pharaohs still stand as a dramatic testimony to their expertise, but the irrigation network feeding off the River Nile also ranks high among their public works. As part of that irrigation system, a canal had been cut eastward across the land of Goshen to what is now known as the Bitter Lakes area of northern Egypt. There, another canal provided access to the Red Sea. Napoleon's military surveyors, probing for a promising route across the Suez Isthmus, found traces of these man-made waterways which had been built almost two millennia before the time of Christ. The Romans had reconstructed the canals during Trajan's occupation of Egypt, but sand and silt had taken their toll during the centuries that followed.

The idea of a canal to link the Red Sea with the Mediterranean did not die with the Caesars, only to be resurrected by Napoleon. It received a new impetus during the Age of Discovery. The sixteenth-century Venetians, whose monopoly of the overland route to the Orient was threatened by Vasco da Gama's voyage to India by way of the Cape of Good Hope, brooded about a water route across Egypt. The enterprise was too ambitious for them, however, and nothing came of it. During the following century other efforts were made to build a canal that would break the British and Dutch hold on commerce with the Orient around the Cape. They all aborted.

A look at a map of Egypt explains why the idea was so tantalizing once Asia was opened up to European trade. Trace the route across Egypt to India: A mere hundred miles of level land separates the Mediterranean from the Red Sea and the open ocean route to India. Now trace the alternative: Vessels must proceed from ports on the Atlantic or the Mediterranean, down the length of the African continent, around the tip of Africa, and then north and east. In the early nineteenth century a steam vessel took 113 days to make the voyage from London to Calcutta. From

Marseilles to Bombay, a ship could save almost six thousand miles if there were a shortcut across Egypt.

But time was not the only penalty a ship paid in its voyage around the Cape of Good Hope. It was a treacherous journey. For his sins, the captain of the *Flying Dutchman* had to sail the waters of the Cape for eternity. The sailors on the *Pequod* could vouch for the awfulness of that penalty: "But, at last, when turning to the eastward, the Cape winds began howling around us, and we rose and fell upon the long, troubled seas that are there. . . . Cape of Good Hope, do they call ye? Rather Cape Tormentoto, as called of yore; . . . we found ourselves launched into this tormented sea."[1]

It was no wonder, then, that a waterway through the Suez Isthmus stirred the imagination and fervor of traders and strategists alike. But imagination and fervor were hardly enough to accomplish the task. A map of Africa and India tells us only about geography—and the geography is deceptively simple. Masked by the short overland distance between the Mediterranean and Red Seas were formidable engineering problems; not visible from an examination of routes and distances were complex political interests and clashing national rivalries. And at least as important as technology and politics, the enterprise was expensive—very expensive. It is hardly surprising the venture lay dormant—more dream than reality—until Ferdinand de Lesseps, skilled diplomat and *entrepreneur extraordinaire,* arrived on the scene in 1854.

De Lesseps had served as a French diplomat in Egypt many years before. Like so many men who preceded him, he had developed a passionate interest in a great ditch across the Isthmus. Unlike many of his predecessor promoters, however, he combined imagination with skill, and fervor with energy.

Contemporary accounts paint de Lesseps in vivid hues, perhaps a shade brighter than life. "In the year 1831," one breathless biographer rhapsodized, "a young Frenchman was seen restlessly pacing the deck of the *Diogine,* the sailing packet from Marseilles to Alexandria. His slight active figure and erect carriage drew attention; yet more, his piercing eye and rapidity of speech and movement, exceeding the vivacity natural to a Frenchman. . . . Besides his native genius, energy and perseverance, de Lesseps derived, of course, peculiar advantages from his early training, his intercourse with statesmen, his knowledge of courts and familiarity with affairs of state."[2] To continue a list of his talents, contemporary accounts note that Frenchmen were awed by his grace in the ballroom and Arabs by his horsemanship.

But grace, verve, and athletic prowess were not necessarily the qualities demanded to meet a great financial and technical challenge. At the outset, at least, de Lesseps had few of the more mundane qualifications one would have thought were required to construct a canal through the Isthmus of Suez. "Known after 1869 as 'The Great Engineer,' he was no such thing. He had no technical background, no experience in finance. His skills as an administrator were modest."[3] Ferdinand may well have been what child psychologists call a "late bloomer."

Building the Suez Canal was by no means his only impressive achievement. At sixty-four, he married a girl of twenty and begat twelve children. And before he died at eighty-nine, he became involved in promoting the Panama Canal* and such other gargantuan schemes as building a railroad across Central Asia and creating an inland sea in the heart of Africa. But even Ferdinand de Lesseps' prodigious talents and vigor would have gone to waste had not fortune shone on him.

Ferdinand's father, too, had been a diplomat in Cairo. In the early nineteenth century, he had influenced the Turkish sultan, head of the Ottoman Empire and, therefore, the ultimate ruler of Egypt, to select Mohammed Ali as pasha, the ranking head of Egypt. When, in his turn, the younger de Lesseps was posted to Cairo as a junior member of the French Embassy, Mohammed Ali took him into his family. During these years Ferdinand befriended and tutored Ali Pasha's favorite son, Mohammed Said. The young Said, de Lesseps later recalled, "was enormously fat, and I made him exercise, much to the delight of his father." Although Ali insisted that de Lesseps review Said's homework at the end of each week, the Frenchman refused. "All I wanted to see was the column showing his weight for the past and for the week. If there was an increase, I should punish him, if there was a decrease, I should reward him."[4] It was this fat little boy who, one day, would play a critical role in transforming the Suez Canal from a dream into a reality.

De Lesseps had another stroke of luck. He was distantly related to the Empress Eugénie and had earned her gratitude when, during popular uprisings in Paris, he escorted her out of Paris to the safety of London. When, later, de Lesseps was seeking the support of Napoleon III for his great enterprise, the mission he had performed for his royal connection was remembered and did him no harm.

For almost a decade during the late 1840s and early 1850s a group of Frenchmen had been trying to obtain a concession from the ruler of Egypt for the right to dig and operate a canal across the Isthmus. But

---

*De Lesseps' daughter Ferdinande broke the first bit of earth for the Panama Canal on January 1, 1880.

Mohammed Ali had died and his successor, his grandson Abbas Pasha, was an unabashed Anglophile. All the French efforts were in vain and all their hopes dashed in the face of the new pasha's stubbornness and indifference. Abbas' death in 1854 marked a new era both for Egypt and Western Europe.

By now, de Lesseps was living in semiretirement in France, still dreaming his great dream. On learning that Mohammed Said, his portly little pupil from the early days in Cairo, had succeeded Abbas, he dashed to Egypt with hopes high and plans ready. He was not disappointed. Said himself welcomed him ashore at Alexandria. With great pomp the royal caravan made its leisurely journey across the sands to Cairo. On the way, de Lesseps instructed his ex-student on the merits of the great enterprise. His enthusiasm was infectious and Said was vulnerable. Soon after de Lesseps touched Egyptian soil he had gained both a concession from Said to build a canal and an all-important ally.

The royal concession to construct the canal was a necessary but not a sufficient step. There was still a long and tortuous journey ahead before Napoleon's abortive project could be set in train. Egypt was a satellite of the Ottoman Empire and owed feasance to Constantinople. Before de Lesseps could legally proceed, the Turks would have to approve the fact as well as the terms of the concession. But Constantinople was beholden for a host of reasons, some rather dark and devious, to London; and so the British as well as the Turkish government would have to be swayed. The British, for their part, were by no means enthusiastic.

Meanwhile, the French government was showing ambivalence as it became aware of the apparent international complications. To add to de Lesseps' problems, the French bankers had gnawing doubts about the financial and technical feasibility of his scheme. But at least de Lesseps had Mohammed Said's backing and was, as a consequence, further ahead than any of the dreamers and schemers who had preceded him.

His next step was to organize an administrative vehicle to finance, construct, and later operate the canal. Under the terms of Said's concession, de Lesseps was authorized to form an enterprise for these tasks. Thus was born the Suez Canal Company in 1856, an international venture with offices in Alexandria and Paris. Four hundred thousand shares in the company were offered for sale in 1858. Eighty thousand, or 20 percent of the total, were reserved in equal amounts for investors in France and England. Sixty-four thousand were reserved for the Egyptian government, and an additional forty-two thousand for Egyptian financiers. The remaining shares were made available for purchase in countries of Western Europe and in Russia and the United States.

In the event, 52 percent of the shares were bought by French financial interests (despite initial qualms) and 45 percent by the Egyptian government. One solitary share was bought by investors in Sweden; five shares were purchased in Germany, seven in Denmark. Great Britain, the United States, Austria, and Russia were the only countries solicited who ignored the opportunity to buy into the enterprise.

The American diffidence is understandable; the nation was then embroiled in the struggle over slavery and there was little capital available for exotic overseas investments. Moreover, the Red Sea was far away and of no commercial or strategic interest. But why had England, the world's greatest trading nation, not picked up even a token of the shares available? The answer lies not in the realm of economics, but of politics—more particularly, geopolitics.

The Suez Canal Company was a private undertaking that had the blessing but, at de Lesseps' insistence, was independent of the French government. De Lesseps' initial attempts to sell large blocs of shares to financiers throughout Europe and in America reflected his desire to provide the venture with a truly international flavor. But the opportunity to invest in the Canal Company was met with astonishing indifference everywhere except in France and Egypt. The disappointed entrepreneur was soon to discover that the highly visible French role in his project not only would result in a British boycott of the stock offering, but would also trigger a nasty case of paranoia in Whitehall. London chose to believe that the Canal Company was a front for French political and military machinations in the Middle East. Whatever the commercial merits of the canal, the British were convinced or professed to be convinced, that de Lesseps' company was an entering wedge for French control over Egypt and an ultimate threat to British communications with India. Lord Palmerston, then prime minister, hinted darkly that Paris would quickly introduce Zouaves, French colonial soldiers from North Africa, disguised as laborers to seize the canal once construction was completed.

In addition to its virtual monopoly of the sea lanes around the coast of Africa, England controlled an overland route, albeit a makeshift one, across Egypt. In the 1830s, an ingenious young Englishman, Thomas Waghorn, established a courier service to carry mail and parcels and to escort travelers between England and India. Several caravans a year utilizing a combination of horses, donkeys, and small craft plodded their way between Alexandria and Suez under Waghorn's watchful and enterprising eye. Passengers landing at Alexandria and embarking from the town of Suez could reach India many weeks earlier than if they sailed around the Cape. "His boats were not only the cleanest and swiftest on the Nile," wrote an admirer, "but such was his surprising influence over the Arabs of the river that he persuaded them to relinquish the semi-nude condition of their race for attire more in conformity with notions of European delicacy; and by a combination of individual daring and resolution, which the denizens of the Desert could well appreciate . . . he indoctrinated them with habits of regularity and docility."[5] Queen Victoria must have been proud.

By 1850 a railroad between Alexandria and Cairo, built and operated by the British, permitted somewhat faster and more comfortable service for at least part of the journey across Egypt. Thus, at the time the Suez Canal Company was being organized, the British had a commercial as well as a political stake in two of their own Europe-to-India routes. If they could kill off de Lesseps' scheme, they could have their crumpets and eat them, too. And that is what they tried desperately to do.

Lord Palmerston, foreign minister for eleven years before he became prime minister, led the British attack on de Lesseps' scheme. Palmerston, according to Winston Churchill, was a "jaunty" gentleman, the embodiment of "Victorian confidence." He was clever, stubborn, and tough— an indefatigable protector of British national interests abroad. Palmerston was not especially popular in the chanceries of Europe. According to a British diplomat of the time, "hesitation in him generally preceded action. . . . Amidst the impulses that impelled him onward, and the resistances that restrained his advance, he sought to steer a course which was rather that of safety than of adventure."[6]

In mid-1855 de Lesseps decided to confront Palmerston face to face in an effort to sway the prime minister. It was a fruitless exchange, but Palmerston, to his credit, was frank. He told de Lesseps that he opposed the canal because "of the fear of seeing the commercial and maritime relations of Great Britain upset by the opening of a new route, which in being open to the navigation of all nations will deprive us of the advantages which we at present possess." Aside from the threat the canal posed to British commercial interests, Palmerston told de Lesseps, he looked "with apprehension to the uncertainty of the future as regards France."[7]

Palmerston's first tactic was to ridicule the chances that the canal could ever be built; his second was to demonstrate that, if built, it would be a financial failure; his third, fall-back position was simply to lollygag on British participation.

The critical front was Constantinople, where the pasha's concession to de Lesseps was awaiting approval by the Ottoman sultan. It was there that Palmerston directed much of his efforts. The British ambassador to Turkey had the ear if not the affection of the sultan. Palmerston charged the envoy with the task of preventing Turkish ratification of Mohammed Said's agreement with de Lesseps. The ambassador did his job well, successfully postponing the sultan's approval for twelve years.

The delay at Constantinople was a nuisance rather than an obstacle; de Lesseps had started to dig seven years earlier. In the spring of 1859 he had personally turned over the first, ceremonial shovelful of sand at the Mediterranean terminus of the canal. The sultan had been outraged. Orders came from Constantinople to cancel the whole enterprise. But de Lesseps, with the timely help of Empress Eugénie, had by now finally received enthusiastic support from the French government—indeed, from Emperor Napoleon III himself. On the strength of this, and the agreement of Mohammed Said, he decided to push on.

In addition to the awkward matter of the sultan's disapproval, de Lesseps soon faced another problem. This was a nasty piece of business that was a product of his own shrewdness. Prior to the start of construction, de Lesseps had squeezed out of the Egyptian government a codicil to the concession of July 1856 that, in effect, required Cairo to furnish the necessary construction workers. In 1861, the British launched a lofty and effective parliamentary protest against this flagrant example of forced labor. They succeeded in keeping the issue before the public as well as the sultan, who, of course, had not yet officially sanctioned the building of the canal. In 1863 the sultan demanded, as a precondition to his approval, the abolition of forced labor. Construction gradually slowed down. But, in 1864, an arbitration commission presided over by Napoleon III determined that the Egyptian government should compensate the company so that the forced labor could be replaced by machines and by paid European and Egyptian workers.

The unsavory smell of that labor agreement would remain to haunt de Lesseps for many years. Thus, in 1880, a history critical of the Suez Canal stressed the pittance paid to Egyptian laborers and concluded on a dramatic note: "Mohammed Said little dreamed that he was consigning upward of twenty thousand human beings to their graves."[8] De Lesseps lost no time in responding to the charge. He was, he wrote, "deeply sensible of the falseness of the accusations. . . . The decree as to the employment of the fellahs . . . is considered a model of justice, humanity and wise foresight. It has closed the mouths of English attacks, which were founded upon supposed forced labor."[9] But de Lesseps avoided the matter of pay scales or the estimate of the number of workers who had met their death while building the canal.

In the meantime, de Lesseps' friend Mohammed Said had died and there was a new ruler in Cairo, the raffish Ismail Pasha. Ismail, a gung-ho enthusiast for the canal, ordered de Lesseps to move ahead. And in 1866 the sultan of Constantinople finally signed on.

The British opposition to the canal did not go unnoticed by one

American diplomat. "You are aware," Charles Hale, the United States consul general in Cairo, wrote to Secretary of State Seward in April 1866, "that the project of piercing the Isthmus of Suez . . . has previously been viewed with the utmost jealousy by the government of Great Britain, and that no expedient has been neglected on its part which diplomacy could suggest for putting obstacles in the way of the work. Without undertaking to say that there has been any change in the feeling of Great Britain in this respect, it may be affirmed that the death of Lord Palmerston and the recall of Sir Henry Bulwer from his post as ambassador at Constantinople have rendered the application of its policy less active; and Mr. Gladstone is even believed to be favorable to the enterprise."[10]*

Despite all the difficulties, the canal inched its way through the desert, south from Port Said** on the Mediterranean and north from the town of Suez at the head of the Red Sea. In the summer of 1869 the two ditches were linked at last and waters from the Mediterranean and Red Sea spilled into the Bitter Lakes about two-thirds across the Isthmus from Port Said. And there it was—the Suez Canal!—ten years and 433 million francs after de Lesseps himself dug his spade into the sand: 100 miles long, 50 to 100 yards wide, 26 feet deep.

The official opening took place on November 17, when a grand flotilla of ships moved in a stately procession from the Mediterranean to the Red Sea. The inaugural ceremonies were a combination of oriental pomp and imperial splendor, and the occasion marked a lavish momentary marriage of commerce and culture. Guests were served truffles in champagne, venison thighs à la Saint-Hubert, and capons garnished with quails. A season of opera in Cairo and the commissioning of Verdi's *Aïda* commemorated the event. An American magazine of the time reported that the harbor of Port Said was crowded with

> . . . the fleets of nearly every great nation, and the flags of the crescent and the cross floated from every mast-head. The Empress of the French, the Emperor Francis Joseph of Austria, the Crown Prince of Prussia, the Princess of Holland, the Khedive of Egypt, and a great number of distinguished men were assembled. A venerable sheik, with flowing beard, took his station in a kiosque and prayed, while the Europeans, in their brilliant uniforms, stood with heads uncovered. Afterwards a procession of Roman Catholic priests ascended a platform prepared for them and conducted their imposing services,

---

*It was around this time that Hale had arrested John Surratt, one of the men involved in Lincoln's assassination. Following a tip from the American ambassador in Rome, Hale discovered Surratt, dressed as a Zouave, in the third-class compartment of a ship arriving at Alexandria from Naples.

**Christened by de Lesseps in memory of Mohammed Said.

while the guns from the ships kept up a salute. The archbishop of Alexandria then delivered a very eloquent sermon, in which he extolled the merits of M. de Lesseps, comparing him to Christopher Columbus, who had, like him, opened the way to a new world.[11]

Although an official U.S. representative was invited, none was present. Congress had not authorized funds for this purpose, President Grant explained to the pasha and, since that body was not in session, he did not feel "himself justified in complying with Your Highness' request."[12] A member of the Boston Board of Trade, Nathan Appleton, however, did manage to attend.

The London *Times* account of the great event was only somewhat more soigné than the American account. Following a report on the opening of the Italian parliament, the *Times* reported that

> . . . on Wednesday night there was high pomp and festival at Ismailia. The dream of years had come true. The ships of two oceans met at the lake harbour in the midst of the Desert, having traversed in their double journey the Isthmus from end to end. A numerous fleet, bearing Imperial, Royal, and illustrious voyagers, had come from the Mediterranean to this half-way resting-place between the two seas, and, simultaneously with these, there arrived from the Gulf of Suez a convoy of ocean-going steamers. The passage of the Canal was thus accomplished. . . . There is no country in the world which has seen stranger processions than the Desert between Suez and the Mediterranean, yet this most ancient of lands saw something totally unlike all that it had ever seen before in the procession of Wednesday. Forty steamers followed one another in single file along the narrow waterway. . . . We rejoice that the undertaking has been completed, and join in doing honour to the man who, under obstacles and difficulties apparently insurmountable, pursued his grand design with unwavering faith to the end.[13]

With the Canal in operation, England became increasingly aware that the time for sulking was over. It would be prudent, even necessary, to recognize not only that the Canal existed, but that it was an imposing feat. De Lesseps was invited to London in 1870, where Queen Victoria presented him with the Grand Cross of the Order of the Star of India.

For the next several years prominent Englishmen would lament British shortsightedness. The Prince of Wales, in a journey to India in 1875, expressed what had long been in the minds of many: The Canal, he wrote to the British foreign minister, "is certainly an astounding work, and it is an extraordinary pity that it was not made by an English Company and kept in our hands because it is our highway to India."[14] Palmerston must have writhed in his grave.

British generals recalled how, during the Indian Mutiny in 1857, troops had to be forced-marched across Egypt rather than sent in transports on the time-consuming route around the Cape. Bankers and merchants had another level of concern: The increasing competition sparked by the Industrial Revolution had reinforced the economic arithmetic that started with the equation Time=Money. And the Canal across Egypt saved both.

It is not surprising, then, that within a year after the Canal opened, two-thirds of all the transiting traffic flew the Union Jack; a few years later, the proportion of British ships was even higher. And meanwhile, London noted wryly, its French rivals were in control of the finances and basking in the glow of international accolades. England would have to find a way to recapture the opportunity it had ignored a decade or so earlier. But how to get a piece of the action? A concurrence of events gave the British their chance.

The original cost of the Canal had been estimated at 200 million francs (about $40 million, then), but the actual expenditures added up to more than twice this amount. Moreover, the work had taken ten years as opposed to the estimated six. And so, although the Canal was an immediate success in terms of attracting customers—almost 300,000 tons of shipping (representing five hundred vessels) passed through in the first full year of operation—its profits for many years to come were committed to paying off short-term construction loans. This, of course, resulted in widespread disappointment in Europe's financial community. By 1871 the value of shares had fallen from the original selling price of 500 francs to about 200 francs.

Before his fateful meeting with de Lesseps, Mohammed Said had been living in the modest circumstances befitting, or at least necessitated by, the poverty of his realm. But hardly had the Canal construction began, when he became mesmerized by the wealth the shipping traffic would bring. He set off, forthwith, on a wild and premature spending spree; counting his tolls before they were collected, Said began to borrow heavily from European banks. He died owing vast sums.

Said's successor, the reckless, charming, fat, and ugly Ismail Pasha, was even more profligate. Despite his public orations on the virtues of economy, Ismail amply indulged his penchant for champagne and jewels. Extravagant tastes, costly playmates, and high jinks forced him to borrow $35 million a year from one or another accommodating creditor. Such trifling matters as interest rates and terms of repayment were beneath his royal concern. By July 1875 Ismail's financial circumstances had become intolerable. He had mortgaged not only himself, but his progeny's progeny as well. His plight was desperate and called for desperate action.

He offered a quick sale of his shares in the Canal—44 percent of the total —to a consortium of French banks. But bankers being bankers, they deliberated and dithered.

Prime Minister Disraeli did not dither. Rather, he dashed. If Palmerston had been cautious and gray, Disraeli was impulsive and colorful. Both men were enthusiastic and tireless in their efforts to maintain England's world position, but they perceived their responsibilities differently. Palmerston was anxious to preserve Victoria's empire, Disraeli to expand it. Disraeli's flamboyance made him vulnerable to shrill criticism from both fellow politicians and fellow writers. "The truth is," one disenchanted observer noted just at the time the prime minister was negotiating for a major share of the Canal, "that Mr. Disraeli has made politics the business of his life, his instinct teaching him that the England of today offered no better field for the display of his peculiar ability. . . . His intellect is the keenest; in power of sarcasm he is unsurpassed by any English orator of any age; he is full of resource, and can keep a cool head when both friends and foes are beside themselves in the turbulent passions of debate. His courage never falters, his pluck and endurance are invincible, and he is the best leader in the world to fight a losing battle."[15]

Disraeli sent his private secretary to Baron Rothschild in Paris with the message that the prime minister needed £4 million (about $20 million) within twenty-four hours. Legend has it that Rothschild thought a moment, nibbled delicately on a grape, and murmured something about "security." The private secretary quickly disposed of that matter: "Sir, the British government is your security." The deal was promptly closed. Disraeli sent a note to his queen: "It is just settled; you have it, Madam."

Ismail Pasha's 177,000 shares permitted the British to take over several seats on the Suez Canal Company's Board of Directors. The Canal was now a joint French-British enterprise, administered by private French banking interests, on the one hand, and the British government, on the other.

London's payment to Ismail was still not enough to get him out of debt. By 1876, the chances of Ismail's paying off his remaining, ever-mounting loans, now amounting to almost £100 million, were so dim that the British and French governments prevailed on the sultan in Constantinople to permit representatives from London and Paris to administer the finances of the Egyptian government, Ismail's protests that Egypt was "now part of Europe" notwithstanding.[16] The pasha was forced to swallow whatever pride he had left and to surrender control over his country's exchequer. Egypt would receive a payment from the Canal's operating revenues, but would have little voice in the management or operations of the company. In the end, Ismail was forced to abdicate. He lived out the rest of his life a poorer but wiser man.

America's perception of England in the early decades of the nineteenth century was colored by unpleasant, recent memories of the War of Independence and, a generation later, the War of 1812. Although the merchants and literati of Boston, New York, and Philadelphia kept in touch with the fads and foibles of England during the Regency and, later, with the more serious accomplishments of the early Victorians, most Americans were preoccupied with more immediate and personal concerns.

British international fortunes had turned during these years. The American colonies had now become the United States of America; Canada's bonds had been loosened as insurance against the disease of revolt; the war with France had sapped much of England's wealth; and the East India Company had pursued such clumsy and shortsighted policies in India that many Englishmen were ready to dump the whole enterprise. But somehow, out of the ashes, the politicians and soldiers and merchants were able to strengthen Britain's hold and expand her reach all over the world. The British flag was soon flying on every continent and over dozens of colonies. By 1880, more than two thousand vessels a year were transiting the Suez Canal, of which 75 percent were of British registry.

There was considerable suspicion of British international motives among many American officials in Washington and diplomats abroad during this period. London's activities in the Middle East were especially suspect. "It is the moral force of the English navy that has for many years kept this country in subjection to the Ottoman rule," E. E. Farman, consul general in Cairo, wrote to Secretary of State Evarts in the summer of 1880. "Egypt could at any time free herself from Turkey with the utmost ease, were it not for the support which the latter would receive . . . from England and France. There have been two reasons . . . for holding Egypt in subjection. . . . First, to strengthen the Ottoman Empire as a bulwark against Russian power and influence in the Orient, and second, because the tribute was really payable to Turkey's English creditors."[17]

In addition to the social differences that then distinguished the societies of nineteenth-century America and Britain and the suspicions each government nourished about the international political and economic designs of the other, both countries were restless and expansionist. This could have boded trouble had it not been that each was concentrating on a different territorial claim. Americans, in pursuit of their "manifest destiny," were flowing first in trickles and then in waves across a vast landmass to create a continental empire; the British, shouldering the "white man's burden," were moving across the seas to carve out a global empire.

Victorian England was then plump and ripe, bursting with the juices of domestic growth and foreign expansion. Englishmen basked in the glow of their queen and slept soundly in the embrace of the Royal Navy and the grace of God. If Victoria was queen, trade was king. Both queen and king flourished from the efforts of active, venturesome men who, with Bibles or guns, made up the vanguard of the trading posts, plantations, and coastal towns that were later to provide raw materials and markets for the pots, textiles, and machinery that poured out of the Midlands factories.

In 1870 John Ruskin pointed the way toward England's future destiny. In a speech that inspired a generation of Oxford men, he charged the young scholars with the need for planting the Union Jack ever deeper into the jungles, ever further across the seas. England, he thundered, "must found colonies as fast and as far as she is able . . . seizing every piece of fruitful waste ground she can set her foot on." In the accomplishment of this great task, de Lesseps' Canal would prove to be indispensable.

Optimism was the reigning mood and hyperbole flourished. The latter half of the nineteenth century was one "destined to rank with the foremost times of England's intellectual activity—to be classed . . . among the few culminating eras of European thought and art as one to which even the title of 'Age' should be applied. . . . We say the Age of Pericles, the Augustan Age, the Elizabethan Age, and it is not beyond conjecture that posterity may award the master epithet to the time of Carlyle and Freud, of Mill and Spencer and Darwin, of Dickens, Thackeray, and their successors, of Tennyson and Browning . . . not only for its wonders of power, science, invention, but for an imaginative fertility unequalled since 'the spacious days' of the Virgin Queen. The years of her modern successor, whose longer sway betokens such an evolution, have been so prolonged, and so beneficent under the continuous wisdom of her statesmen, that the present reign may find no historic equal in centuries to come."[18]

The responsibilities entailed in taking Western civilization to the far corners of the world were mouthed sanctimoniously from the pulpit of the Church of England and from the well of the House of Commons. But the white man's burden was somehow easier to bear when the profits were counted. And if not every adventurer took it seriously once out of range of priest and politician, some, like Sir Henry Stanley, apparently did: "I was compelled to bind myself to [the Zanzibari guides and bearers] on the word of an 'honourable white man,' to observe the following conditions as to conduct towards them: 1st, That I should treat them kindly, and be patient with them. 2nd, That in case of sickness, I should dose them with proper medicine, and see them nourished. . . . 3rd, That in cases of disagreement between man and man, I should judge justly, honestly, and impartially. . . . 4th, That I should act like a 'father and mother' to them. . . . They promised . . . that they would do their duty like men, would honour and respect my instructions . . . and would never desert me in the hour of need. In short, that they would behave like good and loyal children, and 'may the blessing of God,' said they, 'be upon us.' "[19]

This, then, was the spirit of England when Disraeli bought out Ismail Pasha and joined France as a partner in controlling the Suez Canal. And the Canal, providing, as it did, easier access to India, permitted Britain to expand and consolidate its control of that vast subcontinent. The island nation was now, truly, the seat of a great empire. And Victoria was now truly "Queen of Great Britain and Ireland and of the British Dominions Beyond the Seas, Empress of India."

Disraeli's brisk decision was probably the last bravura, self-confident episode of British nineteenth-century foreign policy. The latter years of the century were characterized, at least in the upper reaches of the British policy hierarchy, by hesitation and self-doubt. The practical advantages, if not the intangible prestige, of a continued outward thrust of British power had, by then, begun to pale. By 1890, like the queen-empress and the century itself, the Empire was getting old and tired. The spark was gone, the spunk was missing. And there were other younger and more aggressive nations pushing and shoving for foreign markets, for sources of raw materials, and for flagstaffs on which to hang their banners— Germany, for one.

In retrospect, the procession to commemorate Victoria's Diamond Jubilee in 1897, despite the pomp and color gathered from the four corners of the world, was more a cortege than a parade, a funeral for a dying era. The mood of a mission accomplished rather than of challenges still ahead is evoked in William Watson's bit of verse written a few years before the Jubilee.

> England and her Colonies
> She stands, a thousand-wintered tree,
>   By countless morns impearled;
> Her broad roots coil beneath the sea,
>   Her branches sweep the world;
> Her seeds by careless winds conveyed,
>   Clothe the remotest strand
> With forests from her scatterings made,
> New nations fostered in her shade,
>   and linking land with land.

Compared to the England of Queen Victoria, the France of Louis Napoleon was essentially static. France remained very much a nation of small crafts, individual shops, and tiny farms. The birthrate was dropping alarmingly, harvests were poor, wars in the Crimea and in Italy had taken a heavy toll, and the Church maintained a heavy hand in education everywhere and on life generally outside the big cities. While Great Britain harvested fruits from the Industrial Revolution in the form of textile mills, railways, and engineering plants, mechanics in France were concentrating on ingenious music boxes and other toys for the rich. To be sure, the arts and trade flourished, arches and monuments proliferated, and banking prospered, but rot was apparent everywhere.

England, throbbing, optimistic, and self-satisfied under the motherly, benign reign of Victoria looked with condescension and suspicion at her neighbor across the Channel. A British journal of the time summarized one Englishman's view of France during the Second Empire:

> We have already shown . . . the deplorable ignorance and superstition of the lower order of agriculturists and peasants of France, the endeavors of the clergy and the higher classes to perpetuate their debased condition, the intolerance and bigotry of the ultramontane press in France, the blasphemy of the St. Esprit brotherhood, and the facility with which the people in general resign themselves to any sudden impulse, political or religious, at the instigation of any clever, eloquent charlatan who may possess sufficient power to win the hearts of his hearers. . . .
>
> If we visit the salons of the *parti prêtre,* we shall be told that [Napoleon] has come among men at a time of universal infidelity . . . and that his first crusade is to be against England, the headquarters of the Evil One, the upholder of all the heretical doctrines of republicanism and socialism which have distracted the world during the last three centuries.[20]

During the latter years of the Second Empire, France clearly needed a dose of adrenalin, an exciting triumph to lift up its national pride and to raise its international prestige. Ferdinand de Lesseps provided his emperor and his countrymen with just what was required. By the latter part of the century the Suez Canal turned out to be the most precious jewel in Napoleon III's legacy to the nation.

3

THE LION ROARS

By 1880, England and France had consolidated their economic links with colonies in Asia, and raw materials were flowing toward Europe and manufactures toward Asia in an ever swelling tide. In the last year of the nineteenth century, almost 3,700 vessels, adding up to approximately ten million tons, passed through the Suez Canal. Kipling notwithstanding, East did meet West. And Suez was where they met. The shares of the Canal Company, which originally sold for 500 francs, were selling in 1881 for more than 2,000 francs and on the eve of World War I for more than 6,000 francs.

Although more vessels made the transit through the Canal flying Britain's Union Jack than all other flags combined, the waterway had tremendous significance for virtually every country in Europe and Asia. It established new patterns of trade; it awakened long dormant ports and peoples along busy new shipping lanes; it extended the reach of the world's navies. But for Egypt, the Suez Canal turned out to be a sour bargain.

One lonely contemporary critic of de Lesseps—an American—turned out to have more prescience than his readers at the time may have given him credit for. The Suez Canal, he said, "has proven to all the world —Egypt alone excepted—of great advantage. For Egypt, however, it has turned out to have been a commercial as well as political mistake. It has been the principal cause of her financial ruin, and led to the dethronement of her late viceroy. . . . It was a political mistake because it has placed Egypt upon the highway to India, thus making her an object of jealous solicitude, and of great importance from a strategical point of view to those nations whose power is supposed to be mainly derived from that country, or whose ambitions lie in that direction."[1]

By the early 1880s the situation in Egypt was ripe for trouble. There was widespread if inchoate discontent with the weak, spendthrift Ismail Pasha, who had sold out Egypt's share of the Canal to Britain and had been maneuvered by London and Paris into accepting foreign revenue collectors. The discontented found their champion in Colonel Ahmed Arabi, the first of many Egyptian colonels who would lead Egypt's nationalist struggle. Riots broke out in Alexandria and spread elsewhere. The

British and French soon confronted serious threats to their protégé in Cairo, to their own creditors, and to the Suez Canal itself.

In 1882, British and French warships sailed to Alexandria, but Arabi ignored them. And then, in an act that would change the course of Egypt's history, the French fleet melted away. Just as the French ships were sailing into Alexandria's harbor, the Chamber of Deputies in Paris, which was opposed to cooperating with Britain on any Egyptian venture, insisted the fleet be recalled. The field was left to the British. Undaunted, the British moved shoreward and shelled the harbor. Although the attack did little damage, it served to strengthen Arabi's determination to throw out the foreigners and remove the corrupt and compromised pasha. When Arabi showed no inclination to surrender, the British followed up their shelling with infantry landings at Alexandria. The troops encountered little resistance there and quickly deployed westward to secure the Isthmus of Suez.

Even in those days of gunboat diplomacy, the British attack on Egypt, and especially the shelling of Alexandria, aroused considerable anger both in Britain itself and abroad. In England, Lord Randolph Churchill accused Prime Minister Gladstone of having engaged in a "criminal act" and hoped that the British troops would be thrown out of Egypt "bag and baggage."[2]

In America, the Boston entrepreneur and friend of de Lesseps, Nathan Appleton wrote that "the bombardment of Alexandria during the summer of 1882 was one of the most . . . uncalled for events in modern history. It was a mere excuse to try to seize possession of Egypt and the Suez Canal. . . . The British . . . troops were ordered to attack the poor natives, half naked and armed only with shields and spears! This was a sad day for so-called British civilization and Christianity."[3]

De Lesseps, who had long since retired to France, was outraged at the thought of the British gaining physical control over the project he had worked so hard to complete against opposition from London. He sent a message to Arabi that he was ready to dash to Egypt to assure that "not a single English soldier shall disembark without being accompanied by a French soldier. I answer for everything!" Arabi's reply was polite but not altogether convincing in its expression of appreciation. Nor was it very reassuring; it warned de Lesseps that in order to halt the British advance, the Canal would probably have to be destroyed.

Neither de Lesseps nor Arabi had an opportunity to transform words into action. The British moved swiftly to occupy Port Said and then Ismailia. With control over the Canal assured, they pressed on to trounce Arabi's forces. After a brief interruption, traffic through the Canal was restored under the continued management of the Suez Canal Company.

But now, although the French still had majority control over the Canal Company, the British had exclusive control over the Canal and were in a position to prevent transit by any nation. British forces were based in the Canal area and Egypt became beholden to Britain. Another area of the world would be colored pink on Rand McNally's map.

As far as Egypt was concerned, the British could, at long last, relax —at least momentarily. Churchill put it well: With Disraeli's purchase of Ismail Pasha's shares, "the route to India was safeguarded, a possible threat to British naval supremacy was removed, and—of fateful importance for the future—Britain was inexorably drawn into Egyptian politics."[4] For more than seven decades Great Britain enjoyed the economic and strategic benefits and accepted the political complications that were Disraeli's legacy.

The French, for their part, were irritated and worried at the sudden turn of events that gave the British such dominance over traffic through the Canal. Other maritime nations, too, were concerned. After several years of negotiating, bickering, and haggling, an international conference was called in Constantinople to guarantee free passage to ships of all flags.

The Constantinople Treaty of 1888, signed by nine European powers, gave the Canal its international birthright. It provided for unfettered international transit even after the expiration in 1968 of the concession to the Suez Canal Company. That Egypt itself was not a signatory gave none of the participants much pause. These were, after all, the days of emperors and empires. Egypt happened to be a chattel of the sultan in Constantinople and a ward of the empress in London. With or without Cairo's consent, de Lesseps' ditch had now become, by international agreement, an international waterway. In the stormy decades ahead, the Canal would fare better than any of the signatory nations.

World trade, some pundits tell us, is the outrider of world peace. Possibly so. What these savants frequently overlook, however, is that trade is also often the precursor of vicious competition among nations and economic nationalism within them. The Suez Canal facilitated the international movement of pots and textiles, iron and cotton, to and from Asia and thereby conceivably contributed to world harmony. But the shortcut to India and the Orient also intensified the quest for markets and raw materials among the newly industrialized nations of Europe.

In the event, the Canal turned out to be more than just an artery for goods and travelers. From that moment in the desert when de Lesseps first enlisted the support of Mohammed Said, the Canal was destined to become a strategic prize that would aggravate nationalist rivalries among restive nations. It was a wedge into Asia at the disposal of whatever country controlled Egypt. As shrewd old Lord Palmerston foresaw, control of Egypt was a necessary launching platform for any challenge to England's hegemony east of Suez.

By the turn of the century, a half dozen countries of Europe were pressing to extend their power or their influence into the Middle East. Britain had consolidated its control over the sea-lanes to India by alliances with the sheikdoms bordering the Red Sea. France and Italy had already moved across the Mediterranean to cut large swaths of colonies out of North and East Africa. Germany, recently united and now under the fervently expansionist Kaiser Wilhelm II, was determined to make up for the time and opportunities it had lost during the nineteenth century; it proceeded to establish economic and military footholds in the Middle East and Africa. Russia was casting about to obtain access to the Mediterranean. And, finally, Turkey, smarting from the loss of control over Egypt and too weak to seek revenge on its own, was seeking allies, opportunities, and means to force the British out of the Middle East.

It must have taken little persuasion by Germany to gain Turkish enthusiasm for the construction of a railroad from Berlin to Baghdad. The advantages of such a direct route were obvious: Germany would have fast overland communications into the northern tier of Africa; both Turkey and Germany could quickly move forces to threaten British control of both Egypt and the Canal; and Turkey would be within easy reach of its dependencies, Syria, Jordan, and Palestine. For the rickety Ottoman Empire, all of this seemed worth a great price. But whether it was worth the price Turkey would eventually have to pay is another matter.

Great Britain, sensitive to its vulnerable and critical communication lines with India and already wary of the kaiser's ambitions, was nonetheless tardy in recognizing the threat the proposed German-Turkish railroad posed to its position in the Middle East. Only later, in 1906, did London insist on controlling the section of the railroad between Baghdad and the Persian Gulf.

Although the British were slow to grasp what Germany was up to, their suspicions were eventually aroused when they realized that German officers were training the Turkish army and that German agents were winning (or at least renting) friends on Egypt's borders. German and Turkish intentions became even clearer when, after the British confiscated a Turkish warship being built in a Scottish shipyard, Berlin promptly presented the sultan's navy with two cruisers.

By 1914 any match thrown by anyone almost anywhere on Europe's smoldering continent would have set off the flames. In the summer of that year, an assassin at Sarajevo did the deed.

Turkey hung on to a precarious prearranged neutral perch for the first few months of the war and reminded Britain that Egypt was, and would continue to be, an integral part of the Ottoman Empire. Soon after Turkey joined Germany as a belligerent, London informed Constantinople that it no longer recognized Turkish suzerainty over Egypt; henceforth, the Foreign Office announced in December 1914, "Egypt will . . . constitute a British Protectorate."

For the first time since Britain had taken over control of the Suez Canal thirty years before, this vital link between East and West was threatened. The Canal and the key towns along it—Port Said, Ismailia, and Suez—were the focus of British military activity in Egypt. Enemy ships were cleared from the Canal and tight security was established from one end to the other. All of Egypt was placed under British martial law. What had been a diaphanous overlay of British political administration now became a thick coat of military control.

There was deep concern in London that such a conspicuous transfer of authority from Muslim Turkey to Christian Britain would turn Egyptian troops into a sullen, perhaps dangerous mob. But the British need not have worried; Cairo's army shifted its loyalties, if not its affections, to Egypt's new masters.

The British promptly organized an auxiliary army corps comprised of twenty thousand Egyptian recruits. The move was none too soon. Large Turkish armies were threatening Egypt from their positions in Syria and Palestine and, in early 1915, attacked the Canal. The British Empire troops and their Egyptian auxiliaries beat back the assault. For the next three years the Turks launched occasional harassing raids, but never again seriously threatened the Canal or Egypt itself. And then, in September 1918, the Turks were decisively trounced by an army of British, Australian, and New Zealand troops. The senile, wheezing Ottoman Empire, more than four centuries old, breathed its last in the scorching sands of Palestine. Although the war against Germany was to continue for many more weeks, the fighting in the Middle East was now ended.

The long, awful war left all of Europe prostrate. A whole generation had died and millions more were to live out their lives with damaged bodies, poisoned lungs, missing limbs—or worse. In France alone, a half million buildings and five thousand miles of railroad were destroyed. Inflation, starvation, debilitation—this was the harvest of the Great War for much of Central Europe, France, and Italy. They soon produced a twisted, ugly atmosphere of hopelessness, degradation, and despair. This, in turn, grew into anarchy and tyranny—and into another hideous conflict two decades later.

Although the war had exacted a terrible toll on British life and substance, the United Kingdom emerged better off than many of its continental neighbors. Its parliamentary government and royal house provided a sense of political continuity, its lands and cities had been spared the ravages of the fighting, and its overseas empire remained intact.

Despite the need to reconstruct its economy and regenerate its social structure at home—or perhaps because of it—Britain was determined to expend resources and deploy manpower, both now scarce, in consolidating and expanding its hold over territories in Asia, Africa, and the Middle East. Meanwhile, Russia was in the throes of revolution, Turkey and Germany were effectively sidelined, Italy and France were in political turmoil. As a consequence, much of the Middle East became, in the words of the geopoliticians, "a political vacuum."

London lost little time in filling the vacuum. It moved quickly to strengthen its authority over areas it had long controlled and to stake out new military bases and political enclaves from the lands once presided over by the tributary chiefs of the Ottoman sultans. Iraq, Trans-Jordan, and Palestine became British mandates; British troops occupied Iran; the British secured special military and political rights in the desert sheikhdoms bordering the Persian Gulf and Arabian Sea. And, most important, Egypt, which for decades had been under tight but vaguely articulated British influence, was internationally recognized as a formal British Protectorate under the terms of the Versailles Treaty.

For many Egyptians, the "Protectorate" arrangement was insulting, implying as it did that Egypt, with its thousands of years of history, was incapable of running its own affairs. One Egyptian diplomat put the case eloquently in a letter to *The Nation:*

> Sir, It is unquestionable that the English are a highly practical people. . . . But great as their reputation in this respect may be, in the Nile Valley this practical sense has found itself at a loss . . . .
>
> There exists to-day no other means of winning over the Egyptians than to sincerely seek their friendship, and to base it on a formal agreement to which they would be freely consenting parties. Egypt is the natural guardian of the route to India . . . it is absolutely futile to oppress or to thwart the guardian of one of the most important of the world's corridors.
>
> We refuse to admit that measures as sterile as those that have been applied to Egypt, during a period of almost eighteen months, are a token of political incapacity. . . . We are rather inclined to believe that the errors of English policy in Egypt are due to an ignorance of the veritable situation of the country and

of the state of mind of the Egyptians. . . .

English officials and writers . . . remain slaves of a false notion
of national pride, which by keeping them aloof from the moral and
psychological life of the Egyptians, condemns them to complete
isolation. They ignore everything concerning the people, including
even the social elements of which the nation is composed. . . . From
such an ignorance of the social and psychological conditions of a
whole people, the most unfortunate political conceptions were inevitably bound to spring.[5]

The United States had little direct exposure to the carnage of World
War I. At the war's end, Americans found themselves with an expanded
industrial base, a skilled work force, a high standard of living—and a
desire to wash their hands of Europe and its squabbles.

Scholars and laymen alike often refer to an "isolationist" tradition
in United States foreign policy. But this is an oversimplification. To be
sure, from the early days of the republic until 1917, there had been a
deep-seated desire to shed the problems and the quarrels of the "old
countries"; it was to Europe, not to the rest of the world, that a policy
of "isolationism" applied. Businessmen, missionaries, politicians, and
soldiers were eager to involve themselves and America in Asia and Latin
America.*

It was this American determination to remain aloof from Europe that
President Woodrow Wilson challenged at the end of World War I. But
the determination was too deep-rooted; Wilson was incapable of turning
it around. God knows he tried!

On September 25, 1919, Wilson was in Pueblo, Colorado. He was
there for the same reason he had traveled to scores of towns across
America—to marshal public support against a Congress that scoffed at his
dream of a world united under the League of Nations. Thousands of
people had come from tens of miles away in their tin lizzies, ranch trucks,
and horse-drawn buggies to hear the President talk of war and peace:

Mothers who lost their sons in France have come to me and,
taking my hand, have shed tears upon it . . . their sons saved the
liberty of the world. They believe that wrapped up with the liberty
of the world is the continuous protection of that liberty by the con-
certed powers of all civilized people. They believe that this sacrifice
was made in order that other sons should not be called upon for the
gift of life. . . .

There seems to stand between us and the rejection or qualification of [the League] the serried ranks of those boys in khaki, not only

*Africa was long to remain terra incognita.

these boys who came home, but those dear ghosts that still deploy upon the fields of France.

It was probably the most eloquent of a hundred eloquent pleas Wilson had made in the course of that summer. He rang all the changes. Even the speech-numbed corps of cynical reporters who had accompanied the President on his three-week swing through the West were moved.

But Wilson had shared his dream for the last time. Felled by a stroke, he was rushed back to Washington. The man would linger for a few years, paralyzed, debilitated, but the President and his dream died that day. A year later Warren G. Harding would be elected to preside over America's return to "normalcy."

America in 1919 was not ready for the League. A great war was not enough to cause Americans to forsake a long-standing tradition. But if the American people and their representatives in Congress were reluctant to get involved abroad, American corporations were not. Especially the oil companies. Especially in the Middle East. Soon the Department of State recognized the important American political and economic interests in the area. Stretches of desert and ancient towns leapt from the pages of the Old Testament and became matters of current concern in executive suites of New York office buildings and in newly created offices of the State Department.

Although virtually all of the Middle East on that schoolroom map was salmon pink, a more politically aware cartographer would have taken pains to color some areas a shade less pink than others. For, by the time I reached the third grade, the British, as part of the Protectorate arrangement, had agreed to establish a constitutional monarchy in Egypt and to permit a substantial amount of independence for the Egyptian people— more independence than they had had since the late nineteenth century.

But a "substantial amount of independence" is not the same as true sovereignty. The British still hung on. Britain retained control over the Egyptian Army, and British High Commissioner Lord Allenby remained very much in evidence to assure that Great Britain's interests were not overlooked or compromised in the flush of the new freedom. Under the Protectorate terms, British troops continued to be responsible for protecting the Suez Canal. Further wounding Egyptian pride, His Majesty's soldiers were garrisoned in Cairo, ostensibly because of inadequate barracks and other military facilities in the Isthmus area.

The conspicuous presence of British forces and the less conspicuous but no less irksome role of the high commissioner were obviously anathema to Egypt's nationalists. Even more galling was the growing popular realization that the Suez Canal had been stolen from them decades before by a dissolute Egyptian pasha and a canny British prime minister. And, finally, conditions among the Egyptians themselves were deplorable. In the late 1930s Egypt's mortality rate was among the highest in the world. Less than one percent of the national budget was allocated to education and, as a consequence, only one person in twenty could read or write. It was no wonder that the voice of nationalism was becoming more strident and more effective.

Italy's forays into countries close to Egypt in the late twenties and early thirties gave courage to the nationalists in Cairo struggling for a greater degree of independence and gave pause to His Majesty's ministers in London. Under the shadow of Mussolini's expansionist threats in the Mediterranean and his brutality in Ethiopia, Egyptian nationalists finally gained a place in the sun.

In 1936, in exchange for a British naval base at Alexandria, London agreed to share the defense of the Canal with the Egyptians and to give the government in Cairo the substance as well as the trappings of independence. Under the agreement Egypt gained a modest representation on the Board of Directors of the Canal Company and an annual rental payment for company facilities. Some Egyptian technicians and administrators were given middle-level jobs in the operation of the Canal. For its part, Egypt, recognizing the tense international situation, permitted thousands of British troops to stay in Cairo (where they remained until after the end of World War II).

Hardly had the British extended their control throughout the Middle East in the years after the First World War, when, by the will or the whim of Allah, the importance of the area to all the Great Powers vastly increased. What, only a decade before, had been simply a piece of strategic geography now possessed a resource more precious than gold. Oil had been discovered in Iran a few years before World War I, and extensive exploration was being frenetically pursued throughout the Middle East in the postwar years. At the urging of Winston Churchill, then First Lord of the Admiralty, the British navy had begun to convert from coal to oil in 1913. By the early 1920s most of the world's navies and merchant fleets were following suit. Soon automobiles, with their insatiable appetite for petroleum products, would crowd the highways of Western Europe and North America. And soon, too, large new industrial complexes, electric power stations, and residences would depend on oil for fuel.

If the Suez Canal had been an important waterway for European trading countries in the late nineteenth and early twentieth centuries, it became a strategic, industrial, and commercial artery for every industrialized nation in the decades following World War I. When, during the late 1930s, war loomed again, it was clear to every General Staff that the bountiful reservoir of oil in the Middle East would be a principal ingredient for victory. Control of the Canal and the oil-rich lands in the region ranked high in the planning of a dozen ministries of war.

International rivalries fueled now by new nationalist hysteria were running rampant once more throughout Europe. In Asia, Japan, taken over by ambitious militarists, set the pace. The "war to save democracy" had spawned brutal dictatorships. And the "war to end war" had led to war. It was just as well that Woodrow Wilson did not live to see his dark forebodings come to pass.

World War II burst upon Europe on September 1, 1939, with Hitler's attack on Poland. This time, however, Turkey remained neutral until the war was almost over. It was Mussolini's Italy that posed an early threat to the British position in the Mediterranean. And this time the Middle East, and especially the northern tier of Africa, became a major theater of battle.

Mussolini was an enthusiastic and extravagant purveyor of anti-British and anti-French oratory. But Italy remained a nonbelligerent until June 1940 when, after the smashing of the French lines by the Germans (in the words of Winston Churchill), "the hand that held the dagger plunged it into its neighbor's back."

Before Mussolini's entry into the war, Italian ships, even troop transports and arms-laden warships, were moving freely through the Suez Canal. The British scrupulously observed the terms of the 1888 Constantinople Convention, which provided that ships of all nonbelligerent nations be permitted passage. They did so even though British intelligence knew Rome was reinforcing Italian garrisons in Libya and East Africa and was providing money and supplies to Axis fifth columns in Port Said and Ismailia.

In the spring of 1940, the war, now nine months old, had exploded from a tense, watchful stalemate, to swift, deadly movement—"blitzkrieg." Hitler's divisions smashed into and over Norway, Denmark, Holland, Belgium, and then France.

Britain stood alone in peril. Her army was all but crippled by the hopeless battles on the Continent. Her navy was spread thin over the length and breadth of the oceans. The Royal Air Force, itself understrength, was almost all that remained in the British arsenal. But in May a critical reinforcement arrived from the front bench of the House of Commons. It appeared in the rotund contours of Winston Churchill.

Churchill replaced the discredited Neville Chamberlain as prime minister in the nick of time. The British needed everything they could bring to hand that spring and summer—strength, stamina, the RAF, and Winston Churchill. For many long weeks it was all they had. But more was to come. By late autumn America awoke from its lethargy with a ground-swell of sentiment to provide arms and munitions to hard-pressed Britain.

Franklin Roosevelt sounded the death knell for America's neutrality in the dawn of the New Year. "We look forward," he said in his State of the Union address, "to a world founded upon four essential human freedoms. . . ." Soon after, America threw a lifeline across the Atlantic in the form of the Lend-Lease Act.* A stream of merchant ships loaded with food, equipment, and ammunition began to move in a seemingly endless convoy.

Across the Channel Adolf Hitler felt supremely confident. France and the Low Countries were now out of the war and Great Britain was reeling from air raids and still in shock from its efforts to stem the tide of German armor on the European mainland. This was the time, he was sure, to implement his grand plan for a Middle Eastern and African empire. With Italy now in the war, the Axis powers were ready to mount a formidable combination of forces to knock the British out of the Middle East.

Hitler had great expectations, and they must have seemed well within reach when he met with Mussolini in the autumn of 1940 to plan the war in the Mediterranean. According to their plan, German and Italian war-planes based in southern Europe would first soften up their targets, and then the large Italian fleet in the Mediterranean and the Italian army units already poised in Libya would finish off the job. The place to start, as Napoleon had known almost a century before, was in Egypt. And in Egypt, as many great commanders had long known, the great prize was the Isthmus of Suez. Control of the Canal not only would strike a tremendous blow at vital British military and civilian supply lines, but would also give Germany and Italy access to Middle East oil and prepare the way for Axis armies to occupy the continent of Africa and, in time, the subcontinent of India.

The British had, for months, been anticipating an Italian attack on Egypt. In mid-August Churchill sent a message to his commander-in-chief in the Middle East with detailed instructions about the reinforcement of Empire troops in Egypt. "A major invasion of Egypt from Libya must be expected at any time now. It is necessary, therefore, to assemble

*By an accident of the congressional calendar and with an obvious bit of paper shuffling, the House of Representatives' bill was numbered "H.R. 1776."

and deploy the largest possible army upon and towards the western
frontier. All political and administrative considerations must be set in
proper subordination to do this." He then meticulously listed the forces
that were to be put in place from the pitifully few then available. Among
them were some regiments of British cavalry, "without their horses,"
whose mission it would be to secure the Canal area.[6]

A few weeks later the Italians made their move. They pressed from
Libya into western Egypt and then dug in. British troops, outnumbered
despite the reinforcements, were tied up for precious weeks holding a
line against further inroads by the enemy. Meanwhile, Mussolini's forces
had invaded Albania and Greece, where they encountered unexpected
resistance and heavy casualties.

Despite their problems on the Greek front, the Italians decided to
press forward in Egypt, with the Nile Delta and the Suez Canal as their
targets. But it was an ill-fated move; British, Australian, and New Zealand
troops shoved Mussolini's army back deep into Libya and captured more
than 100,000 prisoners. Churchill had had his share of bitter disappointments during the past many months, and the news from Egypt was the
most encouraging thing that had happened in a long time. In a message
to Prime Minister Menzies of Australia, he crowed, "I am sure you will
be heartened by the fine victory the Imperial armies have gained in Libya.
. . . Remember that I could not guarantee a few months ago even a
successful defence of the Delta and Canal. We ran sharp risks here at
home in sending troops, tanks, and cannon all round the Cape while
under the threat of imminent invasion, and now there is a reward."[7]

It was a narrow escape and a heartening victory, but dangerous days
still lay ahead. The Germans took charge of the battle for Suez. The
hapless Italians would now be subject to orders from Hitler's generals.
Soon the Luftwaffe was dropping mines into the Canal's shipping lanes
and unloading bombs on its terminal facilities. Keeping the Canal open
in the face of the German air attacks was a formidable, dangerous task.
The Canal pilots had to shepherd large ships through the equivalent of
an infantry obstacle course—a sunken wreck here, a live mine there. But
except for one period of twenty-four hours, the Canal continued in operation. It had to: If it had been captured or blockaded, the consequences
for Britain would have been incalculable. After December 1941, especially, when war broke out in Asia, the shortcut made a critical difference
to the movement of Allied supplies and troops to India and Burma.

The network of air defense that the British had contrived to keep
enemy bombers at bay was elaborate and deadly. "Coming from the
North the attackers would meet first the anti-aircraft umbrella at Port
Said, next a barrage of machine gun and Bofors fire, thickened in depth

by heavy anti-aircraft, then rockets with long-trailing wires fired by a naval section; the whole area of Ismailia would be lit up by flares or searchlights, with night fighters operating around them. There was a false channel on the Bitter Lakes and massed fire from anti-aircraft batteries at Shallufa, while Suez was protected by a balloon barrage five sections deep, and its anti-aircraft fire augmented by the guns of a hundred or more ships moored in the bay."[8]

But some German planes got through. For the defenders, the trick was to locate as precisely as they could points where the mines fell so that the explosives could be extricated and then detonated as soon as possible. Observers were stationed every fifty yards along the Canal to pinpoint the location of the mines. And then, with ingenuity born of desperation, a net was stretched each night across vulnerable parts of the Canal. Mines dropped that night were located at daybreak by observing the holes ripped in the net as the missiles fell through.

The land war in the Middle East exploded again in 1942, eight months after Churchill's "fine victory." Now the German Afrika Korps under General Rommel joined fresh Italian troops massing in Libya. Churchill rushed reinforcements to Egypt from every corner of the Middle East and even from across the Mediterranean, where British, Australian, and New Zealand troops were assisting the hard-pressed Greeks.

Rommel launched his attack in May and moved quickly through Egypt's Western Desert to El Alamein. If the forces of the Empire were to save the vital port of Alexandria, Rommel's advance would have to be blocked at Alamein. It was. But the Afrika Korps was halted, not defeated. It remained a formidable force—and it was poised to pounce.

Churchill flew to Cairo in August. He reorganized the Middle East Command and placed General Alexander in overall charge and General Montgomery in command of the Eighth Army in the field. Every soldier and gun that could be spared from other theaters was dispatched to buttress the British and ANZAC troops. Although London was becoming increasingly impatient and chivied Montgomery to launch his counterattack against Rommel, he bided his time while the buildup continued.*

In early October Rommel beat Montgomery to the punch: Aware that the Eighth Army was getting stronger every day and that time was working in favor of the enemy, he attacked. Montgomery's troops bruised Rommel's forces in a sharp but inconclusive battle. And then, following a massive artillery and air assault on major units of the Afrika Korps,

*He would later be sharply criticized by both military historians and his peers for not attacking until he had accumulated an overwhelming numerical superiority and an awesome arsenal.

Montgomery launched a frontal attack and put the Germans to rout. A month later, after one of the most celebrated battles of World War II, Rommel's forces were crushed; Montgomery's "desert rats" had not only relieved the threat to Egypt, but now occupied Libya.

General Alexander's after-action report to Churchill was brief and laconic: "Sir: The orders you gave me on August 15, 1942 have been fulfilled. His Majesty's enemies, together with their impedimenta, have been completely eliminated from Egypt, Cyrenaica, Libya, and Tripolitania. I now await your further instructions."

American troops under General Eisenhower's command had, by now, landed in North Africa and were moving against the Germans from Algeria and Tunisia. Very soon the British and American forces scored their first major success. The stage was set for the invasion of Sicily.

By 1943, Mussolini's regime had collapsed, the Mediterranean was cleared of enemy forces, and the Suez Canal was secure. Supplies were flowing across Iran into the Soviet Union, and men and matériel were streaming from the Mediterranean, through the Canal, to the Allied forces fighting the Japanese in Asia. Two years later, one of the bloodiest wars in history came to a convulsive end with the unconditional surrender of Germany and Japan.

Britain entered its first year of peace since 1938 with pride intact but confidence shaken. As in the case of every other war-shattered nation, its first task was to put its economy in order. Millions of men and women had to be absorbed from the military services or from the now idle munitions factories. A score of cities had to be rebuilt, a dozen ports reconstructed, thousands of industrial factories retooled to meet almost a decade of pent-up demand for consumer goods. Britain, which had been a leading exporter of manufactures since the nineteenth century, faced a major trade challenge after the war; in order to pay for its imports and service its debt, the nation would have almost to double its prewar level of exports.

The government not only faced these herculean tasks, but was also committed to implement an ambitious program of public services designed to eliminate the worst of the country's prewar economic and social inequities.

Over and above their domestic requirements, the British were determined to meet their global responsibilities. Somehow, the government had to find the manpower and the means to contribute British troops to the Occupation forces on the Continent, maintain forces in far-flung territories in Asia, Africa, and the Middle East, and reconstruct its overseas economy. A society that had gone from war to depression to war within one generation confronted an awesome agenda. And the resources at hand were meager.

In the years ahead the British would watch with wonder as Germany and Japan, erstwhile enemies, grew and prospered while their own country staggered and stagnated through the postwar period. West Germany, incidentally, had adequate food supplies by the summer of 1948; Great Britain's food was strictly rationed until 1954.*

Although America's immediate postwar task was less formidable than Britain's and its resources much more abundant, the United States initially proved to be a less than generous peacetime partner. The lend-lease aid that had kept Britain's troops fighting and its war economy functioning was guillotined in Washington within a week after V-J Day. As a consequence, the gloriously victorious British of the summer of 1945 were face to face with bankruptcy by autumn.

Harold Macmillan, reflecting on the United Kingdom's position at the war's end was understandably dispirited: ". . . the financial difficulties seemed almost insurmountable. With huge sterling balances in favour of many Allied and the leading Commonwealth countries—the bitter price for having saved them from enslavement by Hitler which, by a strange inversion of equity, we now had to pay—with small reserves, and large military commitments overseas it seemed a choice between bankruptcy and borrowing."[9] At the last minute London negotiated a $4-billion American loan.

For the tired, threadbare British people the war had been bitter and the victory sweet. But peace presented worries and uncertainties. The bands were still playing "Rule Britannia," but there were few who were singing the words. Proud, unconfident, uncertain. This was the British mood after World War II. Handle with care, psychiatrists warn when confronting an individual with this mélange of emotions. The prescription should apply to nations, as well. But in the flush of postwar power and with inexperience in its exercise, America's statesmen and diplomats ignored such cautions—if, indeed, they had ever been sensitive to them.

When the war ended, France was an economic and political wasteland. More than 300,000 Frenchmen had died. Scores of thousands of factories and commercial establishments and two million housing units were destroyed or damaged. More than four thousand kilometers of railway and almost eight thousand bridges lay in ruin. The task of social

---

*Those British whose lives spanned the two great wars experienced almost twenty years of food rationing between 1914 and 1954. In late 1952, when rations were increased, each person was able to buy somewhat less than a pound of ground meat a week.

and economic reconstruction was horrendous and of political reconstruction, no less so. The Third Republic had disintegrated with France's defeat in the spring of 1940. For the next four years the nation was ruled by the German occupation army in the north and the collaborating functionaries of Marshal Pétain in the south.

After the British-American liberation of France in the summer of 1944, resistance groups headed by General Charles de Gaulle took over the government. In the elections of October 1945 a coalition of Communist, Socialist, and center parties, with de Gaulle at its head, was elected. But de Gaulle, unable to associate himself with the Communists, resigned a few months later.

The Fourth Republic was established in the autumn of 1946. By then the only cohesive political force in France was the Communist Party. Unwilling to accept a Communist premier, the center and Socialist groups allied to elect the Socialist Léon Blum. The year that followed was cursed with poor harvests, labor unrest, and the rise and fall of governments. An ominous start to the postwar era.

One hopeful note was sounded in the summer of 1947 when the nations of Western Europe met in Paris to discuss the Marshall Plan, the American-financed program for European economic recovery. During the next several years, France, while still politically volatile, made remarkable strides in industry and agriculture. In 1945 the country's production was a third less than it was in 1938; in 1953, production had increased to two and a half times the 1938 level. The mood of shame and despair so widespread during the war soon developed into one of pride and hope. France, once again, intended to play an important role in world affairs.

America, too, mourned a long list of war casualties when peace finally came in the late summer of 1945—more than a million young men had been killed or wounded. But in contrast to Europe, America's cities and civilians were unscarred. The United States came out of the war with an enormous industrial plant, a mobile and skilled work force, and a monopoly over nuclear weaponry.

America, in 1945, was the most powerful nation in the world—indeed, the most powerful nation in the entire history of the world. Power *qua* power was something that America did not consciously seek. Riches, yes; influence, yes; affection, yes. But raw power . . .? No. The United States was a *nouveau* in the power game and, like most *nouveaux*, turned out to be careless and imprudent with its newfound wealth.

American soldiers returned home in floods promptly after V-J Day to a country convinced that the defeat of the Axis powers and the birth of the United Nations promised a rosy dawn of long-term peace. The nation's military forces were stripped from 12 million men in January 1945 to 1.5 million two years later. This was the exciting, brief moment when it seemed that the nation could afford, once again, to turn its back on the rest of the world. A job, baby, house, car, and soon a television set were what most Americans set their hearts on.

But 1945 was not 1918. After the Armistice of 1918, despite Woodrow Wilson's pleas, serious politicians could call for and sophisticated citizens could strive for a "return to normalcy." Events following on the heels of V-J Day, however, induced the United States, by default if not by choice, to shoulder worldwide chores and commitments. Soon America would be undertaking even greater international responsibilities than during the war itself. Military occupation of Germany and Japan together with vast emergency relief programs for wartime allies and recent enemies alike was followed by the Marshall Plan for the rehabilitation of Western Europe. Because not only strong national economies, but also strong international institutions were important, America became the host country, the principal funder, and the prime mover for the United Nations Organization and its family of specialized agencies.

But of all the factors that restrained America from taking the nearest exit out of the wider world to the more congenial and familiar surroundings of home, its postwar relations with the Soviet Union were the most important. The guns had hardly been stilled when ominous hints came from Moscow that wartime understandings with respect to occupation zones and troop-withdrawal schedules were open to Soviet reinterpretation. Seek it or not, want it or not, the United States assumed the international role it had long assiduously shunned. Willy-nilly, Americans became drawn into a host of worldwide political, economic, and social problems.

The decade of the fifties was a chilling one for Washington policymakers. The dominant mood was evoked by two short words: "Cold War." And the Cold War, with its violent birth, malevolent adolescence, and stultifying senescence, froze the world between a beckoning hell of another, even more terrible world war and an elusive paradise of stable peace.

The United States rose to the postwar challenges as best it could with enormous economic assistance programs in Western Europe, relief programs elsewhere, and generous financial support for a myriad of new international organizations. Torn between loyalties to its allies in Europe and sympathy for colonies seeking independence, Washington generally (but not always consistently) supported national moves for independence. Yet, the world seemed to be unraveling, year by year.

Soon a kind of paranoia set in. George Kennan reminds us:

> A certain show of bristling vigilance in the face of a supposed
> external danger seems to have an indispensable place in the Ameri-
> can political personality; and for this, in the early 1950s, with Hitler
> now out of the way, the exaggerated image of the menacing Kremlin,
> thirsting and plotting for world domination, came in handy. There
> was, in any case, not a single Administration in Washington, from
> that of Harry Truman on down, which, when confronted with the
> charge of being "soft on communism," however meaningless the
> phrase or weak the evidence, would not run for cover and take
> protective action.[10]

But with or without the "Red scare," there was much to keep the
Truman and Eisenhower Administrations occupied—and worried. A
mere recitation of events can hardly do justice to the noisy and disorderly
procession of international crises that passed the reviewing stand at 1600
Pennsylvania Avenue. There were insurgencies/civil wars/revolutions in
Greece, Palestine, Egypt, Hungary, Indonesia, China, the Philippines,
Malaya, Kenya, India, and Indochina. There were coups and counter-
coups by, for, or against good, bad, or indifferent leaders in Thailand,
Burma, Egypt, Iran, and Iraq. There were Berlin blockades and airlifts.
There was a full-scale war in Korea. There were births and abortions of
defense pacts and counterpacts. There were dramatic intelligence breakthroughs and awkward intelligence scandals. There were generals and
ballet dancers defecting from East to West and diplomats and spies
fleeing in the other direction. And there was the development of a mono-
lithic Communist bloc led by Moscow, followed by breaks in the phalanx,
first by Yugoslavia and later by Albania and China.

Those were the days when presidential advisers whispered of the
dangers of holocaust-by-miscalculation. "Civil defense" was regarded
seriously, yet almost hopelessly. It was a time when Washingtonians
scanned their basements for fall-out shelter possibilities and calculated
the distance between home or office and such likely ground zeros as the
Pentagon and the White House. I remember brooding one evening, while
stalled on the Fourteenth Street Bridge in rush-hour traffic, about the
utter futility of attempting an emergency evacuation from Washington—
or indeed from any other large city. The Quaker maxim to "live each day
as if it were the last" must have crossed more minds than my own in those
dark days of our bright new world.

And so it was that "peace" turned out to be less salubrious than many
had expected. Even powerful, rich, noble America seemed unable to put

things right. The graybeards were baffled and the young, disillusioned.

But all was not lost: By the early fifties there were some who knew what had gone wrong. Armed with The Answer came little old ladies in sneakers—of both sexes and of all ages. Loping up the ramparts and marshaling under the banner of Senator Joseph McCarthy, the zealot in search of a cause, they would save the day. The troops and their leader armed themselves with two potent weapons, the simplistic explanation and the unanswerable question. The Explanation: Somebody had goofed. The Question: Who?

The question would soon become more sharply honed: Who lost China? For, obviously, America once had "had" China. Those who ventured to remind the Senator that Chiang Kai-shek, or his incompetent Nationalist generals or his corrupt Kuomintang party had lost China were supercilious, smart-alecky, un-American. Indeed, they were almost certainly *Communist* smart-alecks; McCarthy had "evidence" that General George C. Marshall and left-wing foreign-service officers and muddle-headed civilian bureaucrats and Communists in the government had, with subversion aforethought, caused the United States to lose China— and were plainly guilty of other, more heinous crimes.

This issue and Senator McCarthy himself had a greater and more persistent influence on the American political scene than many noble causes and better men had been able to achieve. To be sure, the Cold War had started well before McCarthy graced Capitol Hill. And it flourished after his unlamented departure. But riding hard on the anti-Communist sentiment that fed on Soviet postwar bellicosity and American frustration, the shrewd Senator and his manic young associates, Messrs. Cohn and Schine, basked in public attention as they noisily slashed away at one "highly placed Communist" after another.

General Dwight Eisenhower, accepting the nomination of the Republican Party, gave a name to the new postwar campaign: "You have summoned me," he told the Republican National Convention in the summer of 1952, "to lead a great crusade." And a "crusade" it was, with Secretary of State John Foster Dulles leading the legions against the Communist infidels abroad and Senator Joseph McCarthy whipping up the home guard.

This was a time when American forces again went to war—now, to preserve South Korea in the face of an invasion by the North Koreans and the Chinese. And, in a year or so, the ground was laid for yet another war —one that would vainly attempt to preserve non-Communist South Vietnam against a takeover by Communist North Vietnam.

It was a time when the United States was trumpeting its intention to "liberate Eastern Europe"; when a nation was either our friend or our enemy; when a country professing neutrality*—or as it would soon be chic to say, "unalignment"—was obviously not our friend and, therefore, was our enemy. But Secretary Dulles' simple distinction between friend and enemy was destined to break down; in a few years, under the guidance of Dulles himself, the United States would be siding with "unaligned" Egypt against friendly Britain.

World War II brushed Egypt more lightly than most other areas that experienced the fighting at first hand. But there, as in scores of other countries in Africa and Asia, the winds of the war fanned a long smoldering spirit of nationalism. The events of the war years reawakened a latent yearning among many Egyptians to control their nation's destiny.

During the early years of the war, the threat posed by the Italian and German forces from across the Libyan border and the virtual martial law imposed by the British confined Egyptian discontent to grumbling in the public coffee shops, to some pro-Nazi activity by fervent nationalists, and to spirited rhetoric in the privacy of homes and work places. But with the defeat of the Germans at El Alamein and as the focus of British attention shifted to Europe, Egyptian grievances took on a more concrete form and political activity to redress them became more open.

By the end of the war, Egypt was seething. Three issues were dominant: concern over a Jewish state in Palestine, disposition of the Sudan, and continued British military control over the Suez Canal. These thorns would soon be nourished and would grow even more prickly. And others would sprout as well. Together, they would seed the soil of Egypt—and of areas remote from Egypt—to produce a grave international crisis and a turning point in the history of many nations.

*Switzerland's old-fashioned neutrality, of course, was tolerated even by Dulles.

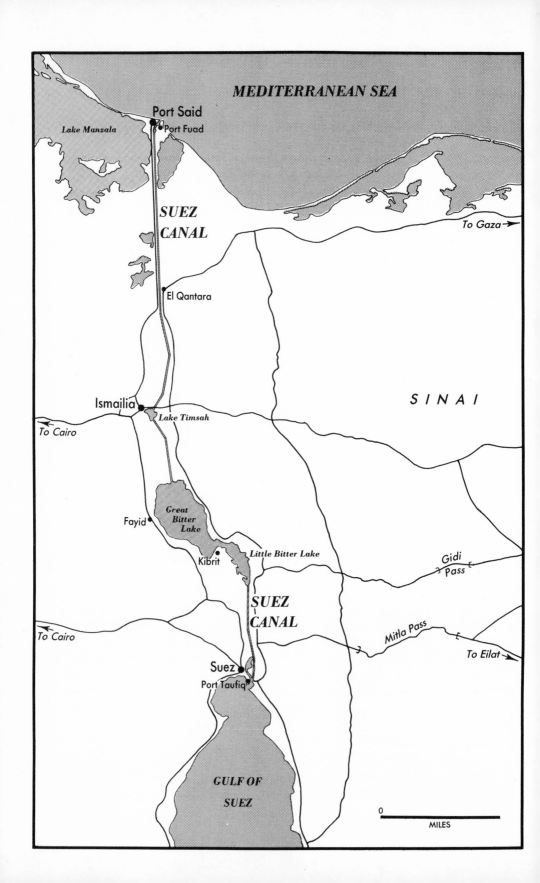

4

SEEDS OF CRISIS

Great international crises occasionally emerge wholly formed like Venus out of the half shell. Some unforeseen and unforeseeable incident—a leader gone suddenly mad; an inexplicable, monstrous miscalculation; a weapon fired accidentally at a sensitive target—may set off a series of awful, irreversible events. But more often, much more often, the roots of trouble can be traced vertically through time and horizontally across national boundaries to the interactions of individuals or groups whose interests or ambitions or styles rub sorely against each other. The resulting friction soon produces a scorching heat which no one involved has the wit or the will to contain.

Looking back, the train of events that culminated in the great international crisis of 1956 seems unavoidable in broad outline, if not in detail. The drama began in the mid-nineteenth century. Industrial revolution and imperial expansion held the plot together. England and France were the principal players. The continents of Europe and Africa provided the setting. Egypt was the victim.

There is no doubt that the economic and political imperatives of the nineteenth century made the construction of a canal across Suez inevitable—if not by de Lesseps, then by someone else. But by a Western European or English, or possibly an American, someone else; not by an Egyptian. And when the Canal was built, it was certain that control over it would be exercised from outside Egypt. In the circumstances of that time, Egypt had little choice but to settle for whatever political and economic participation more wealthy, more powerful countries would deign to relinquish.

The world of the mid-twentieth century was very different from the one de Lesseps confronted as he launched his great enterprise in the hot morning sun at Port Said April 25, 1859. By 1950, the nations of Western Europe were no longer the chief actors, and the countries of the Middle East and Asia were no longer their exclusive stage; England, especially, and Egypt, most especially, had gone through profound changes.

The period of the original Canal concession was ninety-nine years. For geologists this is but a moment; for politicians, it represents a millennium. When President Gamal Abdel Nasser nationalized the Suez Canal in 1956 ("stole it," Prime Minister Anthony Eden preferred to say), there were only twelve more years for the concession to run. But for most Egyptians the eighty-seven years of French and British control had already been too long.

Even if England's postwar world had been a sunny one, the clouds that were gathering over Egypt would have darkened many a ministerial office in Whitehall. But the Egyptian problem was just one of many then besetting the harassed government under Clement Attlee that had replaced that of Winston Churchill.

If London could have concentrated its diplomatic efforts on the issues then threatening its relations with Cairo, and if the government in Cairo could have focused on these issues free from jostling by internal and regional factions, and if. . . . But "ifs" are the stuff of retrospection, the afterthoughts of philosophical observers and of long-retired participants. What *did* happen, rather than what *might have* happened is the historian's task and the politician's legacy. What did happen in these turbulent years following World War II paved the ground for subsequent trouble and trauma.

With the war over and won, the security of the Canal was no longer threatened. Most politically conscious Egyptians resented the continued, abrasive presence of British security forces, now numbering more than sixty thousand troops—more than seven times as many as were permitted under the terms of the British-Egyptian Treaty of 1936. This could be resolved only by a major revision—if not complete revocation—of the treaty, which had been drawn up under the hot breath of Mussolini's foray into Ethiopia and his subsequent military buildup in Libya.

Jewish immigration into Palestine was yet another problem that plagued Britain's postwar relations with Egypt. The matter probably would not have assumed such proportions had not Egypt joined the Arab League—a grouping of Middle East countries organized in 1945 that also included Syria, Jordan, Iraq, Saudia Arabia, and Yemen. Opposition to any increase in the Jewish population of Palestine was a unifying factor for the disparate group of League members. New nationalist leaders and established feudal chieftains of every Middle Eastern state viewed Jewish immigration as a destabilizing and threatening development. Whether his concern was genuine and justified or feigned and exaggerated, every Arab intellectual, sheikh, pasha, and politician quickly discovered that he could prove his loyalty to the greater cause of Pan-Arabism by marching in the vanguard on this issue. Reason and compromise became hostage to bombast and rigidity.

For Egyptians, the fact that Britain could be held responsible made the Palestine issue even more attractive. And, since Egypt's economic and political problems were bad and growing worse, Palestine offered a convenient escape hatch for accumulating domestic frustrations.

This, then, was Egypt in 1946: rampant poverty, disease, and corruption; a dispirited and divided leadership; an incessant jockeying for power in the court of weak King Farouk; a deep desire to be rid, once and for all, of British overlords; a determination to use Cairo's voice and clout to prevent a Jewish enclave in the region. Even a popular and effective leader would have found this a full plate of challenges. But Egypt was not so blessed, and the problems were clearly beyond the government's limited capacity to solve. Postwar Egypt was ripe for plucking by any cohesive nationalist group that could promise economic and political reform, a reordering of external relations, and a restoration of national pride.

Many of the gentlemen who occupied colonial thrones during the nineteenth and early twentieth centuries may have possessed a brain and a spine, in addition to a claim to aristocratic blood. But, in those days, vassal kings who were independent thinkers or gutsy activists had short leases on royal palaces. Rebellious royal inclinations were sublimated by those majesties and highnesses whose crowns and accouterments remained in pawn to the sufferance of faraway masters. Emperor Bao Dai of Indochina was one example; King Farouk of Egypt was another.

Farouk succeeded to the Egyptian throne as a young man in the late 1930s. He strove briefly to exercise the prerogatives of power, but was soon reduced to settling merely for its perquisites. The young king was no match for London's tough Ambassador Sir Miles Lampson (who was wont to refer to Farouk as "that boy"). Whatever leverage Farouk could bring to bear as a consequence of his regal person was soon dissipated by the wartime occupation of the British army. Farouk not only was a monarch without power, he enjoyed neither the affection nor respect of his people. His courtiers were venal, his ministers corrupt. Thwarted by his British overlord and ignored by his subjects, Farouk turned his interests inward—to gastronomy and pornography. In these two fields of royal endeavor, he had few rivals anywhere.

Around his throne surged two rival nationalist parties, the moderate and pragmatic Wafdists, who from time to time gained some measure of power, and the more extreme and fanatically religious Muslim Brotherhood, who were prepared to go to almost any length to attain it. Plots and counterplots punctuated with occasional assassinations enlivened the copy of Western journalists. What rarely caught the newspaper reader's eye in London or New York, however, was the widespread malaise among

Egypt's middle class, the growing frustration of the young officer corps, and the grinding poverty throughout the country—ingredients that were to provide the recipe for revolution.

In early 1942, Egyptian morale was further buffeted when the British ambassador demanded that Farouk replace his prime minister with the current British favorite, the head of the Wafd Party. The king refused. British troops were drawn up in front of the palace, and the ambassador prepared to force Farouk into signing abdication papers. Farouk anxious, above all, to save his throne, caved in. The roots of the Egyptian revolution can be traced to this incident; memories of this humiliation gave strength and cohesion to the movement, a decade later, that overthrew the king.

The first popular postwar uprising was directed not at the government, but at the British. In February 1946, students and workers attacked British property and persons throughout Egypt. Wounded and dead were counted on both sides. Moscow, which had been following events in the Middle East with some interest, was quick off the mark; righteous editorials in *Pravda* demanded the "liberation" of Egypt—a cheap shot from those who, at that very moment, were erecting cages around a half dozen countries of Europe.

The new government in London was a Socialist one more sensitive to the strength of the nationalist tide then sweeping over the world than had been the one headed by Churchill, the last of the great imperialists. It quickly dispatched a high-level delegation to Cairo to renegotiate the Treaty of 1936. But the mood in Cairo was not receptive to negotiation. No Egyptian politician concerned about his career, let alone his life, was ready to compromise. British arguments for the maintenance of military bases as part of a regional defense arrangement against Soviet threats to the Middle East were shrugged off—this despite ominous Soviet moves in Iran. Nothing less than complete British evacuation would be acceptable. In the end, Prime Minister Attlee agreed to withdraw all British forces from Egypt, including those in the Suez Canal area, by September 1949.

All now seemed promising for future British-Egyptian collaboration. Farouk's government had, at last, asserted itself and had neutralized, at least for the moment, the nationalist threat to his throne. There was only one hitch—a hitch that would have profound implications for Farouk himself and for the future role of Britain in the Middle East. It did not appear in the form of a mischief-making politician. Nor did it arise because of dissembling or confusion about the timetable for British withdrawal. Rather, it took the form of a piece of geography—the Sudan. Bordering Egypt to the South, the Sudan is the largest country of Africa.

It was conquered by Egypt in 1821 and, after a brief breakaway under a warring religious leader, was subdued once again in the late nineteenth century and ruled primarily by the British under the euphemism "the Anglo-Egyptian Condominium."

The Egyptians had understood that Attlee's government was prepared to recognize Farouk's claim to be king, not only of Egypt, but also of the Sudan. The British, for their part, had no intention of relinquishing their influence over ten million Sudanese. And the Sudanese, in turn (encouraged to some degree, at least, by the British civil servants who had been administering the Sudan), clearly had no interest in being tied to Egypt, with or without Farouk's invitation.*

The arrangement for British withdrawal had been tortuously worked out and was as delicately balanced as a Swiss watch. But it was now in shambles. The government in Cairo responsible for the aborted negotiation resigned and the nationalist parties once more noisily pressed in on the now beleaguered Farouk. Egypt appealed to the UN, but got short shrift there; despite Moscow's desire to curry favor in Cairo, even the Russians were in favor of self-government for the Sudan. Relations between London and Cairo tobogganed to a new low, although the British withdrew their forces from Cairo, Alexandria, and other outlying areas into more defensible enclaves along the Canal.

On the Palestine front, the situation was even more complex. The British, who had been administering the area under their post–World War I mandate, attempted to restrict Jewish immigration. But Jewish paramilitary forces resorted to terrorism and sabotage in order to open the gates of Palestine to all among the remnants of postwar European Jewry who wished to immigrate. The United States was sympathetic to Jewish aspirations and suspicious (with some reason) that the British were more interested in maintaining a military base in Palestine than in coming to grips with a nasty political and humanitarian problem. Except for France, European nations were preoccupied with their own reconstruction and had little stomach for active involvement in the Palestine issue.

The United Nations, for its part, was anxious to get involved; the mandate, after all, was originally granted by the UN's foster parent, the League of Nations. Moreover, it was important at this early stage of the organization's history to demonstrate that the UN could play an effective

*That the Sudanese were in no mood to accommodate a territorial infringement by the Egyptians was conveniently overlooked by Cairo's more zealous nationalists. At the root of the problem was control over the waters of the Nile, the two branches of which spawn in the mountains of Ethiopia and Uganda, merge into a mighty, life-giving river at Omdurman in the Sudan, and then flow through Egypt into the Mediterranean.

international role. But when, in 1947, the delegates confronted the issue in their temporary quarters at Lake Success, New York, they quickly found themselves tied up in legalistic knots and mesmerized by lofty, empty oratory. When it became clear that both the Soviet Union and the United States were prepared to recognize the new nation, the deadlock was broken. Israel was established as an independent state.

But the strains of "Hatikvah," the old Zionist marching song and the new Israeli national anthem, were all but drowned in the cries of fury from neighboring Arab countries—a fury that was soon transformed from words to war. The Arabs invaded Israel within a week of its independence and were soundly defeated by a nation whose survival depended on victory. The Arab leaders were left to sulk and scheme.

A demoralized, angry Egyptian army limped home. Its anger was directed not so much at the Israelis as toward its own government in Cairo. The king and his ministers had sent it into battle under bumbling generals and with outmoded arms. That ill-fated expedition was to seal the fate of the incompetent, corrupt politicians and the obese, degenerate Farouk. A clandestine Free Officers movement, comprised of young officers, including a Major Gamal Abdel Nasser, in due course would see to that. In the meantime, the fanatics—the Muslim Brotherhood, the Communists, and the remnants of wartime neo-Fascist groups—were rallying around the flag of nationalism. British troops in the Canal Zone, numbering eighty thousand men, soon were heavily engaged in protecting the security of their enclaves.

Clement Attlee was defeated in the election of October 1951. Once again Winston Churchill, still charismatic but now aged and more irascible, took over the leadership. And once again, Anthony Eden, still urbane but now more introspective, became foreign minister. They inherited a host of international problems, not the least of which was the unfinished business in Egypt.

British troops had now begun to counterattack against the guerrilla groups and their allies among the Egyptian police force. In January 1952, they assaulted the Ismailia police station and left scores of Egyptian casualties. Then came the awful morrow—"Black Saturday"—when a large area of Cairo was put to flames. British property was the principal target of the arsonists, but other foreign-owned establishments were not spared. The government in London briefly considered dispatching British troops to Cairo from their garrisons along the Canal, but there was concern that such a step would dangerously expose the Canal to terrorism and sabotage. In the event, the move was unnecessary; the mob and the fires had cooled by nightfall.

The riots not only provided a temporary release for pent-up xenophobia in Egypt, but also demonstrated the impotence of the king and his ministers. The Free Officers Group, headed by Nasser, decided it was time to strike. But Nasser and his brother officers were conscious of their tender years (they were all in their early thirties) and their modest rank (except for Nasser, now a colonel, they were all captains and majors). Worried that neither the Egyptians nor the world outside would take them seriously, they sought an older, more senior officer to lend the movement prestige and authority. Brigadier General Mohammed Naguib agreed to be their titular leader. The revolution was on its way.

Two messages were sent to the American Embassy as the Free Officers set their plan in motion to take over the country. The first, from Colonel Nasser, assured the ambassador that the revolution was purely an internal Egyptian affair and urged the United States not to interfere. The second, from the king, pleaded for American help. The United States stood aside (there was, in fact, nothing else it could do), but Ambassador Jefferson Caffery spent the night with the king in his palace at Alexandria, providing whatever comfort his presence could add.

Churchill's government had a moment of greater uncertainty, a brief brush with temptation. Farouk, surrounded by rebel troops, pleaded with the British ambassador, as he had with the American, for military intervention. But Foreign Minister Anthony Eden, no doubt influenced by the international distaste for Farouk, refused to assist the doomed king. Even if Eden had wished to aid Farouk, British forces in Egypt would have been of little help; the situation in the Suez enclaves was still too precarious to risk moving more than a corporal's guard to Cairo, where the Free Officers had taken control, or to Alexandria, where they had the king at bay. British soldiers remained in their barracks and Farouk was packed off to exile. "In ten years," Farouk told a companion on the deck of his departing ship, "there will be five kings left: Hearts, Clubs, Diamonds, Spades, and England."

Farouk was not the first king to be dethroned in the turbulence of the forties and fifties. Nor was he the last. But he did have the distinction of being among the least loved by his subjects and the least respected by the outside world. On a pass-fail basis, Farouk had flunked the test of royal rule. The only monument he left behind was the world's largest royal collection of dirty pictures.

The Free Officers Group, under General Naguib, now ruled Egypt. Naguib appointed a civilian prime minister and a civilian cabinet; the old soldier regarded the barracks and the field rather than the government ministries as the proper place for military officers. But the arrangement foundered on the issue of land reform. Two-thirds of Egypt's arable land was held by 6 percent of the country's landowners. The officers of the junta, most of whom came from lower-middle-class peasant families, insisted that radical land redistribution be among the first steps taken by the new government. This did not sit well with the civilian ministers, however, and within a few months they were replaced by zealous, activist young officers. Naguib himself took over the prime minister's post, but this, too, was short-lived. Nasser, having led the revolution, was unwilling now to sit on the sidelines, and assumed more and more power as the months went by.

Gamal Abdel Nasser was part of a phenomenon of the 1950s and 1960s. Throughout much of the world, established civilian governments were being muscled out of power by young military officers. Reliable knowns—often corrupt, ineffective knowns—were being replaced by unpredictable unknowns, upsetting American calculations, making a shambles of American plans. "The Colonels" or "the unguided missiles," Washington officials used to call the interlopers.

Some of the Colonels were well-meaning but ignorant; some were malevolent and literate. Many had only a brief moment in the sun; others held on for many years. Each rode into power in the name of nationalism, and each proclaimed a new era of honesty and pride for the nation destiny had called him to lead. All had one major advantage over the tired politicians they had booted out: a strong constituency of armed men.

To some Americans Colonel Nasser seemed the quintessence of the Colonels—a professional soldier from a modest background with a credible military record who had little or no familiarity with life beyond his regiment. But to regard him as an archetype of the young junta leaders emerging then in Africa, Asia, and Latin America was to do Nasser an injustice. He had much more personal charm and popular appeal than most and had genuine aspirations for social change, a sense of self-confidence, and personal integrity.

Nasser was born in Upper Egypt during the closing months of World War I. He came from peasant stock, although his father was a post office clerk and his mother the daughter of a coal merchant. After graduating from high school he briefly attended Cairo University Law School. But Gamal was a poor student, more interested in street demonstrations than books. He did, however, pass the examination for the National Police Force, only to be disqualified on the grounds of his inferior social position. But in 1935 the government relaxed the requirement that entrance to the Military Academy be restricted to young men from upper-class families. Nasser entered the academy in 1937 at the age of nineteen; most of those who were later to join him in the revolution were then his classmates.

Tall and well built, Nasser conveyed a sense of assurance that stood him in good stead as he moved onward and upward. By the time he came to power, he spoke English fluently and was an avid reader of both American and British newspapers. A puritan in his personal life, he provided a startling and welcome change from the king he had ousted. A nonmaterialist, he had an innate distrust of wealth, whether in men or in societies. A man of humble origins, he contrasted sharply with the two aristocrats—Anthony Eden and John Foster Dulles—who would soon cross his path. In short, Gamal Abdel Nasser was a formidable new personality on the fast-moving Middle East scene. Even more worrisome for the men in Whitehall, Quai d'Orsay, and Foggy Bottom, Nasser was an untested unknown.

The new military government in Cairo assumed power on a wave of enthusiasm in Egypt, a wave of encouragement in most other nations— and a wave of apprehension in Great Britain. The British had good reason to be concerned: The delicate renegotiation of the 1936 treaty would now be in the hands of tough young soldiers, rather than tired old courtiers. Naguib's government made it clear that the Canal concession, due to expire in 1968, would not be renewed. In an act of advance planning unusual for any government, Naguib organized a Suez Canal Department to study the operations of the Canal. The announced aim of this group was to prepare for a smooth transition when the concession ran out sixteen years hence.

By 1952 almost a thousand ships a month were passing through the Canal. Although Egypt received a portion of the tolls, the largest share flowed into French banks and the British Treasury. Meanwhile, the government in Cairo was faced with a grave economic crisis: The Egyptian cotton crop fell victim to a sharp drop in world prices and the unsettled political situation cut deeply into the normally thriving tourist trade. To a revolutionary regime anxious to brighten the lot and secure the allegiance of the miserable Egyptian peasant, the sleek, fat Suez Canal Company must have appeared a juicy prize. In the face of the transparent hint provided by Naguib's new department, no government, least of all the British, should have been surprised when Egypt moved against the Canal a few years later.

Although an agreement on the Canal seemed impossible, London and Cairo disposed of one troublesome problem with an accord on the Sudan in February 1953. They agreed to give the Sudanese immediate independence and an opportunity, within three years, to decide on federation with Egypt.* Naguib's reaction to the agreement raised hopes in London: "British-Egyptian relations," he said, "had entered a new era."

---

*In the end, the Sudanese decided to go it alone.

Soon after, Secretary of State Dulles visited Cairo for his first (and last) direct contact with the Egyptian leaders. The Eisenhower Administration had hardly settled into office, but Dulles was already worried about growing Soviet influence in the Middle East and hoped to persuade the new regime that a continued British military presence along the Canal would help Egypt resist pressures from Moscow. Dulles had also been giving thought to a new Middle East Treaty Organization and wanted to sound Cairo out on joining.* The Egyptians countered with a request for arms.

The meeting was educational for the new Administration in Washington and modestly advantageous for the new government in Cairo. Dulles learned that the Egyptians adamantly opposed the British bases on the Canal and returned to Washington with the impression that if the British withdrew from Egypt, Nasser might consider joining the Middle East defense pact. For his part, Nasser was depressed by Dulles' rigid anti-Soviet rhetoric, but he emerged with $40 million of economic aid and a $20-million credit for arms purchases. The only awkward moment of the visit occurred when Dulles, on behalf of Eisenhower, presented General Naguib with a pearl-handled pistol the day after the general publicly referred to Britain as "the enemy."

The Canal talks between London and Cairo resumed in April, not long after Dulles' departure, and eighteen months after negotiations on revisions to the 1936 treaty had broken off. Heartened by the amicability with which the Sudan agreement had been reached, the British were optimistic about an acceptable compromise on Suez. They were wrong. The new Egyptian negotiators picked up where the old ones had left off; nothing less than complete British evacuation would do. Nor were they ready to subscribe to the principle of free navigation. Although Egypt had never allowed Israeli ships to use the Canal, they now insisted that non-Israeli ships carrying Israeli-bound cargo would be denied transit. Naguib's prediction of a "new era" was accurate, but what he had in mind was something much less congenial for Britain than Anthony Eden had earlier assumed.

The talks sputtered on; weeks folded into months. The sessions were frequently interrupted, and occasionally even threatened, by outbreaks of sabotage and violence in the Canal Zone. And they were constantly plagued by the seesaw rivalry between Naguib and Nasser for leadership of Egypt's new government. In February 1954, Naguib was forced to

*Dulles apparently had been brooding about such a defense pact as early as March 1951, when, as ambassador-at-large in the Truman Administration, he sketched out his ideas for "NATOs" in both the Middle East and Southeast Asia.

resign, but he was back three days later—in part, at least, because of his considerable popular support. For the next two months Cairo was wracked with factional dissension, and negotiations on the Canal were virtually halted. In April, the political crisis was patched up—Naguib would be president and Nasser, prime minister. By November, Naguib was out once again, this time, permanently.

In July 1954, more than a year after the talks had begun, the Canal treaty impasse was broken. Recognizing the inexorable march of events, Britain decided to transfer its Middle East military headquarters from Egypt to Cyprus. With this move, the rationale for maintaining large British garrisons in Egypt eroded, and agreement was soon reached for a phased withdrawal of British troops from the Canal Zone by June 1956. For the first time since its construction almost a century before, the territory of the Canal would be under Egyptian control. After the signing ceremony Nasser made London's acquiescence to Egypt's demands somewhat easier for the British to swallow: "We want to get rid of the hatred in our hearts and start building up our relations with Britain on a solid basis of mutual trust and confidence which has been lacking for the past seventy years."[1]

Although the settlement was a triumph for the new regime, the Muslim Brotherhood, which had demanded an immediate and total British withdrawal, regarded the outcome as a sellout to London. A week after the signing, several Brotherhood hoods shot at Nasser. They missed. Nasser was now not only a hero, but also a martyr.* A good combination for an ambitious young leader.

In April 1955, Nasser made his first diplomatic voyage abroad. At Bandung, Indonesia, he met with more than a score of "unaligned" leaders, most of whom had only recently led their nations from colonial status to independence and who, ostensibly at least, had chosen to remain aloof from the increasing tensions then preoccupying the "Soviet bloc" and the "Free World." To the cheers of the Bandung delegations, Nasser announced that, henceforth, Egypt would follow a course of "positive neutrality." As a reward for his good intentions, he came away with a promise from the unaligned nations to back the Arabs against the Israelis.

Nasser's narrow escape from assassination had made him a virtual god at home, and his triumph at Bandung enhanced his prestige throughout the Middle East. He was now *primus inter pares* among Arab leaders. As a neutralist leader of international consequence he was courted ardently by Moscow and warily by Washington. But Nasser's newfound

*This was Nasser's second near-miss. In 1935, he had been wounded in a student demonstration protesting the presence of British troops in Egypt.

international prestige, however flattering, was of little help in solving such pressing domestic problems as the poverty of Egypt's people and the parlous state of the nation's treasury.

A few hundred miles to the northeast of Cairo another national leader also had attracted world attention. This leader, too, found that being in the international spotlight was not a substitute for solving thorny difficulties close to home.

If either Prime Minister David Ben-Gurion of Israel or Prime Minister Gamal Abdel Nasser of Egypt had been a whimsical man, he would have garnered some quiet amusement from reflecting on the similarity of his own plight to that of his enemy. Each had reason to dislike and distrust the British. Each headed a new government manned by inexperienced and frequently quarreling ministers. Each faced the problem of developing his nation's economy to satisfy growing popular expectations and to accommodate expanding populations. Each had to prepare his nation's army for inevitable war.

But neither prime minister had the time nor the tendency to indulge in whimsy. They were both pragmatic activists, too preoccupied with their own challenges to be concerned about the problems of others, especially enemy others.

It is hard to say whether Nasser or Ben-Gurion confronted the graver difficulties in the mid-fifties. Ben-Gurion was surrounded by enemy states which threatened Israel's very survival. Nasser, in turn, had only temporary and uncertain alliances with his fellow Arab leaders. Ben-Gurion had to fashion a nation and a society from a score of nationalities and a kaleidoscope of cultures. But Nasser had to capture the imagination and consolidate the support of millions of apathetic, illiterate rural peasants and urban slum dwellers. Ben-Gurion, presiding over a young and robust democracy, had to placate, if not please, political parties that spanned a spectrum from far left to far right. Nasser sat uneasily as head of a junta, relying heavily on his internal intelligence service to keep him informed of the activities of sullen fanatics in the Muslim Brotherhood, conspirators in the underground Communist Party, and jealous Judases among his own colleagues, any of whom might attempt to snatch his power, perhaps his life.

Ben-Gurion had one advantage, at least, over Nasser. He led a people who realized their economic and national security rested on a fragile base. The feeling of euphoria in Israel after victory in the 1948 war had been short-lived. The armistice a year later simply marked a temporary cessation of hostilities. Arab rhetoric and Arab guerrilla incursions were portents that hostilities would resume sooner or later. The Israelis knew, from this and from bitter memory, that passivity and survival were mutually exclusive: Winning was everything. They had to overcome a harsh natural environment; they had to hold at bay an implacable enemy. If necessary, they would fight and win both battles simultaneously. They were a determined people. And their prime minister was among the most determined of them.

David Green was the son of a liberal-minded, ardently Zionist lawyer who lived in Russian-occupied Poland. In his late teens David was sent to the university at Warsaw, but spent his time, instead, organizing pro-Zionist strikes and demonstrations. In 1906, a few steps ahead of the tsarist secret police, the young Green emigrated to Palestine. For several years he farmed in the malaria-ridden climate and harsh soil of Galilee's death valley.

In 1910, Green moved to Jerusalem to edit a Zionist journal. He changed his name to a Hebrew one—a name he felt was appropriate to his new home and his hopes for the future. Thus, David Ben-Gurion ("David, Son of a Lion") was born. Two years later Ben-Gurion went to Constantinople to study law and to agitate for a Jewish state in Palestine among progressive young Turks who hoped to liberate the Ottoman Empire. He returned to Palestine in 1914, disillusioned, and was soon arrested as a political troublemaker by the Turkish authorities. His death sentence was commuted to deportation, and in 1915 he arrived in the United States. He spent the next three years lecturing and writing. In 1918 he enlisted in the Jewish Battalion of the British army, with which he served first in Egypt and then in Palestine.

After World War I, Ben-Gurion became the prime mover in the Histadrut, the Jewish labor movement. During the period of the British mandate, the Histadrut became the most powerful single Jewish political organization in Palestine and a fine springboard for Ben-Gurion's entry into the wider world of international politics. Soon after the Germans were defeated in the spring of 1945, Haganah, the secret Jewish paramilitary organization, was formed, with Ben-Gurion its civilian commander-in-chief. When, in 1947, the Jewish state was created, it was only natural that the tough, feisty activist David Ben-Gurion should be Israel's first prime minister, under the presidency of Chaim Weizmann, the urbane father figure of the Zionist movement.

As an indefatigable pleader for an independent Jewish state in the chancelleries of the world and as a tough infighter among the squabbling Jewish political factions in Palestine, Ben-Gurion had been known only among Zionist circles. As prime minister of the new state of Israel, however, his short, squat figure and unruly white mane became familiar in scores of countries and every continent. This simple, self-educated, and quick-tempered man had little time for graceful forms; the hard struggle of Israel's survival and development was his single-minded concern. If this meant exacerbating his problems with the Arabs, so be it. Intolerant of mediocrity, impatient with fools, disdainful of poseurs, he proved to be a demanding leader, an uncompromising ally, an unyielding enemy.

The only world statesman he trusted, Ben-Gurion once told a friend, was Winston Churchill. And, like Churchill, he had not become prime minister of his country only to preside over its dissolution. Like Churchill, too, a strong sense of history seasoned his exercise of power—although Ben-Gurion's starting point dated from King Solomon rather than from Queen Elizabeth I.

One basic objective guided Israeli policy under Ben-Gurion: physical and economic security for all Jews who wished to settle in Israel. This meant a strong national economy, retaliation against Arab incursions, and a peace treaty with the Arabs—by negotiation if possible, by force if necessary.

Unrestricted immigration provided both a means and a need for Israel's economic growth. Neither could take place without the other. But both could proceed because world Jewry, especially American Jewry, contributed vast sums for Israel's social, economic, and cultural development.

The reprisal policy, in turn, was closely related to Israel's need for a formal peace treaty. Unless the new nation were to live under permanent siege, its borders had to be secure. There are many who feel now —and some who felt then—that Israel would have increased the odds for a stable, lasting peace if it had been less aggressive in its reprisal policy and less bellicose in its quest for a peace treaty. But Ben-Gurion did not see it that way. Some would say he was an inveterate hawk, others a cold realist. In any event, Israeli punitive expeditions retaliated quickly and brutally against virtually every Arab act of terrorism. Ben-Gurion was a keen student of the Old Testament. "Eye for an eye," the Book of Exodus had said.

For their part, the Arabs would give Israel no rest. Israelis lived day and night with the fear of indiscriminate attack. Like a deadly tennis match, attack and reprisal moved back and forth across Israel's borders. But no one won. And any chance for peaceful accommodation was lost.

Israel's aggressive stance moderated somewhat after November 1953, when Ben-Gurion retired to Sde Boker, his beloved kibbutz, and Moshe Sharett succeeded him as prime minister. Sharett, who had been foreign minister in Ben-Gurion's government, had borne the brunt of unfavorable international reaction to the more robust of Israeli reprisals.

He was by temperament and training more inclined toward negotiation than the fiery Ben-Gurion. Considering the difference between their personalities and their styles of leadership, it is not surprising that Sharett insisted on retaining the foreign ministry portfolio when he became prime minister and that Ben-Gurion had run the Defense Ministry from his prime minister's office.

For the next year or so, there was a marked softening of border tensions. On several occasions during this period, Sharett and Nasser were in secret indirect communication. They both seemed genuinely anxious to concentrate on urgent domestic economic tasks rather than waste effort and substance on costly military programs. But Sharett had a hard row to hoe. Virtually every radio station in the Middle East was maintaining a steady barrage of poisonous anti-Israeli propaganda. Meanwhile, the British agreement to evacuate their troops from Suez and the Russian moves to counter the American and British Middle East Defense Pact promised to reduce Western influence in the area. Israel, it appeared, would be alone in hostile territory.

Adding to Sharett's problem was Eisenhower's determination to shift from Truman's wholehearted support of Israel toward a more even-handed approach to the Arab nations. In the meantime, Israel's hard-liners were opposing Sharett's policies and were being coached and cheered on by Ben-Gurion from his modest bungalow in the desert. By February 1955, Sharett had little choice but to bring Ben-Gurion out of retirement and place him in charge of the Ministry of Defense. Sharett was soon forced out and Ben-Gurion took over, once again, as prime minister. Israel's soft policy was now discarded.

In the early fifties the Cold War—a primitive and, in retrospect, almost adolescent contest between the world's two most powerful nations —was at its height. Any man-made or natural event anywhere in the world —whether salubrious or disastrous, and no matter how trivial—was judiciously weighed by the Great Men in Moscow and Washington in terms of its effect on the "global balance." It was a period of brutish pushing and shoving, of crude threat and counterthreat, of sophomoric name-calling. For Washington it was a time for "containment," not only on the borders between Western and Eastern Europe, but everywhere along the Communist periphery—China on its Indochina border, North Korea at the 38th parallel, and Russia on its southern and western flanks.

Early 1954 saw a culmination of the tension that had marked the postwar era. The winter and spring of that year were full of foreboding in Washington. Fighting continued in Korea despite the cease-fire, and American casualties mounted in a war that was presumably over. Casualties aside, the fact that a war had ended with no discernible American victory was unique in the nation's history. There was outrage and outcry from the right wing. It was at this moment that France's campaign against the Communists in Indochina was being decided at Dien Bien Phu, a tiny French outpost in Vietnam.

On a gray, windy, chilly morning in April John Foster Dulles set out for Geneva. I was sent along as his intelligence aide and briefing officer. The business at hand was to reach a settlement in both Korea and Indochina. Dulles had tried throughout the winter, with all the considerable diplomatic skill and physical energy he could muster, to persuade America's friends and allies not to hold the conference that was now about to assemble. He sensed that Britain was in no mood to stand firm in areas remote from its current, more urgent concerns, and was convinced that France's seven-year war in Indochina had left the French tired and demoralized.

To Eisenhower and Dulles, personifications of the American crusade against Communist expansion, a conference with bellicose Russians, smug Chinese, vengeful Indochinese Communists, and self-righteous Indians promised nothing but disaster. The stakes were high, however, and Dulles had few chips. In the end, he recognized the inevitable: Unless the conference was held and unless the Indochina issue could be resolved at the earliest possible moment, the French government of Joseph Laniel would fall. And the United States was relying on this government to agree to the European Defense Community—a concept initiated in Washington to provide a stronger Allied contribution to the defense of Western Europe. It was a more than usually grumpy John Foster Dulles, then, who took his seat at the Palais des Nations on April 26, 1954.

"Foster looks as succulent as a hunk of Vermont marble," a colleague on the American delegation whispered as he and I trooped into the Conference Chamber behind the secretary.

Dulles was not looking forward to what was about to transpire. To add to his discomfiture, the cochairmen of the conference were to be Anthony Eden—a man he heartily disdained (and vice versa) as a consequence of disagreements during the early days of the United Nations— and Vyacheslav Molotov—a man he deeply distrusted (and vice versa) as a consequence of postwar frictions between Washington and Moscow. But the final ignominy for the secretary of state—and for the President, too—was the presence of Communist China, then Number One on the American hate list, with a delegation two hundred strong. Throughout the conference, Dulles (who returned to Washington after a few days in Geneva) and other high State Department officials made frequent public statements of American policy on the Far East in general and Southeast

Asia in particular. Eden rarely was given advance notice of these and would hardly recover from one unpleasant surprise before another lay in wait. These pronouncements from Washington complicated his task as chairman of reconciling the two sides. No less important to Eden, they also made him look foolish. An uncharitable observer might have said that Dulles was consciously spiting Eden. The observer just could have been right.

For his part, Eden seemed so intent on securing an agreement (some State Department officials at the time would have said *any* agreement) that he appeared to be making unnecessary, even gratuitous concessions. The *New York Times,* on June 1, observed, "Advance predictions that the . . . conference would impose terrific strains on British–United States relations have been borne out." Eden himself was sensitive to this. "I was continually producing proposals," he wrote later, "because if I did not we stuck fast. . . . My activities in this regard were open to every kind of misrepresentation. I was concerned about their effect on Anglo-American relations. . . ."[2] The American delegation pouted and sulked its way through the proceedings and, in the end, disassociated itself from the final agreement, which divided Vietnam into two parts at the 17th parallel.

The strained relations between Eden and Dulles at Geneva deteriorated even further as a consequence of the "Guatemala Affair" that occurred at about the same time. Washington had supported the overthrow of the Arbenz pro-Communist regime. The United States was charged as an aggressor at the UN Security Council in June 1954. To Washington's chagrin, the British (and French) abstained instead of supporting the American position.

The Geneva Conference would appear to have little bearing on what was to transpire two years or so later in the Middle East when the United States and Great Britain would find themselves, once again, at odds. In fact, it had a great deal to do with those subsequent events. For it was at Geneva that Dulles' disdain for Eden blossomed into loathing. And it was there that Eden, in his turn, became successively frustrated by, infuriated with, and suspicious of Dulles.

The friction between the two men was further exacerbated by Eden soon after the adjournment of the conference. In a speech before Parliament, describing the settlement, Eden made reference to "Locarno."* The comparison enraged the Washington hard-liners for whom

---

*The Locarno Pact was a series of post-World War I agreements whereby the Western European powers undertook to guarantee the peace, but Germany did not agree to refrain from aggression.

"Locarno" evoked the image of appeasement and confirmed their suspicions of Eden's role at Geneva.

In a discussion with American journalists in late June, Dulles "confided" that American policy in the Middle East as well as in Asia had suffered because of an American readiness to support French and British "colonialist" policies. He hinted broadly that this would soon change.

No sooner had the conference on Indochina convened than Secretary Dulles began to lobby vigorously in London and Paris for "united action" against further Communist encroachments in Southeast Asia; he hoped to gather Britain and France together with non-Communist countries around the southern rim of China into a Southeast Asian version of NATO. Hardly had the Geneva Conference ended in the early summer when pell-mell preparations were under way to convoke a meeting in Manila to establish the new anti-Communist defense pact. But the concept of a strong regional military organization was watered down even before the conference began. The British and French were reluctant to commit themselves to an Asian NATO, and Dulles himself had some second thoughts. A wan shadow of Dulles' original idea was unveiled on September 6, 1954.

The Southeast Asia Treaty Organization (SEATO) was born, but it had soft gums, rather than strong teeth. Its members included only two countries of the region, Thailand and the Philippines—and the Philippine membership was redundant since that country already had a mutual defense pact with the United States. Within months, France and Pakistan became only nominal members, if that. The United Kingdom, hard pressed in Malaya and elsewhere, could give little more than lip service to the organization. Only the United States, Australia, New Zealand, Thailand, and the Philippines stuck it out to the end. If nothing else— and there was little else—SEATO could be later used by President Lyndon Johnson as one of several justifications for American involvement in the Vietnamese war.

While John Foster Dulles was attempting to whip up enthusiasm for SEATO, his earlier effort to develop a similar arrangement for the Middle East was being pressed in Cairo. There, Nuri Said, the Iraqi prime minister, was urging representatives of the Arab League to align the League militarily with Great Britain and the United States. Prime Minister Said reminded the delegates that an embryo regional pact was already in being; Turkey and Pakistan had signed a defense treaty in April of that year. It was in April, too—a month after Dulles' visit to the Middle East —that Iraq had been promised American arms aid. Nuri Said was anxious to repay Dulles for this expression of faith and, obviously, to reduce his own sense of isolation among the Arab states. But he was unable to deliver the League—and was probably worse off for having tried.

Said's task in Cairo was made more difficult because Nasser was fresh from his victory over Naguib and more than ever distrustful of any association with the West, especially Great Britain. From Nasser's conversations with Dulles six months before, he knew that the Iraqi was simply retailing an idea manufactured in Washington. He lost no time in making known his adamant opposition to Said's proposal. Both leaders began to lobby for support within the Arab League. Said—who, after all, was trying to buck a swelling tide of nonalignment—was soon ostracized by his Arab peers. When, in the winter of 1955, Iraq and Turkey signed a defense agreement in Baghdad, Nasser threatened to expel Iraq from the League.

The Baghdad Pact was the first ray of light the British had encountered in the Middle East in many years. London quickly announced that Britain, too, would join the pact. Aside from starching up the area against Soviet threats, the treaty would enable the British to maintain their RAF bases in Iraq—a matter of no small consequence since there had been recent ominous noises from the Iraqis that the British would have to clear out. It soon became evident, however, that Britain had moved a bit too far, a bit too fast. France, which at first seemed willing to become a member, was unable to overcome its century-long suspicions of British intentions in the Middle East; it not only refused to join, but also persuaded Syria to remain aloof.

Although Eisenhower and Dulles were early enthusiasts of the pact (indeed, Dulles folded the notion into Washington's arms agreement with Iraq), their ardor cooled when Nasser and other Arab nationalists opposed it. Dulles apparently had no compunctions about leaving the British high and dry even though he had pressured a reluctant Anthony Eden to join the Southeast Asia Pact at Manila only a short time before.

This was not soon forgotten. Writing of that period, Harold Macmillan recalled:

> One of the most troublesome of Dulles' experiments in vicarious brinkmanship was his attitude over the Baghdad Pact. He had used every possible pressure upon us to become full members and to give it an active support; but he continued, throughout 1955, to refuse on what seemed somewhat legalistic grounds to commit the United States to membership.[3]

Two years later, when the Soviet position in the region had been strengthened in the aftermath of the Suez debacle, Washington joined the Middle East defense arrangement (by then called the Central Treaty Organization, or CENTO). CENTO turned out to be an even less effective organization than SEATO and was disbanded two decades and many tons of planning papers later.

The planning papers themselves could reveal much about how CENTO and SEATO went about their business. The staff of each organization prepared an annual assessment of the military threat to their respective areas. In the course of one of these assessments—I believe it was 1959—the Pakistanis, who, together with the British and Americans, were members of both SEATO and CENTO—refused to endorse a SEATO planning paper that put the Communist threat to Southeast Asia as "high" because, a few months before, the CENTO staff had overruled Pakistan and ranked the Communist threat in the Middle East as "low." Pakistan needed the reality or at least the fiction of a Communist danger in the CENTO area to make a credible case for more American arms— arms that it wished to use on its borders with India. It was made clear to the SEATO planners that if Pakistan, which was far removed from and had little interest in Southeast Asia, could not have a "high threat" in CENTO, it would not agree to a "high threat" in SEATO. The Pakistanis were promised that the next CENTO threat assessment would be elevated from "low" to "high." Pakistan then agreed that the Communist threat to Southeast Asia was indeed a matter of very grave concern.

But none of this had transpired by the winter of 1955, and Gamal Abdel Nasser had no way of knowing then that the Baghdad Pact would come to naught. He perceived the enterprise as an attempt to make a quick fix in the Middle East by a clever government in Washington and, even worse, as an exercise in international posturing by a desperate government in London. Eden's effort backfired: Nasser was outraged at what he regarded as a clumsy attempt to retain a British military foothold in the region. The Indians, then in the full flush of their self-ordained leadership of the unaligned world and anxious to remain on center stage, took the lead in shrilly criticizing the hapless British. The Russians, not to be outdone, fired off a heavy salvo of threats and propaganda.

Adding to the fluidity, and thus the uncertainty, of the international situation in early 1955, was a change of leadership in Moscow. Georgi Malenkov, the mild-mannered engineer who had succeeded Stalin in 1953, was replaced nominally by the elderly Marshal Nikolai Bulganin, but actually by Communist Party Secretary Nikita Khrushchev.

Any change in the hierarchy of the Kremlin inevitably produced anxiety and insomnia in chancelleries all over the world. But this particular change was especially worrisome. It came as a climax to a power struggle focused on Malenkov's deemphasis of nuclear armament and capital equipment in favor of consumer goods. Foreign Minister Molotov and Secretary Khrushchev had vigorously opposed this policy. Molotov had apparently expected to be named to the honorific senior post, but was removed from the running at Khrushchev's insistence. Khrushchev's views on the Soviet Union's proper international role differed sharply from Molotov's. He regarded the Middle East as a happy hunting ground for the extension of Soviet power, while Molotov viewed the Arab states as unreliable partners in any Moscow-sponsored enterprise.

The unsettled situation in Moscow following the change in government led Western leaders to discount the tough Soviet reaction in late January to the birth of the Baghdad Pact. This was a mistake. Under Khrushchev's prodding, the Russians were now prepared to leap into the Middle East at the first opportunity. And a good opportunity was soon at hand.

During the latter part of 1954 and early 1955 under Sharett's cautious and deliberate policy, the situation on the Israeli-Egyptian border was relatively tranquil. But soon after Ben-Gurion's return from retirement in mid-February to take over the Defense Ministry, Israel embarked on a heavy, bloody, and apparently unprovoked raid into Gaza.

Nasser read the attack, with some justification, as a major shift in Israeli policy and immediately sought to buttress Egypt's army. He began to shop around for modern weapons. The French could not be counted on for additional arms; they were fighting Egyptian-supported insurgents in Algeria and were providing arms to Israel. The British, too, were a problem; they insisted as their price for military aid that Egypt stop its political mischief and propaganda attacks against the Baghdad Pact. Such a move would have jeopardized Nasser's leadership of the Arab League —a risk he was understandably unwilling to take.

Nasser then left a list of his military needs at the American Embassy in Cairo and the ambassador promptly forwarded the request to Washington. But the State Department was apparently preoccupied with other matters. Cairo's request rested undisturbed for many weeks. By early May, however, Nasser was informed that the arms could be made available—cash on delivery. Nasser's response was a "Thank you, but no thank you"; dipping into Egypt's treasury for $27 million would strain the country's finances. He turned down the American offer.*

The Egyptian economy was, indeed, in a frail condition, yet the

---

*Some time before this, while Naguib was still in power, Washington did give the Cairo government a small bundle of spending money, as an earnest token of its friendship. Nasser discovered the $3-million check when he took over from Naguib and regarded both the money and the manner in which it was given as insulting. He built a radio tower with a gaudy restaurant on top with the sum. It is now referred to by irreverent Cairines as "Dulles' last erection."

amount involved in the American arms deal was not very large. If his needs were as urgent as Nasser claimed, it is surprising that he did not agree to Washington's terms. One might suspect he had another, better offer up his sleeve. And one would be right. According to some Israelis, at least, well before Ben-Gurion's raid on Gaza, negotiations had been started to exchange Egyptian cotton for "Czech" heavy military equipment.[4]

In early June, Nasser told the American ambassador that he had an arms commitment from the Soviet bloc. Other things being equal, he confided, he would prefer to be supplied from American sources and would wait for Washington's reaction before sending a purchasing mission to the East. At the ambassador's suggestion, he submitted another, leaner shopping list, this one adding up to $10 million. Washington yawned. It was still yawning when intelligence reports began to flow into the State Department and the Pentagon indicating that a large arms deal (possibly as large as $200 million) was under discussion between Moscow and Cairo. But Dulles was convinced that Nasser "was bluffing" and that the Russians would hardly do something so "contrary to the spirit" of the recent summit conference in Geneva.[5] By August, however, evidence was piling up that Nasser was indeed serious. And that Moscow was, too— Geneva notwithstanding.

The studied indifference in London and Washington toward Nasser's overtures catapulted into a frenzy of activity as soon as they were convinced that an Egyptian deal with Moscow was imminent. The British felt betrayed by Nasser's move. When, in 1954, London had signed the agreement on troop withdrawal, it was on the understanding that the British could use bases on Egyptian territory in the event Egypt was invaded by any power other than Israel—a circumlocution directed at the Soviet Union. But now Cairo was actually courting the Russians!

Secretary Dulles sent two emissaries to Cairo in a last-minute attempt to talk Nasser out of his folly. But by then it was too late—even if Nasser had wanted to call off the negotiations with the Russians, he was probably too far down the road to turn back. In September, Nasser announced that an arms deal had been "consummated with Czechoslovakia." Cairo and Moscow tried to preserve the fiction that the Czechs, rather than the Russians, were the source of arms aid, but it did not take very long before the Czechs' role as front men became an open secret.

Egypt was provided with $250 million worth of heavy equipment to be paid off in Egyptian cotton at low interest over a decade or so. Within a few months Soviet arms and technicians began to arrive in Egypt and Egyptian military officers were sent to the Soviet Union for training.

I was assigned to the American Embassy in London in the late summer of 1955. My job at the embassy was to provide a channel of information and analysis between the American and British intelligence communities. Winston Churchill had, by then, passed the prime minister's seal to Anthony Eden (who had long been poising himself to grasp it), and Harold Macmillan had taken over Eden's portfolio at the Foreign Office. Eden's accession was popular on both sides of the Atlantic. Few national leaders had had the tutelage and the experience in foreign affairs that Eden brought with him to Number 10 Downing Street. "The friendship between Great Britain and the United States is secure in his hands," the New York *Herald Tribune* pronounced shortly after Eden's appointment.

My exhilaration at the prospect of spending a few years in a city I loved and among people I admired receded somewhat during the next several weeks. Something seemed amiss; there was a wispy, enveloping *tristesse-de-vivre* among all I met—from our benighted charwoman to our knighted neighbor. It took the form of bitter little jokes about "Merrie olde . . . ," or of half-finished sentences that ended with a bleak "well, anyway . . ." and a rolling of the eyes, or trailed off drearily with a barely audible "however . . ." and a shrug. For many—rich and poor, Chelsea and Cheapside alike—the Battle of Britain had given London a massive dose of adrenalin, a moment of high purpose and common glory. But everything after that seemed anticlimactic.

And, in truth, much that had happened since V-E Day was a letdown. England in 1955 had only recently been able to shuck off the last of wartime rationing. Taxes were high and salaries were low (our charwoman worked for 35 cents an hour, a high official at the Foreign Office received about $8,000 a year before taxes). Contributing at least as much to the shadowy mood was a sense that glorious victory had been bought at tremendous sacrifice in domestic economic strength and international political influence. "We were always a small country," a friend noted wryly, "but it took a victory over the Axis to make us a small power."

The days remained bright and warm in early September when I first introduced myself to Whitehall. I had gone to pay a call on an official in the Foreign Office and was waiting in his anteroom. "What a lovely day!" I remarked profoundly to a bouncy young clerk sporting a bright smile and sensible ankles. "It is, isn't it!" she chirped. "It's the nicest summer I can remember." "Well," muttered a battered, mustached lady at the other desk, "the summer of 1934 was at least as nice and not as hot. But, anyway . . ."

My new assignment involved attending weekly meetings of the British Joint Intelligence Committee—or at least that part of each meeting

devoted to international events of common concern—as well as the preparatory meetings of the committee's subordinate staff. My first encounter with the Joint Intelligence Staff was mind-boggling. The drama then
taking place in the Middle East was exciting, but I could adjust to that.
What left me in a state of cultural shock was the cast of characters on the
staff, the offstage noises, the props, and "the business."

I learned in due course that British intelligence officers do not have
to be seven feet tall, but when I walked into the meeting room on this,
my first working day in London, it did seem that height was a primary
qualification for employment. As if to emphasize the point, my new colleagues rose as I made my maiden entrance. I was passed from giraffe to
giraffe: "Cooper, y'know—new boy." Each stooped and shook my hand
briskly. "Good show." "Well done." "Poor chap." No name was mentioned except my own. I found myself sitting between two giants wearing
identical black suits (Savile Row), identical blue-striped ties (Eton), and
identical spectacles (National Health).

The proceedings began without ceremony. Somebody handed me a
piece of paper entitled "Work-at-Hand." The businesslike fellow who
had passed me around cleared his throat and sounded off with "Now,
chaps, Item One." Two of my new colleagues groaned, possibly in connection with Item One, possibly not. Three or four engaged themselves
in an independent discussion which consisted almost entirely of laughter.
Someone murmured something from across the room, possibly in connection with Item One, possibly not. Someone else went to the phone and
spent the remainder of the meeting talking to an unknown listener, perhaps in connection with Item One, probably not.

The man on my right passed a paper to the one on my left; it looked
like something from the Sanskrit Vedas. (I later found out it was Greek
pentameter.) A chap stuck his head through the door and bellowed,
"South Africa, fourteen for three!" All groaned. (I made a surreptitious
note in the event this was code for some crisis in Commonwealth affairs.)
"Cricket test match, y'know," somebody shouted to me. All laughed. I
smiled weakly.

The chairman—or I assumed he was the chairman—was saying,
"Now, chaps, Item Five." The chap on my left passed something indeci-
pherable to the chap on my right. He showed it to me: "Not bad, eh?"
I nodded knowingly. (I later discovered it was a Latin translation of the
Greek pentameter.)

I learned on my initial sally into the deliberations of the Joint Intelligence Committee itself that this more senior body conducted its business
formally and briskly under the chairmanship of the able, no-nonsense
Patrick Dean, head of the Permanent Under Secretary's Department of

the Foreign Office.* There seemed to be a wide abyss separating the solemn intelligence chiefs (all of whom had held high official or military positions during World War II) and the breezy young Foreign Office and military staff officers; perhaps the members of the Joint Intelligence Staff would simmer down with advancing age and responsibility. More likely, the difference in comportment might be explained by the principal item on the committee's agenda that day. It was troubling enough to make my new colleagues more than normally grave. For the matter at hand was the Soviet-Egyptian arms arrangement.

I am sure I added little to what my British colleagues already knew. Following the script I had received that morning from Washington, I reminded them that this was the first arms deal the Russians had ever concluded with a non-Communist regime. And I warned that this ominous change in Soviet policy had implications for the long-standing relations the United States, the United Kingdom, and France had with other countries in the Middle East. None of this lightened the atmosphere of the dusty old conference room at Storey's Gate across from lovely St. James Park.

Those first weeks in London not only involved me with a new group of colleagues, they also plunged me into such deep and unfamiliar substantive waters as Cyprus and the Middle East. Unless I had been dozing when these matters had been discussed in Washington, I had not been aware of any heat or interest generated among fellow staff members or senior policymakers during my previous assignment with the National Security Council staff. The Middle East had clearly been a residual claimant on the time of the National Security Council and the Department of State. I suddenly remembered being in the Department before my departure for London and encountering a relatively senior officer from the Near East Bureau who had to ask for directions to Dulles' office.

I was well aware that, for much of the previous year, officials in Washington had been preoccupied with strengthening the non-Communist position in Southeast Asia after the costly war in Korea and the French debacle in Indochina. There had also been much worry about the isolated Western positions in Berlin and Vienna, and much stewing about Chinese Communist threats to Taiwan. Yet another matter of great interest was the growing restiveness in countries of Eastern Europe and, in particular, Yugoslavia's break with the USSR. Either the world had changed drastically in just a few weeks, or London's international concerns were very different from those of Washington.

---

*Later British ambassador to the United Nations and then to the United States.

The Russian arms sale pressed the British into renewed efforts to strengthen and expand the Baghdad Pact. As the dour chief of Naval Intelligence pointed out to the Joint Intelligence Committee, Cairo and Moscow had outmaneuvered the pact. The British, he said, would be on a "sticky wicket" until they could enlarge the membership to include at least one or two more Middle Eastern countries. Jordan seemed a likely prospect since Jordan and Iraq shared Hashemite dynastic ties. More important, however, was the close political and military link the British had had for many years with King Hussein.

Jordan's military force, the Arab Legion, was headed by General Sir John Glubb. Many British officers served in command roles. And so, when Eden learned in November 1955 that Jordan was prepared to join the Baghdad Pact if it received "the necessary backing" from the British, he regarded this as "a moment of opportunity."[6] The Jordanians were promptly given ten late-model British fighter planes. This was soon followed by a visit from Sir Gerald Templer, chief of the Imperial General Staff. All boded well for Jordan's early accession.

But London's satisfaction was short-lived. Jordan's prime minister and three other high officials resigned in protest against the British overtures. King Hussein delicately suggested that Sir Gerald return to London and that the idea of Jordan's membership be shelved. Radio Cairo, the most vitriolic (and effective) anti-Western propaganda instrument in the Middle East, called the Templer visit a "Zionist-imperialist" trick to subvert Jordan's independence. In no small part thanks to Radio Cairo, widespread antigovernment and anti-British rioting broke out in Jordan. According to Eden, Hussein's desire to join the pact was a casualty of two potent weapons—Saudi gold and Egyptian machination.[7]

The British overture weakened King Hussein's influence in Jordan and increased Nasser's suspicion that more was behind the rationale for the Baghdad Pact than an intent to form a cordon around the Middle East against Soviet expansion. Nasser was sure that the pact was designed to counter Cairo's growing influence in the region. Sir Humphrey Trevelyan, the British ambassador in Cairo, was convinced that "the maneuvres over the Baghdad Pact were the main cause of the real deterioration in Anglo-Egyptian relations."[8]

The ill-starred effort stirred up anti-Western feeling in an already restive Arab world, subjected Eden to criticism and ridicule at home, and reinforced Washington's conviction that Great Britain was desperately flailing around simply to maintain the last vestige of its colonial power. Once again, Eden's eagerness to exploit the Turkish-Iraqi defense agreement had backfired; his first important foreign venture as prime minister turned out to be a fiasco.

In the meantime, Nasser had scored another coup. The Egyptians and Syrians signed a defense treaty in mid-October which they noisily advertised as the Arab nationalist challenge to the Baghdad Pact.

The British intelligence chiefs and the ministers in Whitehall were not alone in their concern about Soviet activity in the Middle East. The French had barely extricated themselves from Indochina when they were confronted with another, even graver threat. By the autumn of 1955 the Liberation Front had turned the Algerian countryside into a virtual battlefield. Before long, it would be mounting major terrorist attacks on Algiers itself. While the FLN professed to be "unaligned," there was little question that the left wing of the Front had close ties with the USSR. It was also clear that the governments in Moscow, Peking, and Eastern Europe had more than an abstract intellectual stake in the success of the Algerians' "war of liberation." And there was no question as to where Cairo's sympathies rested.

The reaction in Paris to news of Nasser's arrangement to buy weapons and equipment from Moscow stirred the French to respond to Israel's quest for arms. Their first move was to sell late-model Mystère fighter planes to Israel and then, following the British lead, they canceled their existing military contracts with Nasser, including the sale of spare parts for French weapons already in the Egyptian inventory.

In Israel, the Soviet arms deal signaled that Nasser was preparing for early war. The conciliatory policy of Moshe Sharett was now regarded as a failure (the fact that Egyptian terrorist attacks had slackened until the massive reprisal at Gaza was conveniently ignored). At the same time, the military activists led by Ben-Gurion argued that the Egyptian-Soviet agreement provided a timely moment for challenging Cairo's sanctions on Israeli use of the Canal.

As for the United States, its approach to the area was dominated by three major—and not always consistent—forces: The powerful pro-Arab oil interests urged that Washington do nothing to anger the regimes in the oil-rich anti-Communist Arab feudal states. The influential pro-Israeli constituency argued that the United States should provide unstinting and unquestioning support to Israel. And the secretary of state pushed for a policy—almost any policy—that would reward pro-Western regimes and punish those who professed to be neutral. The entry of the Soviet Union into the Middle East through the gates of Egypt touched exposed American nerves on all sides. Washington, which had mistakenly chosen to regard Nasser's hints of a possible arms deal with Russia as a crude form of blackmail, was now exasperated and angered.

The year 1955 closed on a dolorous note for the British government. Even without its problems in the Middle East, an increasingly worrisome Greek-Turkish-Cypriot struggle in Cyprus and a growing insurgency in far-off Malaya would have been ample cause for concern. But there was more—and worse—in store.

5

THE CRISIS GROWS

January 1, 1956, was cold and windy in Washington, chilly and rainy in London—a fitting start to what would be a dreary year. But New Year's Day or not, the world's business went on, for good or for ill. In every national capital, in every embassy, someone had to stand the watch. And on that day, at the American Embassy in London, that someone was I. As I counted off the lonely holiday hours sitting in my office, I felt no need to apologize for feeling morose. For while my colleagues were asleep or at play, I had plenty of time to brood—and much to brood about.

During their free moments, young diplomats take pleasure in amateur psychoanalysis. The unwitting subjects, more often than not, turn out to be their colleagues or their chiefs. And so, sitting by the telephone and staring out at the dreary, empty park in Grosvenor Square, I reflected on the men destiny and the American electorate had made me serve. There was my immediate chief, of course, but he was just an older, more senior officer; I knew what made *him* tick—a combination of brass and brains. More puzzling were the two big chiefs—Secretary Dulles and President Eisenhower. But it was really only John Foster Dulles who interested me; the President seemed to have little talent and less concern for the complexities of foreign affairs.

It was Secretary Dulles (or, as my superior called him, "Foster") who, virtually single-handed, managed the foreign policy of the United States. As Sherman Adams, then chief of Eisenhower's White House staff, had said, Eisenhower gave Dulles

> . . . more trust and confidence than any President in modern times had bestowed on a Cabinet member, so that the Secretary's opinions and decisions would be accepted around the world *and at home* as the opinions and decisions of the President. In the quiet of Eisenhower's home, Dulles had talked about this relationship before they had begun their official association. "With my understanding of the intricate relationships between the peoples of the world and your sensitiveness to the political considerations involved, we will make the most successful team in history."[1]

The secretary had had a long apprenticeship. It was astonishing, I mused, that Mr. Dulles had been, one way or another, associated with American foreign policy since the Wilson Administration. He had been instrumental in negotiating the peace treaty with Japan and had played an important role in organizing the United Nations. Although he had had a long career as a corporation lawyer, John Foster Dulles came to the oak-paneled suite of offices in Foggy Bottom better prepared than most of his predecessors. Perhaps that might help to explain why he was such a vain, sublimely confident man—a loner who sought little advice from his colleagues or his staff.

Dulles was broad physically, but narrow in almost every other regard. He was an ardent if not elegant swimmer, but had no known hobbies, no sense of humor, few interests outside his work, and few intimate friends. His relationship with his wife, Janet, was one of his few endearing qualities. Both criticism and praise were beneath his notice. "His was the informing mind, indeed almost the sole keeper of the keys to the ramified web of understandings and relationships that constituted America's posture of categorical anti-Communism and limitless strategic concern."[2]

The secretary's brother Allen, the director of the Central Intelligence Agency, was a very different sort—bluff, extroverted, tweedy. He was a good listener, a talented raconteur, a compassionate paterfamilias. Both men were lackluster administrators, caring little for how the great agencies beyond their immediate entourages were organized, and even less for the details of management. Allen was a leader, liked and respected by his subordinates. But Foster was a boss, remote and insulated from all but a very few.

How did the two brothers get along? I did not then know, but I got a hint several years later, at the beginning of the Kennedy Administration. In early 1961, my colleague William Bundy* and I were sitting in Allen Dulles' office when Walt Rostow, a member of Kennedy's new White House team, dropped in to "pay his respects." After a moment of polite chitchat, Allen said, "Walt, there's something I've always been curious about: How do you and your brother Gene get along? You are both distinguished professors, and are both involved in public affairs. Is there any rivalry between you?" Walt hesitated. And then he said, "Bill, how do you get along with your brother Mac? After all, he's younger than you and is now the President's chief national security adviser." Bill looked thoughtful for a moment and murmured, "Well . . . Allen, how did you get along with Foster?" Silence. And then Dulles' voice boomed across the room, "Walt, if there's anything I can do to help you or the White

*Later assistant secretary of state, and now editor of *Foreign Affairs*.

House staff, I hope you'll let me know." End of visit.

It was Allen who finally pushed Joe McCarthy down the slippery slope toward oblivion; he refused to permit any CIA employee to appear before the senator's kangaroo court. Allen was the first to say No. But Foster was among the first to say Yes. He had given McCarthy a hunting license in the State Department and then exacted a pledge from his dispirited subordinates, not of "loyalty," but of *"positive* loyalty."*

This insistence on "positive loyalty" may have reflected the fact that John Foster Dulles was a zealously religious man—a Presbyterian with a Calvinist outlook—who was confident that he knew what was right and what was wrong: Anti-Communism was right; pro-Americanism was right; Communism was wrong; neutralism was wrong. He also knew *who* was right and *who* was wrong: Konrad Adenauer, Ngo Dinh Diem, Chiang Kai-shek, Syngman Rhee were right; Pandit Nehru, Mao Tse-tung, Ho Chi-minh, and Marshal Bulganin were wrong.

But this was too simplistic a catalogue of Dulles' friends and enemies. Take Anthony Eden, for example—what to make of the secretary's view of him? Dulles seemed to be fed up with what he regarded as Eden's conciliatory approach toward the Russians, and he was clearly suspicious of Eden's efforts to hang on to the British colonies. (How Dulles could believe that anyone could simultaneously pursue a soft Soviet and hard imperialist policy was a good question. I wondered whether anyone in Foggy Bottom would have the temerity to raise it with the secretary.)

Complicating Dulles' relationship with Eden was his conviction that, of all "neutralists," the worst were those, like Nasser, who, wallowing in Soviet promises of military and economic aid, became "neutral on the side of Moscow." And so, on the one hand, Dulles was pulled by a strong anti-Communist fixation to make life difficult for the Nassers of the world. On the other, because of his deep personal dislike of Eden, he was inclined to give only grudging aid and comfort to the British, who were by then having second thoughts about wooing Nasser and were moving, instead, toward confrontation. Eden had other enemies in the Department of State. Under Secretary Herbert Hoover, Jr., could not abide the prime minister, and another senior official had said of Eden that he "had never met a dumber man."[3]

In terms of protocol, at least, Foreign Secretary Selwyn Lloyd was the secretary's opposite number in Great Britain. In reality, Anthony Eden was Dulles' counterpart; Lloyd seemed to count very little in the present order of things. To be sure, he had been a successful lawyer and had a

---

*Perhaps Dulles was inadvertently echoing Nasser, who, in a spirit of excessive zeal, committed his country to "positive neutrality."

splendid war record. And, although barely fifty years old, he had already held several important government posts—the Number Two job at the Foreign Office, Minister of Supply, Minister of Defence, and, now, foreign secretary. But as foreign secretary, thus far, at least, he was neither very obtrusive nor very effective. Some of the old Whitehall hands referred to him as "a junior minister in a senior Cabinet post." Perhaps that was why Anthony Eden had selected him the previous spring to replace the tougher-minded Harold Macmillan. Eden was the man to worry about. When he moved into 10 Downing Street, he kept one hand clutched on the government's foreign affairs portfolio, especially with regard to the Middle East.

In 1915, when he was eighteen years old, Anthony Eden went to war. Two years later he was a brigade major, the youngest of his rank in the Royal Army. He had a distinguished record and was awarded the Military Cross, one of Britain's highest military honors. He then entered Oxford, where he studied Arabic and Persian. He made little impact on his fellow students there and was not regarded as a "comer."[4] But, after leaving the university, Eden rose quickly in both politics and diplomacy. He resigned his post as a junior minister in early 1938 in protest against Chamberlain's appeasement of Hitler, and was later made foreign secretary in Churchill's war cabinet. Eden was then forty-three—a wunderkind. There was no question in most people's minds, least of all Eden's, that he would succeed Churchill as prime minister; it was only a question of time. After all, Eden had been singled out as early as 1931 by Prime Minister Stanley Baldwin as a potential resident of Number 10. And during the war Churchill had made Eden de facto prime minister-designee in the event of his death.

From the moment of the Conservative victory in October 1951 and Sir Winston Churchill's return to Downing Street at the age of seventy-seven, it was assumed by the British public, by the British politicians, and by Anthony Eden himself that Churchill would soon step down in favor of his long-time pupil and colleague. But months passed and years passed and Anthony Eden remained a gentleman in waiting. There were moments when Churchill hinted broadly to Eden, or to those he knew would pass the word to Eden, that he was planning his imminent resignation. And then, on the morrow, he would change his mind—if, in fact, he had really been serious on the day before. Time after time, Eden would rise eagerly to the bait, only to retreat gamely back to the Foreign Office when it was snatched away.

Yet Sir Winston seemed honestly of two minds regarding the wisdom of abdicating in favor of Anthony Eden, his crown prince. In mid-1954, explaining to a confidant why he had once more postponed his resignation, Churchill mused, "It is not as if I were making way for a strong young man. Anthony seems to be very tired. I detected strain in his telegrams [from the Far East conference in Geneva]. Sometimes he sends 3,000 words in one day—and there is nothing in them."[5] And, later, after he finally resigned, "I wonder—I wonder if he can do it. Courage— Anthony has courage. He would charge . . . but would he charge at the right time and in the right place?"[6]

The waiting kept Eden on edge. Like an athlete confined to the bench, an understudy kept in the wings, he watched anxiously for the signal that would mean the great moment had come. It did him no good. He became a tightly coiled spring, and the tension aggravated the damage already done to his spirit and his health by a series of operations he had undergone in 1953 and bouts of illness he suffered through 1954 and 1955. At one point, in desperation, Sir Horace Evans, Eden's physician, consulted Churchill's. Eden "did not know where he was," Evans told his colleague. "The Prime Minister had written as if everything was at an end and that he [Eden] would have to take over; and now he is behaving as if nothing had happened."[7] My patient's well-being, he said in so many words, depends on your patient's health; when Churchill decides he is too old or ill to continue in office, Eden will recover markedly.

Finally, on April 6, 1955, the signal came, the long-awaited day arrived. After spending half his life in politics and most of his political career in the shadow of Winston Churchill, Anthony Eden became prime minister.

Society reporters frequently referred to Eden as "polished"—to them, and even to more sophisticated admirers, he epitomized the model English diplomat: trim, handsome, cool, charming, articulate. These were the qualities that were readily discernible. There were other less obvious sides to Eden, however, and in the end, they would bring his spectacular career to a dead halt.

In the realm of international affairs, Eden was the most self-confident of men, no doubt a result of his many years as foreign minister and prime minister-in-training. He kept his own counsel and remained aloof from colleagues and subordinates. World politics was his passion; gardening and quiet evenings with his wife, Clarissa, provided his only escape from official duties. He found solace and relaxation in sunbathing and sought whatever opportunities he could to indulge himself in this innocent sensual pleasure. If he was blessed with a sense of humor, this was kept secret even from those who knew him well. He was a diligent, compulsive worker, frequently pushing himself and his subordinates to the raw edge of exhaustion.

Winston Churchill's son, Randolph, no admirer of Eden, would later write: "It has been said of him that he has no enemies and few friends. There is something in this. He is not at all what Dr. Johnson called a 'clubbable man.' "[8]

Many of the things I had heard and read about Sir Anthony Eden were reminiscent of what I knew about John Foster Dulles. But Eden seemed the weaker man. He was thin-skinned and high-strung, while Dulles was insensitive and tough. Although Dulles was in his late sixties, he seemed strong as a bull. And Eden—only fifty-eight that New Year's Day—had a debilitating stomach and liver ailment which was sometimes better and sometimes worse, but which never seemed to be entirely absent.

It is surprising, I thought as I stared out the window at a lone, unsteady wanderer on windswept Brook Street below, how much alike Eden and Dulles are; each is convinced that he knows the solution to the world's problems. What was troubling was that their "solutions" seemed to be different. A bad omen; the year ahead looked unpleasant enough without frictions between the secretary and the prime minister.

There were many, in both Britain and America, who felt that the style and thrust of Eden's leadership smacked of the old days—the Edwardian era when the map of the globe was mostly pink and Britannia ruled the waves. "The Prime Minister had not adjusted his thoughts to the altered world status of Great Britain, and he never did," recalled one high American official who had worked with Eden over the years.[9]

Eden's early perceptions of Britain's role in the world may have been shaped by his youth in the salad days before World War I. And his outlook later may have been molded by his mentor Churchill, the last British prime minister for whom the British Empire represented a current reality, rather than a historical concept. One influence certainly must have reinforced the other. In any case, his approach to areas of the world that had once paid homage to the British raj made even the conservative John Foster Dulles suspect that Eden, and the British in general, wanted to turn back the clock of history—or at least to slow it down.

This matter had been troubling Dulles for a long time. Soon after he had returned home from his visit to the Middle East in the spring of 1953, Dulles privately noted that "the days when the Middle East used to relax under . . . British protection are gone . . . we must convince the Arab States that the U.S. operates on a policy of its own. . . ."[10]

But if Sir Anthony had old-fashioned ideas about Africa, South Asia, and the Middle East, he had a sharper sense than Dulles of the future as it applied to Eastern Europe, the Soviet Union, and Communist China. These were new forces, Eden recognized, that could not be ignored; the

Poles, the Russians, and the Chinese had their own sense of destiny and their own vital interests. Dulles' stubborn refusal to recognize this maddened Eden.

Eden had an early premonition that the secretary would be an unreliable and overbearing partner. He tried, soon after Eisenhower was elected, to lobby against Dulles' appointment. Now he was still smarting from his unhappy experiences with Dulles at the 1954 conference in Geneva* and the more recent moves by Dulles, which had left him politically exposed and Britain militarily vulnerable on the Baghdad Pact issue. "In recent years," Eden reflected some time later, "the United States has sometimes failed to put its weight behind its friends, in the hope of being popular with their foes. The practical consequences of this uncertain diplomacy are illustrated by United States treatment of the Baghdad Pact. . . . An ounce of [American] membership . . . would have saved a ton of trouble later on."[12]

Only a few weeks before the Prime Minister had referred to the Secretary of State as "that terrible man." It was rumored around the Foreign Office that this had become Eden's synonym for Dulles in the Prime Minister's conversations with his Whitehall colleagues. But, for better or worse, unless either the Conservatives or Republicans were thrown out of office in the coming year, it was certain that Eden and Dulles were bound to see much of each other during 1956.

The old year had left both Washington and London a dubious legacy: A meeting at Geneva in November of British, French, American, and Soviet foreign ministers, which, it was hoped, would result in the unification of Germany, had produced nothing. The Western position in Berlin was exposed and vulnerable. As for the Baghdad Pact, its balance sheet was long on liabilities and short on assets: It had weakened Jordan's pro-Western King Hussein; isolated Iraq's pro-Western Nuri Said; stimulated a defense pact between Egypt and Syria; and buffeted Eden's prestige both abroad and at home. Elsewhere in the Middle East, the Israeli borders had become feverish with attacks and reprisals; the British position throughout the Persian Gulf was becoming increasingly shaky; violence by and against the British in Cyprus and the French in Algeria was escalating month by month. Meanwhile, the Russians had gained an important presence in Egypt and were collecting bouquets from nationalists everywhere in the Middle East as a result of the arms deal with Nasser.

It was time for Washington and London to take stock. In mid-Janu-

---

*Harold Macmillan characterized Dulles' behavior at the time as "elephantine obstinacy."[11]

ary, American and British diplomats were summoned home for consultation. At the end of that month, Anthony Eden and Selwyn Lloyd set off
for Washington to review the state of play and lay their future plans. For
the prime minister, the meeting offered an opportunity to secure American support for British policy in the Middle East. For the secretary of
state, the conference would permit a chance to demonstrate that he had
been dead serious when he implied, eighteen months earlier, that the
British could no longer take American support for granted.

Sir Anthony hoped that the Americans would agree to convince
Nasser that Washington and London would, if necessary, guarantee Israel's borders. Eden's move was dictated only in part by sympathy for
Israel; he was more concerned about the difficulties that would flow if
Jordan's British-supported Arab Legion were forced to move against the
Israelis. Such an attack might be forestalled, he thought, by conspicuous
(even if cosmetic), to-ing and fro-ing by British and American military
forces in the area. Dulles gave this idea short shrift; international commitments involving the possible use of force, he told him, would require
congressional approval.*

Eden's other major objective in Washington was to persuade the
United States to use its influence to stop Saudi Arabia's funding, via
Egypt, of revolutionary (and anti-British) movements in Jordan, Iraq, and
Lebanon. But Dulles parried this request, too; such a move might alienate
King Saud, America's best friend in the Middle East. Moreover, Saud
might someday become an important regional counter to Nasser.

Eden elaborated on the results of the meeting on his return to
London. "On the Baghdad Pact," he told Chancellor of the Exchequer
Harold Macmillan, "the U.S. have moved a long way and will give us all
support, moral and material, short of membership."[13] Surely, this was a
thin little thing to emerge from a three-day conference among a President, a prime minister, and senior members of their respective cabinets,
but Eden professed to be pleased. Macmillan, whose threshold of satisfaction was higher than Eden's, observed, "Like so many of these conversations, there was little tangible result."[14]

Sherman Adams, Eisenhower's assistant, was even more candid:

> Eden's visit to Washington did not resolve one serious differ-
> ence between the American and British positions on the Middle East
> question; our firm opposition to colonialism made us sympathetic to
> the struggle which Egypt and the other Arab States were making to

---

*The deployment, a decade later, of hundreds of thousands of American troops,
airmen, and sailors to Vietnam without benefit of Congress' blessing must have given Eden
a wry smile, but he was too polite to raise the point when I interviewed him.

free themselves of the political and economic control that the British felt they had to maintain in the Middle East in their own self-interest.[15]

The meeting Eden had been so anxious to arrange turned out to be a nonevent—except for one matter, one he alluded to in a message to London after his first session with Eisenhower on February 3:

> The future of [American-British] policy in the Middle East depended to a considerable extent on Nasser. The Americans thought that the present talks about the Aswan Dam with Mr. Black [Eugene Black, President of the World Bank] might indicate [Nasser's] state of mind.[16]

The "Aswan Dam"—innocent-sounding, even romantic in its evocation of the Nubia. But, of all the issues related to the Middle East then preoccupying officials in London and Washington, Egypt's Aswan Dam was the most pregnant with troublesome implications.

The young Egyptian officers who had ousted Farouk in 1952 had aspirations loftier than the mere attainment of power. Their humble origins made them sensitive to the misery rampant in Egypt's rural areas. They were conscious of the economic responsibilities implicit in their revolution. Egypt, a largely desert country about the size of Texas and New Mexico, had a population of 21 million people reproducing themselves at the rate of 4 percent a year. One-half of 1 percent of the population received 50 percent of the national income. The average individual annual income amounted to less than $100.

If Nasser's hopes for a high dam at Aswan came to fruition, vast areas could be irrigated and an enormous new source of electric power could be made available. The dam, Nasser said early in 1955, would "increase agricultural output by almost 50 per cent . . . it will be the highest dam [with] the largest reservoir in the world. It will cost $516,000,000 [and] will increase national production by $50,000,000 and will add an annual government revenue of $60,000,000."[17] To Nasser, the dam was the key to raising Egypt's living standards; it was his most cherished project, ranking at least as high as modernizing the Egyptian army.*

The ambitious plan to harness the Nile at Aswan rivaled in scale the Pyramids and the Suez Canal; it would be one of the greatest civil works projects undertaken during the past century anywhere in the world. Although the idea predated Egypt's revolution, it was not until Nasser and

---

*In the end, Nasser turned out to be optimistic. The dam's net advantages to Egypt became a matter of considerable controversy.

his brother officers assumed power that the first positive steps were taken.

On the heels of West Germany's payment of approximately $800 million to Israel as reparations for Nazi crimes, the Egyptians asked Bonn to assist them in planning and constructing the High Dam. By the end of 1952, two West German firms had begun on-site planning. It soon became clear, however, that the enterprise was far too ambitious and costly for the Germans alone to handle.

In the autumn of 1955 Nasser appealed to the World Bank. On the basis of Egypt's early discussions with Bank officials it was generally assumed that the work would proceed in two stages. The first would involve preparatory engineering work including the building of coffer dams and diversionary canals. This phase was estimated to cost $70 million in foreign exchange* and was to be funded by the United States and Great Britain ($55 million from the Americans, $15 million from the British). Stage two, the construction of the High Dam itself, would follow in about five years. This phase would cost $400 million** and would be financed half by the Bank and half by the Americans and British. But before the project could start, economic, engineering, and agricultural experts of the World Bank would have to agree that the venture was feasible.

London and Washington were anxious to counteract the Moscow-Cairo arms pact, and it took little persuasion to convince Eden and Dulles that the sum involved in the first stage was a fair price to recover ground recently lost to the USSR. When it became known that Moscow had followed up its military agreement with an offer to finance the High Dam, London and Washington became even more anxious to participate. In November 1955, Nasser was assured that British and American funding would be forthcoming if the Bank's experts came up with positive findings. There were only two explicit conditions: The High Dam would be given priority over other Egyptian civil works projects, and construction contracts would be awarded on a competitive basis. Although discussions with the Egyptians concentrated on crisp economic and administrative matters, the negotiators from Washington and London, at least, knew that Nasser's political cooperation with the West was an implied additional condition.

The meeting between British and American officials in January 1956 had reviewed Nasser's probable response not in terms of a yes or a no, but in terms of some visible moderation of his anti-Western policy. Dulles and Eden regarded their commitment to the first phase of construction

---

*This, too, was an optimistic estimate; the actual cost turned out to be $100 million.
**In the event, this phase cost nearly $1 billion.

as Nasser's reward for good conduct. If Nasser was aware that he was being tested during the early months of 1956, however, he gave no sign of it.

A few weeks after Eden returned to London from Washington, King Hussein fired General Sir John Glubb. Although Glubb had headed the Arab Legion for fifteen years, he was given only two hours to gather his family and get out of Jordan. Hussein claimed that the decision was his alone; he had sacked Glubb because the general was planning to remove several Jordanian officers who happened to be active nationalists. But Eden was convinced that Nasser was behind Glubb's dismissal.[18]

Circumstantial evidence, at least, bore Eden out.

Cairo Radio had been incessantly pounding away on the theme that Glubb was the real ruler of Jordan and that Hussein was his submissive lackey. But the Egyptians were not the only ones who took that line: London newspapers had long romanticized "Glubb Pasha." A hero-starved English public had been treated to extravagant accounts of this remnant of the Victorian era, and genuinely believed that Glubb was at least as important a figure as King Hussein.

In any case, the issue of Glubb had reached a climax at a difficult moment in Jordan. The young king had barely squeaked through the violent opposition on the occasion of General Templer's visit. Dumping Glubb may well have saved his throne. Indeed, Glubb himself later expressed sympathy for Hussein's dilemma.

Britain's alliance with Jordan had been carefully worked out from the moment Britain created the state immediately after World War I. Britain's influence in Jordan had depended on the British-educated Hussein, the British-financed Arab Legion—or more precisely, the Arab Legion under the command of Glubb and his cadre of young British officers—and British subsidies. The Legion was not only Hussein's palace guard, but the mainstay of Jordan's military forces. And in 1955, after British bases along the Suez Canal had been evacuated, Jordan had become one of the few remaining British footholds in the Middle East. Now the London-Amman alliance seemed to lie in ashes. Eden's discomfiture was especially acute because during the past two years he had strongly advocated strengthening the Legion and pursuing a pro-Jordan policy, even at the risk of jeopardizing British influence in Israel.

During the week following Glubb's removal, Hussein received an offer from the Russians and another from a Saudi-Egyptian-Syrian consortium to replace the British subsidy. This was hardly stuff to make Eden and his ministers in Whitehall feel any easier about the British future in Jordan. And yet Eden made no move. To be sure, he met with his cabinet, he consulted with American Ambassador Winthrop Aldrich, and he talked at length with General Glubb. But to his critics, now a growing number of Members of Parliament and the press, Eden appeared to be floundering. When, at last, on March 7, he spoke to the House of Commons, his speech betrayed the uncertainty and indecision that had marked the days immediately following Glubb's dismissal. "I must tell the House bluntly that I am not in a position to announce tonight, in respect of immediate policy for Jordan, definite lines of policy . . . because I am sure that to attempt to do so now, with such information as we have, would not only be premature but probably dangerous to our own interests."

Eden, himself, was rueful about this performance. "The speech . . . was regarded as one of the worst in my career. I have no doubt it was, from the parliamentary point of view." But the speech was part of a more elaborate effort to keep his lines open to Hussein: ". . . as diplomacy, the speech served its purpose. It broke no bridges with Jordan. . . . It was an occasion for doing nothing."[19]

If the prime minister kept his temper as far as Hussein was concerned, he went into a frenzy at the mere thought of Nasser. It seemed to Eden that all his efforts to preserve some vestige of British presence in the Middle East consistently ran afoul of the Cairo colonel. According to Anthony Nutting, then minister of state in the Foreign Office, Eden had "declared his own personal war against Nasser," following the dismissal of Glubb.[20] When, a month later, Foreign Office analysts urged the government to keep its powder dry with regard to Egypt in order to "neutralize" Nasser, Eden exploded, "I don't want Nasser neutralized, I want him destroyed!"[21] Anthony Nutting, an associate of Eden at the time, described him as "hysterical."

In early 1956 Nasser was first referred to in the Joint Intelligence Committee as the "Middle East Mussolini," or the "new Mussolini." (He would later be called a "petty Hitler.") The pejorative was apparently coined by Foreign Secretary Selwyn Lloyd who, by an unfortunate shake of the dice, was traveling through the Middle East on his way to Pakistan when the Jordanian crisis blew up.

Nasser was entertaining Lloyd and Ambassador Humphrey Trevelyan at dinner on the evening of Glubb's dismissal. The ambassador was given a message at the dinner table but waited until they had left Nasser's residence before telling Lloyd that Glubb had been fired. Lloyd was sure that his host had known about it in advance, especially since he had made some disparaging remarks about Glubb at dinner. Nasser actually did not learn about the incident until the following morning and accused Lloyd, when he saw him later that day, of having withdrawn Glubb.[22]

Soon after Lloyd's awkward dinner in Cairo, he was the target of an ugly stone-throwing attack by nationalists in Bahrein—a British protectorate on the Persian Gulf. The foreign secretary was convinced (probably correctly) that Nasser was behind virtually all of the nationalist movements in the Middle East, although he probably would not have claimed that Nasser played any direct role in encouraging the mob attack in Bahrein. A shaken Lloyd returned to London convinced that his government would have to face down the "new Mussolini."

Events moved quickly during that fateful spring. Marshal Bulganin and Chairman Khrushchev journeyed to London in April, having first paved the way with some conciliatory signals. The USSR, they said before leaving Moscow, was interested in a "fair settlement" of the Arab-Israeli problem. Eden took the occasion of the visit to administer a heavy dose of British concerns about Soviet moves in the Middle East. He bore down heavily on the British need for a continuing flow of oil. So critical was Middle East oil, Eden said bluntly, the British would "fight for it," if necessary. John Foster Dulles himself could not have put the matter more plainly. The Russians were taken aback. Khrushchev warned Eden of engaging in threats. What neither Eden nor the two Soviet leaders realized then, of course, was that the time would soon come when Sir Anthony would have to make good his threat.

Eden also warned his guests of the dangers of an arms race in the area. He urged them to join an East-West embargo of military equipment as soon as Moscow had completed the deliveries entailed in its current arms agreement with Egypt. Khrushchev and Bulganin pointedly reminded Eden that the arms were "Czech, not Russian," but they seemed impressed with Eden's general argument. On leaving London, Khrushchev told the press that his government would be prepared to participate in a UN arms embargo of the Middle East.

The Anglo-Soviet meeting was something less than a diplomatic success, but it was about par for the Soviet-Western course in the tension-laden days of the mid-fifties. At the nonofficial level, the visit must have been unpleasant for the men from Moscow. Although they had tea with the queen at Buckingham Palace, they got a lukewarm reception from London's man in the street. Even worse, their dinner with members of the opposition Labour Party ended in a donnybrook over the issue of Social Democrats imprisoned in Eastern European jails. Khrushchev was later heard to remark wryly, "Bulganin can vote for the Labour Party, but I'll cast my vote for the Tories."

Whether the Russians' host was a polite Eden or the rambunctious Socialist opposition party, the Cold War remained close at hand. In addition to the items on the official agenda and the argument with Labour leaders about prisoners, their visit was marked by a tragicomic spying episode; a Royal Navy frogman disappeared suspiciously near two Russian naval vessels that had escorted the Soviet officials to England. Her Majesty's government lamely explained that he was on a training exercise and that his proximity to the Soviet ships was an unfortunate coincidence.

Commenting on the final communiqué, *The Times* of London observed, "The statement records general agreement on wide aims—but nothing substantial or concrete. Inevitably, it will disappoint many, but immediate important results were not to be expected."[23] The best that could be said for the Bulganin-Khrushchev visit was that Anglo-Soviet relations were no worse than before.

Spring is the season of hope—or so the poets claim. But the spring of 1956 was merely a continuation of dark cold despair for British officials charged with advancing Her Majesty's interests in the Middle East. If anything, the outlook during the mild sunny days of April and May must have seemed even more bleak than it had in dreary February.

Guy Mollet, the French prime minister, was also in deep trouble that spring. For eighteen months, French troops had been fighting an army of irregular forces in Algeria. Civilian and military casualties were mounting. Many Arab leaders and some interested parties outside the region were anxious to rid North Africa of its last remaining colonial ruler, but Nasser, by his own account, had set the Algerian nationalists off to a good start. "Ben Bella [the head of the Algerian nationalist movement] said that on the 31st of October [1954] the revolution will begin in Algeria. We sent him arms."[24]

Upon the disintegration of the Ottoman Empire after World War I, France staked out economic and political claims in several choice pieces of Middle Eastern and North African property—Syria, Lebanon, Morocco, Tunisia, and Algeria. At the close of the Second World War Syria and Lebanon were given their independence, but France refused to budge elsewhere on the littoral. By the early fifties, however, the virus of nationalism had taken a firm hold in Morocco, Tunisia, and Algeria. In the summer of 1954, Prime Minister Mendès-France had hardly completed the Indochina negotiations at Geneva when he had to turn to the task of working out the process of Tunisian independence. Mendès-France's government fell before the business could be completed, however, and it was left to his successor, Edgar Faure, to continue. In the meantime, the situation in Morocco and Algeria deteriorated. In early 1956, both Tunisia and Morocco became independent. But in Algeria, the French *colons* applied their political weight to the politicians in Paris, and the Faure government decided that France would pursue a policy of repression rather than accommodation toward the Algerian nationalists.

In January 1956, Edgar Faure fell from grace. The next government in the dizzy succession that marked the Fourth Republic was formed by Guy Mollet. It seemed doomed from the start—a grudging coalition between the Radicals and the Socialists—but it lasted longer than any since the end of World War II. Algeria was the prime election issue, just as Vietnam would be the burning problem in the American election of 1968.

Mollet came to power hinting of some compromises with the Algerian nationalists. His investiture speech referred to the "Algerian personality," which immediately aroused the French settlers in Algeria. They feared Mollet would soon negotiate directly with the nationalists. The new prime minister visited Algiers a few weeks after taking office and was greeted by mobs of rioting, egg-throwing Frenchmen. A shaken Mollet returned to Paris convinced that his government would have to stand fast in Algeria.

Anthony Eden and John Foster Dulles had both led sheltered and privileged lives. Guy Mollet, on the other hand, had a background of turmoil, of rough and tumble. In this regard, at least, he had more in common with David Ben-Gurion, even Gamal Nasser, than with either Eden or Dulles. Mollet was orphaned at the age of twelve during World War I and had been brought up as a charge of the state. He became a student of the English language and later taught English and wrote textbooks on English grammar. Mollet was a militant Socialist and combined his teaching with labor union activity. He was active in the liberation movement during World War II. In 1942 he was captured by the Germans and was sent to Buchenwald for his sins. After the war he resumed his activities in the Socialist Party and was elected to Parliament in 1946.

Guy Mollet had not held a senior government post until he became prime minister. As the key figure in the Socialist Party, he wielded a great deal of backstage power and played an active role in making and breaking the series of governments that ruled France in the decade after the war. Although a Socialist, he was firmly opposed to the Soviet Union. "The USSR is not left, but East," he was wont to say. Withal, Mollet was not regarded as a consequential personality—"a vain and timid man," one observer called him.[25]

Mollet came to power on a rising tide of French nationalism. "My country, right or wrong," evoked the mood of France in 1956. The trauma of the ignominious departure from Indochina following the fall of Dien Bien Phu was a watershed for France; Algeria, at least, would remain "French." Almost 250,000 French troops, most of them conscripts, were fighting to assure that would be so. But by early 1956, Algeria and the fate of more than a million French settlers hung in the balance. Indeed, the stability of France itself seemed at hazard.

By the spring—that season of "hope"—the situation had so worsened in Algeria that 150,000 reservists were called up and dispatched to reinforce the embattled French troops. If any Frenchman had doubted that France was, once again, at war, his doubts were now dispelled.

Paris had been pursuing a pro-Zionist policy since the end of World War II. The French were motivated not so much by lofty moral or philosophical considerations but by stronger forces of national interest. The objective of reducing British influence in the Middle East had preoccupied French politicians for a century. The French had been supporting Zionist, anti-British paramilitary groups in the years before Israel's independence. After the State of Israel was created, the French regarded the Israelis as a useful counterweight to growing Arab nationalism, especially in French North Africa.

Within a month after the Anglo-Egyptian agreement of July 1954, Israel had secretly initiated arms purchases from France. After Egypt closed the arms deal with the USSR in late 1955, and after America and Great Britain refused to get involved in a Middle East arms race, Ben-Gurion naturally turned once more to France for planes and tanks. Against the background of Paris' growing suspicion and hatred of Nasser, it should have come as no surprise that Ben-Gurion was able to procure a full measure of military hardware.

In the late spring of 1956 relations between Cairo and Paris were more strained than ever. France now knew that the Algerian revolution had reached the point of no return. French armies in Algeria were desperately trying to keep the roads open and the cities and towns secure against an army of 100,000 Algerians. Casualties mounted and macabre atrocities became a hideous commonplace on both sides. French settlers, who thought of themselves as being front-line troops in a dirty war, became increasingly impatient with what they regarded as inadequate support from the metropole. And the French officer corps, still haunted by their rout in Western Europe sixteen years before and their recent defeat in Indochina, were making ugly sounds of protest against any French politician suspected of being conciliatory toward the Algerian nationalists.

Guy Mollet was sure that the man behind all France's troubles was Gamal Abdel Nasser; unless Nasser was contained and his mouthpiece, Cairo Radio, was silenced, the whole Middle East, perhaps France itself, would become a battleground.

In the United States, the onset of spring came on a lighter note. Americans across the country looked forward to the beginning of another presidential campaign and the quadrennial promise of drama and excitement. Washington officials, who peered out at the world through a wider lens than did their counterparts in London and Paris, found the season mildly hopeful. In Vietnam, where the United States had put all its chips on President Ngo Dinh Diem, Washington sensed the beginning of a "miracle"; Diem had consolidated his power over the rival warring sects and a strong, stable, pro-American government was just over the horizon. In Eastern Europe, Yugoslavia had firmly established itself as a dissident Communist regime; Poland and Hungary were showing signs of restlessness against tight Soviet control.

To be sure, the situation in the Middle East was tense and potentially dangerous. But except for Israel, with whom the United States had a special political relationship, and Saudi Arabia and Iran, where there were special economic ties, America felt less directly involved in the region than did either Britain or France. There was little concern for British problems in Jordan and French difficulties in Algeria. As for Nasser, he was regarded as more of a nuisance than a threat.

Cairo Radio could trumpet the most shocking insults, deliver the most outrageous lies, and the secretary of state would shrug them off. Nasser could engineer unrest against British allies and threaten British territories in the Middle East, and Dulles would murmur gratuitous advice to Anthony Eden about the sins of colonialism. And Cairo could boast of its support to the Algerian nationalists fighting the French, and the secretary would look the other way.

It was not that Dulles deprecated the importance of the Anglo-American or the Franco-American alliance; he—and, of course, Eisenhower—regarded a strong NATO as the key to American policy in Western and Eastern Europe. But to Dulles, British and French military diversions in the Middle East weakened Allied strength in Europe, the main theater where the line would have to be held against Soviet encroachments.

Washington's forbearance with the storm and fury emanating out of Egypt did not reflect a particular fondness for Nasser. Indeed, for Dulles, Nasser's neutralist stance complicated and blurred the neat black-white global picture that formed the basis of Washington's foreign policy. For all Dulles' rigidities, however, he recognized a strong political force when he confronted one. Nasser was such a force in the Middle East. It was better to try to domesticate and to learn to live with him than to banish him, snarling and vengeful, into the "Soviet camp."

There was another reason why Washington remained relatively unruffled by the plight of the British in Jordan and the French in Algeria: Neither London nor Paris had much of a constituency in the United States. But peace did. Especially in an election year.

In mid-May, however, Nasser went a step too far. And with that step he trod on John Foster Dulles' most sensitive corn: He recognized Communist China. The enormity, the gross calumny, of such a step snapped whatever goodwill John Foster Dulles harbored toward Gamal Abdel Nasser. For the secretary, recognition of China had come to assume almost religious significance; it was just short of devil worship. And Dulles was not alone in this view. For a vocal, powerful segment of American opinion, American policy with regard to China could be summed up as "isolation and ostracism." To attain this end, American ambassadors abroad were instructed to use every diplomatic (and, on occasion, nondiplomatic) means at hand. But there was another side of this coin: Any leader of any country in Africa, Asia, and Latin America could, and often did, demonstrate his independence of the United States by simply implying that "someday" his government intended to recognize Peking. Such a hint frequently paid off; a delivery of goodies was likely soon to arrive from Washington as insurance against hasty action.

Either Nasser did not know the implications of his recognition of the Peking government during the Aswan negotiations (which is unlikely), or he knew and was resigned to the angry winds from Washington (which is possible), or he scarcely gave Washington's view a second thought (which is probable). In any case, he sprung his announcement on an unprepared White House and Department of State. And this, of course, added insult to Dulles' injury.

At a press conference following Nasser's recognition of Peking, Dulles revealed that he

> expressed a regret of [Nasser's] action extending recognition to Communist China. I have also indicated that we are sympathetic with whatever action he reasonably takes to emphasize the genuine independence of Egypt. And to the extent that he is spokesman for Egyptian independence, we have sympathy with his point of view; but to the extent that he takes action which seems to promote the interests of the Soviet Union and Communist China, we do not look with favor upon such action.[26]

Although Washington felt that Nasser's ineffable act came out of the blue, this was a reflection on American intelligence information rather than on Nasser's reliability. Ever since the Bandung Conference in April 1955, the matter of recognizing Communist China had certainly been on Nasser's mind. The Chinese must have taken pains to keep the question before him. The issue for Nasser then was not so much *whether* to proceed, but *when*. His decision was made in late April when, in deference to Eden and to the delight of Dulles, the Russians implied that they would join a UN arms embargo of the Middle East—if, in fact, the UN adopted such an embargo. Nasser's public announcement was triggered when he learned that France had agreed to sell weapons to Israel.

If arms for Egypt were in danger of being cut off by the USSR and by other members of the UN while Israel was obtaining new equipment from France, Nasser must have reasoned that his only prudent course would be to find a source of guns outside the UN. Communist China, not then a member of the UN, was a logical candidate. That China, however willing, was in no position to provide Egypt with modern arms did not escape Nasser's notice. Indeed, Premier Chou En-lai apparently told him as much at Bandung. But Nasser hoped to use China as a middleman for Soviet weapons. In the end, of course, there was no UN arms embargo, China was not called upon for military matériel, and Nasser did get into trouble with Washington.

Although the projected official American share of the foreign exchange cost for the Aswan Dam was less than half the total, the whole arrangement hung on Washington's decision; the British would not go forward—indeed, could not afford to go forward—without the American contribution, and World Bank funding was contingent on American–British participation. It would be inaccurate to say that Nasser's precipitate recognition of China alone jettisoned the American–British–World Bank financing of the High Dam; there were too many other factors and actors in play during the spring of 1956. But it would be fair to say that Nasser's bravura act chilled Secretary Dulles to the bone. And a chilly Dulles was a dangerous Dulles.

At least well into May, Nasser, Eden, and even President of the World Bank Eugene Black were optimistic about American approval. The Administration was obviously anxious to forestall further Soviet inroads into the Middle East. As early as the previous December, a State Department paper had stressed that "Western financing [of the dam] is necessary to avoid the threat of Soviet penetration" and that Egypt would accept Moscow's assistance if the West did not come through.[27]

Preliminary technical discussions with American, British, and Egyptian representatives in December had gone well. Moreover, the World Bank had given the enterprise a rigorous examination and a passing grade. By the spring of 1956, the odds in favor of the High Dam were good—but not good enough. Those who knew Washington well, especially the Washington of the mid-fifties, would have hedged their bets.

The first warning signal that might have caught the eye of the wary would have been the size of the eventual financial commitment. Nasser was relying, after all, on a Republican Administration that was then professing concern, ad nauseam, about the reckless spending and unbalanced budgets of its Democratic predecessors. Those were pinch-penny days in Washington. My own exposure to Republican appointees at the National Security Council staff level had taught me a surefire way to project the image of a sound fellow while killing an idea I was reluctant to criticize on its merits: When the discussion, pro and con, had all but run its course, I would simply ask, "How much will it cost?" When a number—any number—was mentioned, I needed only to raise my ample eyebrows, suck in my breath, and then utter a barely audible, "Wow!" But even in periods when Micawber rather than Scrooge ruled the roost in Washington, the commitment to go ahead with the High Dam would have occasioned consternation.

There was another reason for caution about the prospects for the High Dam: Legislators did not then (nor do they now) appreciate being locked into a long-term commitment of funds. They prefer annual appropriations based on yearly justifications. State Department bureaucrats, too, dislike such a long-term arrangement, for it is they who have to make the difficult case that the program is of such overriding importance that it warrants exceptional congressional treatment. They would have been reluctant to assume this chore at any time for such a sensitive area as the Middle East. But an aid program for Egypt that, once approved, would have to extend over many years was hardly a succulent political morsel to throw before Congress in the election year of 1956. No wonder, then, that deep in the bowels of the Department there was little enthusiasm for the dam.

These blinking yellow danger signals should have given pause. And yet they were hardly enough in themselves to cause the High Dam advocates to abandon ship. The ultimate price tag would be in the hundreds of millions, but the immediate decision called for only $55 million over several years. Aid to Korea in 1955 was $207 million and to Indochina $216 million. Congressional justification would be a nuisance, but it was manageable. Secretary Dulles, the most powerful personality in the cabinet, could have coped with both of these problems—if he had wanted to.

The real problem—the one that sharply decreased the odds on approval—was that Dulles did not want to fight over the dam. Though it was not then discernible to the naked eye, the Aswan High Dam, as such, did not make John Foster Dulles salivate. What did was the hope that American assistance could be exploited to achieve other, more important ends.

One such end, of course, was the preemption of further Soviet penetration into the Middle East. American funding of the Dam would help achieve this. Dulles' other objective was more ambitious: He wanted to use the prospect of American (and therefore British, and therefore World Bank) funding to exact concessions from Nasser that, together with pressure on Israel, would force a settlement of the Arab-Israeli conflict. If the secretary had had a guarantee that both his objectives would be achieved, the dam would have filled him with ardor.

Dulles' approach to Egypt's request was by no means a shiny innovation in international relations. It has long been used by one nation against another and has been variously described as "blackmail," "strings-attached," or "linkage." Businessmen refer to it as "reciprocity."

Thus it was, that in the autumn of 1955, within weeks after American, British, and Egyptian representatives had met for preliminary discussions on the dam, Dulles launched a vigorous but unsuccessful drive to bring Israel and Egypt together on a compromise territorial and political arrangement. He dispatched a special emissary, the Texas oil magnate (later secretary of the treasury) Robert Anderson, to undertake the thankless mission of arranging the mating dance. This was the bargaining process Eden had in mind when, a few months later, after his meeting in Washington, he noted that negotiations on the High Dam would depend on Nasser's "response." But the Israelis could not be persuaded to yield on important issues simply to help Nasser get his dam. And Nasser was furious at the thought that the Americans were trying to link aid for the High Dam with concessions toward Israel. So much for the secretary's attempt to tie aid for the dam to an Arab-Israeli treaty. And so much for whatever dreams he may have had of winning a Nobel Peace Prize.

Negotiations on the High Dam continued, however—albeit with less fervor than might have been the case if Dulles' peace plan had worked. But it was heavy going; the path toward American participation was strewn with anti–High Dam lobbies. There was, for a starter, the Cold War lobby: Why should the United States spend hundreds of millions of dollars to help the avowed friend of her avowed enemy? And then there was the cotton lobby: Egypt was already exporting cotton at cut-rate prices; why should the United States spend hundreds of millions to reclaim land in Egypt that would be planted to cotton and further compete with American farmers in a shrinking world market? And the pro-Israel lobby: Why should the United States help Nasser at all? And the one-man Senator-Morse-of-Oregon lobby: Why finance a giant dam in Egypt instead of one—or several—in America's own Northwest?

Those who thought in the spring of 1956 that the omens boded well for American funding of the High Dam could not have known the tough sledding the Aswan advocates were having. Except for Eugene Black, the dam had few strong proponents in Washington. Black's readiness to proceed was obviously a necessary condition for Washington's eventual approval, but it was by no means a sufficient one. Black was head of the World Bank, not a member of the Eisenhower Administration. Dulles was the key, not Black.

Nasser himself delivered the coup de grace in mid-May. His recognition of Communist China sapped whatever remaining enthusiasm Dulles had for the enterprise and confronted the secretary with the strongest lobby of all—the powerful China Lobby headed in the Senate by Minority Leader William Knowland of California. Knowland gave the secretary some friendly advice: The government's overall foreign aid bill would soon be voted in Congress. The Administration had professed interest in two controversial country programs: assistance to Nasser, the Communist-lover, and assistance to Tito, the Communist. He, Knowland, heartily disliked both gentlemen, but would not be unreasonable. Dulles could choose one or the other. But unless the Administration was ready to risk jeopardizing the overall aid bill, Dulles would be wise not to press for both. The secretary chose Tito, who, after all, was trying to consolidate his divorce from the men in the Kremlin, rather than pursue a courtship with them.

Soon after, American funding of the Aswan High Dam was a dead letter. But how and when should the British and the World Bank, the would-be partners in the enterprise, be told? And what of informing that part of Washington that existed outside the State Department's executive offices? Finally, and most important, how best to break the news to the Egyptians? Dulles did what came naturally—he kept his cards close to his chest. But, inevitably, some faint rumors of his closely guarded hand emerged.

In late May, Egyptian Ambassador Hussein, a skilled diplomat with a good nose for trouble in the air, had begun to sense a changing mood. He dashed off to Cairo to warn that prospects for American approval were dim. Dulles, he told Nasser, could probably have dealt with the cotton lobby and the pro-Israeli interests, but Egypt's recognition of China had shaken the secretary. If Nasser still wanted American funding, some assurances were in order, Under Secretary Herbert Hoover, Jr., had told the ambassador just before Hussein left for Cairo. First, Egypt would have to halt its arms purchases from the Soviet Union; the Administration was worried that Egypt would be unable to pay Moscow and still repay the Aswan loan. And then Nasser would have to move the Arabs toward peace with Israel. If Nasser could agree to these, American approval might yet be obtained.

According to Egyptian newsman Mohamed Heikal, a confidant of

Nasser, Hoover's conditions "came as no surprise." Nasser had discovered a month earlier that "the Americans were going to renege on their pledge. He knew because one of his secret agents had provided him with all the top secret minutes of the meeting of Foreign Ministers of the Baghdad Pact in Teheran in the middle of March."[28]

Ambassador Hussein, who apparently had been kept in ignorance of Nasser's source of information, returned to Egypt again in late June to report that Dulles was facing heavy congressional opposition to the loan and that the secretary needed the guarantees sought earlier. He found Nasser in an ebullient mood. The British had by now completed their final withdrawal from Suez, the Russians had recently renewed their earlier offer to help Egypt finance the dam, and Nasser had just been "elected" president of Egypt. "Tell Dulles," Nasser said to Ambassador Hussein, "that you have accepted all his conditions and watch his reactions. . . . I give you carte blanche. Go and tell him that we have accepted everything. . . . Because we are not going to get the High Dam."[29]

Hussein returned to the United States on July 17. He told reporters on his arrival that "all the decisions now are up to Washington and London." Egypt had decided to "take assistance from the West. It all depends on them."[30]

Even before Hussein's press announcement, Dulles had become aware through the American Embassy in Cairo that Nasser was apparently ready to go along with the two American conditions and realized that his hand would soon be forced. Much to Dulles' embarrassment, his own scenario had not taken account of this. He had been counting on Nasser's losing his temper over Washington's insistence that he stop buying Soviet arms and make peace with Israel. According to Dulles' script, Nasser would rant and rave against American interference and, in a spate of anger, announce he was turning to Moscow for the loan. If only Nasser had obliged, it would have made the secretary's task infinitely easier.

Dulles had one remaining high card to play: Soviet Foreign Minister Dimitri Shepilov had visited Cairo in mid-June to participate in the ceremonies celebrating the departure of the last British unit from Egypt. Following his meeting with Nasser there had been carefully orchestrated leaks indicating that Moscow was ready to extend credits for the dam on more favorable terms than the West.[31] Indeed, a position paper was prepared in the Department of State that raised the possibility of a Soviet offer to finance the dam. In such an event, Washington should "let nature take its course, but be prepared for the possibility that the Egyptians and Soviets would conclude a deal." In any case, the memorandum noted, the United States had no funds "immediately available" for the dam.[32]

Dulles hoped that, somehow, it could be shown that Nasser was trying to blackmail the United States. But he needed the right lever and that would take time. Meanwhile, Dulles' first task was to inform Eisenhower that Nasser was pressing for an immediate decision.

On July 13 the secretary drove to the Gettysburg farm where the President was recuperating from a six-week bout of ileitis. The tortured, stop-and-start Aswan Dam negotiations were hardly important enough to have concerned the ill Eisenhower, and he had been barely aware of what had been going on. Cairo's readiness to comply with the American terms, Dulles told the President, might mean that Nasser's discussions with Shepilov had not gone as well as earlier accounts had indicated.[33] But, he reminded his boss, the Administration was already facing difficulties pushing the overall foreign aid bill through Congress, and a request for funds to finance the dam would rock the boat.

Eisenhower, who had displayed scant interest in the Aswan matter, left the decision to Dulles. He would support the secretary either way, but was obviously unenthusiastic about going ahead. It was, after all, an election year, and America's participation in the High Dam consortium would win him few votes.

An appointment with the secretary was arranged for Ambassador Hussein on July 19, two days after his return from Cairo. On July 18, Dulles called the British ambassador to the Department. He broadly implied, but did not flatly tell the ambassador, that he planned to inform Hussein the deal was off. This was not the first indication the British had received. Cabot Lodge, the U.S. ambassador to the UN, had warned Anthony Nutting (who was then in New York) that Dulles "would in all probability renege on the Aswan Dam loan."[34]

Upon receiving the news from the British Embassy in Washington, Eden and Lloyd immediately contacted Dulles urging him to avoid precipitate action. The same cautionary note had been sounded a day or two earlier by the French ambassador to Washington, Maurice Couve de Murville. De Murville, who had previously served in Cairo, reminded the State Department that Nasser was a volatile personality. It was by no means unlikely, the ambassador warned, that Nasser would take over the Suez Canal in direct response to Washington's abrupt cancellation of the Aswan negotiations.

The British and French warnings apparently made little impression on Dulles. He was ready to bite the bullet. And he bit it at his meeting with Ambassador Hussein on July 19.

In due course, Hussein gave Dulles his opening. Urging the United States to approve the loan, the ambassador patted his pocket and archly implied that a firm Russian offer was figuratively right there. Dulles played his high card: America would not be blackmailed; let Cairo go to Moscow. As a matter of fact, Dulles continued, the United States had grave doubts about Egypt's ability to undertake the economic burdens of repaying the loan. The deal was off.

The official statement following the meeting elaborated on the American rationale—a rationale that emphasized the economic risks of the loan (which, at best, had been a marginal consideration) and carefully avoided the political problems at issue: Developments since December, when the preliminary offer had been made, the Department noted, "have not been favorable to the success of the project and the United States Government has concluded that it is not feasible in present circumstances to participate in the project. Agreement by the riparian states (e.g. the Sudan) has not been achieved, and the ability of Egypt to devote adequate resources to assure the project's success has become more uncertain than at the time the offer was made."[35]

Eugene Black was no less furious than Nasser on learning that Dulles had backed off. And, of the two, Black was the more surprised.

Black had a right to be angry; no American official had shown him the courtesy of providing even a few hours' advance notice of the decision —or even that a decision was imminent. Hussein had seen him a day or two prior to the fateful meeting with Dulles and reported that Nasser had accepted the American conditions. Hardly a week before, Black had told an American audience that the World Bank was now convinced that the High Dam was an economically sound investment. And now Dulles was leaning on the economic-fragility argument to rationalize the American position. With considerable justification, Black felt ridiculed and betrayed.

But Black and his Bank were expendable casualties in Dulles' view. And Black was not the only key figure who was kept in the dark. Robert Murphy, under secretary for political affairs and the third-ranking official in the Department of State, was also taken by surprise. The secretary confided in no one except the President—and even Eisenhower was not informed of the final decision until the very morning of Hussein's appointment.[36]

John Foster Dulles had decided on his own to say "No"—finally, brusquely, decisively. His advisers, other interested parties, and other considerations were secondary. Time would take care of them. And time did, as time almost always does.

The British, too, had become increasingly disenchanted with the Aswan scheme. Nasser's support of troublemakers in Jordan and else-

where was at the root of their change of heart, but publicly Eden professed that he, like the Americans, was troubled by the economic risks:

> As the months passed [following the winter of 1956], a growing
> proportion of Egyptian revenues was directed to meeting payments
> for arms from behind the Iron Curtain . . . it became more and more
> doubtful whether the Egyptian government would be able to cover
> their part of the inevitable expenditure for the dam project. . . .
> There was a point beyond which we could not go on financing this
> venture . . . the State Department shared both our doubts for the
> present and our apprehension for the future of the scheme. . . . In
> mid-July . . . the Government came to the conclusion that they could
> not go on with a project likely to become increasingly onerous in
> finance and unsatisfactory in practice.[37]

Eden was thus not opposed to the American decision, but he was
sorely miffed about Dulles' tactics and style. "I would have preferred not
to have forced the issue. There was no need to hurry." But "we were
informed, not consulted and so had no prior opportunity for criticism or
comment."[38]

It is a moot question whether Lodge's warning to Nutting and Dulles'
exchange with the British ambassador added up to London's being "informed" or being "consulted." Although Eden's plea for caution was
ignored, he had a last-minute opportunity to warn Washington against
hasty action.

Eden's recollection that concern about the economic wisdom of the
enterprise tipped the scales in London against the High Dam smacks
more of an excuse than an explanation. Cairo's mischief making and
vituperative anti-British propaganda had become standard items for discussion on the weekly menu of the various Whitehall meetings I had been
attending that spring and early summer. No one—not even the economic
intelligence experts—gave Egypt's financial situation more than passing
mention. Nor, to give my own colleagues and bosses in Washington their
due, did I get any inkling from them that Egypt's economic prospects
were high on the list of American concerns. Nasser had been causing
sleepless nights for analysts and policymakers in London and Washington, but it was not his credit rating that preoccupied them.

Even America's closest allies were mystified over the rationale behind Dulles' renege. On the day following the American decision, a
Canadian diplomat told his State Department colleague that "the United
States has seemed in the Aswan matter to have rebuffed Nasser as he was
moving towards the U.S."[39]

At the Joint Intelligence Committee meeting following the announcement of the American decision I was pressed hard to explain why we had turned Nasser down. As a loyal civil servant, I did my best to mouth some platitudes about Egypt's grave population problem and unpromising economic outlook, but I knew that the official Washington explanation was far from the real reason. And my British friends knew that I knew. We were all very uncomfortable—but not as uncomfortable as we soon would be.

Nasser heard the news in Yugoslavia on his way back to Cairo from a meeting with Tito and Nehru—hardly the most propitious time or occasion. Perhaps he would have reacted differently if he had received Hussein's message and read the hollow American communiqué in the familiar surroundings of his Cairo headquarters. But probably not; his was not an equable temperament under the best of circumstances.

Nasser treated Washington to a taste of his venom and gave a hint of worse to come a few days later when he dedicated the new Suez-Cairo pipeline. He accused the United States of lying about the Egyptian economy: ". . . we shall not pay any attention to the imperialists . . . to those who have been trying to exercise control over us and our potentialities . . . we are determined to live proudly and not to beg for aid."[40]

Washington reacted with a strong official protest—but it turned out to be strictly pro forma, as the State Department must surely have known it would. And then, on July 26, Nasser played the ace of trumps. He took over the Suez Canal—locks, stocks, and barrels.

6

BUYING TIME

As January spun into July I knew little of what was unfolding in Number 10 Downing Street, the presidential palace in Cairo, or the executive offices on the State Department's seventh floor. Even if I had known much more than I did, I could hardly have guessed what it all would mean. And so, in blissful ignorance, I bundled myself and my family off on July 21 for an extended holiday at a small village on a remote Norwegian fjord.

London was now only a few days behind us, but we already felt relaxed and refreshed in the country inn on the road from Bergen to Oslo. Although it was early evening, the sun was still high as we returned to the inn after a long day of swimming, sailing, and picnicking. Our daughters giggled their way up the path as first one and then the other extravagantly imitated the ladies they had seen on the beach maneuvering their way in and out of bathing suits from under their dresses.

The Bergen paper was resting on its usual place on the foyer table. Ordinarily I barely noticed it, but this afternoon a two-inch headline leapt out at me. My Norwegian was only marginally better than my Pushtu, but "Nasser" and "Suez" emerge as "Nasser" and "Suez" in any Romanized script. Although there was an intervening word dotted with Ø's which I could not decipher, the exclamation point at the end of the three-word headline made it clear that whatever had happened was worthy of special emphasis.

I tried to ignore what I knew I had seen. A puritan conscience and a decade of Washington conditioning, however, made this a losing battle. I then attempted to fall back on the thin assurance that the embassy would get in touch with me if there was a serious crisis. But I remembered that no one in Grosvenor Square had a clue as to where in Norway I was. I procrastinated as long as I could, but after dinner I called London. A harassed-sounding duty officer confirmed my suspicions; Nasser had taken over the Canal. "Should I come home?" "How the hell do I know? Somebody will probably call you in the morning now that we know where you are." Somebody did. I was on the next flight out of Oslo for London.

On the plane I read the nationalization speech in *The Times* and was struck by Nasser's apparent neurosis about the late M. Ferdinand de

Lesseps: "I began to look at Mr. [Eugene] Black . . . imagining I was sitting before Ferdinand de Lesseps"; "In 1954, Ferdinand de Lesseps arrived in Egypt . . ."; "I was again carried back to Ferdinand de Lesseps"; "We have complexes from de Lesseps . . . ." There were seven references to that memorable Frenchman in the first few hundred words of Nasser's speech. Several years later I learned that "de Lesseps" was a code word between Nasser and the man he had picked to carry out the Canal take-over. If Nasser used it at the opening of his speech it would signal that he had decided to proceed with nationalization. Egyptian technicians were then to move immediately to occupy key installations along the Canal.[1]

Having repeated the key word enough times to assure that the message would be understood, Nasser then settled down to the business at hand:

> . . . we aim at the eradication of past evils which brought about our domination, and the vestiges of the past which took place despite ourselves and which were caused by imperialism through treachery and deceit.
>
> Today the Suez Canal . . . has become a state within the state. It has humiliated ministers and cabinets. . . .
>
> Do you know how much assistance America and Britain were going to offer us over 5 years? Seventy million dollars. Do you know who takes the 100 million dollars, the Company's income, every year? They take them of course. . . .
>
> We shall not repeat the past. We shall eradicate it by restoring our rights in the Suez Canal. This money is ours. This Canal is the property of Egypt. . . . The Suez Canal Company in Paris is an imposter company. . . .
>
> But history will never repeat itself . . . we shall build the High Dam. We shall restore our usurped rights. . . .
>
> Thus, today, citizens, when we build the High Dam, we are actually building the dam to defend our dignity, freedom and pride, and to eradicate humiliation and submission.
>
> Egypt—the whole of Egypt—one national front—one unified and solid front—will fight to the last drop of its blood. . . . We shall not let warmongers, imperialists or those who trade in human beings dominate us. . . .
>
> Therefore, I have signed today the following [nationalization] law which has been approved by the Cabinet:
>
> . . . Today, citizens, rights have been restored to their owners. Our rights in the Suez Canal have been restored to us after 100 years. . . .

Today, citizens, the Suez Canal Company has been nationalized.
. . . On embarking upon the fifth year of the Revolution, as Farouk
was expelled on July 26, 1952, the Suez Canal Company will depart
on the very same day. . . . Sovereignty in Egypt will belong only to
her sons. . . .

Now, while I am speaking to you fellow countrymen, brothers
of yours are taking over the administration and the management of
the Canal Company, the Egyptian Canal Company not the foreign
Canal Company. They are taking over the Canal Company and its
facilities for the direction of navigation in the Canal, the Canal which
is situated in the territory of Egypt, is a part of Egypt and belongs
to Egypt. We now perform this task to compensate for the past and
build up new edifices for pride and dignity.[2]

By the time Nasser had finished his speech, the Suez Canal was under
Egyptian control. Nasser had avenged the Aswan Dam decision; if the
West would not finance the dam, Egypt would do it through the revenues
of the Canal. The department that Cairo's revolutionary government had
established to anticipate the expiration of the Suez Canal Company concession had done its work well. Its plan was ready twelve years ahead of
schedule.

I went from Heathrow directly to the embassy. Awaiting me was a
culling of material from the Egyptian press and radio. Washington's
official explanation for turning down the Aswan loan had fooled few
Egyptian commentators. One broadcast was uncomfortably close to the
truth: The American explanation was "a fabrication, a poor attempt to
conceal the real reason—resentment over Egypt's independent foreign
policy and a determination to exert pressure on the Egyptian government." There were other, more vituperative reactions to Dulles' decision:
Colonel Anwar Sadat, then the managing editor of a semiofficial newspaper, charged that the United States and Great Britain "suck the blood of
human beings for the sake of their prosperity and trifle with the security
of the world for the sake of their caprice and pacts."[3]

Attacks on the United States in the Egyptian press were one thing;
Nasser's caustic statements were quite another. A copy of the State Department's reaction to Nasser's speech was on my desk. The wording was
just barely on the sunny side of diplomatic discourse. Under Secretary
Hoover had called in the Egyptian ambassador immediately after the
speech and told him that "the United States was shocked by the many
intemperate, inaccurate and misleading statements made with respect to
the United States by the President of Egypt. . . . Such statements were
entirely inconsistent with the friendly relations which have existed between the two Governments and peoples. . . ."[4] If Nasser actually read

the text of the American protest, he apparently ignored it. There was no reply from Cairo.

I wondered whether the initial Western reaction to the nationalization might have been more sympathetic, or at least less violent, if the tone of Nasser's remarks and the manner of his delivery had been less vitriolic. After all, it was not the first time during those hectic postwar years that the property of Western nations had been taken over by a nationalist regime. Just a few years before, in Iran, large British oil installations had been nationalized; London had swallowed hard, but accepted it. But Nasser's nationalization speech seemed calculated to exact the highest possible quotient of fury in London, Washington, and Paris.

Nasser spoke extemporaneously, referring only occasionally to a few hastily scribbled notes. His audience at Manchia Square in Alexandria, the scene of his close brush with assassins two years before, had whipped itself into a frenzy of excitement in the expectation that something special was in store. They were not disappointed. The anniversary of the Egyptian Revolution was a made-to-order occasion for Nasser to vent his long-smoldering anger. His remarks—taunting, insulting, sarcastic, bombastic—brought cheers from his countrymen all over Egypt.

An hour or so after I arrived at the embassy, I called the Foreign Office to tell the chairman of the Middle East "working party" (which had been established soon after the Jordanian crisis) that I had returned to London. But he was still in Switzerland on his annual six-week summer holiday. My friend finally cut his holiday short—he returned to London in late August. For months afterward he would regale not altogether sympathetic listeners with the problems involved in his "precipitate" departure from Switzerland. Nasser did not realize it, but he had a special adversary at a strategic point in Whitehall.

Our evening at that peaceful Norwegian inn had been spoiled by the news from Alexandria. But this was trivial compared to the discomfiture Nasser had created the previous night at 10 Downing Street. Prime Minister Eden and Foreign Secretary Lloyd received the report of the nationalization while they were entertaining Nuri Said of Iraq at a state dinner. Lloyd, who just a few months before had been dining with Nasser when General Glubb was thrown out of Jordan, was, by now, an old hand at finding unexpected courses on the menu. He took the news calmly. But Sir Anthony seemed a victim of spontaneous combustion. Those who knew him well had never seen him so angry. His nerves had been on edge for several tension-ridden weeks and the escalating problems with Nasser had taken their toll.

Eden's aide was sent scurrying to round up as many civilian and military advisers as could be found in London on a summer night. Dinner was cut short. Port and cigars were dispensed with. And Nuri Said made a hasty departure. Within the hour, a mixed bag of British officials—guests from the State Dinner in white ties and tails; others, who had not been so favored, in casual summer garb—convened in the Cabinet Room. Among them were the counselor from the American Embassy (Ambassador Winthrop Aldrich was unavailable) and the French ambassador.

Eden got to the point without ceremony: The Egyptians had engaged in an aggressive act; a sharp, quick response was called for; the Foreign Office was to examine the possibility of legal redress. And then he turned to the chiefs of staff. What could be done militarily? It was a big, anxious question, but it elicited a small, agonized reply: Nothing—or at least nothing very soon. British troops were fighting the EOKA in Cyprus, the Communists in Malaya, and the Mau Mau in Kenya. Major elements of the army were assigned to the NATO forces in Germany. There was little left to permit an early move against Nasser.[5]

Most of those who filed out of 10 Downing Street on that July night felt helpless and frustrated. Was the supine acceptance of an act of international piracy by a petty Mussolini to be the fate of once powerful Britain? Was this to be the harvest of Britain's costly, glorious victory just over a decade before?

That meeting at Downing Street marked a milestone in Britain's journey from an island nation, to a world empire, to a small European power. For on that night, in that place, it was revealed that the empire had no clothes.

Not everybody realized this then, of course. Not the Tory backbenchers; they had already been seeking Eden's political scalp because he had agreed to withdraw British troops from the Suez Canal Zone. Not the outraged press: "The British Government can prove that its legs are not completely palsied by getting up on them and raising hell," screamed the Daily Sketch; Nasser's act, The Times scolded, was "a clear affront and threat to Western interests. . . . The time has arrived for a much more decisive policy." And not Anthony Eden; he felt both betrayed by Dulles' sudden cancellation of the Aswan Dam offer and trapped by Nasser's unexpected nationalization of the Canal.

Nasser was threatening not only the future of his government but also the very security of Great Britain. Eden was unwilling to resign himself to inaction, unable to exercise patience. Perhaps Churchill egged him on. "We can't have that malicious swine sitting across our communications," Sir Winston had said, on hearing the news of Nasser's takeover. "What will the Americans do?" he was asked. "We don't need Americans for this!" Churchill snapped.[6] Eden insisted that his government must seek immediate legal redress, or make a military response, or both.

Looking back, it is tempting to ascribe Eden's outrage to personal pique which had been exacerbated by the injured amour propre of the Victorian-minded imperialists surrounding him. But that would be only part of the picture. A fairer judgment would take cognizance of Britain's historic stake in the Suez Canal. No further evidence need be offered than the sacrifices made in the Second World War to prevent that waterway from being controlled by unfriendly nations. The United Kingdom itself had been stripped of precious soldiers and scarce weapons to ward off an Axis threat to the Canal.

Britain had to trade to survive, and the route to Asia through the Suez Canal was vital to Britain's economy. Twenty-five percent of total British imports came through the Canal. And for decades the shortcut to the oil fields of the Middle East had been recognized as a great strategic prize. ("The Canal is an oil pipeline, an economic lifeline," editorialized London's *Star* on July 27.) Finally, the United Kingdom was a major partner in the Suez Canal Company. Forty-five percent of the Canal revenues flowed into the British treasury. Britain counted on these revenues to bolster its hard-pressed exchequer in the twelve years still remaining before the Suez concession was to expire.

On July 27, the day following the abortive state dinner, Eden reassembled his chief advisers. In a more structured and less emotional session, the prime minister heard the gloomy overnight reports from his legal, economic, and diplomatic aides.

The legal experts had concluded that Her Majesty's government had a puny case. Nasser was apparently ready to abide by the 1888 Convention of Constantinople, the international treaty that had guaranteed all nations unfettered transit through the Canal; foreign shipping would continue to proceed through the Canal without interference. The Israelis, of course, would be excluded, but they had been prevented from using the Canal even under the regime of the Suez Canal Company. Moreover, the lawyers stressed, Nasser had taken over the Canal *Company;* the Canal itself lay in Egypt's sovereign territory. Finally, he had *nationalized* the Company, not *confiscated* it; shareholders would be compensated.

A hasty examination of other options had turned up nothing very promising. The Russians, on the one hand, were offering large loans at low interest and the Saudis, on the other, were a source of ready cash. And since American and British assistance for the High Dam was already a dead issue, the cupboard was practically bare of economic sticks or carrots. If the prime minister wanted to move against Nasser, he would have to rely on either diplomatic or military action; the legal route and economic sanctions were nonstarters.

But diplomatic pressure also promised little.* There was obviously no hope of support from either the Communist or the unaligned nations. Even among the Commonwealth nations, there would be only a few staunch supporters. Military action, despite the grim report of the chiefs on the forces available, seemed to be the only feasible course.

Following that meeting, Eden sent telegrams to President Eisenhower and Premier Mollet suggesting that their personal representatives come to London to consider the next move. Premier Mollet, who had called Eden immediately after the takeover, had Foreign Minister Christian Pineau on his way within hours.

That afternoon Eden told an anxious House of Commons: "The unilateral decision of the Egyptian Government to expropriate the Suez Canal Company . . . affects the rights and interests of many nations. Her Majesty's Government are consulting other governments immediately concerned. . . . We are in touch with the United States Government and the French Government. . . . I would ask the House not to press me to say more than this at the moment. . . ."

Eden's next message to the White House summed up the situation as it appeared to him on the morning after.

> This morning I have reviewed the whole position with my Cabinet colleagues and Chiefs of Staff. We are all agreed that we cannot afford to allow Nasser to seize control of the Canal . . . in defiance of international agreements. If we take a firm stand over this now we shall have the support of all the maritime powers. If we do not, our influence and yours throughout the Middle East will . . . be finally destroyed.
>
> We should not allow ourselves to become involved in legal quibbles about the rights of the Egyptian Government to nationalize what is technically an Egyptian company, or in financial arguments about their capacity to pay the compensation which they have offered. . . . We should take issue with Nasser on the broader international grounds.
>
> . . . We are unlikely to attain our objectives by economic pressures alone. . . . We ought in the first instance to bring the maximum political pressure to bear. . . .
>
> . . . My colleagues and I are convinced that we must be ready, in the last resort, to use force to bring Nasser to his senses. For our part we are prepared to do so. I have this morning instructed our Chiefs of Staff to prepare a military plan accordingly.
>
> However, the first step must be for you and us and France to

---

*A note of protest had already been sent to the Egyptian government; it was returned a few hours later to the British Embassy in Cairo.

exchange views, align our policies and concert together how we can best bring the maximum pressure to bear on the Egyptian Government.[7]

The President, still recovering from a debilitating illness, was alarmed at the tone of Eden's telegram. With Secretary Dulles in Peru and not scheduled to return to Washington for a few days, Eisenhower felt isolated from the fast-moving developments in London. Moreover the presidential election campaign was warming up; the Democrats were scheduled to meet on August 17 and the Republican Convention was barely a week later. He welcomed Eden's suggestion that he send a personal envoy to coordinate American, French, and British policy and told Under Secretary of State Robert Murphy to leave for London immediately.

Murphy arrived on the following evening, Saturday, July 28. He became quickly aware of the public mood. "The time for appeasement is over," the *Daily Mail* had warned that morning. "We must cry 'Halt!' to Nasser as we should have cried 'Halt' to Hitler. Before he sets the Middle East aflame, as Hitler did Europe." The newspapers he saw at breakfast on Sunday were no less shrill and were a foretaste of what lay in store when he met with Lloyd and Pineau later that morning and with Harold Macmillan at dinner. As the days passed, the Nasser-Hitler analogy would soon become common parlance in the press, the House of Commons, and the government.

When Murphy met with Eden a day or two later he sensed that Her Majesty's government was prepared to retrieve the Canal by force. To assure that both British and Egyptians understood how seriously London regarded Nasser's move, Eden told Murphy that he intended to call up thousands of reserve troops and to reinforce the British fleet in the Mediterranean. "It became increasingly evident," according to Murphy, "that there was serious and perhaps imminent prospect of Anglo-French military action."[8] The under secretary would have been even more concerned had he known that Premier Mollet had already broached the possibility to Eden of a combined French-British-Israeli attack on Egypt.[9]

The exploratory talks in London in late July provided the first chance for officials from Washington to size up the new French foreign minister. Under Secretary Murphy was not impressed. He was especially disturbed by Pineau's undiplomatic approach to a diplomatic crisis. The minister was "far more aggressive than Eden," accusing Murphy of discounting the seriousness of Nasser's move against the Canal. To make matters worse, Pineau was openly contemptuous of the United States and blamed the American refusal to finance the High Dam for the present crisis.[10]

Murphy and his colleagues in Washington should not have been taken by surprise; Pineau had given earlier hints of his attitude. In March he had revealed to the Anglo-American Press Association in Paris his "utter disagreement" with Western policy. "Despite alliances, despite affirmations, there is no real common French-British-American policy." He recited such examples as the refusal of Britain and the United States to support the French in North Africa, the unwillingness of the United States to cooperate with France in Indochina, and the fact that Paris was not consulted about the Baghdad Pact. He implied that if the Atlantic alliance fell apart, France would make its own deal with the USSR. (Mollet, despite his anti-Soviet inclinations, had already announced his desire to establish closer relations with the Russians and was scheduled to visit Moscow with Pineau the following May.)

Although Pineau did not refer to the Anglo-American summit meeting held in Washington earlier in the year, many reporters who heard his remarks felt that the foreign minister was signaling his pique that he and Mollet had been ignored by Eden and Eisenhower. Learning of this, Eden had promptly invited Mollet to London. Whether the President and his secretary of state were aware of it then or not, they had a difficult new partner across the Atlantic.

Upon completing his formal training as an economist, Christian Paul Francis Pineau had been employed by the Bank of France. But, like Mollet (and Ben-Gurion), he found that labor union activity was more to his liking than banking. Fired by the bank for trying to unionize its employees, he became a mover and shaker in the Socialist Party. During World War II he joined the French Resistance, was captured by the Germans, escaped, and joined the de Gaulle government-in-exile. He served in the National Assembly and held posts in several French governments as minister of public works, of tourism, and of transport. After the fall of the Mendès-France government in early 1955, he made a bid for the premiership, but lost out to Edgar Faure. Until his appointment as foreign minister in December 1955, Pineau's experience as minister of tourism was as close as he had come to international affairs.

Despite his relative innocence in the field of diplomacy, however, Christian Pineau was a man of parts. Aside from being an economist, a labor organizer, and a politician, he wrote children's fairy stories—some with Socialist ideological overtones, some not. One of his most fanciful told the tale of a boy stranded on a desert island who made friends with a man-eating serpent. Some of his adult readers wondered whether the story was inspired by Pineau's interest in détente with the USSR.

Pineau was not regarded with much affection among the professionals at the Quai d'Orsay. He raised havoc at the higher levels of the French diplomatic service by his capricious appointments, transfers, and firing. But in the eyes of France's career diplomats his cardinal sin was his habit of chasing off on missions abroad without benefit of professional advice. A prime example was his visit to Cairo in June 1956. Nasser promised, he told the National Assembly on his return, to halt Egyptian aid to Algeria. When it became clear that such assistance was continuing and when the situation in Algeria had worsened, Pineau felt personally betrayed by Nasser—a matter that would assume increasing importance in the months ahead.

"An interesting man," a French international lawyer told me. "But the worst foreign minister in the Fourth Republic." A formidable personality, another observer noted, "resolute and respected as the toughest minister intellectually" in Mollet's cabinet.[11]

During his tense meetings in London with Eden and Pineau, Murphy advised caution. He argued that force should be held in abeyance until efforts at a negotiated or diplomatic resolution had been tried and proved wanting. In particular, he urged that Eden convoke a meeting of the signatories to the international Convention of 1888.

Concerned about Murphy's reports, Eisenhower wrote a worried letter to Eden on July 31. (It was probably drafted by Dulles, who by then had returned to Washington.)

Dear Anthony:
From the moment that Nasser announced nationalization of the Suez Canal Company, my thoughts have been constantly with you. . . . Until this morning, I was happy to feel that we were approaching decisions as to applicable procedures somewhat along parallel lines. . . . But early this morning I received the messages, communicated to me through Murphy from you and Harold Macmillan, telling me on a most secret basis of your decision to employ force without delay or attempting any intermediate and less drastic steps.

We recognize the transcendent worth of the Canal to the free world and the possibility that eventually the use of force might become necessary in order to protect international rights. But we have been hopeful that through a Conference, in which would be represented the signatories to the Convention of 1888, as well as other maritime nations, there would be brought about such pressures on the Egyptian government that the efficient operation of the Canal could be assured for the future.

. . . I cannot over-emphasize the strength of my conviction that some such method must be attempted before action such as you contemplate should be undertaken. . . . Public opinion . . . would be outraged should there be a failure to make such efforts. Moreover, initial military successes might be easy, but the eventual price might become far too heavy.

I have given you my own personal conviction . . . as to the unwisdom even of contemplating the use of military force at this moment. Assuming, however, that the whole situation continued to deteriorate to the point where such action would seem the only recourse, there are certain political facts to remember. . . . Employment of the United States forces is possible only through positive action on the part of the Congress. . . . There would have to be a showing that every peaceful means of resolving the difficulty had previously been exhausted. Without such a showing, there would be a reaction that could very seriously affect our people's feeling toward our Western Allies. . . . This could grow to such an intensity as to have the most far-reaching consequences.

I realize that the messages from both you and Harold [Macmillan] stressed that the decision taken was already approved by the government and was firm and irrevocable. But I personally feel sure that the American reaction would be severe. . . . On the other hand, I believe we can marshal that opinion in support of a reasonable and conciliatory, but absolutely firm, position. So I hope that you will consent to reviewing this matter once more in its broadest aspects. It is for this reason that I have asked Foster to leave this afternoon to meet with your people tomorrow in London.

. . . the step you contemplate should not be undertaken until every peaceful means . . . has been thoroughly explored and exhausted. Should these means fail . . . then world opinion would understand how earnestly all of us had attempted to be just, fair and considerate, but that we simply could not accept a situation that would in the long run prove disastrous to the prosperity and living standards of every nation whose economy depends directly or indirectly upon East-West shipping.

With warm personal regard and with earnest assurances of my continuing respect and friendship,

> As ever,
> DE[12]

Eisenhower's letter did little to soothe Eden's spirits. His hopes for American backing of early military operations were dashed. Moreover, Murphy's unpromising proposal for dusting off the 1888 Convention was now being pushed from the White House, a quarter virtually impossible to ignore. But Ike's note acknowledged at least one point Eden had raised with Murphy: Since the Americans had not signed the Constantinople treaty, the Prime Minister had told Murphy, they could hardly play a leading role in a conference of the signatory nations. Eisenhower now suggested a meeting, not only of the signatories, but also of "other maritime nations." Because of the President's firm disapproval of early military action, however, this was thin gruel—all the more so in light of the imminent arrival of "Foster," whose presence in London, albeit necessary at this time, would do nothing much for Eden's blood pressure or his bile.

As the prime minister contemplated the delay implied in convening a large international conference, he drew some small comfort from the realization that, in any event, Great Britain could not mount an early attack against Egypt. His chiefs of staff had just informed him that it would take at least several weeks before the necessary military forces were readied.

The French, Eden had learned, were in no better position. Mollet had been told by his minister of defense that the sole French aircraft carrier then in the Mediterranean had only a handful of planes that could cope with the Russian MIGs in Nasser's air force. Almost two weeks would be needed before squadrons of Mystères with their maintenance equipment could be transferred from their NATO bases in Germany and before the French fleet could move into the eastern Mediterranean. Most disturbing, however, was the French Army's situation. The troops in southern France and those that could be spared from the fighting in Algeria had virtually no landing craft available. And although there were two brigades of paratroopers in Algeria, they had had no jump training since early 1955. Until British and French forces could be readied, Eden concluded, it would be advantageous to demonstrate, both at home and abroad, that peaceful efforts had first been explored.

Secretary Dulles' departure for London was preceded by warnings to Whitehall from the British Embassy in Washington that the Department of State was remarkably unconcerned about Nasser's seizure of the Canal. London's worry that Nasser would halt free world traffic through the Canal was apparently not shared in Washington.

If Nasser wanted to finance his High Dam from Canal tolls, the American reasoning went, he would be unlikely to move against the major maritime powers. British, French, and American shipping amounted to almost half the tonnage plying the Canal; British ships alone represented almost a third of the total. Nasser himself had recognized this: "The nationalization . . . in no way affects Egypt's international obligations," he announced soon after he took over the Canal. "Freedom of shipping . . . will in no way be affected . . . there is no one more anxious than Egypt to safeguard freedom of passage and the flourishing traffic in the Canal."

Washington's lack of passion was made apparent by the secretary on his arrival in London on the first of August. Dulles once again treated Eden to a lecture on the American constitutional process: American troops could not be sent into action on foreign soil without congressional approval—and Congress was then in summer recess. Moreover, as Eisenhower had admonished in his letter, if the case for force was to be made on Capitol Hill, careful legal groundwork would have to be laid.

Dulles then raised a new issue: A clear distinction had to be made between the Suez Canal and the Panama Canal; Washington was concerned lest an international precedent be set that might encourage the Panamanians to take over the Panama Zone or that would inhibit the use of American troops should such an event occur.

The secretary reiterated the Administration's worry about the Panama Canal at an embassy staff meeting early the next morning. It was nearly ten o'clock when that session adjourned. Within a few minutes I was due at a meeting of the Middle East working group several miles away at Storey's Gate. As I clambered into a waiting car, the thought struck me that I knew next to nothing about the historical and legal background of the Panama Canal and the relationship, if any, between Panama and Suez. I ran back to the embassy library and hastily read in the *Encyclopaedia Britannica* that the Panama Canal was considered to be an American rather than an international waterway.

I arrived at the working group late and disheveled, but the fifteen minutes spent in scholarship proved worthwhile. "Chet," the chairman asked a few minutes after I took my place, "what is so bloody special about your Panama Canal?" "Well," I said, "it's like this. . . ." I would like to think I registered surprise that anyone could be uninformed on so obvious and important a matter of diplomatic history and international law. Such are the minor triumphs of meetingsmanship.

While Dulles was urging prudence, his French counterpart was pressing for action. When all was said, Pineau argued, the Canal had been a French enterprise. It was de Lesseps who dug the ditch in the first place. The British came in later. And the Americans, he pointedly reminded Dulles, had played no role. In addition, France, like Britain, was dependent on Middle East oil; its economy, which had just recovered from the war, would grind to a halt without it. Moreover, French banks had large holdings in the Suez Canal Company. And, at least as important, the French position was becoming desperate in Algeria. An Egyptian diplomatic victory and a French defeat would boost FLN morale and lower French prestige there.

Pineau did not endear himself to Dulles by his insistence on an early, tough response. Especially galling was Pineau's repetition of the charge that had earlier angered Murphy: Reneging on the Aswan Dam deal had caused the present predicament. Whether Pineau went beyond this to remind the secretary that the French ambassador to Washington had warned the State Department that Nasser would seize the Canal if the loan was summarily rejected is lost in the dust of history. In any case, Dulles heatedly denied Pineau's accusation. Nasser, he insisted, was simply waiting for a pretext. If it had not been Aswan, Nasser would soon have contrived another excuse; he was sure that nationalization could not have gone as smoothly unless it had been planned long in advance.

The session was a stormy one, Pineau recalls. "Eden detested the American Secretary of State. I will not repeat certain harsh remarks made about him, in order not to tarnish Eden's legendary reputation for courteous behavior." As the talks went on, according to Pineau, "Eden grew increasingly angry and Dulles became increasingly colder."[13]

Yet for all his cautionary lectures and despite the friction between them, Dulles gave Eden reason to be encouraged. The secretary agreed that it was "intolerable" for Egypt to control the Canal without international supervision. Force was not out of the question, but it should be employed only as a last resort. And certainly not before all diplomatic means had been tried and found wanting. As a first step—and as a way of establishing the difference between the international regime for the Suez Canal and America's exclusive arrangement with regard to the Panama Canal—the Constantinople Treaty signers should be assembled. To Eden, the most heartening aspect of Dulles' discussions was the secretary's point that Nasser must be made to "disgorge" the Canal. "Those were forthright words," Eden recalled. "They rang in my ears for months."[14]

The meeting of the three foreign ministers revealed their individual perceptions of national and Allied interests. As Dulles and Eisenhower had indicated time and again over the past two years, American policy would increasingly tend to diverge from the British on issues that carried "colonial" overtones. As for the French problems in Algeria, the Americans had already demonstrated their indifference to Paris' attempts to hang on to its last territory in North Africa. On a more mundane, but nonetheless sticky point, the United States had little concern about who collected the tolls so long as the Canal remained open to international shipping. And so the Administration was reluctant to insist that American shipowners change their normal practice and pay their tolls to the Suez Canal Company's offices in London or Paris rather than to the toll collectors at Port Said or Ismailia.

Robert Murphy summed up the American view:

Pineau was dead wrong about the degree of importance which all of us in the United States Government attached to the Suez incident. . . . The material interest of the United States was not identical with that of either France or the United Kingdom. France and Britain had very substantial holdings in the Canal Company. American holdings were insignificant. France and Britain were directly dependent on the flow of Middle East oil. The United States was not nearly so dependent. But . . . we certainly were fully aware of the importance of Western prestige in the Middle East.[15]

Inevitably, Paris and London, on the one hand, and Washington, on the other, identified and weighed the available options in profoundly different ways.

In the end, Dulles' views prevailed; Eden agreed to call a meeting of nations which had signed the 1888 treaty plus certain others who had not signed it, but who had a major commercial stake in the Canal. Eden was, of course, influenced by the reality that early armed action against Nasser would require American political support, if not military participation. But another warning signal also led Eden down the path of negotiation; his initial enthusiastic support from the press and from the Opposition had begun to erode as the scale of British military preparations became evident.

August 2 was a critical day for the prime minister. It was the last time the House of Commons would meet before its long summer recess. There would be difficult, even dangerous, weeks ahead. Unless Eden could win support, not only from his own party, but also from the Opposition, a tough anti-Nasser policy could be pursued only at considerable political risk. And since such a policy, including the probable use of force, was what he had in mind, it was important that he have Parliament behind him.

Earlier that day he had told his cabinet of the steps under way to prepare for military action, if the need arose. And, as if to underline this eventuality, several high-ranking French naval officers had arrived in London that very morning to discuss the deployment of the French and British fleets.

When Eden appeared at Commons later that day, he described the broad outlines of his discussions with Dulles and Pineau. Then he informed the members that "Her Majesty's Government have thought it necessary . . . to take precautionary measures of a military nature." He told them of his plans for sending naval and military elements to the Mediterranean and calling up some reserve units.

Hugh Gaitskell, leader of the Opposition, took the floor. His speech was all Eden could have wished. Nasser's takeover of the Canal, he said, "must be recognized as part of the struggle for mastery of the Middle East . . . it is all terribly familiar. It is exactly the same as we encountered with Mussolini and Hitler in the years before the war." He approved of Eden's efforts to coordinate British policy with Washington and Paris and agreed that a conference of "concerned nations" should be convened. Economic sanctions and an arms embargo against Egypt were justified. With regard to the use of force, "I do not object to the precautionary steps which the Prime Minister has announced. . . . I think we were right to react sharply. . . . While force cannot be excluded, we must be sure that the circumstances justify it and it is . . . consistent with the UN charter."

The debate that followed the two major speeches was calm and displayed considerable agreement with Eden's position. Captain Charles Waterhouse, a hard-line Tory, triumphantly announced that "we got Colonel Nasser on the run and he must be kept on the run." Another Tory complimented both Eden and Gaitskell and noted that their speeches reflected "the united view of the House and indeed of the country." Herbert Morrison, a onetime Labour foreign secretary, said that Nasser's action was "morally wrong." "The matter should be taken to the UN, but after the UN dealt with the matter, if force was necessary, I would support it." Denis Healey, the principal spokesman for foreign policy for the Labour Party, scolded Eden for the "total confusion" of his Middle East policy and warned that force should be used only if Egypt tried to prevent free transit through the Canal. Finally, one MP wryly remarked that "Nasser has succeeded in uniting the House of Commons."[16] He was right, if only momentarily so.

Within hours of his speech to the House, Gaitskell was attacked by left-wing members of his party. He quickly began to trim his sails. In endorsing Eden's speech with his reference to use of military force, Gaitskell lamely explained in private to Eden and then in public, he really meant that the British would have to appeal their case to the United Nations before there was any resort to force.

In the meantime, some of my colleagues in the British intelligence establishment and in the Ministry of Defence—first an order-of-battle specialist and a photointerpreter, then an economist and a Nasser-watcher—suddenly "left town." One of them told me, with more or less of a straight face, that he was off for a "summer holiday." French military experts, too, one heard, were "vacationing."

My friends filtered back one by one, surprisingly pale and fatigued for people who, presumably, had been resting in the sun. In fact, they had seen little sun and had found little rest. They had spent all their days and some of their nights underground in the secret chambers that had been tunneled under London during the early days of World War II.

There, in uncomfortable, confined quarters, the plan for an attack on Egypt had been prepared. Targets had been mapped, land, air, and sea logistics arranged, manning tables calculated, force dispositions worked out, reservists mustered.

On August 8, plans for a joint British-French attack on Egypt were completed. The enterprise would be commanded by a British general with a French general as his deputy. General Sir Hugh Stockwell would lead the British forces; General André Beaufre, the French. It was dubbed Operation Musketeer in honor of Stockwell's grand mustache. The plan called for a sea-based attack on Alexandria. From there, British and French forces would move toward the Canal and then toward Cairo. Although the primary mission would be to seize the Canal, Cairo Radio would also be an early target. And so would Nasser's government.

The enterprise was now cooked and canned; it was put on the shelf to await the moment when Eden and Mollet were ready to serve it up. But it would be many weeks before the signal would, in fact, be given. And when it was, much of the careful advance planning would have to be jettisoned in favor of frenetic improvisation.

Although military preparations appeared to be proceeding at a gratifying pace, Eden became increasingly uneasy about his political rear. From early August on, starting with Gaitskell's public retreat from his speech in the House of Commons, Eden realized he could no longer count on support from the Labour Party. With Parliament in recess until October 23, the prime minister had to rely solely on the media to publicize the government's position. While this permitted him to avoid rough-and-tumble exchanges in Commons, in the end he might have fared better if the major problems he had to deal with could have been subjected to Parliamentary debate.

In an effort to rally the support of the British people, the prime minister made a nationwide broadcast on August 8, the day Operation Musketeer was born:

> The alternatives are clear for all to see. If we all join together to create an international system for the Canal and spend its revenues as they should be spent . . . there will be wealth for all to share, including Egypt. There is no question of denying her a fair deal or a just return. . . . Meanwhile we have too much at stake not to take precautions. We have done so. That is the meaning of the movements by land, sea, and air of which you heard in the last few days. We do not seek a solution by force, but by the broadest possible agreement. That is why we have called the conference.[17]

The signatories of the Convention of 1888, as well as other maritime nations, convened at stately Lancaster House in London on August 16. The conference was to work out a formula—or rather approve a formula earlier decided upon by London, Paris, and Washington—for an international agency to operate the Canal "consistent with legitimate Egyptian interests." All together, there were twenty-two delegations. Greece had been invited but refused to attend; its relations with Great Britain were strained because of the troubles on Cyprus. Egypt was also asked, but ignored the invitation; instead, it ridiculed the conference formula as an exercise in "collective colonialism."

A few days before the American delegation departed for London, Eisenhower and Dulles, concerned at the high state of emotions in Britain, France, and Egypt, warned congressional leaders of possible hostilities in the Middle East. Congress, they said, might have to be recalled from its summer recess to share responsibility with the Administration if American involvement appeared imminent. Sherman Adams, then special assistant to President Eisenhower, recalls that the President was "serious" and the secretary "grim" as Eisenhower concluded his briefing of key senators and congressmen. "There are so many possibilities involved that I shudder to think of them." The important thing, Eisenhower told them, was to strive for a peaceful settlement and for the world to "know that we are doing so."[18] He informed the legislators that arrangements had already been made for massive emergency oil shipments to Western Europe in case of an interruption of oil shipments from the Middle East.

It was indeed a "grim" John Foster Dulles who boarded his VIP plane for yet another trip across the Atlantic. He arrived in London on a wave of public statements by the President obviously designed to reiterate earlier warnings to Eden that the United States could not be counted on for military support in the event Britain and France initiated an attack on Egypt. "I can't conceive," Eisenhower told the press on August 8, "of military force being a good solution, certainly under the conditions as we know them now." "Does this mean," a British correspondent asked, "that you are opposed to the use of force under any circumstances?" "I said," Eisenhower replied tartly, "every important question in the world in which more than one nation is interested should be settled by negotiation." Whatever satisfaction Eden had eked out of Dulles' earlier references to making Nasser "disgorge" the canal was short-lived.

In response to instructions from Washington, Charles Bohlen, ambassador to Moscow, explained the American position to Marshal Bulganin. Bohlen, too, found himself falling back on the Hitler analogy.

"Nasser's action," he told Bulganin, "seemed . . . a revival of Hitler's tactics. . . . Hitler, too, had unilaterally denounced treaties."[19] Bulganin seemed unimpressed.

The Russians grudgingly agreed to attend the London Conference, but raised several procedural objections (including a complaint about the United States' being included as an "inviting Nation" even though it had not signed the 1888 treaty). The signals out of Moscow promised little prospect of Soviet cooperation. Bohlen was, once again, instructed to see Bulganin. This time his message was more pointed: The Soviet leadership, Dulles wanted the Kremlin to understand, would be under a "grave delusion" if it assumed that the United States would not associate itself with its allies, Britain and France, if the conference failed.[20]

When the sessions actually got under way, the Russians removed any remaining doubts about their attitude: "We believe," Foreign Minister Shepilov told the conference, "that the Egyptian Government . . . was acting within the norms of international law . . . and therefore [Suez] cannot be the subject of discussion either at this or any other international conference."[21]

The Soviet delegation was not the only one that promised to be awkward. The Indians had begun to develop considerable capacity to create difficulties for the West, especially when the issue under discussion smacked of maintaining the worldwide distribution of power. Foreign Minister Krishna Menon in particular was, with some justification, regarded by London and Washington as a pesky gadfly and an energetic mischief maker. The United States had had an earlier dose of Menon's righteous oratory, gleeful wheeling, and incessant dealing at the 1954 Geneva Conference on Indochina.

At the Bandung Conference of Unaligned Nations held barely a year before the London meeting, Krishna Menon was in the full ripeness of his self-appointed role as spokesman for the "neutralist world." And how he spoke! During most of his adult life Menon had been a London barrister. He had an enviable ability to smother his audiences under a richly embroidered, highly intricate oratorical blanket. The Canal issue was just his cup of tea. It lent itself ideally to weaving a woof of brightly hued arguments against imperialism, nationalism, the white man's burden, and exploitation with a warp of more mellow strands in praise of economic development and self-determination. The presence of Menon as head of the Indian delegation was one more cross the Americans, British, and French would have to bear over the next many days.

But Menon and his prime minister, Pandit Nehru, intended to do more in London than simply sound the klaxons of anti-imperialism. They were determined to defuse the British and French efforts to wrest control over the Canal from Nasser. To the Indians—and indeed to Indonesia and Ceylon, the other Bandung conferees present—Nasser's seizure of the Canal was a welcome, timely blow against the remaining vestiges of Western Europe's nineteenth-century exploitation of Africa and Asia.

The fact that Nasser was not present at the conference, Mohamed Heikal, Cairo journalist and Nasser's confidant, later wrote, "did not mean that Egypt was not represented. . . . We had our friends there, particularly the Indians in the person of V. K. Krishna Menon, who spoke passionately on Egypt's behalf, and the Russians, represented by Foreign Minister Dimitri Shepilov."[22] Ashraf Ghorbal, then Egyptian counselor of embassy in London and later the ambassador to Washington, was the contact for the daily briefings provided by Menon and Shepilov. He recalls that most of his telegrams to Cairo started with "At the Conference today, the Americans [or the French, or the British] deem it necessary that Egypt. . . ." For years after, he was referred to among his colleagues as "Mr. Deem-It-Necessary."

On the morning of Dulles' arrival in London, a trim, amiable, taciturn young man showed up in my office. He carefully closed the door and pulled a chair close to my desk. "We've got one of our guys on one of the unfriendly delegations," he announced without any preliminaries. "Who's 'we'?" "You, me, the company!"

The fog cleared; the visitor, whom I had never laid eyes on before, was from CIA—a colleague from the Operations side. "You from Washington?" I asked. "Nope." "Who the hell is this 'guy'? Shepilov? Krishna? The Indonesian foreign minister?" My visitor grinned. "Not yet. Give me time." Then he was all business: "Look, this is how we'll work it. I meet my guy someplace at two AM every day. You get here about six thirty. I'll tell you what some of the big wheels are reporting and what their instructions are. Don't ask me how. Then you tell old Johnny F. what to expect. OK?"

Of course it was OK. In fact, if his predawn appointments produced anything, it would be very damn good. Moreover, the timing was just right. Dulles wanted to keep abreast of current international events in general, and the Middle East situation in particular. I was scheduled to brief him in the ambassador's residence every morning at breakfast.

When I arrived at my office early the next morning, my friend was already draped over a couch. He was bleary-eyed and needed a shave, but excessively chipper and none the worse for what must have been a very short night's sleep. He handed over a couple of pages of foolscap. "This is what the Ceylonese, Indonesians, and Indians will say at today's meeting. Burn it after you've hoisted it in. Cafeteria open yet? See you tomorrow." He was off.

I decided that it would be premature to mention the caper that morning to Dulles. I wanted to make sure that I wasn't being led astray. And, in any case, there seemed nothing dramatic in what purported to be the unaligned foreign ministers' opening statements to the conference. At the meeting later that morning, however, they did indeed speak along the lines that had been sketched out in the hastily scribbled notes I had read earlier. My new friend might yet turn up something important; it would be useful to have a few hours of advance notice.

On the following morning I was presented with another sheaf of papers. These seemed more interesting: The Indians were planning to introduce their own alternative to the Big Three proposal. Instead of having an international body *control* the Canal, such a group would have only advisory and *consultative* functions. The Indonesians, the Ceylonese, and the Russians would be meeting with Menon in a few hours, and they would all support the Indian plan.

I told Dulles about all this an hour or so later. "How do you know?" "Courtesy of your brother Allen, sir." Dulles was skeptical and I thought slightly annoyed; he had not detected any hint of a new Indian initiative the day before. "Let's try an experiment, sir. You and the Indonesian foreign minister are going to meet privately later in the day. Tomorrow I'll tell you what went on." The next morning after seeing my friend, I told the secretary what he had said. "Well, the son-of-a-bitch! That's not quite what I said, but it's interesting to know what he says I said." It was the first time I had ever heard Dulles swear.

The Indians introduced their proposition a day later, on August 20. The Russians, Indonesians, and Ceylonese promptly endorsed it. None of this came as a surprise, thanks to my friend. Nor did the news that Shepilov was having daily skull practices with Cairo's "observer."

The meetings adjourned on August 23. The conferees were split eighteen to four on the British-French-American proposal that an international organization control the Canal. Since the Russians had refused to permit the proceedings to operate on a majority-rule basis, the result had no binding force. The outcome was hardly a ringing success for the sponsors, but Eden put a brave face on it. "Thank you," he cabled Eisenhower after the conference had adjourned, "for all the help Foster has given. . . . It was, I think, a remarkable achievement to unite eighteen nations on an agreed statement of this clarity and force."[23]

Eden may or may not have been genuinely grateful "for all the help Foster" gave, but some Americans who witnessed Dulles' performance during those days in London were not impressed. Charles Bohlen, who attended the sessions, felt that "Dulles was at his worst at this meeting. He shaded the edge of downright trickery and even dishonesty. . . . He talked out of both sides of his mouth. To the British and French, he talked as if he favored them; to the Russians, he sounded anti-British and anti-French." The secretary, he said, "was too slick, seeking to make points in the manner of a Wall Street lawyer." Dulles "saw the Suez as a dying gasp of imperialism."[24]

There was one remaining piece of business; at British insistence a delegation from among the "Eighteen" would go to Cairo to convince Nasser to accept the majority proposal as a basis for negotiation. Since the idea of organizing an international control commission had been initiated by the United States, Eden urged Dulles to lead the mission. But the secretary would have no part of it. "I think it is preferable," Dulles cabled Eisenhower, "that we should become less conspicuous."[25] Robert Menzies, foreign minister of Australia, volunteered.

No one, least of all Eden, Dulles, and Menzies, had illusions that the mission would succeed. Their sights were set much lower than securing Nasser's agreement to turning over the Canal to an international body. A waltz to Cairo, however, was an essential part of the choreography designed for the London Conference. At the very least, Menzies and his partners—representatives from Ethiopia, Iran, Sweden, and the United States (Assistant Secretary Loy Henderson acting for Dulles)—would get a firsthand sense of Nasser's mood.

Nasser agreed to meet with the conference emissaries on September 3. But he had already made up his mind not to yield an inch. He had ample evidence of the divided opinion among the people and politicians in Britain and of the cautious view with regard to the use of force in Washington. Nasser's estimate of the mood of the Eisenhower Administration was reinforced on August 29, well before Menzies landed in Cairo. At a press conference on his arrival in Washington from London, Dulles confided to Nasser and to the world at large that "the United States is not dependent to any appreciable degree at all upon the Suez Canal." And on the very day Menzies started his negotiations, Eisenhower told the press that the United States was "committed to a peaceful solution of this problem." Hearing of this, Nasser joked to an aide, "Which side is he on?"[26]

Meanwhile British and French military preparations quickened. General Stockwell had by now received cabinet approval for a landing at Alexandria. By mid-August, British troops, some of whom had been withdrawn from NATO's British Army of the Rhine, were being airlifted to Cyprus, where they were joined by French forces. The military deployments were well publicized to give credibility to Menzies' warnings in Cairo that serious consequences might follow a failure to resolve the dispute through diplomatic means. To underline the sense of official gravity, London and Paris advised British and French citizens to leave Egypt, Syria, and Lebanon.

Eden's and Mollet's actions may not have frightened President Nasser, but they scared the hell out of President Eisenhower. Hostilities in the Middle East were the last thing he wanted now that the election campaign had started in earnest. Although Dulles was later to deny it, domestic political considerations clearly dominated Washington's policy throughout the next few months. Robert Murphy subsequently wrote that "Dulles . . . was acutely aware that a commitment to support hostilities could have a disastrous effect on Eisenhower's candidacy."[27] After all, it was the Democrats, the Republicans were wont to claim, who always managed to march the United States into war. Adlai Stevenson, the Democratic candidate, would be an easy target. Unless . . .

Just as Menzies was arriving in Cairo, Eden received a reply to his letter from Eisenhower. The President had flashed some warning lights across the Atlantic.

> I am afraid, Anthony, that from this point onward our views on this situation diverge. As to the use of force or the threat of force at this juncture, I continue to feel as I expressed myself . . . some weeks ago . . . new military preparation and civilian evacuation exposed to public view seem to be solidifying support for Nasser. . . . I must tell you frankly that American public opinion flatly rejects the thought of using force. . . . I really do not see how a successful result could be achieved by forcible means. . . . Before such action were undertaken all our peoples should unitedly understand that there were no other means available. . . . Seldom, I think, have [we been] faced by so grave a problem. . . . We must put our faith in the processes already at work to bring Nasser peacefully to accept the solution along the lines of the 18-nation proposal. . . . [28]

If Menzies had a sword in his scabbard when he agreed to embark for Cairo, Dulles and Eisenhower snatched it from him along the way. He and his colleagues had three sessions with Nasser, all fruitless. On September 9, Nasser dismissed them. They were probably pleased to leave the dust of Cairo behind them.

Eden held no false hopes that Menzies' mission would change Nasser's mind. He had agreed to go through the motions, much the same way a thrown steeplechase rider will scramble after his horse, brush himself off, remount, and gamely complete the course. It was the sporty follow-through, the well-bred Thing To Do.

The issues at stake in Suez were too important to be left in limbo after the abortive effort of Australia's foreign minister. Alternative courses of action had to be pursued. A joint British and French appeal to the United Nations Security Council was prepared, warning that "a threat to peace" was hanging over the Middle East as a consequence of Nasser's action. London and Paris hoped that the Security Council would agree to persuade Nasser to negotiate on the basis of the Eighteen Nation Proposal.

Washington's support would be critical if the resolution were to have any chance of approval. But the United States, and Canada as well, were cool to the idea. Both Secretary Dulles and Foreign Minister Pearson were sure that the UN would vote against the resolution and that Eden and Mollet would then feel justified in pursuing their military plans. Instead of making a formal appeal which would involve action by the Security Council, Dulles urged that Britain and France send a letter simply informing the Council of the present situation and avoid asking for a vote. Although the French ridiculed Dulles' suggestion—it was like "leaving a visiting card," one Frenchman remarked—Eden and Mollet had little choice but to follow Dulles' advice.

Washington's refusal to back its allies in an appeal to the UN was a critical turning point in the Suez saga. Up to now there had been a frank exchange of views—as befitted three partners in an enterprise. After their inability to gain American support for their UN initiative, Eden and Mollet realized that the United States had its own concerns and con-ducted their business more privately—as befitted two partners who did not quite trust the third. On September 12 London and Paris sent a joint letter to the Security Council warning that Nasser's unwillingness to accept the Eighteen Nation Proposal as a basis for negotiations ag-gravated the tension which "if allowed to continue would constitute a manifest danger to peace and security."

In the end, the British-French warning to the UN was overtaken by yet another delaying tactic which Dulles dreamed up over the Labor Day weekend. Dulles was desperate lest the dismal failure of the Menzies mission and the UN's pro-Egyptian sympathies provide Eden and Mollet with an excuse to plunge ahead with an armed attack on Egypt. The London Conference and the follow-up sessions in Cairo with Nasser had intensified their feeling of frustration. Dulles knew well that both men had only reluctantly agreed to the ill-starred meeting of the 1888 signato-ries. Somehow, further efforts had to be generated from Washington to buy more time.

Time for what? Time to permit Nasser to demonstrate that the Egyp-tians would operate the Canal without interfering with international traffic. Time to erode Eden's remaining domestic support for military action. Time to make yet another try at forcing Nasser either to "dis-gorge" the Canal or, more likely, to share his control with some mutually acceptable international body. Time, above all, to get the Administration through the remaining sixty days of presidential campaigning without a Middle East war.

All these factors must have pressed heavily on Dulles' mind during the long weekend in early September at his Canadian retreat on Duck Island. How much weight each of them carried probably varied hour by hour. But he was surely driven by the news of escalating military prepara-tions in Britain and France. He spent his brief holiday brooding about yet one more diplomatic effort to resolve the Suez Canal problem.

Finally, in the peace and quiet of Lake Ontario, Dulles contrived a plan for another conference. Soon after his return to Washington he shared his new idea with the British ambassador. It took the form of organizing a "Users Association." It would comprise the major shipping nations and would, in effect, set up its own Suez Canal authority.

Eden replied to Eisenhower's ominous letter of September 2 a day or so after his ambassador sent him the first sketchy reports of Dulles' new brainstorm:

> . . . we must have some immediate alternative which will show Nasser is not going to get his way. In this connection, we are at-tracted to Foster's suggestion, if I understand it rightly, for the running of the Canal by the users in virtue of their rights under the 1888 convention . . .
>
> The seizure of the Suez Canal is . . . the opening gambit in a planned campaign designed by Nasser to expel all western influence and interests from Arab countries. . . . If Nasser is allowed to defy the eighteen nations, it will be a matter of months before revolution breaks out in the oil-bearing countries and the West is wholly de-prived of Middle Eastern oil. . . .
>
> We are conscious of the burdens and perils attending military intervention. But . . . if the only alternative is to allow Nasser's plans quietly to develop until this country and all Western Europe are held to ransom by Egypt acting at Russia's behest it seems to me our duty is plain. We have many times led Europe in the fight for freedom. It would be an ignoble end to our long history if we accepted to perish by degrees.[29]

Eisenhower had read the situation accurately; the British and Ameri-can positions had begun to "diverge." In the light of this exchange of letters, neither the President nor the prime minister should have been surprised when the divergence later took the form of deeds rather than words.

Eisenhower elaborated on the American position in a letter to Eden on September 8:

> Whenever, on any international question, I find myself differing even slightly from you, I feel a deep compulsion to re-examine my position instantly and carefully. But permit me to suggest that when you use phrases in connection with the Suez affair, like "ignoble end to our long history" in describing the possible future of your great country, you are making Nasser a much more important figure than he is. . . .
>
> The use of military force against Egypt under present circumstances might . . . cause a serious misunderstanding between our two countries because I must say frankly that there is as yet no public opinion in this country which is prepared to support such a move, and the most significant public opinion . . . seems to think that the United Nations was formed to prevent this very thing.
>
> It is for reasons such as these that we have viewed with some misgivings your preparations for mounting a military expedition against Egypt.
>
> At the same time, we do not want any capitulation to Nasser. We want to stand firmly with you to deflate the ambitious pretensions of Nasser and to assure permanent free and effective use of the Suez waterway. . . .
>
> It seems to Foster and to me that the result that you and I both want can best be assured by slower and less dramatic processes than military force. There are many areas of endeavor which are not yet fully explored because exploration takes time.
>
> We can, for example, promote a semi-permanent organization of the user governments to take over the greatest practical amount of the technical problems of the Canal, such as pilotage, the organization of the traffic patterns, and the collection of dues to cover actual expenses. This organization would be on the spot and in constant contact with Egypt and might work out a *de facto* "co-existence" which would give the users the rights which we want. . . .
>
> Nasser thrives on drama. If we let some of the drama go out of the situation and concentrate upon the task of deflating him through slower but sure processes . . . the desired results can more probably be obtained. . . . We could isolate Nasser and gain a victory which would not only be bloodless, but would be more far reaching in its ultimate consequences than could be anything brought about by force of arms. In addition, it would be less costly both now and in the future.
>
> Of course, if during this process Nasser himself resorts to violence . . . then that would create a new situation and one in which he and not we would be violating the United Nations charter.

I assure you we are not blind to the fact that eventually there may be no escape from the use of force. . . . But to resort to military action when the world believes there are other means available for resolving the dispute would set in motion forces that could lead, in the years to come, to the most distressing results. . . .

As ever your
friend,
DE[30]

Neither I nor my American or British colleagues knew of the letters between the President and the prime minister. But most of us at the embassy sensed the growing irritation with the British that had been creeping into the telegrams from the State Department. Nor could we possibly miss the growing impatience of our contacts in Whitehall.

My friend on the Middle East working party had by now returned from his holiday in Switzerland. Much had happened in his absence, but he had had the advantage of a long, albeit abbreviated, summer vacation and a fresh approach. Both would be needed for a situation that was getting increasingly untidy, even somewhat out of hand. He invited me to drop by his Mayfair flat one evening for a "gossip" and a drink. "Just between two old boys," he asked, "what is Washington up to? Every proposal, whether it had to do with bashing the Gyppos or appealing to the UN gets knocked down in Foggy Bottom. Chums in Downing Street tell me our old boy is feeling queer and is all nerves. Your friends at home had better come up with something constructive pretty soon." I agreed, but did not say so. Instead, I reminded him that Dulles had already passed on the outlines of a Suez users' initiative to the British Embassy. "What about *that?*" I asked with more bravado than I felt. "Well, what *about* it? How many guineas would *you* put on that horse?" I shrugged. He changed the subject. We had another drink. I left.

Virtually at the same moment my friend was pressing me, his boss was pressing mine—possibly a coincidence. "What does the United States have in mind?" Selwyn Lloyd cabled Dulles. Washington had rejected every British suggestion for dealing with Nasser, but had itself not served up anything very nourishing. Soon, on September 10, the British had their answer. Fortuitously, Mollet and Pineau had come to London that day to concert their next step with Eden and Lloyd. The British and French together had an opportunity to review Dulles' elaboration of the Suez Canal Users Association.

The Association would be organized to achieve "the most effective possible enjoyment of the rights of passage given by the 1888 Convention" and would "promote safe, orderly, efficient and economical transit of member-controlled vessels." It would have its headquarters in Rome and would be run by an executive group comprising the five nations (Australia, Iran, Ethiopia, Sweden, and the United States) represented on the Menzies mission to Cairo. The Association would hire its own pilots from among the non-Egyptian staff of the old Suez Canal Company, would collect tolls from the users, and would pay Egypt a fair price for services provided. Its activities would be based at the two entrances of the Canal; if Egypt refused to permit this, the operation would be conducted from ships anchored offshore.

Eden, although irritated by yet another American diversion, decided it was worth a try. He later recalled that it appeared to him to be "a possible interim scheme."[31] He insisted, however, that vessels belonging to Association members, including all American-owned ships (regardless of the flag under which they sailed), should pay their Canal tolls into the Association account rather than directly to Egypt. He also asked that the principal Canal users, France and Great Britain, be represented on the board of directors.

Mollet and Pineau were more suspicious of American motives and more skeptical about Dulles' new idea. They would have much preferred, now that the London Conference had accomplished nothing, to avoid any further diplomatic approaches and move militarily to seize the Canal. The Eden-Mollet meeting in London ended on September 11 with agreement "that the refusal of President Nasser to negotiate created a very grave situation." The communiqué noted that the two leaders "discussed the further measures to be taken and reached full agreement upon them." One of the "measures" was to participate in Dulles' meeting of the "Suez Canal Users Association." Eden, anxious as ever to carry the United States with him if force ultimately had to be used, evidently had persuaded a reluctant Mollet to go along.

A conference was scheduled for September 19 to organize the new Association. But no sooner had the date been set than, once again, Eden felt the ground becoming slippery underfoot.

Eden and Mollet had scarcely digested Dulles' new proposal when, on September 11, Eisenhower, in yet another of his mischief-making press conferences, responded to a question as to whether the United States would back Britain and France if they eventually resorted to force: "Well . . . I don't know exactly what you mean by 'backing them.' As you know, this country will not go to war ever while I am occupying my present post unless Congress . . . declares such a war; and the only exception to that would be in the case of unexpected and unwarranted attack on this nation . . . so, as far as going into any kind of military action under present conditions, of course, we are not." Regarding economic sanctions: "A program of economic sanctions has never been placed

before me as of this moment, never." Regarding an appeal to the United
Nations: "I am certain that it will be referred to the United Nations before
anything you would call a more positive, material-physical positive steps
[sic] are taken. I don't know whether this is the exact time."

Eden went to a special session of the House of Commons on September 12 to announce the new step toward a negotiated settlement. Ambassador Aldrich, whose admiration for Dulles was not unbounded, tried to
warn Eden against excessive optimism; Dulles was a "devious" man he
said. But the prime minister pressed forward with his own interpretation;
the concept of SCUA took on a stronger cast in its translation from
American to English. The difference between Dulles' and Eden's interpretation would hasten the time of trouble.

Eden, as if to warn Eisenhower that the United States could not take
the British entirely for granted, told Parliament that "if the Egyptian
Government should seek to interfere with the operations of the association . . . Her Majesty's Government and others concerned will be free to
take such further steps as seem required. . . ." When pressed as to what
he had meant by "further steps," Eden refused to elaborate.[32]

On the following day Dulles presented *his* interpretation of the Users
Association idea to the press. He acknowledged that it was only an interim solution and then removed whatever bloom there may have been
on the rose by admitting that a Users Association would probably be even
less acceptable to Nasser than the Eighteen Nation Proposal. "We recognize," Dulles said in his introductory remarks, "that what is now suggested represents no permanent solution. We shall be unremitting in our
efforts to seek by peaceful means a just solution giving due recognition
to the rights of all concerned, including Egypt." So far so good. But then,
in response to a question about alternative arrangements should the
Users Association fail, he administered a coup de grace to Eden's hopes
for American support in the event force was necessary: "If we cannot
work out . . . a program for getting ships through the Canal on acceptable
terms . . . the alternative for us at least would be to send our vessels
around the Cape . . . we do not intend to shoot our way through. . . ."

Toward the end of the press conference a reporter pushed the secretary hard: "Mr. Secretary, with the United States announcing in advance
it will not use force, and with Soviet Russia backing Egypt with its propaganda, does that not leave all the trump cards in Mr. Nasser's hands?"
Dulles gave a limp reply concluding with a vanillalike homily: "I do not
know what are the 'trump cards' that you refer to other than the fact that
there has been, and I hope will be, a continued loyalty of the great nations
to their obligations under the Charter of the United Nations."[33]

There were additional inauspicious omens that darkened the prospects for Mr. Dulles' Duck Island inspiration. One came from Cairo on September 15: In a fiery speech President Nasser referred to the Canal Users Association as "in truth [an organization] for declaring war." Two days later another came from Moscow: In a letter to Eden, Bulganin warned against the use of force to wrest the Canal from Egypt.

While Dulles was backing and filling, Eden and Mollet decided to take the initiative. The failure of the first London Conference, the doubts about the success of the Users Association, and the all too obvious reluctance of Washington to sanction any military measures made them determined to find some way to tighten the screws on Egypt. At their meeting in London, Eden and Mollet decided to repatriate British and French employees of the nationalized company. These represented by far the largest proportion of Canal pilots and technicians. Six hundred of them packed up and left Egypt. Within a fortnight, only a handful of foreign and two score Egyptian pilots, out of a normal complement of more than two hundred, remained in the employ of the new regime. Eden and Mollet had been assured by the president of the former Suez Canal Company that this step would be effective; the Egyptians, he predicted, could not possibly operate the Canal.

Much of the informal chitchat in the various committees, working groups, and lunchtime sessions I attended during mid-September revolved around the difficulties the "Gyppos" would have in keeping the Canal operating without the assistance of the foreign pilots. Amusing accidents were piled on ludicrous disasters. Amateur artists vied with one another as they sketched their impressions of what the Canal would be like by Christmas. One I remember in particular drew his picture on the United Service Club's linen tablecloth. His piece of art portrayed the Canal solidly stacked with upright ships, bows or sterns stuck deep in the silt.

On occasion, a Royal Navy officer would inform the company that piloting a ship through the Canal was not much more difficult than maneuvering a motorcar on a holiday weekend through the Staines bypass outside of London. On occasion, too, someone would remind the group that American and British intelligence analysts had concluded that the Canal could be operated without foreign help. But such killjoy remarks were brushed aside as just another example of poop-deck sang froid or of an intelligence officer's bookkeeping mentality; it was much more fun to ignore the sobersides and to wait gleefully for the next comic Cassandra to top the tale of the last.

As the days passed, however, the story lost its edge. On the eve of the Second London Conference, the news came that forty-two ships had safely transited the Canal, as opposed to the normal prenationalization average of thirty-nine. A report that fifteen Russian pilots had arrived at Suez just about this time provided yet another piece of evidence that Nasser would be able to run the Canal without benefit of the veteran British and French employees.

Traffic, in general, moved more slowly through the Canal during the early autumn than it had prior to nationalization, but it moved—and without much difficulty.

"They were such snobs, the French and the British," an Egyptian pilot recalled many years later. "They insisted you couldn't pilot this Canal without two years' training." He had been hired during the summer of 1956 and was shepherding ships through the Canal without incident after thirteen days of tutelage.[34]

Few international conferences since World War II have had as bad advance notices as the one that convened in London on September 19 to organize an alternative arrangement for the operation of the Suez Canal. And deservedly so. It was hastily contrived, inadequately articulated, and internally inconsistent. It was a giddy brainstorm conceived in a desperate effort to buy time. In the event, time was bought. But there was nothing positive to show for the high price of its purchase.

7

IMPASSE

John Foster Dulles may have genuinely believed that a Suez Canal Users Association, as he perceived it, might defuse the Canal crisis. And Anthony Eden may have sincerely hoped that a Users Association, as *he* perceived it, might resolve the Canal problem. But Guy Mollet and Christian Pineau felt that, whether the organization took Dulles' soft or Eden's hard form, it was too rickety a notion to rely upon—even if Nasser would accept it. Which he clearly would not.

Most people at the American Embassy, including, I am sure, Ambassador Aldrich, were more inclined toward Paris' view than to that of either Washington or London. In short, the Association seemed to us a dumb idea. Within a few days after Dulles first conjured it up, the acronym "SCUA" was irreverently being referred to as "SCREWYA." In the event, Britain, fatalistically, and France, grudgingly, agreed to go along with the American initiative—stark evidence of the minimal bargaining power they then had in Washington.

And so, on September 19, a host of great nations once again assembled in London. Only this time there were eighteen, not twenty-two. Among those absent were the Indians. "Nominally absent" would perhaps be a more accurate description of their status. New Delhi had sent an observer group (including Menon, of course) to be available in the hope that their advice or their good offices would be sought and to provide Cairo with a listening post.

My shadowy connection with the "Third World" showed up again on the morning of the first session. "What have you got?" I asked him. "Negative. Old Dulles may have to make this one on his own." "I thought you practically ran the joint out there." He organized a thin smile. "Not quite. My guy's boss back in Shangri-La said he had been raising hell and keeping late hours when he was in London last month. Made him stay home with his wife and kids." He hung around for a day or two and then disappeared without even a good-bye, apparently chagrined at his inability to provide an encore to his earlier performance. Dulles sighed when I told him we would have nothing special from the underground. But I couldn't determine whether it was a sigh of disappointment or relief.

The conference lasted three days. After his opening remarks Dulles faced a barrage of questions from a covey of bewildered foreign ministers. He soon found himself in deep water: "I would be glad to take more time and then could perhaps answer [the questions] better, and what I say now is subject to correction." The Japanese foreign minister asked how the use of the Association's pilots could be reconciled with a situation in which Egypt insisted that only *its* pilots be used. Under such circumstances, Dulles responded, "I don't see that the pilots of the Association would practically have very much to do, and that part of the plan would have collapsed."[1] Many delegates were concerned about the relationship between the conference and what might eventually develop at the UN as a result of the British-French letter to the Security Council. Here Dulles, one of the original architects of the United Nations, was more confident: "What we are suggesting is a mechanism for the kind of a provisional solution which is precisely the kind the United Nations could seize hold of."[2]

The conference was far from being a love feast indulged in by eighteen like-minded allies. Beneath the cosmetic unity of the communiqués and the surface smiles of the delegates, there was hostility (France), suspicion (Norway), skepticism (Japan), and bewilderment (many). There was also irritability—especially on the part of the British: When a Yugoslav representative queried the use of force, he was told by a senior Foreign Office official, "Britain is not used to getting advice from small Balkan powers"; a Swede who was presumptuous enough to raise the same point was asked, "What did your country do in the last war?"[3]

Although few, if any, of the delegates thought that SCUA held any promise, they listened solemnly to the litany of John Foster Dulles and the lofty speeches of Selwyn Lloyd. In the end, it was left to these two men to pull and tug at the most critical issue: whether the condition for membership would involve obligatory or voluntary adherence to the Association's decisions. Depending on how this was resolved, the Users Association could either exert effective pressure on Nasser or merely be an international debating society.

Dulles had thrown down the gauntlet in his opening statement to the conference: "Membership in the Association would not, as we see it, involve the assumption by any member of any obligation. It would, however, be hoped that members . . . would voluntarily take such action with respect to their ships and the payment of Canal dues as would facilitate the work of the Association. . . . This action, I emphasize, would be entirely a voluntary action by each of the member governments, if it saw fit to take it."[4] Dulles warned his British and French colleagues that if, in fact, the voluntary nature of the participants' involvement was not explicitly set forth, the United States would not sign the agreement.

The most sensitive and critical matter implicit in Dulles' objections to obligatory responsibilities for the Association members had to do with the payment of Canal tolls. The British and French felt that unless Nasser were denied the revenues, the Users Association would have no clout. The Americans, on the other hand, did not want to be responsible for ordering American shipowners, including those whose ships sailed under flags of convenience, to pay their tolls to a remote agency of uncertain authority rather than, as was their usual arrangement, to settle directly with the established collectors at Port Said or Ismailia. Nor, perhaps, did Dulles really wish to endow SCUA with clout.

At one point in the conference there ensued a seemingly endless discussion of tolls, dues, tonnages, and trade volumes. To the naked eye, this turgid arithmetical exercise was necessary so that the proportion of the cost of the new Association to each member could be assessed. But there was another, more devious reason: The West was anxious to conjure up a formula that would make Communist countries, in general, and the USSR, in particular, ineligible for membership. Like schoolboys, the delegates, pencils and notepaper at hand, were studying (dozing over?) a smorgasbord of statistics catered courtesy of State Department researchers.

It took a stronger stomach and a more disciplined psyche than I possessed to sit quietly while senior officials droned and nattered on about who should pay how much to whom, if and when the airy-fairy Users Association ever got organized. I slipped out of the conference room into the welcoming arms of the tea lady in the lounge. Alone in a corner reading a newspaper was the foreign minister from Ethiopia. "Are you, too, absent without leave?" I asked. He grinned and shrugged. "It's too much, you know. My Foreign Office consists of myself, a few assistants, and a half dozen clerks. Perhaps those figures they're looking at are right, perhaps they're wrong, but I do not know and couldn't possibly find out. I'll just wait until they decide on Ethiopia's dues. If they are too much, we just won't pay. In fact, we may not bother at all. Incidentally, if I can break away and go to the theater tonight, what would you recommend?" I had found a soul mate. We spent a pleasant hour discussing the London stage, being careful, however, not to dwell on the farce being performed a few steps away.

Meanwhile, in the conference chamber, Dulles, once again, got his way. The final Declaration of the meeting read in part:

"SCUA shall have the following purposes: . . . to receive, hold and disburse the revenues from dues and other sums which any user of the Canal *may* [italics added] pay to SCUA."[5] The specific issue of tolls was left hanging. The secretary carried the field and the Association shakily embarked on its appointment with history.

On October 1, the Association had its first meeting, but by now there had been further attrition; three countries—Japan, Pakistan, and Ethiopia—of the original SCUA varsity eighteen opted out. It occurred to me later that I missed scoring a point or two by not forewarning the State Department of Ethiopia's desultory interest in the enterprise. I comforted myself, however, knowing that in explaining how I learned of the possible defection, I would have had to confess my own dereliction.

The maiden SCUA session was attended solely by the local ambassadors from the member countries rather than the foreign ministers. It was a listless affair. Everyone present knew he was involved in a tacky sideshow rather than in the main event, which was then being prepared three thousand miles away. As host and chairman, the British faced the difficult task of making something out of nothing. A lugubrious Elizabethan-looking Foreign Office acquaintance nicely summed up the whole enterprise: "I don't know whether I'll make it through this process; I'm a one-ulcer man in a two-ulcer job."

For whatever it was worth, by early October the Suez Canal Users Association was a living, breathing thing. But a wan and helpless thing.

On September 23, a week before SCUA's organizational meeting, the scene had shifted to New York. Eden and Mollet had requested a Security Council session to consider the appeal they had made on September 12 but which, at Dulles' urging, they had left in limbo. The prime minister and premier made their move while Dulles was flying back to Washington from London and could not be consulted or even informed. In the light of their recent experience, Eden and Mollet must have found this timing quite convenient.

In response to Eden's and Mollet's request, a meeting of the Security Council was called for October 5. But once again, the British and French would set forth on a series of delicate negotiations uncertain of the support they would receive from their American ally. On September 26, Secretary Dulles had been asked by the press if the United States would back Britain and France at the UN. "Well," the secretary said, "I think in general that we will." On October 2, just after the SCUA organizational meeting had convened in London, Dulles, in another one of his indiscreet news conferences, acknowledged that the United States had fundamental differences with Great Britain and France on the Suez problem. America, he said, intended to remain aloof from its allies' "colonial problems." Then came an even more savage blow: When asked whether he had "pulled the teeth" from SCUA, by insisting that payments by member countries were a voluntary matter, he replied that SCUA "never had any teeth."

The long-suffering Prime Minister Eden was enraged. The secretary of state's public disavowal of the organization that he himself had conceived and then shoved down Eden's throat was infuriating enough. But then Dulles made Eden gag by implying that Suez was just another "colonial problem." Anthony Nutting was with the prime minister at Downing Street when Dulles' remarks came over the teletype. "With a contemptuous gesture, [Eden] flung the piece of paper across the table, hissing as he did so, 'And now what do you have to say for your American friends?' "[6]

"The representatives of the Users' Association countries were then assembled in London," Eden later wrote, "confidently awaiting the United States decision to pay the Canal dues to their organization. These were the teeth. Mr. Dulles' statement was in conflict with the Users' understanding of the United States Government's intentions."[7] For Eden this was the last straw. Nothing else that Dulles would say or do over the next several weeks would convince him that he could rely on American support.

The Jordanian and Egyptian crises were not the only burdens Eden had to bear that autumn. British troops were fighting off insurgents in two far-flung areas of the old Empire. In Malaya, an English colony since 1874, thousands of British soldiers had been involved in a "police action" against Communist guerrillas for seven years. By October 1956, there had been more than two thousand casualties and the end seemed nowhere in sight.

In Cyprus, an English colony since 1878, an Athens-inspired force of tough Greek Cypriot farmers and fanatic schoolboys (and perhaps some undercover Greek troops, as well) were tearing the island apart in the cause of annexation with Greece. Ten thousand British forces were heavily engaged in trying to restore law and order.

Of the two, the problem of Cyprus was the more awkward and demanded much more time and attention from Whitehall; Malaya was dealt with largely by British civil servants, police officials, and military officers on the spot.

Complicating the British problem on Cyprus was the political and spiritual leader of the insurgents. A man of the cloth and a man of the people—or at least the Greek Cypriot people—Archbishop Makarios was a skillful politician, a shrewd strategist, and the most powerful religious personality on the island. More than that, Makarios was regarded throughout the world, together with Tito and Nasser, as a founding father of the nonaligned movement. An effective combination of the profane and the pious. "Black Mac," the British called him. In desperation, the British snatched him up in March 1956 and placed him under confinement on one of the tiny Seychelles Islands in the Indian Ocean.

At the moment when Eden was having his other troubles across the Mediterranean, Makarios' forced exile was complicating the resolution of the Cyprus problem and fueling political restiveness in England itself. Parliament was noisy with speeches about the ineptness of the government. Trafalgar Square was seething every Sunday with angry pro-Cypriot crowds. Driving into Sussex one autumn Saturday, I saw busloads of county constables moving in the other direction to reinforce the London police then being stretched thin coping with pro-Greek and anti-Greek, pro-Makarios and anti-Makarios demonstrations.

The prime minister, whose health had been frail for several years, was being ground down by the accumulated tensions of the summer. Cyprus, Malaya, Jordan, Egypt weighed heavily on him. Deteriorating relations between London and Washington had also taken their toll. As the Security Council debate was about to begin in early October Eden fell seriously ill. He was briefly hospitalized with an alarmingly high fever. While the principal responsibility for the discussions at the Security Council would, in any case, have fallen on Foreign Minister Selwyn Lloyd, the prime minister would have directed the overall strategy. But Eden was out of touch with Lloyd during the early, important days of the session.

Much more important than the immediate problem in New York was Eden's illness. This would have a critical bearing on shaping the delicate and dangerous weeks ahead, for, according to those who worked closely with him then, Eden had apparently gone through a change in personality.[8] Eden's father had been famous for his temper tantrums and Anthony had inherited the tendency to indulge in intense bursts of anger. But throughout the Suez crisis the prime minister was strangely calm. This may have resulted from the bout of 106° fever, or from his tortured liver and his jaundice, or from the medication he took to ease the excruciating pain.* No matter; the fact was that Eden seemed to alternate between phases of sublime confidence and dreadful misdoubt during the months of crisis and trauma. He was acutely sensitive to everything that was happening, but seemed sometimes unaware of and sometimes excessively obsessed by the dire consequences that dogged his every move. Eden appeared to be functioning on a level 10 percent removed from reality. It was a critical 10 percent and virtually guaranteed that his Suez policy, flawed as it was, would turn into a grave national and personal tragedy.

What of his partners across the Atlantic—the two men who were responsible for the other side of that now strained and contorted special Anglo-American relationship? To most people who saw him in those days, John Foster Dulles looked as strong as an ox. Bent and gray, perhaps, but of late that had been the usual posture and pallor of American

---

*Pathologists and physicians believe it could be any one, or all, of these.

secretaries of state even after only a few months in office. But Dulles, too, was sick, very sick. Few people, and certainly not Eden, knew that Dulles was ill with cancer. And then there was Eisenhower: Despite the sunny smile, he, too, had barely recuperated from serious illness. So it was that a great and tragic international drama was about to be played out by three afflicted men.

The Security Council debate opened on October 5 with a proposal by Lloyd, supported by French Foreign Minister Pineau, that Egypt should negotiate a new agreement on the Suez Canal, based on the Eighteen Nation Proposal and including an international control board. Until such a new agreement was reached, Lloyd urged, Egypt should cooperate with SCUA even though Nasser had already rejected the Eighteen Nation Proposal out of hand and regarded SCUA as anathema. The Lloyd-Pineau proposal was, as expected, strongly opposed by the USSR. Dulles generally endorsed the British and French stand, but attempted to introduce some maneuverability into their position; the Eighteen Nation Proposal was not immutable and there were probably other ways to meet the requirements of Britain and France while, at the same time, not infringing on Egypt's sovereignty. The debate had gotten off to a predictable, unpromising start.

On October 8, it was the Egyptian foreign minister's turn to address the delegates. Fawzi spoke in a vein that seemed to reveal a new spirit of compromise. "It is probably advisable," he told the delegates, "if we agree—as we seem to do—on negotiating a peaceful settlement of this question, to establish a negotiating body of reasonable size, and more important still, to put for the guidance of that body a set of principles to work by and objectives to keep in mind and attain."[9] He then summarized several general principles with regard to the Canal that were sure to appeal to all the delegates, especially Lloyd and Pineau.

The mood in New York changed markedly after Fawzi's speech. None of the Security Council members actually dissolved into a state of euphoria—each of them was too seasoned by years of shifting diplomatic winds and tides to regard one speech as a landfall—but most of them, including some members of the British delegation, felt optimistic that an eventual compromise was on the horizon.

International meetings rarely make progress in the noise and heat of plenary sessions. It is in the corridors, lounges, and private offices that the bargains are struck and the breakthroughs are made.* This was the case in New York. After the formal opening speeches in which the oppos-

---

*My tea-lounge conversation at Lancaster House with the Ethiopian foreign minister is not necessarily the model I have in mind here.

ing parties staked out their negotiating turf, representatives of Britain, France, and Egypt gathered in Secretary-General Hammarskjöld's office to seek some common ground.

The Security Council membership in the autumn of 1956 did not include India, but the peripatetic Krishna Menon had come to New York, via Cairo, to offer his help. He was armed with a proposition of his own (which he must have first cleared with Nasser). This involved fiddling with the 1888 Constantinople Convention to permit some loose form of international oversight for the Canal. The idea got nowhere, but Menon was everywhere. Everywhere, except where he wanted to be—in Hammarskjöld's private office with foreign ministers Lloyd, Pineau, and Fawzi.

Under the patient prodding of the secretary-general, the three foreign ministers met privately from October 9 to October 12. Out of their sessions came a more precise articulation of the principles that Fawzi had formulated earlier. Lloyd then incorporated them in his speech to the Council on October 12: (1) "Free and open transit through the Canal"; (2) respect for "the sovereignty of Egypt"; (3) "The operation of the Canal should be insulated from the politics of any country"; (4) tolls and other charges should be fixed "by agreement between Egypt and the Users"; (5) "A fair proportion of the dues should be allotted to development";* (6) disputes arising from unsolved questions between the Canal Company and Egypt "should be settled by arbitration, with suitable terms of reference and suitable provisions for the payment of sums found to be due."

It was agreed that representatives of Britain, France, and Egypt, together with the secretary-general, would meet again at Geneva on October 29, for further private discussions and, it was hoped, a final agreement. "To say the least," Anthony Nutting recalled later, "the discussions in New York produced the makings of an agreement on the future of the Suez Canal which Lloyd felt at the time, and later publicly admitted, gave us substantially what we required in the way of guarantees that the Canal would be operated in the interests of all who used it."[10]

But the "makings of an agreement" was not what Anthony Eden or Guy Mollet had in mind. At that moment, in London and in Paris, plans were being made to produce not a compromise, but an impasse.

Eisenhower and Dulles were torn, that autumn, between domestic political considerations and the need to demonstrate Western strength

---

*This was of major concern to many Canal users who were worried that Nasser would direct all revenues to Egypt's domestic requirements and skimp on the maintenance of the Canal.

in the Middle East. Eden and Lloyd were torn between preserving close ties with Washington and standing up to Nasser. Mollet and Pineau had no such sense of ambivalence; they were certain of their objectives, assured about where their interests lay. They were operating in terms of blacks and whites, rather than various shades of gray.

The Mollet government had been installed only six months before the nationalization of the Canal. It came to power pledged to find a satisfactory resolution of the full-scale war in Algeria. For Mollet and Pineau, the seizure of the Canal presented an opportunity, not a problem —a welcome chance for direct military confrontation with Nasser, the noisy and troublesome supporter of the Algerian Liberation Front.

Foreign Minister Pineau had made it abundantly clear in his first meeting with Under Secretary Murphy in London many weeks before that the Mollet government, unlike the Eden government, had no sentimental hang-ups about a "special relationship" with the United States. The French were dubious that the Canal could be wrested from Nasser through diplomatic means and that America would support military action if diplomacy failed. In any case, French public opinion and a majority in the Assembly were pressing for a tough stand against Egypt. They wanted Gamal Abdel Nasser's blood, not his goodwill. Indeed, the continued existence in office of the Mollet government depended on bringing Nasser to his knees, not to a conference table. No wonder Murphy had regarded Pineau as "aggressive"!

And so, while the ailing Eden was preoccupied with the care and feeding of John Foster Dulles and with keeping his own political house in order, Mollet and Pineau, under the hot breath of a hawkish French public opinion, were cultivating and encouraging another ally, Israel.

Unknown to London, some cautious, tentative contacts had taken place in mid-September between Paris and Jerusalem. A meeting had been arranged by the French to explore the possibility of Israel's participating in joint British-French military action against Egypt. Ben-Gurion hesitated for several days. Cooperation with France, Israel's friend and supporter, was one thing; cooperation with Great Britain, Jordan's sponsor and ally, was quite another. But on September 23, he instructed Shimon Peres, the Israeli defense minister, who was then in Paris, to inform the French defense minister that Israel would favorably consider the French proposal. Israeli forces would move toward the Canal and against Sharm el-Sheikh, the Egyptian fortress astride the Gulf of Aqaba.

Peres immediately returned to Israel and told Ben-Gurion and Moshe Dayan that the French seemed prepared to go to war against Nasser on their own, although they were convinced that once they made that decision, the British would join them. The French would welcome Israeli participation.[11]

On September 26 Eden and Lloyd went to Paris to concert their approach at the forthcoming Security Council meeting and to inform the French that Iraqi forces would soon move into Jordan to strengthen the Arab Legion against Israeli attacks. Eden reports that the French were "skeptical about the United Nations and more skeptical still about the Users Association. . . . They felt that the American Administration was not keeping its promises."[12] They agreed to participate in the Security Council meetings, if only to demonstrate that nothing helpful would emerge, but strongly opposed the British plan to deploy Iraqi forces into Jordan. The French did not mention their discussion with the Israelis a few days before. The obligatory communiqué following the meeting referred to discussions about the "European Common Market"—a matter that would cause Eden some embarrassment later when anti-Common Market members of his Conservative Party pressed him hard for details of the discussions in Paris.

General Moshe Dayan was sent by Ben-Gurion to Paris at the end of September, accompanied by Foreign Minister Golda Meir and Shimon Peres, to meet with Christian Pineau and his military advisers. The Israelis presented a shopping list for more arms to the French chief of staff, General Ely. The first definitive discussions of a joint French-Israeli military operation against Egypt took place at this meeting. Christian Pineau set off for the UN discussions in New York later that day.

Eden may have been informed of the French-Israeli arrangements when Pineau passed through London on his way to New York. If so, he apparently chose not to share this choice morsel of information with his foreign minister. Selwyn Lloyd, unaware of the extent to which the French had already committed themselves to the military track, pushed hard and constructively for a compromise. Pineau, on the other hand, seemed strangely blasé, even indifferent. It was as if he were just going through the motions of the exercise—which, in fact, was all he was doing. One day, during this period, for reasons he did not then understand, Abba Eban, the Israeli ambassador to the UN, was asked to arrange a meeting between Pineau and the Israeli chief of military intelligence, who was then visiting the United States.[13]

On October 12, Eden's political hand was strengthened by an enthusiastic vote of confidence at the annual autumn bash of the Conservative Party. He told his fellow Tories that some progress was being made at the Security Council "due to the firmness and resolution we . . . have been showing throughout this crisis."

But not all of the prime minister's colleagues supported a bellicose approach toward Egypt; during the party conference, Eden's minister of defense, Sir Walter Monckton, resigned from his post.* He was replaced by Viscount Antony Head, who exhibited more enthusiasm for Eden's enterprise. Although Monckton did not then reveal that he had disagreed with the government's military preparations, the Eden-watchers on Grosvenor Square regarded his resignation as a symptom of something worrisome going on in Whitehall. It was duly noted at an embassy staff meeting, soon after, that Her Majesty's government might be moving into dangerous waters under the guidance of a shaky navigator.

In the Middle East, meanwhile, brisk skirmishes were already taking place. Israeli reprisal raids against Jordan in late September had escalated in a matter of weeks to the point where it became clear to Eden that honoring Britain's defense pact with the Jordanians could lead to a British-Israeli military confrontation—hardly a desirable circumstance in the light of the plans to move against Egypt. The situation almost came to a head on October 10 when there was a particularly nasty bit of border fighting in which a few Israeli Air Force planes took part, and it appeared that the Royal Air Force would have to be called upon to back up the Jordanian forces. An anguished Eden was spared the need for making a decision when the fighting broke off. But the effect of British vacillation in the face of Jordan's moment of danger was felt in a few days; a nationalist, anti-British, pro-Egyptian group took over the government in Amman. Less than two weeks later Jordan would sign a military treaty and agree to a joint command with Egypt and Syria.

This, then, was the state of play in Paris, London, and the Middle East as the United Nations Security Council delegates left their conference chamber in a moderately optimistic mood after Selwyn Lloyd's speech on the evening of October 12.

The last thing Mollet and Eden wanted in New York in mid-October was to be faced with the prospect of any UN agreement short of one involving Egypt's complete acquiescence to the Eighteen Nation Proposal. They had been worried that some mischievous stroke of fate or a wily Nasser would create a spirit of general, inconclusive harmony which would tie their hands for weeks ahead. Now, just such an awful development seemed imminent, and under the worst possible circumstances. Looming on the morrow in the Security Council was a compromise-in-hiatus. And the world would expect it to be massaged and beaten into negotiable form before representatives of Britain, France, and Egypt met with the secretary-general in Geneva on October 29.

*He remained in the cabinet, however, as paymaster general.

If the two prime ministers were apprehensive about the developments at the Security Council on October 12, Eisenhower was bubbling over with a sense of relief. Only two weeks before, a Gallup poll had reported that 46 percent of those queried had designated "threat of war, Suez, foreign policy" as the most important problems facing the country. And the election was less than a month away. The President wasted little time in sharing the good news from New York. In a television appearance on the evening of October 12, he told his audience that he had "the best announcement that I could possibly make to America tonight. The progress made in the settlement of the Suez dispute this afternoon at the United Nations is most gratifying. . . . It looks like here is a very great crisis that is left behind us. I do not mean to say that we are completely out of the woods, but . . . in both his [Dulles'] heart and mine, at least, there is a very great prayer of thanksgiving."

Ike was on the campaign trail and obviously had laced his remarks with a generous dash of hyperbole. Nevertheless, his optimism was genuine. The Administration in Washington clearly felt it was over the hump of the Suez crisis.

As Anthony Eden and Guy Mollet assessed the situation evolving at the United Nations, they probably reckoned that they had only two options available. The first involved swallowing their pride and jettisoning their plans for attacking Egypt. This would mean joining with Dulles to exploit the hints of flexibility emerging from Cairo and pressing forward toward more robust, perhaps conclusive, diplomatic concessions. The second entailed insisting on terms that were more favorable than they knew Fawzi could agree to. This would court international opprobrium, but would provide a rationale for subsequent military action.

Of the alternatives, one was hypothetical, the other foreordained. The decision for war had gathered too much momentum in London and Paris to be stopped by halfway concessions. Eden was driven by his determination to destroy Nasser. Mollet, for his part, knew that his government would fall if he flouted the National Assembly's mounting demands for confrontation rather than compromise. Moreover, he had already gone far down the road toward joining Israel in an attack on Egypt—an attack that would have to be launched soon, lest the element of surprise be lost. But first, they would have to choke off the emerging feeling throughout the world that Egypt's stance was changing from one of stubborn resistance, to compromise, to sweet reasonableness. The only way to accomplish this would be to introduce an element into the discussion that would be guaranteed to change the mood and invite a deadlock.

On the night of October 12, Lloyd and Pineau received new instructions. These were designed not to expand but to contract the circumference for diplomatic maneuver. The resolution they had drafted was revised to incorporate not only the agreed-upon "six principles," but also a section that was tailor-made to scuttle the whole agreement. It stated that if Egypt would not accept the Eighteen Nation Proposal Nasser must submit concrete suggestions for implementing the six principles, and urged, to boot, that Egypt be required to cooperate with SCUA pending a final settlement. Some friendly foreign ministers tried to take some of the sting out of the British and French position. Thus, Dulles emphasized again that the Eighteen Nation Proposal was not the only basis for a settlement; there were doubtless others that all could agree upon. But the final result turned out to be everything Eden and Mollet could have wished: The "six principles" were agreed upon unanimously, but the new provisions were vetoed by the Soviet Union.

Eden would later claim that the defeat of the British and French resolution in the UN brought his government's Middle East policy to a point of no return. "We were left with six principles . . . they just flapped in the air. . . . The way was open to endless procrastination by Egypt. Worse, it also lay open to her to renew her aggressive designs in other fields. . . . The truth was starkly clear to me. Plunder had paid off."[14]

London and Paris had clearly pulled the switch on what might well have been the beginning of a negotiated solution to the Suez problem under the umbrella of the UN. But, in the end, did their last-minute, damaging intervention make a difference? Was a golden moment of diplomacy and reason wantonly cast away? Secretary-General Hammarskjöld seemed to think it had been. So did Selwyn Lloyd. And so did Anthony Nutting: "In his negotiations in New York Lloyd appeared to have gotten from Fawzi effectively all we needed to safeguard our interests in the Canal."[15]

But these were views expressed in the immediate aftermath of the crisis by disappointed men. Reflecting on the event much later, Robert Bowie, who had been Secretary Dulles' chief planner and special adviser, is not entirely certain. "Letting Fawzi explore a compromise might have suited [Nasser's] tactical situation, though he may not have intended to follow through. But Egypt could well have been serious, responding to the various pressures already mentioned. And the Fawzi concessions were compatible with the basic refusal to 'give up' operation of the Canal, while offering safeguards consistent with Nasser's earlier assurances."[16]

If the British and French had demonstrated some flexibility in New York in early October, could the Egyptians have done the same at Geneva several weeks later? Probably not even Nasser or Fawzi knew. Egypt was under pressure, economic primarily, to reduce the level of tension in its relations with the West, but Nasser may well have felt that with Soviet and Third World support, he could ride out his problems. After all, he had the Canal, and the British and French had SCUA—as disproportionate a distribution of bargaining power as one could imagine. Adding weight to the desirability of procrastination by Cairo was Washington's obvious willingness to keep talks—almost any kind of talks in any kind of forum —going indefinitely. Eden's instincts that an agreement in New York would turn out to be merely temporary and cosmetic may well have been right. And yet . . .

And yet, the British and French had already lost the game in late July. Whether or not Eden and Mollet could bring themselves to face it, the world had already accepted the nationalization of the Suez Canal as a fait accompli. In October they might have salvaged something of their interests if not their pride—providing, of course, that Nasser could have been persuaded to follow through on his offer to permit the establishment of an international advisory board comprised of SCUA nations. But wars have been fought over insults to national pride as frequently as over threats to national interests. And in the autumn of 1956, the question of pride overrode many seemingly more logical considerations.

The Security Council debate adjourned on October 14. In the interim between the New York meeting and the informal session scheduled for October 29, Hammarskjöld hoped to consolidate and then broaden the area of agreement between the opposing parties. On October 24, in preparation for the Geneva meeting, the secretary-general wrote to Fawzi outlining what had already been agreed upon—an arbitration and fact-finding body composed of Egyptians and members of the Users Association. He proposed that this form the basis for Fawzi's forthcoming discussion with Lloyd and Pineau in Geneva.

Fawzi replied on November 2—too late for the secretary-general to act. With one exception, he subscribed to Hammarskjöld's interpretation of the area of accord: He was not happy with the clause which stated that if an offending party refused to honor its responsibilities to pay an award made by the international tribunal, "certain limited 'police action' would be permitted even without recourse to further juridical procedures." If the meeting of October 29 had taken place, it might well have stalled on this issue; the British and French were now gun-shy of agreements without "teeth" and the Egyptians were in no mood to agree to "police actions," however "limited."

Eden and Mollet, too, were busy in the days following the New York meeting. But not on preparations for the session with Fawzi. Within hours after the Security Council had adjourned, the first minister of Her

Majesty's Government voluntarily, indeed with some enthusiasm, slid down the slippery slope. On October 14 at Chequers, the prime minister's country residence, Anthony Eden received a detailed account of what the French and Israelis had been up to. It was then and there that he decided to accept an invitation to join their enterprise.

Two French emissaries—a cabinet minister and a general—slipped into Chequers that Sunday morning and for several hours briefed Eden on the French-Israeli "scenario." Except for Eden, only Anthony Nutting (sitting in for the foreign minister who was still in New York) and Eden's private secretary were present.*

The two Frenchmen described a plan that, in essence, called for an invasion across Sinai by the Israeli armed forces, which by now had been strengthened with new deliveries of French arms and airplanes. The Israelis would streak toward Suez, but when they were virtually at the east bank of the Canal, France (and Britain, if Eden agreed to join), professing concern lest the Canal become a battleground, would occupy Port Said, Ismailia, and key points in between. In the course of all this, Cairo Radio might just happen to be silenced and Nasser overthrown. But that could not be helped—fortunes of war and all that.

All could go according to plan, the two French officials noted, if Britain would accelerate its military timetables and if Israel were not diverted from its attack on Egypt. The latter point was urgent and critical; unless Eden called off the Iraqi reinforcements for Jordan, the Israelis, worried about terrorist raids across the Jordanian border, might decide to scrap the Sinai invasion and launch a preventive move against Jordan instead. Then the British, to honor their defense treaty with Amman, would have to unleash the RAF against an Israeli Air Force possessing several score brand-new French Mystère fighter planes. (Eden was later to refer to this prospect as a recurrent "nightmare.") Eden had a choice, his visitors grimly told him: He could persuade Nuri Said to keep his forces home or he could forsake this chance, with the help of the Israeli Army, to settle the score with Nasser. The prime minister had no difficulty deciding. Nutting later reported that Eden agreed to "ask Nuri to suspend his move temporarily."[17]

The fateful meeting ended with a request by the French emissaries for an early RSVP. The prime minister promised he would let Paris know his decision as soon as possible. But Eden knew then what his decision would be. Much to Nutting's despair, so did he. And much to the two emissaries' relief, so did they.

---

*The private secretary, like all efficient representatives of this genre, was dutifully taking notes, until Eden stopped him.

October 16 was another momentous milestone on the fateful journey. Eden, with a worried Lloyd in tow,* flew to Paris where he agreed in principle to the French plan. Some details were worked out, but the actual date for D day was left for later discussion.

Although the decision called for complex military and political arrangements, only a handful of men in Britain, France, and Israel were informed of it. In Israel, the tension on the border with Jordan provided Ben-Gurion with a useful diversion. On October 14, the Israeli cabinet (obviously not knowing what was transpiring between London and Paris) met to discuss Britain's apparent readiness to attack Israel on behalf of Jordan. "The Government heard with concern and astonishment the threat of the British Foreign Office that Britain would invoke the Anglo-Jordanian Treaty against Israel . . . if Israel should oppose a change in the *status quo* in this region by the stationing of Iraqi troops in Jordan."[19]

On the following day Israeli ambassadors throughout the world were summoned home to discuss the Jordanian crisis.** And just as Eden was leaving for Paris on October 16, Ben-Gurion reassured the Israelis and warned the Egyptians. Israel, he said, was rearming and would take stern steps against the fedayeen raids. Moreover, Egypt's blockade of the Gulf of Aqaba and its prohibition of Israeli ships in the Suez Canal would "disturb the stability of the peace in the Middle East."

Eden does not report his Paris seduction in his memoirs, of course, but he does sidle aesthetically up to the point: ". . . we had to pool our information and consider the action we must take in the light of developments in the Middle East, itself, and in particular the growing menace of hostility by Egypt against Israel . . . the fedayeen raids on Israel were started up afresh."[20]

On October 18, Eden met with his cabinet and reviewed the events of the Paris meeting—or at least those aspects of the meeting he felt he could reveal. Once again, he was elliptical and cautionary about impending Israeli developments. "We [i.e., Eden and Lloyd] described the increasing tension in the Middle East with the growing danger that Israel, under provocation from Egypt, would make some military move."[21]

Meanwhile, the SCUA meetings were sputtering on in London. The cables from the State Department hedged as to whether the Administration would pressure American shipowners to pay their Canal tolls to

*When Lloyd heard of the Chequers meeting on his return from Washington, he told Nutting that Britain "must have nothing to do with the French plan."[18]

**At the airport in London where he was changing planes, Abba Eban, Israel's ambassador to the UN, saw Lloyd and Eden. Eban later learned that the two British officials were rushing off to Paris.

SCUA rather than, as Dulles used to say, put "cash on the barrel head."

An American decision on this score was not as simple as the French and British professed to believe. Ships flying the Union Jack or tricolor had always followed the pattern of paying their tolls periodically to the Canal Company's agents in London or Paris. American ships, on the other hand, settled their bills directly with the toll collectors at the Canal on a pay-as-you-go basis. It would be American shipping, primarily, then, that would have to change its mode of payment. And this could be done only if Washington officially instructed American shipowners. As a consequence, Dulles was genuinely concerned that the United States would bear the principal onus for directly removing revenue from Nasser's coffers. A further complication hung on the fact that about half the American-owned ships were registered under such flags of convenience as Liberia and Panama. This would involve considerable pressure on third countries, many of whom could be expected to be sympathetic to Nasser.

It would have been one thing for Eisenhower and Dulles to assume these risks or to draw on their stock of political capital if they had had a stake in making SCUA a strong bargainer in its dealings with Nasser. But as was evident by now, they regarded SCUA as simply a means for diverting the British and French from doing anything rash—at least until after the election.

And so, as the days went on, the discomfited American representative at the SCUA meeting talked around, under, and above the tolls issue, while it became increasingly clear to everyone that Washington had no intention of doing anything to change the status quo.

A syndrome that frequently distorts the perceptions of diplomats posted abroad is "host-country-itis." A good diplomat, of course, should always lean over backward to understand the point of view of the country to which he is assigned. There is a subtle but critical difference, however, between this and being insensitive to his own country's position. It is not unlikely that many of us at the American Embassy in London that autumn were afflicted with at least a mild case of host-country-itis. And it is at least possible that some of us were not as obsessed with the need to reelect Dwight Eisenhower by a landslide as was John Foster Dulles. Be that as it may, we were white with rage and red with embarrassment. It was not that we would necessarily have disagreed with a clear-cut decision by the secretary against paying American Canal tolls to SCUA. What pushed us to distraction was the zigging and zagging, today-we'll-say-we-will-and-tomorrow-we'll-say-we-won't tactics that Dulles had adopted.

If the secretary was driving us at the embassy around the bend, it was nothing compared to what he was doing to our friends in Whitehall and even to the rank and file of Englishmen. The *New York Times* reported from London on October 9 that "informed public opinion, politicians of both parties and the press are highly critical of the Secretary of State. . . . Within a few hours a lawyer, a Conservative Member of Parliament, an actor, and an oil tycoon asked one American what in heaven's name Mr. Dulles thought he was doing. . . . Those who are the most offended are usually the United States' best friends." On the same day there was a cartoon on the front page of London's *Daily Express* that carried the caption: "Well, even if he is nothing but a crazy, mixed-up corporation lawyer, at least he could make up his mind exactly which river he's selling us down!"

Asked about reports of British dissatisfaction the next day, President Eisenhower told the press that he had queried Dulles about "whether he [Dulles] had even any intimation from anyone in British officialdom whom he met that they were dissatisfied with our stand in this thing or thought that we have been vacillating and not carrying forward as we started out. He hasn't and I assure you I haven't." The fact was, of course, that both had, but neither cared.

Since 1945, no government, or at least no government of a large nation, has lived out its allotted time free from shock and turmoil. Internally, national leaders have had to grapple with growing inflation, escalating public expectations, deteriorating cities, expanding populations, and worrying social tensions. Externally, presidents, prime ministers, and junta chiefs have had to deal with East-West competition, North-South rivalries, and have–have not frictions. The responsibilities of national leadership are heavy, but those who seek them are hardly unaware of this. What many would-be leaders are unable to anticipate, however, and what their constituencies are unable to appreciate, is the wrenching, tearing, soul-destroying, day-in day-out personal toll such responsibilities entail.

Those who survive their terms in office to enjoy the fruits of less hectic days are the leaders who have been adept at delegating authority to their subordinate ministers. They are also the ones who have thoughtfully selected the problems requiring their direct involvement and, too, the moment at which their involvement becomes essential. By and large, such careful discrimination has been easier to exercise in the case of domestic than of foreign crises. Great departments of government with large resources at their disposal can cope with labor strikes, droughts, epidemics, or natural disasters. But external crises can quickly escalate into situations beyond the ability of foreign offices to handle. When this happens, not only the full attention of the foreign secretary, but also of the chief executive is required. For here, commanding issues of national prestige, even of war and peace, are at stake.

There is another facet to the problem, a more subtle one. Many prime ministers and presidents—most often, it seems, *American* presidents—find more satisfaction and more fun (although they would deny the latter) in spending precious time on international problems than on domestic ones. Trying to fit pieces of the world jigsaw puzzle together may be more complicated, but it is greater sport than trying to get the mail delivered on time; one-shot summit meetings with other potentates may be hard on the waistline, but they are easier on the nerves than constant exposure to quarreling national-interest groups.

It is no wonder, then, that the absorbtive capacity for handling international crises is limited. Washington, for example, is notorious for being a one-crisis-at-a-time community.* Even in more compact, less constricted governments, the circuits of foreign policy decision making can quickly become overloaded. And this is what happened in the United Kingdom in the autumn of 1956.

For almost a year Eden's government had been juggling the delicate problems of Jordan and Iraq—and had alienated important segments of British public opinion in the process. For several months the prime minister had been grappling with the separate, but related problem of Egypt —and had expended a tremendous amount of precious time and energy with nothing to show. He insisted on taking personal charge of these consuming issues. He became the Middle East desk officer. Meanwhile, the world went on, buffeting Britain's economy at home, bruising its interests abroad. But all of these problems—sluggish economic performance, faltering national welfare programs, terror by night in Cyprus, jungle fighting by day in Malaya, steps toward economic and political integration in Western Europe—were residual claimants on the time of a distracted prime minister.

The great nationalist movements of the post–World War II decade were variants of a single romantic, indeed heroic, theme: a search for identity by peoples who had long been the pawns of remote kings and queens. But each search was destined to be played out on a larger stage, as part of a grander, complex plot, with more powerful characters forcing the action. The great rivalry between East and West, between "Communism" and the "Free World," distorted and poisoned many a high-minded quest for self-determination in the forties and fifties. What might

---

*From 1964 until 1974, Vietnam preoccupied Johnson and Nixon, Rusk and Kissinger; no international event short of a full-blown crisis could attract their attention away from Southeast Asia.

have been poignant local struggles between the yearnings of the ruled against the die-hard, nineteenth-century attitudes of their rulers turned out, more often than not, to be ugly, dangerous peripheral battles of the great Cold War then so virulent in the main arena of Eastern and Western Europe. And lurking always in the background was the specter of another and infinitely more hideous world war.

It was this that gave the great men in Washington, London, Paris, and Moscow—and hundreds of millions of ordinary folk everywhere— restless nights and worried days. Prime Minister Eden, no less than any other leader in the West and East, was sensitive to the danger. But perhaps more than any other, he found himself relying on the delicate art of balancing the threat of force with the prospect of compromise. In the last analysis, Anthony Eden was a diplomat—not a general, not a lawyer, not really a politician. And the country he led could not, in the postwar era, make its mark by pressing nasty international situations to the brink of war; unlike either the Soviet Union or the United States, Britain was too weak for such a tactic, even if it chose to adopt it. But neither was Britain prepared to run for cover in the face of every noisy threat; like the Soviet Union and the United States, it had worldwide economic, political, and strategic interests. It was, at least in its own eyes, still one of the postwar Big Three.

By October 1956 the prime minister was facing formidable physical and mental strains. Medication, determination, and sheer guts got him through each day. As the tortured Anthony Eden surveyed the world and all the troubles then besetting him, the overshadowing tensions that were part and parcel of the Cold War colored his judgments, intruded on his thoughts, complicated his policies: The nationalist extremists in Jordan were backed by the new revolutionaries in Egypt, who, for their part, were militarily supported by the tough-minded men in Moscow. The Enosis movement in Cyprus was not a simple matter of Greek expansionism, but had the sympathy (and perhaps more) of Moscow. The insurgents in Malaya were not Malayan nationalists, but *Communist* Chinese nationalists backed (inadequately and ineffectively, as it was to turn out) by the tough-minded men in Peking. And they, in turn (it was a matter of certain knowledge then), were closely allied to the Soviet Union. No wonder that Eden referred time and again in his correspondence with Eisenhower to the ominous designs of the "Russian Bear."

The prime minister had additional reasons to worry about Soviet motives in the Middle East. The Kremlin had been leaning over his shoulder for more than a year. In early August Bulganin wrote to Eden and Mollet protesting the "repression" of Egypt. In mid-September he wrote again accusing Britain and France of threatening force to wrest away Egyptian sovereign rights. Later in the month he wrote once more, criticizing the Users conference. Eden cabled Eisenhower shortly after he had read that letter from Moscow: "You can be sure that we are fully alive to the wider dangers of the Middle East situation. They can be summed up in one word—Russia. . . . I feel sure that anything which you can say or do to show firmness to Nasser at this time will help the peace by giving the Russians pause."[22]

Bulganin and Khrushchev had not been having a salubrious time of it either during 1956. The search for national identity throughout the world did not leave the Kremlin untouched. And the Soviet leaders' problems were much closer to home than the Middle East. They started early in the year when, at the Twentieth Party Congress, Chairman Khrushchev denounced the erstwhile untouchable Josef Stalin. Such a step is not taken lightly, nor without breaking a great deal of crockery. As dramatic as the denunciation of Stalin was, however, other events occurring later in the year overshadowed it. What Chairman Khrushchev did not anticipate was the effect his speech would have outside the Soviet Union.

By the fall of 1956, Yugoslavia had weathered several years of tension following its break with Moscow. Marshal Tito was a beacon to other would-be dissidents and a warning signal to Moscow's subordinate leaders throughout Eastern Europe. Two regimes, in particular, were vulnerable to the faint breeze stirred up by Tito.

Hardly had the first shock waves of Khrushchev's assault on Stalin's memory passed when, in June, Polish workers in the industrial city of Poznan threw down their tools and rampaged through the streets. High prices and low wages triggered the demonstrations, but the bread-and-butter issue quickly escalated into an anti-Communist and anti-Soviet protest. There were angry confrontations between the workers and the police. And there was bloodshed.

The riots were quelled after seventy-two tense hours. But it took the clubs and guns of special troops rushed in from Warsaw to do it. For a few months Poland remained quiet, but foaming. The hard-liners were unable to keep the lid on for long; the Poznan riots had increased the dissension that had boiled up among the Polish Communist Party's movers and shakers following the Soviet Twentieth Party Congress. By mid-October Wladyslaw Gomulka was released from jail to head a new, more moderate Polish government. It was he who greeted the astonished Khrushchev on October 19 when the Soviet leader made a surprise visit to Warsaw. Although Russian troops were then moving toward the city, Gomulka stood up to Khrushchev's demands that Poland once more toe

Moscow's line. On October 21 Poland embarked on a policy of "national Communism" and on a "Polish path to Socialism."

Moscow had barely squeaked through this crisis on its Eastern European front when another explosion occurred, this one in Hungary. The Hungarians had been restive since 1949, when Moscow replaced their coalition government with a tightly controlled Popular Front. In response to Tito's defection, Moscow was determined to keep Hungary in line, and replaced the more nationalist Communist leaders with Moscow-controlled men. On October 20, students, intellectuals, and workers, inspired in part by the bloody riots in Poland, drafted demands which included the abolition of the secret police, the withdrawal of Soviet troops stationed in Hungary, the reinstallation of nationalist leaders, and the bringing to trial of the current, hard-line, Moscow-dominated leadership. On October 23, suppressed in their attempt to broadcast the manifesto, the dissidents battled with the die-hard secret police and now unenthusiastic army units.

On the following day, the Hungarian politburo installed Imre Nagy, a nationalist-moderate Communist as head of the government and then forced him to call on the Soviet army for help in restoring order. Russian tanks entered Budapest. This set off a widespread revolt of students, workers, and even elements of the Hungarian army. The riots quickly took the form of violent protest against Moscow rather than against Moscow's agents in Budapest. Two members of the Soviet politburo slipped into the city to take over control of the situation from their now impotent Hungarian colleagues. They arrived in time to see a violent battle between the demonstrators and the secret police. There were heavy casualties on both sides. Fighting continued for a few days, but Nagy eventually managed to restore some semblance of order. On October 29, Soviet troops were withdrawn—momentarily.

The events in Poland and Hungary put the lie to Moscow's assertions that the people of Eastern Europe were willing partners in the cause of a great Communist empire ruled from the Kremlin. Which is not to say that either the Poles or the Hungarians necessarily wanted to return to the old days of a capitalist-feudalist society. What they were yearning for —and were denied—was what Moscow was then advocating for Egypt and other countries of the Middle East. They wanted to seek their own way; they wanted, in the words of the Poznan rioters, "Bread and Freedom."

The mood was by no means as gloomy in Washington as it was in London, Paris, Jerusalem, or Moscow during the latter part of October. Election Day was looming close and the odds favored an Eisenhower victory by a comfortable margin—providing no unforeseen crisis intervened. The Middle East, except on the Israeli-Jordan border, seemed momentarily quiet—strangely so—and the Suez principals were ostensibly preparing for the Geneva meeting at the end of the month. On October 27, Dulles told the Dallas Council on World Affairs that the situation in the Middle East was "grave" and that he could not "predict the outcome." But if the British, French, and Egyptians reached an agreement at the forthcoming meeting in Geneva, "they will deserve the praise which world opinion and history will surely bestow on them." The British and French, for their part, had been restrained in word and deed, at least to the naked eye, since mid-October. In Washington this was regarded as all to the good.

The Administration and its international affairs experts were transfixed with the situation in Eastern Europe during those days in late October. Washington's spotlight had momentarily shifted from Egypt and Israel to Poland and Hungary. Since the beginning of Eisenhower's presidency, a major rhetorical theme had been the "liberation of Eastern Europe." And now that this seemed about to happen, Secretary Dulles appeared to have lost his nerve. The United States watched and waited and tried desperately to keep its powder dry—at least until after the election. By the end of the month Gomulka had stared the Russians down and the new government in Budapest seemed to have matters under control. Washington heaved a sigh of relief.

Despite outward appearances, however, all was *not* quiet on the Middle East front. The clock was ticking away the hours that still remained between peace and war.

The choreography of the attack on Egypt was finally settled at a secret meeting held outside Paris in late October. The broad outlines, of course, had long been informally agreed upon by the French and the Israelis. But when the prime minister was briefed by his visitors at Chequers in mid-October, there were critical aspects of the plan that troubled him. He was hag-ridden with the prospect that he and his government would be tagged with the scarlet letter "A" for aggressor. Eden was also uncomfortable with the notion of directly allying British forces with the Israelis, who, after all, were the enemies of Britain's allies, Jordan and Iraq. If he was to proceed together with Mollet against Nasser, as he had now decided to do, he would have to contrive to make Britain (and, by extension, France) appear on the side of the angels.

Eden had not spent half his life in the diplomatic service without learning a few tricks. He had arrived in Paris for his meeting with Mollet and Pineau on October 16 armed with a plan that would, he thought, provide the British and the French with all the advantages of an attack on Egypt and few of the disadvantages: Israel, which had its own incentives, would attack across Sinai and move toward the Suez Canal; Britain and France, who had a major stake in preserving the Canal from the damage of war, would issue an ultimatum warning the belligerents to keep their distance from either side of the Canal. Then, on the assumption that Egypt and/or Israel would not accept the ultimatum, Britain and France would introduce their own troops. If it became necessary for French and British forces to engage Egyptian or Israeli troops, this would be a sacrifice London and Paris would make to preserve a vital international waterway. The Anglo-Egyptian Treaty of 1955 provided that British forces could return to the Canal Zone in time of war. By "war" both sides had in mind hostilities involving the USSR, but for London's present purpose an Egyptian-Israeli war was as good as any other. It could later be said that the British operation had some, albeit flimsy, basis in international law.

But the Israelis were not quite the innocents Eden may have assumed. Ben-Gurion was furious when he learned, through the French, of the British idea. In his view, it required Israel "to mount the rostrum of shame so that Britain and France could lave their hands in the waters of purity."[23] The British commitment not to come to the aid of Egypt in the event of an Israeli attack and not to assist Jordan if the Jordanians attacked Israel was hardly a sufficient sweetener. Compounding Israel's distrust of Eden's scenario was Britain's Middle East policy during the past several years under both Labour and Tory governments.

The bargain was struck and sealed in an atmosphere replete with the trappings of international intrigue. A wealthy and trusted friend of the French premier conveniently had business requiring his temporary absence from his villa in the out-of-the-way village of Sèvres near Paris. There, on October 22, modest, inconspicuous automobiles whisked a few high British, French, and Israeli officials. Everyone involved, participants and servants alike, was sworn to secrecy. What took place at that rendezvous was later to be referred to by the ugly word "collusion."

The first meeting at Sèvres was hardly an auspicious beginning for a common enterprise carrying considerable military and political risk. Selwyn Lloyd and his assistant seemed unwilling to taint themselves with any direct contact with the Israelis. They confined themselves to one room of the villa; Ben-Gurion, Pineau, and their aides were in another. The French shuttled back and forth between the two rooms.

Three matters had to be resolved. The first dealt with the objectives of the campaign. Here the French and the British were at odds with the Israelis. Ben-Gurion insisted that the war should end with a comprehensive political settlement that would cover Israel's military and political problems with all its Arab neighbors. In the end, however, he agreed that this was too ambitious a goal and settled for more modest territorial objectives, with a settlement to come some time later.

The second item on the agenda was the timing of the attack. On this matter, strangely enough, the British and the Israelis were allied against the French. They were both sensitive to Eisenhower's need to get through the next two weeks without a crisis and wanted to launch the attack after election day. But Pineau's insistence that early action was necessary carried the day.

Finally, there were the scenario outlining the Israeli attack, the London-Paris "ultimatum," and the subsequent British-French intervention. These questions found the Israelis quarreling with the British. Lloyd urged that the Israelis' military action "not be a small-scale encounter but a 'real act of war,' otherwise there would be no justification for the British ultimatum and Britain would appear in the eyes of the world as an aggressor."[24] For his part, Lloyd agreed that British and French bombers would attack Egyptian airfields immediately after the twelve-hour ultimatum had expired. Although Ben-Gurion was generally satisfied with the course of the discussion, he was outraged that the ultimatum as it was then worded would lead the world to view Britain and France as "cops" and the Israelis as the "robber."[25]

The final give and take occurred late in the evening when the British at last deigned to join the French and Israelis. According to Moshe Dayan, "Britain's foreign minister may well have been a friendly man, pleasant, charming, amiable. If so, he showed near-genius in concealing those virtues. His manner could not have been more antagonistic. His whole demeanor expressed distaste for the place, the company, the topic."[26]

The meeting on the twenty-second resolved most of the outstanding difficulties and misunderstandings. Lloyd, with relief, fled back to London. French and Israeli military representatives spent the following day discussing logistics, and Pineau went to London for consultations with Eden. On October 24 the three delegations reassembled at Sèvres to review the broad operational plans and to address, once again, the issue of the "ultimatum."

Selwyn Lloyd chose to avoid this final session. Instead, he instructed Patrick Dean to fly to Paris, where he would be told the site of the meeting. A civil servant rather than a politician, Dean could hardly have been delighted with this awkward assignment. He had been given only the sketchiest idea about what was to be discussed. He walked into the session at Sèvres, a hostage of decisions already made by Eden and an heir to Israeli animosity that had been stirred up by Lloyd. But at least he had with him a revised version of the ultimatum that satisfied Ben-Gurion; the new wording would place the onus for withdrawing from the Canal solely on the Egyptians.

The meeting on the twenty-fourth wrapped up the plan for action: The date for the Israeli attack was set for October 29, the ultimatum would be issued the following day, British and French forces would move twelve hours later. Before he left Paris that night General Dayan cabled his military headquarters to begin immediate preparations. On October 27 Ben-Gurion discussed the Sèvres accord with members of his cabinet. There was no turning back now.

In retrospect, I should have known that the curtain on the Suez melodrama was about to open. For a week or so there had been fewer meetings of the Middle East working group. When they were held I was excused after a few moments of embarrassed anodyne discussion. My embassy colleagues were also seeing less of their British counterparts during the latter part of October. There was nothing one could put his finger on, but there seemed to be a sudden noticeable cooling of relationships.

Two more hints fell in my lap, but I was too obtuse to piece a story together. The first occurred on the evening of October 24. A stag, black-tie dinner was arranged for a visiting CIA official at the home of Patrick Dean. The guests were greeted by Mrs. Dean—sans husband. "Pat has been called away suddenly," she said. She was a charming substitute for the absent host, but was unable to dispel the air of mystery that surrounded her husband's whereabouts. She wouldn't have told us, of course, even had she known, that Dean was then at Sèvres.

The second clue was more direct and appeared at the eleventh hour. I did what I could with it, but it wasn't enough. Washington ignored my message. And it had come too late, in any case.

Sunday, October 28, was cold and dreary. Rain clouds hung low. Par for the London course. The Cooper and Dean families had had a long-standing date for a drive into the country, a picnic, and a walk across the Downs. Just as we were leaving to pick up the Deans the phone rang. It was Pat; he had been called to an urgent meeting with the foreign minister. The session was set for noon; perhaps he'd be free later. He sounded distraught and I suspected that he'd be tied up for the remainder of the weekend. We decided to lunch at home.

Rain was not all that was threatening that Sunday. Within the past week, the Israeli-Jordan border had been set afire, King Hussein had allied Jordan with the Egyptian-Syrian defense pact, and the French had captured (or rather shanghaied) five of the leading Algerian nationalists. But it was Eastern Europe that was receiving the lion's share of press and official attention in Washington and in most capitals of Europe. Although Soviet troops were still in Hungary, there were reports that they would soon depart. The White House and the State Department were frenetically absorbed in following this situation and in adjusting old policies to the new regimes in Budapest and Warsaw.

I went to the embassy after the disturbing phone call from Dean. The overnight telegrams revealed little new. The Israelis were still mobilizing and Hungary was still smoldering, but the incoming cable traffic had no smell of an imminent explosion. Adding to the feeling that all was quiet, albeit momentarily and uneasily so, was a telegram from the ambassador to Washington: Aldrich had seen Lloyd on Saturday evening and had been assured that the British were committed to a peaceful solution of the Canal problem and the avoidance of force in the Middle East. I returned home and read the Sunday papers by the fire. Dean again called about two thirty; the meeting was over, he'd very much like to get out of London. Could we pick them up and drive up to Greenwich for tea? We could and did. It turned out to be a glum, silent afternoon. I had never seen my friend so morose, so preoccupied.

We returned to London about eight o'clock. I dropped off the Deans, took my family home, and drove, once again, to the embassy. I sent a message to Washington that is etched in my memory: "Spent family afternoon with Patrick Deans. Dean just had apparently difficult session with Lloyd. Very tense. Pressed him for reason—Hungary? Middle East? Dean replied: 'You and I are in for much trouble, and it won't be because of Hungary.' He volunteered nothing further. Will check this worrisome matter again in morning."

While in the cable room sending out my message I discovered that between my morning and evening trips to the embassy, Eisenhower had told the press of "disturbing reports from the Middle East [which] involved information that Israel was making a heavy mobilization of its armed forces" and had warned Ben-Gurion of "forcible action which would endanger the peace." But Jordan, rather than Egypt, seemed to be Eisenhower's primary concern. There was also a report that the State Department had advised all nonessential American civilians to leave the Middle East.

In Budapest that Sunday, the weather was sunny and warm. The crowds that had for several days been swarming the downtown streets were now swollen with thousands of additional demonstrators. According to *The Times* (London) "trustworthy reports reaching London leave no doubt that the people of Hungary, with the exception of some members of the secret police, were by the weekend united to a man in passionate resistance to the Soviet forces. . . . The uprising has not only spread through the country but has been astonishingly successful." The new nationalist Hungarian prime minister, Imre Nagy, promised that Soviet troops would be withdrawn from Budapest, and by Sunday afternoon Russian tanks and armored cars were moving to the outskirts of the city. Across the border in Austria a mass burial was given to a score of freedom fighters. Notably absent from any of the banners and signs carried by the mourners was the hammer and sickle. Budapest radio announced that Hungary would not compete in the Olympic Games.

While the situation was heating up in Hungary, things were cooling off in Poland. The hated Russian Marshal Rokossovsky was relieved as commander-in-chief of the Polish armed forces and had "taken leave" in the Soviet Union; Stefan Cardinal Wyszynski, for decades the Roman Catholic primate of Poland, was released from prison, where he had been incarcerated for three years; a Warsaw newspaper called for an "independent foreign policy based on Polish national interests."

Meanwhile, in New York, the UN Security Council met to consider the Hungarian question and to indict the Soviet Union for "violently repressing the rights of the Hungarian people." Nine members joined the condemnation, one (Yugoslavia) abstained. The Soviet delegate claimed, inter alia, that France and Britain were trying to divert world attention from their actions in Algeria and Cyprus and that the United States was fomenting the uprising in Hungary. "Tommyrot" was Dulles' prompt response.

Abba Eban, Israel's ambassador, assured the UN on Sunday night that "Israel will start no war"; recent mobilization steps, he said, were purely defensive.*

Elsewhere in the United States, the air was thick with domestic politics, football, and the usual weekend trivia: Eisenhower was pronounced in "excellent health" after a physical examination at Walter Reed Hospital, but he would forsake golf for the remaining days of the campaign; Democratic presidential candidate Adlai Stevenson outlined his plans for a "New America"; Vice-President Nixon was campaigning strongly in California, realizing that the loss of his home state to the Democrats could impair his chances for running for President in 1960; the New York Giants beat the Philadelphia Eagles and Oklahoma trounced Notre Dame. The Statue of Liberty celebrated its seventieth birthday, and Elvis Presley was given a polio vaccine shot.

In London that weekend, there was an unusual spate of official activ-

---

*Eban was telling the truth as he knew it; he had not been told of the imminent Israeli invasion or of the secret discussions with Britain and France.

ity, some public, some private. A spokesman at Downing Street expressed British "sympathy and admiration for the Hungarian people's struggle." Direct British intervention was ruled out, but a donation of $25,000 was given to the International Red Cross for Hungarian relief. The Foreign Office professed to know nothing about exploratory talks on Suez scheduled for Geneva on the following Monday. The prime minister's press secretary, William Clark, returned from a two-week vacation abroad and checked into his office at Downing Street shortly after noon. A meeting was in progress, but when he attempted to enter the conference room where Selwyn Lloyd, Patrick Dean, and other civilian and military officials were in session with the prime minister, he was refused entry by a policeman.[27] He submitted his resignation later that day.

Paris was in a state of excitement, not only because of the developments in Hungary, but because Ben Bella and the other Algerian rebel leaders kidnapped by the French had just been transferred from Algiers to a Paris jail. Newspaper editorials in France and elsewhere regarded the French move as a victory of the Middle East hard-liners against those who were ready to conciliate the nationalists. Meanwhile, the NATO council, headquartered outside of Paris, was meeting to consider possible NATO moves in response to the events in Hungary.

In the Middle East, Syrians set fire to a French school, Jordanians set fire to the French consulate in the Arab sector of Jerusalem, and Egyptian workers went on a twenty-four-hour general strike to protest the French seizure of the Algerian nationalist leaders. A news report from Cairo described the "new" Egyptian Army as being "strong" and having "high morale."

On that day, too, the innocent British chargé in Israel, acting on the instructions of his innocent superiors in the Foreign Office, warned the Israelis that an attack on Jordan would bring immediate British military reprisal. At that moment Ben-Gurion was warning his cabinet that large-scale military operations were imminent. But—as Eden and Lloyd well knew—Egypt, not Jordan, was the target. And in Tel Aviv, Jerusalem, and Haifa, a call went out for donations of blood.

Sunday, October 28, was a busy day for many people in many places. As for myself, I returned home from the embassy late that night, deeply puzzled, a little worried, very tired. I slept well—the last night that would happen for quite a while.

8

THE GRIM HARVEST

Monday, October 29, was the day when the foreign ministers of the United Kingdom, France, and Egypt were to have met with the secretary-general of the United Nations in Geneva to carry on the exploratory talks which had been adjourned in New York two weeks earlier. But Her Majesty's Foreign Office had apparently decided that such a meeting would serve no useful purpose.

Monday was also the day I had promised Washington to follow up the tantalizing hint of a brewing crisis in Anglo-American relations I had received the previous afternoon. I arrived early at the embassy and skimmed through the overnight harvest of telegrams. Washington had not reacted to my message of Sunday evening. Neither CIA's watch officer nor the State Department's Secretariat had apparently felt the telegram reporting my encounter with Dean was worth bringing to the attention of either Allen or John Foster Dulles. Walworth Barbour, the second-in-command at the embassy, urged me to pursue the matter. Meanwhile, he would make his own inquiries.

I called Dean, but he was "at a meeting." Indeed, it seemed that every official in Whitehall spent all day Monday at a meeting. So far as I can remember, no one in the embassy—diplomats, military attachés, or intelligence officers—had much luck that day in seeing any British official of consequence. In the end, I spent much of Monday making fruitless phone calls and catching up on the events in Eastern Europe and the Middle East.

The situation in Hungary had improved somewhat with the removal of most Soviet troops from Budapest. There was still shooting in the city, however, and Noel Barber, correspondent for the London *Daily Mail,* had been hit by trigger-happy Soviet soldiers. A general strike, now in its fifth day, was still in effect throughout much of the country. Elsewhere in Eastern Europe, crowds of Poles cheered the release of Stefan Cardinal Wyszynski and the Polish Communist Party formally announced its support of Hungarian demands for the removal of Soviet troops; Marshal Tito told the Hungarian people that their fight for freedom might destroy Socialism in Hungary and endanger world peace; and East Germany was reported to be in a "state of tension."

In the USSR, government leaders denied that Soviet forces in Hungary were being reinforced. The remaining troops would be withdrawn, they said, when the rebels had laid down their arms. Western observers in Moscow reported that the Kremlin was preparing the Soviet people for a major ideological retreat with respect to Eastern Europe.

In the United States, the Longshoremen's Union refused to handle Soviet cargo until Moscow pulled all its troops out of Hungary; American, French, and British representatives discussed the next step concerning the Soviet actions to be taken at the UN Security Council; the Soviet mission to the UN was picketed by hundreds of Hungary's sympathizers; and a group of Russians who had come to the United States to observe the elections were attending a Nixon rally in San Francisco where they heard the vice-president liken their government to the Nazi and Fascist dictatorships.

That Monday was a gloomy autumn day in Washington. But Secretary Dulles had little opportunity or inclination to gaze out his window at the gray Potomac or the muted fall foliage lining the Virginia bank. For soon after he arrived at his desk news came of an Israeli feint against Jordan followed shortly by a major attack on Egyptian positions in the Sinai. The first reports told of a paratroop landing at Mitla Pass, approximately thirty miles from the Suez Canal. Soon after, there was news of an Israeli attack on El Kuntilla, a fortified Egyptian border position and a key stronghold on the route across the desert to Suez.

Ambassador Abba Eban was at the State Department explaining to Assistant Secretary William Rountree that the Israeli mobilization was strictly a defensive measure when news came of the invasion of Sinai. Eban was taken as much by surprise as Rountree. "I'm certain, Mr. Ambassador," Rountree said sarcastically, "that you will wish to get back to your embassy to find out exactly what is happening in your country."[1]

President Eisenhower was on the campaign trail and learned of the Israeli attack as he was flying from Jacksonville, Florida, to Richmond, Virginia. He made a hasty speech in Richmond—racial equality should be undertaken on a local and state level rather than through federal intervention—and rushed back to Washington. His national security advisers were already at the White House when he arrived. The President was livid: "All right, Foster, you tell 'em [the Israelis] that, goddamn it, we're going to apply sanctions, we're going to the United Nations, we're going to do everything that there is so we can stop this thing."[2]

A suitably stern message was dispatched to Ben-Gurion urging him to return his troops to Israel. UN Ambassador Cabot Lodge was instructed to ask for an emergency Security Council meeting the next morning. Congress, then in recess, was put on notice to stand by for a special session.

Later that day Adlai Stevenson, campaigning in Boston, did nothing to reduce Eisenhower's ire: The President, he said, "had given Americans reassurances about the Middle East that had been tragically less than the truth." Meanwhile, American evacuees were in the process of leaving Jordan, Israel, Syria, and Egypt.

In London, the cabinet met in what the press reported to be a mood of "deep concern" about the possibility of war in the Middle East. In fact, the mood was not only one of "concern," but also of anger. Eden read the text of the British-French ultimatum which he planned to deliver to the Israeli and Egyptian ambassadors. He asked for cabinet approval. Although the ministers had been told of the British-French-Israeli plan immediately after the Sèvres meeting and had had an opportunity to discuss the ultimatum at that time, several of them resented Eden's attempt to railroad through what was, in effect, a declaration of war. But they had little choice; they could accept the prime minister's wording, however grudgingly, or they could resign. Eden later assured the House of Commons that the cabinet had discussed and approved the ultimatum. There were no new resignations, but Eden left behind a reservoir of bad feeling, which would do him no good in the tension-filled days ahead. Reflecting on this later, an American Anglophilic lawyer remarked that "Eden violated the basic tenets of the British cabinet system."[3]

In Paris, the news of the ultimatum was greeted by an outpouring of official and popular sympathy for Israel and enthusiasm for the opportunity, at long last, to get at Nasser. Mollet, incidentally, was even more cavalier with his ministers than Eden was with his; the French cabinet was not given an opportunity to discuss the ultimatum until after it had been made public.

The Security Council convened at 11 AM on Tuesday, October 30. At the request of the Israelis, the British, and the French, it adjourned after a few minutes and was rescheduled to meet several hours later. The reason for the request was soon to become apparent.

At the Council meeting the United States was determined to invoke the Tripartite Declaration of 1950, in which the United States, Great Britain, and France undertook to oppose aggression by either Israel or the Arab states. Washington instructed its ambassadors in London and Paris to inquire of Selwyn Lloyd and Christian Pineau how they planned to implement the Declaration. When the message was received in London, many of the ambassador's subordinates—and I suspect Aldrich himself—regarded such an inquiry as a fruitless exercise; after all, only two days before the Israeli attack Lloyd had told Aldrich that the British were pressing for a negotiated settlement. But Dulles' instructions could not be ignored, fool's errand or not. After he had seen Lloyd later that morning, the ambassador reported to Washington that the foreign minister had talked vaguely of British plans to label Israel as an aggressor at the Security Council. But London and Paris would want to consult beforehand, and Lloyd had been unable to get in touch with Pineau; would Aldrich return in the afternoon? In due course, Aldrich retraced his steps. Although only an hour or two remained before the Security Council was scheduled to meet, the ambassador felt there would still be time for the three parties to the Declaration to coordinate their positions.

Lloyd was in the House of Commons when Aldrich returned to the Foreign Office. The permanent under secretary greeted the ambassador with a copy of the British-French ultimatum. His timing could not have been worse. For, at that very moment, the text of the ultimatum was being carried over news tickers across the world.

Knowing what we now do of the discussions at Sèvres just a week before, it is clear why the Israelis finally agreed to accept the wording of the ultimatum. It ordered them to do just what they had intended to do, but gave the Egyptians twelve hours to abandon the Suez Canal to French and British occupation forces:

> The Governments of the United Kingdom and France have taken note of the outbreak of hostilities between Israel and Egypt. This event threatens to disrupt the freedom of navigation through the Suez Canal on which the economic life of many nations depends.
>
> The Governments of the United Kingdom and France are resolved to do all in their power to bring about the early cessation of hostilities and to safeguard the free passage of the Canal.
>
> They accordingly request the Government of Israel:
>
> (a) to stop all warlike action on land, sea and air forthwith;
>
> (b) to withdraw all Israeli military forces to a distance of ten miles east of the Canal.
>
> A communication has been addressed to the Government of Egypt, requesting them to cease hostilities and to withdraw their forces from the neighbourhood of the Canal, and to accept the temporary occupation by Anglo-French forces of key positions at Port Said, Ismailia and Suez.
>
> The United Kingdom and French Governments request an answer to this communication within twelve hours. If at the expiration of that time one or both Governments have not undertaken to comply with the above requirements, United Kingdom and French forces will intervene in whatever strength may be necessary to secure compliance.[4]

Hearing the terms of the ultimatum while at the Security Council meeting, the astonished Abba Eban mused that "since we were nowhere near the Canal, we would have to 'remove ourselves' forward in order to obey."[5]

While the ultimatum had been cleverly composed to fit French, British, and Israeli plans, it was too clever by half for much of the rest of the world. It fooled few and angered many—not the least, the President of the United States and his secretary of state. But for Anthony Eden and Guy Mollet, the ultimatum ended months of frustration, waiting, shilly-shallying. Time had been running out for both their governments; the on-again, off-again orders to their military high commands had been debilitating; the Americans were proving to be unsympathetic, even unreliable partners; and Nasser's domestic and international position was growing stronger every day. Now, at long last, Eden and Mollet could take matters in their own hands. And, they reasoned, if they moved quickly enough, neither friends nor enemies would notice or care how transparent was their guise as selfless international guarantors of free passage through the Canal.

Hardly had news reports of the ultimatum reached Washington when British Chargé John Coulson* and French Ambassador Hervé Alphand appeared in Dulles' office. They bore messages from their prime ministers to President Eisenhower explaining why the United States had not been consulted or even warned. The British note was weak and defensive: "My first instinct," Eden said, "would have been to ask you to associate yourself and your country with the declaration. But I know the constitutional and other difficulties in which you are placed . . . it would help . . . very much if you found it possible to support what we have done at least in general terms. We are well aware that no real settlement of Middle East problems is possible except through the closest cooperation of our two countries. . . ."[6]

As Mollet later described it to the Assembly, "When our American friends asked us why [Mollet or Pineau did not warn them of the ultimatum] I told them: You would have stopped us. I even added: We did not want you to be late; we did not want to go through the same periods of waiting that we went through from 1914 to 1917 and from 1939 to 1941."[7]

The White House issued a statement shortly after noon, Washington time. Although restrained, it barely hid Eisenhower's wrath: "As soon as

---

*Roger Makins, the British ambassador, had left Washington early in October. His replacement, Harold Caccia, did not arrive until November 8. The timing of this changing of the guard was obviously not accidental.

the President received his first knowledge, obtained through press reports of the ultimatum . . . he sent an urgent personal message to the Prime Minister of Great Britain and the Prime Minister of the Republic of France. The President expressed his earnest hope that the United Nations Organization would be given full opportunity to settle the items in the controversy by peaceful means instead of by forceful ones. . . ."

Eisenhower's message to Eden addressed him not only as "head of Her Majesty's Government," but as "my long-time friend." He then asked Eden to explain "exactly what is happening between us and our European allies—especially between us, the French and yourselves. We have learned that the French had provided Israel with a considerable amount of equipment . . . in excess of the amounts of which we were officially informed [and] in violation of agreements now existing between our three countries. . . . Last evening our Ambassador to the United Nations met with your Ambassador. . . . We were astonished to find that his government [i.e., Great Britain] would not agree to any action whatsoever to be taken against Israel. He further argued that the tripartite statement of May, 1950, was ancient history and without current validity.

"Egypt has not yet formally asked this government for aid. But . . . if the United Nations finds Israel to be an aggressor, Egypt could very well ask the Soviets for help . . . and then the Mid East fat would really be in the fire . . . we may shortly find ourselves with a de facto situation that would make all our present troubles look puny indeed. . . ."[8]

There were stories floating around the embassy in London that, in addition to the message referred to in the White House press announcement, Ike had telephoned Eden and had given him unshirted hell. Eden denied this,[9] and Eisenhower does not mention it in his memoirs. Eden's memory may have been selective on this score, however, and Eisenhower's account may have been discreet. Ike, it appears, did call Downing Street, but mistook one of the prime minister's aides, who answered the call, for Eden himself. By the time Eden got to the phone, Ike had finished his tirade and hung up.[10]

But whether Ike conveyed his displeasure with his "long-time" friend orally or in writing, there must now have been little doubt in the mind of the prime minister that he had underestimated the effect of the ultimatum on Anglo-American relations and on his own position at home.

It was six o'clock, Cairo time, when the news ticker in the British embassy tapped out the text of the Eden-Mollet ultimatum. This was the first Ambassador Trevelyan had heard of his government's virtual declaration of war on Egypt. He met with President Nasser and Foreign Minister Fawzi a few hours later. Trevelyan tried to defuse the bombshell, referring to the message from London and Paris as a "communication."

But Nasser was no fool: "We take it as an ultimatum." When the ambassador gamely tried to reassure the Egyptians that Britain and France were simply trying "to stop the fighting and protect the Canal," Nasser replied angrily that "we can defend the Canal and tomorrow we shall be defending it from more than the Israelis." The confused and discomfited ambassador took his leave. Looking down from a balcony, one of Nasser's aides watched Trevelyan walk out of the president's residence. The aide was "half grinning, half frightened, like a gargoyle on the keystone of a Medieval arch." The embassy staff spent the night burning official papers.[11]

The Egyptians, as expected, formally rejected the ultimatum. In a letter to the president of the Security Council later that day, Nasser stressed "the imminent danger of, within a few hours from now, British and French armed forces . . . occupying Egyptian territory." He requested an immediate meeting of the Council. "In the meantime and until the Security Council has taken the necessary measures, Egypt has no choice but to defend itself and safeguard its rights against such aggression."[12]

In Eastern Europe the situation remained tense and unpredictable. Although events in Poland and Hungary were crowded out of the headlines by the crisis in the Middle East, observers across the world sensed that the new regimes in Warsaw and Budapest were playing a dangerous game with Moscow. Premier Gomulka was demanding payment of huge, uncollected Soviet war reparations and a renegotiation of outstanding Polish-Soviet economic agreements. Premier Nagy had defied the Kremlin by promising free elections and the end of one-party rule. Moscow, for its part, was obviously delighted that public attention had shifted to the Middle East and hoped to keep it that way. It enthusiastically endorsed an immediate meeting of the Security Council to deal with Israel's attack on Egypt and the French-British ultimatum.

When the Council met, the United States introduced a resolution that condemned Israel—and by implication, Britain and France—and directed Israel to withdraw its forces from Egypt. The impact of the American position at the UN was reinforced by reports that Washington was considering halting all economic aid to Israel. This was a risky step for the Administration to take on the eve of a presidential election, but Eisenhower and Dulles were angry men on Tuesday, October 30.

The American resolution was intended to leapfrog the ultimatum and seize the initiative away from London and Paris. It was promptly endorsed by the Soviet Union and vetoed by Britain and France—the first time that either nation had exercised its veto since the UN's establishment more than a decade before. The Russians then introduced a modified resolution which softened the anti-British, anti-French tone, but retained the provisions directed at Israel. This, too, was vetoed.

The outcome of the debate found Washington supported by Moscow and at odds with its two old friends and partners in NATO. Washington had allied itself with the USSR against America's allies just a few hours after it had led the UN attack on Moscow's aggression in Eastern Europe. This was an awkward and uncongenial moment for Eisenhower, but he had the support of most Americans and much of the world. And he was convinced that, however ironic the immediate circumstances, he was in an unassailable moral position. He was reacting to his deeply felt abhorrence of war. It was no accident that, despite Washington's bellicose rhetoric directed toward Moscow and Peking, despite the Administration's trumpeting for the "liberation" of Eastern Europe, despite Dulles' "brinkmanship," the United States had carefully avoided major military ventures during the previous four years.

That autumn the White House was especially determined to avoid war, except in the face of a direct threat to American national security interests. But now the Administration was suddenly confronted with the possibility that America would be dragged into hostilities by Britain and France. To make matters worse, Eisenhower and Dulles were convinced that America's old allies had launched a desperate attempt to preserve what remained of their pre–World War II colonial positions in the Middle East.

In Paris, Premier Guy Mollet felt relieved of a heavy burden. During three months of unproductive diplomacy the situation in Algeria had worsened and Nasser had taken over the Canal. Mollet had had a surfeit of words. Now France would be embarking on a course that French public opinion had long been demanding. On Tuesday the National Assembly had given him an enthusiastic vote of approval and, on the strength of this, Mollet and his government could ignore criticism from the outside. A warning from someone in the American Embassy that France and Britain had only twenty-four hours to call off their threatened attack on Egypt or face U.S. intervention was shrugged off; the Administration in Washington, the French were sure, would not take such a move before the Presidential election.[13]

Anthony Eden, for his part, had the worst of both worlds. He faced deep divisions at home—the Labour Party leadership, which had been left in the dark about all that had been going on, had given him a stony reception in Commons. Even more worrisome was the angry public and official reaction in the United States and the British Commonwealth. But he knew there was no pulling back from the course he had set.

Mollet and Eden were still in the preoperational stage of their joint enterprise on Tuesday, October 30. But Ben-Gurion, ill with influenza, had been at war for twenty-four hours. On Sunday he briefed his cabinet on the forthcoming Sinai campaign and then called in members of the opposition parties. Finally, he explained to the Israeli public the reason for the large-scale mobilization. His announcement was carefully designed to prepare his countrymen for dark days ahead. There was danger, he said, from his sick bed, of surprise Arab attacks "from the south, the north and the east." He concluded with the Old Testament warning, "Behold, he that keepeth Israel shall neither slumber nor sleep."[14] Ben-Gurion, despite his illness, then took charge of the campaign.

On Monday evening the Israeli government announced that "Israel this evening resorted to security measures to eliminate Egyptian commando bases in the Sinai Peninsula."[15] By Tuesday morning Israeli troops had taken the eastern end of the Mitla Pass (less than thirty miles from the town of Suez) and three key Egyptian posts along the border of Israel. On that morning, however, Cairo Radio assured its listeners that the Israelis had been repulsed. "The enemy plan to advance with major forces inside Egyptian territory has failed."[16]

The British-French ultimatum expired on Wednesday, October 31, at 6 AM Cairo time (4 AM London time, and 11 PM, on October 30, Washington time). The gravity of the moment was underscored by reports from Malta that British marine commandos in full battle kit were boarding LSTs and that British and French air transports were landing on Cyprus. There were reports, too, that the largest naval concentration since World War II was assembling in the eastern Mediterranean. Included in the fleet were a French battleship and five British and French aircraft carriers.

Heightening the mood of impending war was the announcement from Washington that the American Sixth Fleet based in the Mediterranean was being reinforced by a submarine "hunter-killer group" (an aircraft carrier, two submarines, eight destroyers, and a tanker) which had been cruising off the Dutch coast. There was a rumor that the Sixth Fleet had orders to intercept British and French warships sailing toward Egypt. At the Pentagon in Washington maps of the Middle East were in such demand that they had to be rationed. Stocks fell and commodities rose on international markets during that Wednesday—a typical threat-of-war performance.

Traffic through the Suez Canal was still moving normally on Wednesday despite the expiration of the ultimatum; a thirty-six-ship convoy, the largest ever to make the northbound trip, arrived at Port Said on schedule. This, despite an unidentified (and grossly premature) radio report that British and French troops were already landing in Egypt.

The Sèvres script called for British bombers to attack Egyptian air-fields soon after Cairo rejected the ultimatum. On the basis of this, the Israelis took a calculated risk by employing their own planes to provide an air umbrella for their thinly stretched infantry. Although the risk to Israeli cities was hedged by the presence of two French air squadrons which had flown to Israel just before the invasion of Sinai, Jerusalem, Tel Aviv, and Haifa remained vulnerable to Egypt's two score attack-bomb-ers, which had been provided by the USSR.*

The first Royal Air Force strikes against Nasser's air force were to start on the morning of October 31, but the appointed hour came and went without an attack. Ben-Gurion and Dayan had some anxious mo-ments and deep suspicions about their new ally. They did not know that the first RAF sorties had been turned back in mid-flight when the British learned that U.S. planes were then on Cairo's airfields loading American evacuees. But at dusk the British and French started their bombing and continued it around the clock for several days.

The assault on Egyptian airfields may have been a welcome relief to the Israelis, but it shocked much of the rest of the world. There had been no indication in the ultimatum that the British and French contemplated air attacks; the prospect of Anglo-French military intervention along the Canal was worrisome enough. And while London, Paris, and Tel Aviv knew that the bombing was to be confined to airfields and military targets, no one else—in Cairo, in Washington, in Moscow, at the UN in New York —could count on this.

Dulles had been feeling ill all that week. The news of the air attacks utterly unnerved him. To someone who saw him late that day, he ap-peared "almost totally exhausted, ashen-gray, heavy-lidded, shaking his head in glazed disbelief."[18] Eisenhower, too, was taken aback by the new development. "Bombs, by God!" he exploded. "What does Anthony think he's doing? Why is he doing this to me?"[19]

Nasser was, of course, even more shaken. Despite his apparent self-possession during the meeting with Ambassador Trevelyan on the eve-ning before, the news of Britain's alliance with Israel had taken him completely by surprise. It was a contingency he had earlier considered, but discarded in the light of Britain's ties with Jordan and Iraq.

Then came bombing. At least as disturbing to Nasser as the unex-pected air attacks was the Soviet Union's reaction to this turn of events. After approximately fifty Egyptian planes had been destroyed on the

*According to one source close to Ben-Gurion, the United States Air Force "obligingly organized an air lift from Florida to France" to supply the French planes with extra fuel tanks so they could be flown directly to Israel without refueling. Apparently this was done without Eisenhower's knowledge.[17]

ground, Moscow ordered the Ilyushin bombers it had supplied to be removed to safety. The bombers were flown to remote fields in upper Egypt and to sanctuaries in Saudi Arabia and Libya. Nasser was now left without an offensive air arm.

Assuming that the bombing was a prelude to major ground attacks on Alexandria and Cairo, Nasser vowed, in terms reminiscent of Churchill's stirring speech fifteen years before, that Egypt would never surrender, but would wage guerrilla war on the invaders. "We shall fight bitterly, O compatriots. We shall not surrender. . . . Each one of you is a soldier in the National Liberation Army. Orders have been given for the issue of arms—and we have many arms. We shall fight from village to village and from place to place. Let each one of you be a soldier in the Armed Forces so that we may defend our honor, dignity, and freedom. Let our motto be: 'We shall fight, not surrender. We shall fight, we shall fight, we shall not surrender.' "[20]

On that Wednesday the Israelis, according to plan, had accepted the ultimatum and consolidated their positions east of the Canal. After halting their advance toward Suez, they concentrated on seizing the area bordering the Gulf of Aqaba, which had always been their principal objective. If they could break the Egyptian blockade of the port of Eilat, Israel would, at long last, have access to the Red Sea and Indian Ocean.

While the bombing of Egyptian airfields continued, the French and British commands put the finishing touches on plans for their ground force attacks. This turned out to be more difficult than one might have assumed, considering that their military planning had been going on since August.

A major shift in both objectives and strategy had been forced on the Cyprus headquarters by London only shortly before the Israeli invasion of Sinai. All through the late summer and early autumn plans had gone forward on the assumption that forces would land at Alexandria and then fan out toward the Canal and Cairo itself. But reactions both in Britain and abroad to the prospect of a military attack on Egypt and his own state of physical and nervous exhaustion caused Eden to blow hot and cold as D day loomed ahead. He became especially concerned, indeed obsessed, about the possibility of heavy casualties—among either Allied troops or Egyptian soldiers and civilians. As a consequence, Eden had second—and more cautious—thoughts. He ordered that the paradrops and beachheads be confined to strategic points along the Canal.

This reversal would turn out to be only the first in a series of last-minute modifications that would have to be made in response to orders from Eden; schedules, targets, and deployments were constantly changed to accommodate the shifting political developments in New York, Washington, Paris, and—especially—in London. In the officers' mess of the Royal Scots, one of the regiments in the expeditionary force, a favorite quip was "of the twelve different invasion plans prepared, Eden chose the thirteenth."

By Wednesday morning, October 31, diplomatic relations were virtually broken between Washington and London. Ambassador Aldrich was called home and embassy officers were told to keep their distance from Whitehall. A weary Minister Walworth Barbour summoned me to his office and gave me my own marching orders: Because the intelligence link to the British was too important to jeopardize, I was to continue to maintain contact with British intelligence officials. Moreover, I would be the channel to Her Majesty's Government for whatever other business could not wait until the skies cleared. On the way to the Foreign Office to tell Dean of Barbour's instructions, I asked my cab driver what he thought of the developments in the Middle East. "Well, guv'nor," he said, "I'm with the PM all the way. No bloke can fight a cold war in a hot climate."

Overnight reports from the Middle East indicated that the war as well as the climate was "hot": The joint British-French military headquarters at Nicosia was now directing what British military spokesmen referred to as "The War."

In the Gulf of Suez an Egyptian frigate was sunk by a British cruiser in the first naval engagement of The War. Cairo Radio announced—either in error or with malice aforethought—that British aircraft had bombed the cities of Cairo, Alexandria, and Ismailia; Selwyn Lloyd later explained to an anxious House of Commons that RAF missions were confined solely to military targets. And among such targets would be Cairo Radio.

On the Sinai front, Israeli troops had begun to attack the heavily defended Egyptian positions at Rafah on the southern end of the Gaza Strip and had broken through toward El Arish on the coast of the Mediterranean. An Egyptian frigate was damaged by Israeli jets and towed into Haifa harbor with the Star of David flying triumphantly at its masthead.

That Wednesday was a busy day for Anthony Eden. He was not only personally involved in planning the attack on Egypt, but he was also trying to patch up deep fissures on his home front. This was a war that seemed unlikely to close political and class ranks; my cab driver spoke for some, but by no means all of his countrymen. To be sure, no love for Nasser exuded through the streets of London. Children had added a twist of their own to the song from Disney's *Snow White:* "Whistle while you work; Nasser is a twerp." And Nasser's effigy was substituted for Guy

Fawkes' on many a bonfire that All Saints' Eve. But in my travels around the city, I sensed some validity to the statement made that day by Hugh Gaitskell. "The majority of Britons," he said, "were shocked by Eden's aggressive policy."

In his speech to the House of Commons that evening, Eden attempted to explain why he had withheld information about British plans from Washington. The problem of the Suez Canal, he told the House, was one of "survival" to Britain and France, but only of secondary concern to America. "Indeed, Mr. Dulles, himself, made this clear on 28th August, when he said the United States' economy is not dependent upon the Canal. . . . Throughout all these months this fact had inevitably influenced the attitude of the United States . . . as compared to ourselves and France. I do not think," he went on defensively, "that we must in all circumstances secure agreement from our American ally before we can act ourselves in what we know to be our vital interests. . . . We have expressed our preoccupations and our reasons [to the United States] dating right back to the Suez Canal seizure, why the matter seemed to us of such overwhelming importance. We have done this at all stages. . . . I do not think that . . . I have anything to repent, because it is sometimes a Government's duty to take decisions for its own country." He then described the three goals that he felt warranted the government's course: Preventing Nasser from achieving the mastery of the Arab world "through a series of palace revolutions"; an "enduring solution" of the differences between Israel and the Arabs; a "just solution" of the Suez dispute.[21]

Eden's speech to the Members of Parliament was interrupted by shouts of support from his party, especially from among those backbenchers, the "Suez Group," who had long been clamoring for robust British action against Nasser. But after he had finished he experienced what was described in the press as a "hammering" from furious Labour Party speakers. Caught in between were many Conservative MPs who were appalled at the deterioration in relations between London and Washington and some Labour MPs who were distressed at their party's refusal to back Israel.

When, in answer to Opposition demands, the prime minister was unable to tell the House whether or not the nation was actually "at war," the Opposition became so enraged that the noise of their shouts drowned out the wretched Eden's further remarks. The mood in the House became so angry, anguished, almost hysterical that the speaker suspended the session—for the first time in thirty years.

Aggravating Eden's concern about the political reaction in Britain was the barrage of criticism from abroad that cascaded on London, Paris, and Tel Aviv that Wednesday. India, Greece, Italy, Norway, and Sweden added their denunciations to those of the Arab and Communist countries; Canada and West Germany announced a suspension of their aid to Israel.

Events taking place in Washington were particularly troublesome for the prime minister. Although President Eisenhower had taken pains in a nationwide broadcast to point out that American disapproval of British, French, and Israeli actions in the Middle East did not imply any change in American "friendship" with those nations, he reiterated that the United States "was not consulted in any way" about the current developments, "nor were we informed of them in advance." The *New York Times* solemnly reported from Washington that "serious and well-informed" officials felt that the United States had "lost control of events in areas vital to her security." A Washington *Post* editorial called the Israeli invasion and the British-French ultimatum a "collusive" action. "What has happened to the Atlantic alliance?" the *Post* asked. "Can there again be a full measure of confidence between Washington and London and Paris?"

The political decibels in America were further heightened by candidate Stevenson's charge that the Republicans' foreign policy in general, and Middle East policy in particular, had "plunged the world to the brink of war," and by ex-President Truman's that the United States "had been misled by the Eisenhower Administration." All this carried ominous portents for the Eisenhower-Eden relationship, especially with the election less than a week away. Eden had dipped deeply into his political capital with the Administration.

Meanwhile, it had become apparent that any further consideration of the Middle East crisis by the UN Security Council would be subjected to French and British vetoes. Eisenhower hinted at the next step in a speech on Wednesday evening: Despite the French and British vetoes, "the processes of the United Nations . . . are not exhausted. It is our hope and intent that the matter will be brought before the United Nations' General Assembly. . . . There can be no peace without law. And there can be no law if we were to invoke one code of international conduct for those who oppose us and another for our friends."

Coached by the Indians (who were then not members of the Council), the Yugoslavs (who were) requested that the matter be moved from the Security Council to an Emergency Special Session of the General Assembly under a procedure adopted several years before during the Korean War. The "Uniting for Peace" resolution received the necessary seven votes in the Council; the United States and the Soviet Union joined forces once again to vote "Aye."

On Thursday, November 1, my two daughters simultaneously developed "bad headaches" as they were donning the shirts, blazers, and boaters that comprised the uniform of young female scholars at the Saint Nicholas Montessori School. Could they stay home that day? And perhaps tomorrow, as well? Close questioning revealed their ailment to be anticipatory rather than actual. On the previous day their schoolmates had berated Joan and Susan for being "beastly" to England. We had a serious chat about the complexities of foreign policy, the need to show the flag, and the importance of getting an education. But the clincher was Susan's remembering that Thursday was "singing-sewing-and-sliced-meat day." They went down the road, resigned if not joyous, to cope with their personal and disagreeable share of the Suez crisis.

I had my own trials that day. In addition to my usual pro forma appearance at the daily Joint Intelligence Committee meeting, I had been given an unpleasant errand. For reasons hard to fathom, someone in the Department of State suddenly became concerned about London's policy on Cyprus, particularly about the incarceration of Archbishop Makarios. I was instructed in my new capacity as chargé-at-large to make a "stern case" for the immediate release of the archbishop—an unwelcome task for the appropriate embassy officer even in the best of times. But I was a pinch hitter—and it was the worst of times.

I called on Dean and explained my errand. He turned me over to a youngish desk officer who, it seemed, had been looking for an opportunity to unburden himself to an American. Eden's move against Egypt was not only idiotic, but disastrous, he blurted. "God only knows where it will end!" I heard him out and then put my question. "Makarios? Christ, tell Washington we'll bring the chap back to Cyprus soon enough. We have to—we're running out of small boys." I passed on the first part of his remarks. As for the second, I felt that relations between London and Washington were strained enough without adding an extra fillip, however juicy it might be.

We had been invited to dinner that evening at the home of a Foreign Office friend. Although the invitation dated from more tranquil days, we were determined to go in the same spirit we had urged upon our children earlier in the day. It turned out that we were the only Americans present among a dozen or so guests. The Dutch wife of a British official greeted us with an awkward welcome: "How nice to see someone other than dreadful Englishmen!" We quickly disassociated ourselves from her person and her views, and the evening turned out to be less of an ordeal than we had anticipated. It became evident that deep passion and divided opinions surrounded the Suez venture even among Britain's civil servants. In the heated arguments between colleagues, and even between husbands and wives, our alien presence was all but ignored.

The shrill voices in support of or in opposition to Eden and his Suez policy at that dinner party were symptomatic of the general mood in England by midweek. "Never since the Boer war," an Oxford professor mused over lunch on Thursday, "have the British people been so divided." Friendships were broken, marriages strained, political alliances rent. There were pervasive undertones of wrath in the civil service, harsh words in St. James Street clubs, heated hyperbole in staid newspapers. By Thursday, Britain was virtually being torn apart by ugly demonstrations of students, shrill calls from the Opposition for the government to resign, and sharp queries from church leaders about the morality of Eden and his advisers.

Meanwhile, the bombing continued. Twenty Canberras dropped their bombs on Cairo Radio's installations—but missed. According to the press, warships were closing in on the Egyptian coast, although there was no hint from any official source that British and French forces were about to land. That day, American planes were sighted over the convoys and that night, American warships, lights blazing, passed through the French fleet.[22]

On the eastern front, Israeli troops broke out of an Egyptian trap in the Mitla Pass with heavy casualties and expanded their positions. El Arish, the principal depot for Egypt's Sinai army, was captured, as were key positions along the Gaza Strip. By nightfall, the Israelis controlled the northern Sinai. But, as Ben-Gurion and Moshe Dayan well knew, time was of the essence: "At the head of the campaign against the Suez-Sinai operations stands the Government of the United States . . . and of course . . . the Soviet Union. Those two 'soloists' are accompanied by an assorted choir of 'peace-at-any-price' enthusiasts. . . . There is no doubt that time is working against us and the pressure on Britain and France . . . and certainly on us . . . to halt our military action will become more and more acute. Who knows how many more campaigning days are left to us?"[23] Elsewhere in the Middle East, several developments threatened to widen the area of conflict: Nasser was urging the Syrians to blow up foreign-owned oil pipelines; Iraq ordered full mobilization; Jordan and Syria announced their readiness to go to Egypt's aid if Cairo asked for their help.

Thursday, November 1, was a black day in Eastern Europe. Taking advantage of the diversion offered by the crisis in the Mediterranean, Moscow decided to bring a quick end to the revolt in Hungary. Two Soviet tank divisions moved across the border to advance on Budapest while other armored units sealed the city off from the rest of the country. Premier Nagy appealed to the UN, announced Hungary's withdrawal from the Warsaw Pact (the USSR–Eastern Europe counter to NATO), declared his country's neutrality, and demanded the withdrawal of Soviet reinforcements. But the tragic situation in Hungary was virtually ignored as the Middle East crisis gained momentum.

The military action in Egypt and the desperate plight of the Hungarian freedom fighters were overshadowed on Thursday by Secretary Dulles' call in the United Nations General Assembly for an "immediate cease-fire" in Egypt and "a halt to the movement of military forces and arms into the area." Earlier that day, Nasser asked American Ambassador Raymond Hare to forward a request to Washington for help. Eisenhower replied that he would do all he could through the United Nations.[24] The cease-fire resolution was obviously what the President had in mind. It was passed after midnight by a resounding vote—65 for, 5 against (France, Britain, Israel, Australia, and New Zealand), 6 abstentions.

On the American domestic political front, Eisenhower and Stevenson continued to exchange charges and countercharges. The President asked the nation to judge whether it would feel secure in the present world crisis under Stevenson's "design for disaster" (i.e., the banning of further H-bomb tests). Stevenson, in turn, called the Middle East crisis a product of the "abysmal, complete, and catastrophic" failure of the Administration's foreign policy. The *New York Times,* examining the campaign from a somewhat more detached perspective, reported a consensus among its political correspondents that the anti-Soviet revolts in Eastern Europe and the Suez Crisis had strengthened Eisenhower's bid for re-election. Its editorial that day endorsed the Administration's posture of "peace with justice" in the Middle East.

Lost in the noise level on that busy Thursday was a report from Avery Brundage that assured the world that even though Britain, France, and Egypt were at war, they could all participate in the 1956 Olympic Games.

On Friday, November 2, I realized no one I had talked to during the course of the week had provided even an inkling of what he thought might happen in Egypt once the British and French troops had landed. Suppose the Suez operation succeeded: *What then?*

After the perfunctory few minutes that I had recently learned to expect in my daily exposure to Britain's senior intelligence officials, I dropped in on the members of the intelligence staff. In their crowded and less austere quarters, the atmosphere was relatively more relaxed. "Who's going to run Egypt if you chase Nasser out?" I asked. There was a collective shrug. They then confirmed what I had already suspected: Since virtually no one except the cabinet, the chiefs of staff, and a few senior civil servants had prior knowledge of the British and French venture, little advance political planning had been done. The staff assumed that there would be a military occupation and that General Naguib might be willing to take over from Nasser. We agreed that this would be undesirable for more than a brief period. Why not get through to Foreign Minister Fawzi? Lloyd and Pineau seemed to have gotten along with him in New York hardly two weeks before. Perhaps he might be persuaded to head an interim Egyptian government. "Jolly good idea." The staff would prepare a "minute" as soon as they could get to it. And that, I reflected on my way back to the embassy, was just about the way the Suez enterprise had been carried out.

As for the war itself, the Israelis had now taken heavily defended Rafah and were in the process of mopping up Egyptian troops in the Gaza Strip. The battle for Sinai was virtually over; thousands of Egyptian troops had been either killed or captured, or were wandering aimlessly and hopelessly in the desert. The British and French claimed they had neutralized Cairo's air force; more than one hundred Egyptian planes had been destroyed or damaged, including scores of the most modern Soviet-built fighters and bombers. But the Egyptians had their own triumphs. They had scuttled seven ships in the Canal, blocking passage in both directions. And their Syrian friends had blown up three pumping stations of the pipeline that carried Iraqi oil through Syria to the Mediterranean ports.

Round-the-clock bombing of Egyptian military targets, reports of warships and landing craft moving toward the Egyptian coast, and ominous-sounding war communiqués emanating from the Cyprus headquarters indicated that an assault was likely at any hour. But the hours went by and there was no sign of a landing force. A representative of the French military attaché's office had come to see Moshe Dayan Thursday night. The French command on Cyprus, he told Dayan, was frustrated by the inability or unwillingness of the British to move. Unless the British advanced the scheduled invasion date—then set for November 6—by forty-eight hours, the French might proceed on their own.[25] The French officer's visit reflected the impatience evident in Paris itself. On Thursday morning, the French headquarters in Cyprus received a telegram from General Ely, the French commander-in-chief: "The Egyptian army appears to be routed in Sinai. . . . The situation should be exploited as soon as possible. . . . The political situation necessitates the landing of some allied forces in less than twenty-four hours."[26]

To a cynical observer, the scurry of military activity seemed primarily verbal. I was reminded of the scene from *The Pirates of Penzance* in which the policemen are on the wharf and presumably about to embark to do battle with the pirates. "Go, ye heroes, go to glory," sing their ladies.

"Away, away!" orders their chief. "Yes, yes, we go," the policemen respond, still standing fast. "Then do not stay." "We go, we go." "Then why all this delay?" "All right—we go, we go, yes forward on the foe." "Yes, but you *don't* go!" "We go, we go, we go—Tarantara-ra-ra!" As of that Friday, the "policemen" were still on the wharves and airfields of Cyprus, and I among others was not at all sure that they would, in fact, ever really "go."

After the passage of the American-sponsored cease-fire resolution, attention at the United Nations shifted, once again, to Hungary, where reinforced Soviet tank units were now battling ragtag liberation groups on the streets of Budapest. Premier Nagy had appealed to the UN secretary-general late Thursday to guarantee Hungary's neutrality and to bring the issue before the General Assembly, where the Soviet Union could not use its veto. The Security Council met in emergency session and, over Soviet objections, the Western Powers called on the UN to take measures against Moscow's aggression. No decision was reached, however, and another meeting was scheduled for Saturday afternoon. Further heightening the tension in Budapest, Soviet troops had prevented a convoy of American diplomatic personnel and their dependents from leaving the city.

Elsewhere in Eastern Europe, there were reports of large-scale Soviet troop movements across Poland into East Germany. In Rumania and Bulgaria, the Communist regimes had ordered tight security precautions against "counterrevolutionaries" and expressed their support for Moscow's actions in Hungary.

The deteriorating situation in Eastern Europe gave London and Paris little respite from the worldwide clamor for a Middle East cease-fire. Eden rejected a Labour Party demand for an immediate stand-down of attacks on Egypt. Pineau made a hurried trip to London that Friday to press for moving up D day and to consult about a French and British response to the UN. Although there was no official announcement following the meeting, it was "reliably reported" that the two governments would not comply with the UN's demand for a cease-fire until after British and French troops had gone ashore. Landings were expected on Saturday.

Israel, too, was racing against the clock. While its troops had taken control of eastern and central Sinai, they were still fighting their way to Sharm el-Sheikh, the Egyptian base that sat astride the narrow strait controlling the entrance to the Gulf of Aqaba and the shipping lane to the port of Eilat. An Israeli spokesman warned that Israel would not pull back from Egypt until there were guarantees that terrorist attacks from Arab countries would end and Israeli ships had free passage through both the Canal and the gulf.

In Washington, the President was reported to be so confident of victory in the following Tuesday's election that on Friday he decided to stop campaigning. This was just as well, since there would be much over the next few days to keep him fully occupied at his desk in the Oval Office.

Each day of that interminable week seemed to be more tense than its yesterday. I awoke every morning to a feeling that this would surely be the Moment of Truth: The British and French forces would land at Suez and the battle would be joined; and/or there would be a cease-fire; and/or Eden would resign; and/or the Russians would either leave or subjugate Hungary. But the days passed and the tension mounted, and the relations between the United States and its old friends continued to deteriorate, and tempers continued to rise in Britain, and Eden hung on, and the Russians tightened their vise on the Hungarians. It was hard to distinguish between the bad dreams of restless nights and the nightmares of frenetic days.

The five-hour time difference between London and Washington did little to improve the quantity or quality of sleep for folk at the American Embassy. At about seven o'clock in the evening in Washington weary officials had begun to order their thoughts. This meant that telegrams of instruction or information would arrive at the embassy's code room at about 2 AM London time. Most of these messages could obviously wait until the beginning of business, but in the predawn hours of every day there always seemed to be a few that the duty clerk felt (frequently, I was sure, with sadistic satisfaction) needed an immediate reply. And so the phone would ring: "Mr. Cooper, something just came in that looks pretty urgent." "What's it say, what's it about?" I would ask, already knowing the response. "Gee, sir, I don't think I ought to say over the phone." "Can it wait until I arrive later?" And then the inevitable, "That's up to you." There was no going back to sleep and so I would yawn, dress, exchange waves with the now familiar prostitutes shivering on the corner a few feet from my house, and drive to Grosvenor Square.

Sometime before dawn on Saturday, November 3, the telephone rang. It was the code room, of course, but this time the message was different: "Come down to the embassy right away. Washington wants to talk to you on the secure phone." A half hour later I had a long conversation with Robert Amory, CIA's deputy director. He was in a fit of exasperation. "Tell your friends," he shouted so loudly that I could have heard him across the Atlantic without a telephone, "to comply with the goddamn cease-fire or go ahead with the goddamn invasion. Either way, we'll back 'em up if they do it fast. What we can't stand is their goddamn hesitation waltz while Hungary is burning!"

"Back up" the British if they invaded? This was a new twist and I was anxious to discuss it with Minister Barbour. But when I returned to the embassy at about nine o'clock, another piece of news preempted the titillating information I had gleaned several hours before. Secretary Dulles had been taken to the hospital during the night. There were no details except that he was in great pain and needed surgery. The operation later in the day revealed abdominal cancer. And so, at the most critical moment of crisis in both Hungary and the Middle East, John Foster Dulles was taken out of action. Responsibility now rested with a well-meaning, but basically uninterested President and with an unimaginative, relatively inexperienced, reportedly anti-British acting secretary, Herbert Hoover, Jr. It would be two months before Dulles returned to the Department.

Later in the morning I squeezed what I could from Amory's thin hint that, despite all the events of the past week, the British still had friends in Washington. "Cease fire or get on with the landings," I urged the Joint Intelligence Committee when it was my turn to speak. "Present Washington with either an overnight stand-down or a fast fait accompli, and everything will be OK again soon. This isn't just my personal view. I'm not speaking without instructions." The men around the table nodded coolly, but volunteered nothing about the timing of either a cease-fire or an assault.

A day or so later I realized that that angry predawn telephone call had reflected a reconsideration of policy taking place throughout Washington. By the weekend, the Administration was softening its recriminatory approach toward London, Paris, and Tel Aviv and seemed anxious to close the breach in the Western alliance.

Saturday was the day when the British and French landings were expected. The British bombing attacks, which by now had all but wiped out the Egyptian Air Force, shifted to ammunition dumps, military barracks, and weapons depots. Cairo Radio was targeted again and, this time, was hit. But there was no hint of imminent paratroop drops or seaborne attacks. And so when I left the JIC meeting room that morning I sought out an acquaintance on the committee's secretariat. He was the liaison officer between the intelligence chiefs and the military staff. "What's going on?" I asked him. "Is there going to be a landing or not?" He glumly escorted me upstairs to a temporary operations center which had been set up in the area where the Joint Intelligence Committee used to meet. "Cooper wants to know where the hell our troops are," my escort explained to a harassed colonel behind a makeshift, overflowing desk. The officer flung aside a curtain to reveal a large map of the Mediterranean. He pointed to a patch of blue. "Our troops? There they are. In the middle of the bleeding Med!" On the map were dozens of colored pins, each representing a British or French warship or troop transport—halfway between Malta and Egypt. What the chart did not show, but what I discovered later, was that the sole New Zealand warship in the flotilla had dropped out; the cabinet in Wellington had overruled its prime minister and ordered the cruiser to return to home waters. London's papers that morning were carrying reports from Cyprus of paratroopers packing their gear and troop carriers being readied, but the colonel had had no word of a firm zero hour.

The fortunes of the Suez expeditionary force turned out to be at even greater hazard than the operations map implied. As of Saturday, five days after the Israeli move on Sinai and four days after the British and French ultimatum, the high command on Cyprus was still waiting to hear from London and Paris about the date and even the precise points for the landings!

And that very morning the commanders had received a message that left them in no doubt about Eden's limited concept of the action against Egypt. Invading troops, the message said, were to concentrate solely on the Canal; under no circumstances was any unit to move beyond the narrow confines of the Canal.

The message to Cyprus that Saturday enraged General Beaufre, the French commander. In his view the whole venture had shrunk overnight from a major assault on Egypt and Nasser to a minor attempt to secure a beachhead at the Canal.[27]

By the weekend a distraught Anthony Eden was being torn asunder by friends and enemies both at home and abroad. The noisiest and most insistent voices came from those demanding that Britain obey the UN's call for a cease-fire. But there were other voices, British as well as French —important and by no means lonely—urging him to get on with the job of finishing off Nasser's regime and restoring the Canal to British and French control.

On Saturday London and Paris rejected the UN's cease-fire resolution. Later that day Eden gave a nationwide TV-radio speech explaining, yet again, the government's position. But this time, the prime minister introduced a new and critical point. "The Israeli invasion," Eden said, was likely to lead to a "widespread flare-up in the Middle East. If you see a fire the first question is not how it started, but how to put it out. . . . What we did was to take police action at once. Action to stop the fighting and separate the armies. . . . Before long it will become apparent to everybody that we acted rightly and wisely. . . . Our friends inside the Commonwealth and outside could not . . . be consulted in time." He then flashed an important signal to New York: "If the United Nations would take over the police action, we would welcome it."[28]

The speech confirmed General Beaufre's worst fears: a "police action" instead of a "war"; and an invitation to the UN to "take over." No wonder the invasion was confined at the last moment to the Canal area. The mounting pressures against the Suez venture had clearly given the prime minister sober second thoughts. But the backtracking hardly satisfied Eden's angry critics.

Opposition leader Hugh Gaitskell demanded and received "equal time." He told the British people that they were "at war," urged Conservative members of the House of Commons to help their Labour Party colleagues to depose Eden. "I don't believe the present Prime Minister can carry out this policy. . . . His policy this last week has been disastrous, and he is utterly, utterly discredited in the world. Only one thing can now save the reputation and the honour of this country. Parliament must repudiate the Government's policy. The Prime Minister must resign. The Labour Party . . . are a minority in the House of Commons. So, the responsibility rests with those Conservatives who . . . want a change. . . . We undertake to support a new Prime Minister in halting the invasion of Egypt, in ordering the cease-fire and complying with the decisions and recommendations of the United Nations."[29]

Anthony Eden did not resign, but Anthony Nutting did. Nutting had already told Eden that he disagreed with the government's Middle East policy. Now he realized he was unable "to defend the Government's position either in Parliament or the United Nations." The resignation had been offered on Wednesday, but not accepted and announced until Saturday.

The day had one bright spot for the beleaguered prime minister: Winston Churchill publicly declared his support. "I am confident," he wrote to the chairman of the Conservative Party, "that our American friends will come to realize that, not for the first time, we have acted independently for the common good. World peace, the Middle East and our national interest will surely benefit in the long run from the Government's resolute action." But privately, and somewhat later, Churchill was less than enthusiastic. "I am shocked by what he did, and I'm an Anthony man," he told his physician, Lord Moran.[30]

Throughout Saturday, November 3, the reaction to the Middle East crisis continued to gather steam. From Delhi came the news that the prime ministers of five key Asian nations would soon convene to plan "joint action" with respect to the crisis. A prominent Indian politician called for India's secession from the Commonwealth. From Peking, Communist China told London and Paris that they would be faced with "inestimable grave consequences" if their troops were not "withdrawn immediately from Egypt"—an ominous if premature warning. And from very close to home, the General Council of the British UN Association (of which Anthony Eden was chairman) resolved that Britain had "lost a great part of our moral standing in the world" as a consequence of the attack on Egypt.

Eleanor Roosevelt, however, defended Israel's invasion of Sinai. And George Kennan, in a letter to the Washington *Post,* bitterly criticized the Administration's actions in the UN, although he acknowledged that the British and French move was "ill-considered and pathetic." Looking beyond the immediate crisis, Vice-President Nixon predicted that out of the current turmoil in the Middle East would emerge a "more stable area in which the Soviet Union would not be a decisive influence." The *New York Times* editorial stance was judicious, but generally pro Britain, France, and Israel; the Washington *Post* was more outspoken and critical of the three countries.

Matters were in precarious balance in the Middle East that Saturday; one war seemed about to start, another about to end; the British and French confrontation with the Egyptian Army was then still in the future, the Israelis' was now almost over. Israeli forces controlled Sinai and Gaza and were headed toward their last, most important objective, Sharm el-Sheikh. In Cairo, meanwhile, the withdrawal of Egyptian forces from Sinai and the bombing notwithstanding, the populace seemed to be going about its business with an astonishing air of fatalism.* The Air Ministry in Whitehall had had early illusions that the RAF, single-handed, could topple Nasser, but these must have been dispelled by November 3.

In Hungary, there were reports of "almost total anarchy" in the southern part of the country and of the murder of Erno Gero, the former first secretary of the Hungarian Communist Party. But the struggle was turning dangerously, possibly irreversibly against the freedom fighters. By late Saturday afternoon there were signs of an imminent definitive showdown. Additional Soviet forces were moving across the Hungarian border, despite Prime Minister Nagy's pleas to Moscow and an eleventh-hour message from Eisenhower to Bulganin. "It is especially shocking," the President told the marshal, "that this renewed application of force against the Hungarian Government and people took place while negotiations were going on between your representatives and those of the Hungarian Government. . . . I urge in the name of humanity and in the cause

---

*An Egyptian who lived a few miles from the airport during that period remembers the whole city shaking with explosives and that early in the bombing there was great concern that attacks would be made on Cairo itself. But one morning there were leaflets stuffed in every mailbox of his apartment house, presumably prepared if not delivered by the British, reassuring the people that they were in no danger.

of peace, that the Soviet Union take action to withdraw Soviet forces from Hungary immediately." Meanwhile, Peking came out in strong support of Moscow's action; New Delhi turned away queries about its attitude with a "no comment."

The United Nations had never before, and has never since, experienced a moment of crisis, a sense of impending disaster such as characterized the weekend of November 3–4. The General Assembly was in session throughout the night on Saturday debating the situation in the Middle East, while the Security Council was addressing the situation in Hungary. And meanwhile, John Foster Dulles, the helmsman of American foreign policy, was hurting and helpless in Washington's Walter Reed Hospital.

Only a week had passed since the aborted picnic. It was a week made up of seven long, terrible days: The political map of the Middle East had been changed; the revolt against tyranny in Hungary had been all but crushed; the prime minister of the United Kingdom had started his swift slide into oblivion; the secretary of state had been hospitalized with terminal cancer; Anglo-American relations had sunk to a lower level than at any time since the American Civil War; the Suez Canal was blocked. On a more personal level, friendships had been broken, my daughters ostracized at school, my wife insulted by shopkeepers. As I left my house for Grosvenor Square on Sunday morning, November 4, I wondered whether the end of the grim harvest would ever come.

Too late for the Sunday papers but in time for the early morning BBC broadcast came a report that provided one of the most poignant moments of a poignant week. It was a translation of Premier Nagy's speech made at dawn over Budapest Radio: "This is Imre Nagy, Chairman of the Council of Ministers of the Hungarian People's Republic speaking. In the early hours of the morning Soviet troops have started an attack against the Hungarian capital with the apparent purpose of overthrowing the lawful democratic government of the country. Our troops are engaged in battle. The government is in its place. This is my message to the Hungarian people and to the whole world."[31]

Later in the day there was another message from Hungary—a heart-rending cry for help: "This is Hungary calling. This is Hungary calling. Early this morning the Soviet troops launched a general attack on Hungary, we are requesting you to send us immediate aid in the form of parachute troops. . . . For the sake of God and Freedom, help Hungary!"[32] And then . . . nothing. But those who could help—even if they had been willing—were otherwise engaged.

The Russians had seized Nagy and his cabinet during the day and installed their own government headed by Janos Kadar, who had bolted to the Soviet side at the moment of showdown. Marshal Tito, who knew better than anyone in Eastern Europe the limits of Moscow's tolerance, issued a statement that evening supporting the new regime in Budapest. According to Tito, Kadar would negotiate the withdrawal of Soviet forces and, at the same time, preserve Socialism in Hungary.

Few people in Britain thought much about Hungary that Sunday. Most were preoccupied with the Middle East. Many were angry, and Anthony Eden, not Nikolai Bulganin, was the target of wrath.

London's Hyde Park is an ideal place for leather-lunged orators to share their various and competing prescriptions for the achievement of every human aspiration, from eternal peace to eternal youth. Trafalgar Square, on the other hand, provides a fine setting for a more purposeful, more organized effort to right wrongs. Here the attention of a large crowd can be focused on a particular, immediate issue and the roads feeding into the square provide a tempting invitation to move from oration to demonstration. The stone platform that supports the towering statue of Lord Nelson offers a convenient rostrum for speakers and honored spectators. The square is a few minutes march to Whitehall. Although the American Embassy is somewhat farther removed, it is still only a half hour's walk away on Grosvenor Square. But on Sunday, November 4, it was Downing Street rather than Grosvenor Square that was in the dock.

The National Council of Labour had organized a rally to protest Eden's Middle East action. Twenty thousand people gathered under the banner "Law, not War!" Speaker after speaker berated the government. One proclaimed that the government was endangering world peace and the structure of the United Nations "merely to satisfy the conceit and vanity of that foolish man, Anthony Eden." But it was the fiery Labour MP Aneurin Bevan who captured the afternoon's laurels for polemics: "If Eden's sincere in what he is saying—and he may be—then he is too stupid to be prime minister. He is either a knave or a fool. In both capacities we do not want him." The meeting broke up with a march toward Downing Street, which was finally diverted to Parliament Square by mass formations of London policemen. There were many arrests, many injuries.

Eden's wife, Clarissa, went to Trafalgar Square for a firsthand view, but left quickly when she was recognized. Lady Eden was encouraged by the sight of many progovernment banners and by the heckling directed at the Labour Party speakers.

Cairo had broken diplomatic relations with Britain the day before, and Councilor of Embassy Ashraf Ghorbal had strolled down to the square as his last act of official business before leaving for Egypt. His reaction contrasted sharply with Lady Eden's. He reminisced many years later about how inspired he had been with the outpouring of British sympathy for his country.

I, too, went to Trafalgar Square. What I saw that day was a depth of feeling on the part of young university students, of old manual workers, and of many ages and classes in between that I had not realized existed in Britain. The vast majority was loudly and passionately opposed to Eden and his Middle East policy. Lady Eden was right about the presence of people carrying pro-Eden signs and hecklers, but the police removed them from the square when they appeared to be in danger of being drawn and quartered by the angry crowd. The march toward Number 10 had ugly overtones; large-scale violence seemed likely if the demonstrators broke through the cordon of police.

One indication of support later gave Eden some small satisfaction. A London bus driver wrote of his admiration and told Eden that "eighty per cent of the crowd were of foreign extraction so that was no true census of opinion and can be ignored."[33] We were all acting out the fable of the blind men and the elephant.

Trafalgar Square was not the only site of protest rallies that Sunday. Meetings were held at universities throughout the country to oppose or support—mostly to oppose—the Suez action. At Oxford several hundred students and dons signed a petition calling the venture "morally wrong" and a danger to the Commonwealth, the Atlantic Alliance, and the United Nations. A similar petition was signed by more than six hundred students at Cambridge.

The prime minister was in trouble and he knew it. If the government ever had a consensus for a policy of regaining control of the Suez Canal, it had worn paper thin by Sunday. The Trafalgar Square rally marked one of the few times in modern British history that a street demonstration would directly influence government policy.

At the United Nations, too, the spotlight on November 4 was turned toward Suez rather than Budapest. To be sure, the General Assembly had voted "to investigate" the situation in Hungary after the Security Council wrangled its way through the night. But as the secretary-general, Marshal Bulganin, and all the other great men were aware, there was nothing consequential that the United Nations could do, or would try to do, to help the Hungarians or punish the Russians. If the organization was to prove that it had any capability for dealing with a world crisis, the Middle East, rather than Eastern Europe, would provide the test.

Lester Pearson, Canada's wise minister of external affairs, found the key. It was he who suggested a way out for Eden. The prime minister's speech on Saturday broke the logjam: "if the United Nations will take over the police action. . . ." And it was Pearson who introduced the resolution to set up a UN Emergency Force "to secure and supervise the cessation of hostilities."

By Sunday, Israeli forces had taken Sharm el-Sheikh. The war, as far as Israel was concerned, was over. Israel's ambassador to the United Nations was instructed to announce Tel Aviv's readiness to accept an immediate cease-fire, providing Egypt did the same. The British and French were surprised and angered by the Israeli announcement. Their expeditionary forces were still at sea; an Israeli cease-fire before the landing would make a mockery of their whole enterprise. London and Paris immediately pressured Tel Aviv to continue fighting and later that day, with great embarrassment, Israel withdrew its offer. Nonetheless, at the general headquarters of the Israeli Army a military spokesman reported that "All operations in the Sinai Peninsula have stopped. The job is complete and done." Egypt and other Arab states were invited to engage in peace negotiations. On Sunday night cities throughout Israel once again were lit up.

On Sunday, too, France, Britain, and other countries of Western Europe must have sensed that, however and whenever the war ended, Egypt's corking up of the Canal and Syria's sabotage of the pipelines threatened an imminent oil shortage. But Eden and Mollet could derive at least some satisfaction from knowing that emergency petroleum supplies had been arranged in Washington.

Russia, confident that its Eastern European flank was secure and justifiably unconcerned about a UN "investigation" of the Hungarian situation, had become even more righteously indignant over events in the Middle East. Moscow sent a sharp protest to London and Paris, calling their closure of certain parts of the Mediterranean and Red Seas an "act of aggression." The notes were ignored. Perhaps Moscow expected them to be. But as the Kremlin knew, and the rest of the world did not, this was but an opening salvo. In due course, the Russians counted on grabbing the attention of Anthony Eden and Guy Mollet.

9

MOMENT OF TRUTH

Early Monday morning, November 5, Britain and France invaded Egypt. After all the months of mobilization, preparation, and planning, the operation was a handsome, albeit modest effort. Six hundred paratroopers of Her Majesty's 3rd Parachute Battalion dropped on a small airfield at El Gamil a few miles west of Port Said. Five hundred men from the 2e Régiment de Parachutistes Coloniaux dropped near the waterworks at Port Fuad, on the outskirts of Port Said to the south. Egyptian resistance was brisk but short-lived on both fronts. British and French reinforcements later in the day consolidated and expanded the invaders' holdings. By early afternoon the paratroopers were closing in on Port Said. At 4:30, the Egyptian commander of the town put out some tentative feelers regarding arrangements for surrender.

The next several hours were marked by confusion. General Stockwell and General Beaufre, the two commanders of the invasion, had their headquarters on separate ships. Communication between them was so faulty that the terms of surrender could not be arranged until ten o'clock that night. Nevertheless, the headquarters on Cyprus, obviously overeager for good news, flashed a report to London late in the afternoon that Port Said had surrendered. In Parliament that evening, Eden enjoyed a brief moment of satisfaction when he read to an enthusiastic House a telegram from Cyprus headquarters reporting the "surrender." But the news was premature—the Egyptian commander, on his own initiative or by orders from Cairo, had changed his mind.

On the day of the invasion Anthony Eden confronted a difficult dilemma. His military establishment, powerful MPs of his own party, and his French ally were insisting ·that the operation proceed until at least some concrete military results were achieved. On the other hand, there was strong pressure, both in Britain and abroad, in favor of his announcing an immediate cease-fire. Unless he took the former course, all the political losses he had incurred would have been for naught, all the military preparation that had been made since late July would have to be written off. Unless he took the latter course, he would have to face the wrath of the United Nations, the United States, and even of the Commonwealth. On that very day he received a message from Ottawa that was later described as "the most blistering personal telegram ever to pass between two Commonwealth Prime Ministers."[1]

The terrible choice would have challenged the mental stamina and inner resources of the most healthy, rested, and resilient of men. But Eden was now frail, exhausted, and taut. Compounding the agony were his sense of frustration and his pangs of conscience as the United Kingdom, then one of the strongest powers in Western Europe, helplessly watched Soviet tanks snuff out the revolt in Hungary.

These were not his only trials on that black Monday. He faced two grave additional threats: one to the nation's financial stability, and one to the nation's very existence.

The British economy had been suffering from anemia since World War II and by the mid-fifties was still in need of tender care and constant feeding. Even without the financial strain of Suez, 1956 would hardly have been regarded as a vintage year. But the Suez venture had racked the stability of the pound. In September, Britain's foreign exchange reserves fell by $57 million, in October by another $84 million. "These were tolerable figures," recalls Harold Macmillan, then chancellor of the exchequer. "No doubt confidence was sustained because the Americans still seemed to be active in our support."[2] But in the first few days of November, there was a fearsome run on the pound: $279 million were withdrawn—15 percent of Britain's total dollar reserves. The sterling crisis was the worst the nation had experienced in the postwar decade.

The draw-down on reserves was in part occasioned by India's coincidental need for sterling to fund its new Five Year Plan; in part by a withdrawal of Communist Chinese deposits for the disposal of the Egyptian government; in part by the transfer of funds from British to Swiss banks by the Middle East oil nations;[3]* and in part by a large disposal of pounds by speculators on Wall Street and by the Federal Reserve Bank. With regard to the sale of sterling in the United States, Macmillan comments, "How far this was due merely to the desire to avoid loss and how far this followed the lead of the United States Treasury is hard to know."[4]

Macmillan had put the matter delicately. The fact was that Secretary of the Treasury George Humphrey, with Eisenhower's encouragement, was applying the bluntest weapon in America's nonmilitary arsenal, a financial squeeze. But the British had, or should have had, advance warning that the Administration would not hesitate to use economic pressure to push London to the wall. Washington's contingency plans to provide

*The effect of the transfer of funds to Swiss banks was not as serious as it might have been. Since British banks were paying about 7 percent interest and Swiss about 2 percent, the Swiss bankers promptly redeposited the transferred funds in London banks.

emergency supplies of oil to Western Europe, worked out soon after the nationalization of the Canal, were being held in suspense well after it became apparent that Europe was facing a serious oil shortage. And, then, when Britain, in an effort to rescue the pound, applied to the United States for a loan of $1 billion and to the International Monetary Fund for $500 million—loans that would normally have been approved as a matter of routine—Humphrey refused to go along unless London first agreed to a cease-fire. Britain's financial situation was so desperate at that point that Harold Macmillan appealed to a visiting journalist from Washington to write a personal letter to Secretary Humphrey urging him "to go easy on the pound."[5]

Harold Macmillan, a stalwart early supporter of Eden's Suez policy, the man who said that he would rather pawn the National Gallery than be humiliated by Nasser,[6] was faced with an awful decision. But he knew there was no choice. As chancellor of the exchequer, he told the prime minister he could not guarantee the stability of the pound unless Britain called off the fighting.

There was another threat, an even more brutal one, that confronted the prime minister on Monday. It arrived that night from Moscow. The Russians, with the crisis in Hungary now safely behind them, had sent a thinly veiled warning to Washington, London, Paris, and Tel Aviv and to the chairman of the UN Security Council. The fighting in the Middle East, Bulganin reminded President Eisenhower in Washington, could lead to "world war." He urged joint American-Soviet military action against France, Britain, and Israel to "curb aggression" against Egypt. Moscow's message was rejected out of hand. Bulganin's letter, the White House said, was "an obvious attempt to divert world attention from the Hungarian tragedy; [it] makes the unthinkable suggestion that the United States join with the Soviet Union in a bi-partite employment of their military forces to stop the fighting in Egypt. . . . Neither Soviet nor any other military forces should now enter the Middle East area except under United Nations mandate. . . . The introduction of new forces under these circumstances would violate the United Nations Charter, and it would be the duty of all the United Nations members including the United States to oppose such an effort. . . . The first and most important step that should be taken to ensure world peace and security is for the Soviet Union to observe the United Nations resolution to cease its military repression of the Hungarian people and withdraw its troops."[7]

So much for Bulganin's note to Eisenhower. But Moscow was determined to gain as much mileage as possible out of its new and self-proclaimed role as the guardian of peace in the Middle East. And so, shortly after midnight New York time, the Security Council met yet again in emergency session to consider a resolution forwarded to the president of the Council from Foreign Minister Shepilov. Moscow proposed that Britain, France, and Israel cease all military activity in the Middle East within twelve hours after the passage of the resolution and withdraw their forces within three days. If the "aggressors" did not comply, Shepilov suggested in terms similar to Bulganin's message to Eisenhower, "all member states of the United Nations, especially the United States and the USSR . . . should give military and other assistance to the Egyptian Republic . . . by sending naval and air forces, military units, volunteers, military instructors."[8] The Council gave the Soviet proposal short shrift; the resolution was voted down within thirty minutes of its reading. So much for Shepilov's letter to the United Nations.

Bulganin's messages to Tel Aviv, London, and Paris were closer to the bone. He warned the Israeli government that it was "criminally playing with the destiny of its country and people—which raises the question of the whole existence of Israel as a state." Bulganin then informed the government that he was recalling the Soviet ambassador: "We hope the Israeli Government will duly understand and evaluate this warning of ours."[9]

Ben-Gurion was enraged. "What particularly infuriated him," according to Moshe Dayan, "was the difference between the letters to Britain and France and the letter to Israel. The one to us was couched in terms of contempt and scorn, and it threatened the very existence of Israel. The messages to France and Britain [had] none of the coarse mockery that marked the text of the ultimatum to Israel."[10]

Bulganin's warnings to London and Paris were a bit more subtle to be sure, but, nonetheless, tough and ominous. The British and French action, he said, "has the most dangerous consequences for the cause of general peace." And then, after a lecture on their aggressive aims, came an awful, if implied, threat: "There are countries," Bulganin reminded Eden, "that are so powerful they need not attack Britain and France by naval or air power," but by other means "such as rocket technique. If rocket weapons had been used against Britain and France they probably would have called this a barbaric action. Yet in what way does the inhuman attack made by the armed forces of Britain and France on the nearly unarmed Egypt differ from this? . . . We are fully determined to crush the aggressors and restore peace in the Middle East through the use of force."[11]

The Kremlin underscored its outrage by moving against targets close to hand. On the day its ugly messages were sent, mobs besieged the British, French, and Israeli embassies in Moscow. This was the first time

in the history of the Soviet Union that street demonstrations were un-
leashed against foreign governments.

On November 6, the second day of the British-French invasion, the
plans and words and deeds that Nasser's nationalization of the Suez
Canal had set in motion in world capitals on three continents came to a
head. Tuesday provided the long-awaited moment of truth.

Early that morning newspapers reported that British and French
commandos were swarming over the beaches to reinforce the paratroopers in the Port Said area. What none of the readers or, for that matter,
the swarming soldiers knew was that the landings had taken place and the
fighting had intensified several hours after Eden had decided to comply
with the UN's call for a cease-fire. For, in the predawn hours of November
6, the prime minister of the United Kingdom lost his nerve.

The Soviet threat, in and of itself, probably would not have tipped
the scales toward a quick cease-fire, but it added to the burdens the
physically ailing and emotionally drained prime minister had to bear.
This and the combination of domestic political divisions, an international
run on the pound, American and Commonwealth opposition, Third
World vituperation, and United Nations pressure finally became too
much for Eden. Sometime after midnight he called Premier Mollet in
Paris and told him that, as far as Britain was concerned, the jig was up.
Mollet refused to accept Eden's sense of hopelessness, interpreting it
solely as a reaction to the Soviet threat, and asked Douglas Dillon, the
American ambassador, to meet with him immediately. Dillon dressed
quickly and drove through the cold, early-morning darkness to Matignon
Palace, Mollet's official residence. There he found several French cabinet
members. The premier told Dillon of Eden's call. Would the ambassador
ask Washington to guarantee that the United States would come to the
aid of Britain and France in the event of a Soviet attack? The conversation
was interrupted by a call from London. It was the restless, tortured Eden
again; he had now definitely decided to order British troops to cease
fire.[12]

It had been a sleepless night for Eden—yet another in a long procession. At ten o'clock on Tuesday morning he assembled his cabinet and
told his colleagues of his decision. It was then noon in the Middle East;
British and French troops were now strengthening their positions in the
area around Port Said. Mollet and Pineau were not unsympathetic to
Eden's problems but were horrified that he was prepared to order a
cease-fire before "we could get a good position along the Canal that
would put us in a good negotiating position."[13] When Eden called Mollet
to tell him of his meeting with the cabinet, the premier asked him to delay

the order for "two or three days." Eden refused. At best, he could wait for twelve hours—that is, until midnight London time; 2 AM, November 7, Cairo time.

Chancellor Konrad Adenauer was in Paris at that moment. In a conversation with Ambassador Dillon, he predicted that neither Paris nor London would be targeted by the Russians, but rather Berlin. Later, at a meeting at the Matignon Palace, he urged Mollet to accept the cease-fire.

Soon after his telephone conversation with Mollet, Anthony Eden sent a message to the secretary-general of the United Nations. "If the Secretary-General can confirm that the Egyptian and Israeli governments have accepted an unconditional cease-fire, and that the international force to be set up will be competent to secure and supervise the attainment of—[the cease-fire and the reopening of the Canal]—Her Majesty's Government will agree to stop further military British and French operations." And, then, after urging that the United Nations permit British and French technicians to begin at once to clear the Canal, the message concluded with a statement that "Her Majesty's Government are ordering their forces to cease fire at midnight GMT unless they are attacked." Premier Mollet sent a similar message, although he urged that "a meeting of the Security Council . . . be called at the ministerial level as soon as possible in order to work out . . . a settlement of the problems of the Middle East."[14]

While from his office in Downing Street Eden was proceeding head-long down the cease-fire track, events elsewhere in London, across the Channel, and in the Middle East were moving ahead on their own momentum.

At sunrise on Tuesday morning French warships were scheduled to open a bombardment of Port Fuad in preparation for amphibious landings. At the last moment word got to the flagship that French paratroopers had fought their way into the town during the night. The British fleet, whose mission it was to fire at nearby Port Said, was unaware that the French now held Port Fuad. Some British shells found their way into areas occupied by the paratroopers. Luckily, there were no casualties. Tuesday had not started well.

All that morning forces waded ashore, guns held high, under protective air cover. Although the beaches had not been mined, the port was dotted with wrecked ships and this, plus some Egyptian resistance, made the landings somewhat trickier than anticipated. But one young officer remembered having actually enjoyed the experience: "It was just like the films I had seen of World War II landings—only ours was by no means as dangerous.''[15] For another, the attack was almost an anticlimax. His battalion's heavy equipment and stores had been loaded at Southampton in early August. The battalion finally sailed for the Mediterranean on October 31. Although the soldiers were told their mission was to separate Israeli and Egyptian forces, the propaganda aboard ship was directed solely against "Johnnie Gyppo."[16]

Another battalion was given ten days' notice to prepare for operations against Egypt while it was "chasing EOKA terrorists" in the central mountains of Cyprus. "There were considerable difficulties to be overcome," the commander recalls. "It is not easy to switch troops of however high caliber from mountain antiguerrilla tactics to set-piece modern operations involving armor, artillery, and aircraft. The troops just managed to have very sketchy conversion training.

"We arrived off Port Said by ship at six in the morning, but for some still unexplained reason we did not come into the harbor and disembark until three in the afternoon. Our job was to go straight through the town and down the west bank of the Canal, to clear it, and to capture Ismailia. By this time the only opposition in Port Said itself was a few snipers. We moved steadily southwards but at about ten o'clock that night we received a message that a cease-fire would be in effect at midnight."[17]

By late afternoon on Tuesday British and French troops occupied several square miles of the Port Said area and thus controlled the northern entrance to the Canal. The commanders were laying plans for a quick movement on the following morning to the south toward the Canal town of El Qantara. But their plans were for naught.

Meanwhile, the relations between the two allies-of-convenience, Britain and Israel, were showing signs of additional strain. Shortly before the paratroopers landed in Egypt on Monday, Eden announced that "once British and French forces have occupied the key points on the Canal, Her Majesty's Government will ensure that the Israeli forces withdraw from Egyptian territory." British officials in London told reporters that the Israeli withdrawal should take place "even before a peace settlement." But Ben-Gurion had no intention of pulling out of Sinai and told Eden so. According to one journalist, "Ben-Gurion . . . couldn't accept the idea of Israel being treated as the moral equivalent of the Egyptians. . . . The idea of Israel being the sole aggressor was abhorrent to him."[18] But this was not the only fissure in store on November 6; the Entente Cordiale, the historic alliance between Britain and France, was endangered by what took place later that day.

Washington regarded Bulganin's warnings with considerable concern. The *New York Times* reported that "it would be difficult to exaggerate the extreme tension that gripped the United States government. . . . The United States took the Soviet threat 'to use force to crush the aggressors and restore peace in the Middle East' very seriously." There were "reliable reports" that the Air Defense Command in the Washington area had been put on an emergency alert.

Some accounts well after the event imply that officials in London discounted the Soviet threat. But that is not the way I remember the reactions at the time. "Nuclear blackmail" rather than "diplomatic bluff" were the words I heard during the twenty-four hours following the announcement of Bulganin's message to Eden over Moscow's radio—an announcement, incidentally, that preceded Eden's actual receipt of the communication. Some British intelligence officers, to be sure, were skeptical that Moscow could throw nuclear missiles from Soviet territory into Britain—but they were not *certain.* And they knew the consequences of their being wrong were grave indeed.

Political and military officials in London apparently felt sufficiently concerned about the Soviet warning to transmit their anxiety to the forces fighting in Egypt. Accompanying the order to cease fire at midnight, one commander remembers, was a warning that if they did not do so "there was a risk of Russian nuclear attacks on London and Paris. At the time I thought it was a bit unfair of the authorities to put in this message to the field what almost amounted to blackmail. 'If you don't stop we in London and your families may suffer.' "[19]

Ben-Gurion sent Golda Meir and Shimon Peres to Paris to consult about the Soviet threat. Pineau apparently took Moscow's words at face value. "We have no means of defense against missiles," he told the Israelis. "I suggest that you do not belittle Bulganin's warning."[20]

Later that day, the Swiss government invited heads of state of the United States, Britain, France, the Soviet Union, and India to meet in Geneva as soon as possible to defuse "the danger of 'World War III.' "

I can make no claim to cool insouciance about the Soviet threat to rocket London and Paris. I called my Washington boss, Robert Amory, on the night of November 5 and told him I would not attend the Joint Intelligence Committee meeting the following morning unless Washington lifted its embargo on intelligence information to the British. Washington, I knew, would be assessing Bulganin's warning. That assessment should be shared with the British. If the embargo was not lifted before I had to leave for Storey's Gate, I told Amory, I would not go. I did not intend to sit silently when the Soviet threat was discussed. Instead, I would pack, return to Washington, resign. Brave words, but I meant what I said. When I returned home that night I told my wife that we might be leaving for America within a day or so.

Perversely enough, there were no mid-night phone calls from the code room that night. And when I arrived at the embassy early the next morning the message I was looking for was not there. At about nine o'clock (4 AM Washington time) I called the watch office at CIA's Washington headquarters. "Keep your shirt on," someone I knew who had the duty on that shift told me, "there's something coming."

Since World War II, the United States and Great Britain had each shared a large part of its secret information with the other under the umbrella of the Anglo-American special relationship. In part because of this, my British military and civilian associates had begun to regard me as an "old boy." Our encounters at the Joint Intelligence Committee had evolved into a series of informal, frank exchanges until of a sudden the "special relationship" had melted away.

At the end of October, Washington had stopped the flow of almost all intelligence to the British. London, in turn, had virtually blacked out the Americans. No information relating to the Mediterranean and the Middle East was being exchanged in either direction.

As a consequence, I no longer was treated as an overseas partner in a joint enterprise, but rather as just another representative of another government. Actually, not just *another* government, but a government currently treating Britain as a pariah. There was courtesy, of course; the British are rarely rude. But there was also coolness. Bitterness, too. And the feeling was reciprocated. They felt let down by the Americans, I felt betrayed by the British. We were both right.

Day after day, I had been taking my place at the table in the Joint Intelligence Committee conference room and had sat mute as the committee discussed the situation in, or bearing on, the Middle East. "What do the Americans have on this?" Chairman Dean would ask hopefully. "Nothing, I'm afraid," I would say. The litany had, by now, become mechanical—but each question, each response, was freighted with despair nonetheless.

The first meeting in that awful series was the worst. Just a week before, on Tuesday the thirtieth, I was accompanied by an associate, a retired admiral. He—my God, I still recoil from the memory!—responded to Dean's query by standing up, rocking back on his heels, closing his eyes, and reciting a bit of doggerel that ended with something like "a friend to the end." He left for Washington soon after, the only bright moment in two dreary weeks.

I was brooding about this that Tuesday morning as I walked out of the bright sunlight into the dark, dank Ministry of Defence building at Storey's Gate. I waited in the gloomy anteroom for my invitation to join the Intelligence Committee. Every day during the past week I had experienced a malevolent feeling of disorientation; a tolerated intruder in a troubled house. But now, at ten o'clock, November 6, 1956, I sensed that, whatever lay ahead, at least one aspect of the old special relationship would be restored. In my pocket were Washington's last-minute instructions to share the American assessment of Bulganin's rocket threat with the British. The embargo was over.

The buzzer sounded for the committee clerk. She disappeared into the conference room. "You may join them now, sir," she said coldly on her return. As I rose I reflected on *this* symptom of the new mood. In happier days, she had given me a wink and a smile and a "Get-along-with-you-now."

The gloomy conference room was a complement to the mood of that season. A single grimy window looked out on St. James Park, sparkling and crisp today in the autumn sunshine, but the blind was drawn as if to cut off the sight of another, more pleasant world. A fortnight before, the committee had been ejected from its comfortable, relatively cheerful quarters two floors above; that area had now been converted into a makeshift military operations center. (It was there, on the previous Saturday, that I had been granted a quick, surreptitious look at the disposition of the laggard invading fleet.) Instead of a hollow square of cozy individual writing desks, this room was graced with but one long table. Instead of the familiar colorful charts that brightened the old room, there was now just one map of the Middle East (hastily shrouded as I entered). The only familiar sight was the green baize cloth thrown over the table, the ritual covering that marked every Whitehall meeting of consequence. It was, in its way, an altar cloth, transforming an assembly into a congregation.

I found my seat at the foot of the table facing the chairman. Tension weighed heavy that morning, seven days after the British forces had first set sail for Egypt, twenty-four hours after the landings near Port Said. It was different from the tension I had sensed in Whitehall and in the streets and houses of London during that week. This was not the strain of frustration, nor of waiting, nor of anger. This had the smell of foreboding. I had recently become used to seeing these men, my friends, gray with exhaustion. Today they were ashen. They were worried. Really worried. For the past many hours they had been grappling with Moscow's unexpected, hideous threat.

As I looked about, the rectangular table seemed to transform itself into a menacing triangle. Patrick Dean was at its base; his associates were divided along each side; I was at the apex. I exchanged grave good-morning nods with one, and then another. Not a word from anyone. And then, just as Dean cleared his throat to speak, the bells of St. Margaret's, a block away, began to peal. So oppressive was the atmosphere at that moment, anything seemed possible. A wild thought knifed through me —was this an omen of something terrible and imminent? Were there church bells ringing alarms or dirges all over Britain?

Dean waited for the bells to come to rest. And then, finally: "Chet, we have been discussing the Soviet rocket threat. Is there anything that you can tell us of the American view?" Eyes bore down on me from both sides of the triangle.

"Yes, Mr. Chairman," I said hoarsely. "I have something to say: The United States Intelligence Board had an emergency meeting last night. They are convinced that the Russian nuclear rocket threat is a bluff. They seriously doubt that Moscow has either the long-range missile capability or the nuclear warheads to threaten Britain and France. They want you to know they do not believe there is any real danger."[21] The room seemed brighter. And the tension eased. "Thank you," Dean murmured. "Tell Washington we are grateful for their views."

On my way out of the soot-covered old building into Storey's Gate and the sunlight a half hour later, I learned that I had been wrong about the bells. They had been striking joyous notes of marriage rather than ominous notes of war. Altogether, it had been a good morning—perhaps a portent of better days ahead.

On my way back to the embassy, my car was diverted from the Horse Guard's Approach to make way for the queen. That Tuesday marked the opening of the new session of Parliament. Elizabeth was on her way to deliver her "Speech from the Throne." The queen revealed the government's deep concern about the state of Britain's relations with its overseas allies. She called for "worldwide cooperation" with the United Kingdom to settle the dangerous crisis in the Middle East.

Later that evening the House assembled again for its regular session, still in the dark that the Suez venture was about to end. The members, Conservative and Labour alike, cheered Eden when he told of his firm rejection of Moscow's threat. "I have received with deep regret," Eden had written Bulganin, "your message of yesterday. The language . . . made me think at first that I could only instruct Her Majesty's Ambassador to return it as entirely unacceptable. But the moment is so grave that I feel I must try to answer you with those counsels of reason with which you and I have in the past been able to discuss issues vital for the whole world. . . . Our aim is to provide a peaceful solution, not to engage in argument with you. . . . It ill becomes the Soviet Government to speak of the actions of Her Majesty's Government as 'barbaric.' The United Nations have called on your Government to desist from all armed attack on the peoples of Hungary. . . . The world will judge from your reply the sincerity of the words which you have thought fit to use about Her Majesty's Government."[22]

It was Anthony Eden's proudest moment in the two sad weeks that had passed since that conspiratorial meeting in the suburbs of Paris. The fruits of his long service to his country were harvested in that gutsy response to Moscow's crude attempt at blackmail.

At sunset on November 6, a bare thirty-six hours after their operation had begun, the British and French commanders learned, first from a special broadcast over the BBC and later from official telegrams, that London, Paris, and Tel Aviv had agreed to comply with the UN's demand for a cease-fire. The British officers were disappointed, but not surprised; they were aware of Eden's state of mind. The French commanders were furious; troops were ashore and their beachhead secure, but the forces were nowhere near achieving even the modest, scaled-down objective of taking over the Canal. General Beaufre, the commanding general of the French forces, regarded the cease-fire as "an irretrievable error" and "considered the possibility of disobeying." He did not, of course.[23]

Some time after midnight, with the end of the war at hand, the Egyptian military command received a message from Egypt's military attaché in Moscow: "Khrushchev told the ambassador that Russia cannot offer material help because of geographical obstacles. He said [for us] to strengthen our will to resist."[24] Nasser was probably not surprised: He already had a report from Syria's President Kuwatly, who was in Moscow when he learned of the air attacks on Egypt on November 1. Kuwatly begged Khrushchev and Bulganin to help, but the Russians claimed that military intervention was impossible. They promised only to exert political pressure on France, Britain, and Israel through the United Nations.[25]

At 2 AM, November 7, Cairo time, the cease-fire went into effect. The Suez war was over. The human toll: more than 100 Israelis, almost 3,000 Egyptians, 26 British and French. And the political reckoning: the Israelis suffered embarrassment, but now were secure along the Gaza border, controlled the entrance to the Gulf of Aqaba, and occupied all of Sinai; the Egyptians won an important diplomatic victory and incurred a disastrous military defeat on their western front and a local defeat at Port Said; the British and French experienced a profound diplomatic defeat and gained a trivial military victory. The United Nations proved that it could cope with an international crisis—a much needed demonstration, coming as it did on the heels of its abject failure in Hungary. The Russians came off best of all; they gained a long-sought influence in the Middle East.

In Britain, France, and Egypt, Tuesday, November 6, was the last day of the war. In Israel, it was the first day of peace. In the Soviet Union,

Bulganin was busy keeping international attention focused on the Middle East and away from Eastern Europe. In Hungary, it was a time of mourning. In New York, November 6 was the day when world statesmen watched the United Nations structure teeter and wondered whether it would be a successful experiment or, like its predecessor, the League of Nations, a noble failure. But in America—for both those who could find Budapest and Cairo on outline maps of Europe and the Middle East and those who could not—Tuesday was Election Day.

During the past week, developments in Hungary and Egypt had been as prominently discussed in the nation's media as were the presidential candidates. Americans had only recently experienced a terrible war in Korea. They had come to know the meaning of "invasion," "aggression," "cease-fire," "armistice." In addition, there were large American Jewish and Eastern European communities with high stakes in the outcome of the war in the Sinai and in the streets of Budapest. Dwight Eisenhower and Adlai Stevenson had had much competition in their quest for the limelight. But in the excitement of Election Day, interest in events abroad was momentarily, at least, put aside.

Enough people "loved Ike" enough to reelect him by a landslide. Despite his tough stance with respect to Israel, he won even New York, with its large Jewish population, by a handsome margin. "Modern Republicanism," Eisenhower said in his victory speech, "has now proved itself and America has approved of modern Republicanism." It was hardly a sentence that would go down in history as a precious jewel in the treasure chest of political rhetoric, but, as the election had demonstrated, the people wanted a good politician rather than a skilled rhetorician.

The President had reason to be pleased that day even before he was certain of his reelection. On his return to Washington from Gettysburg, Pennsylvania, where he had cast his vote, Eisenhower learned of Eden's decision to order a cease-fire. He could now approach his next four years at the White House without war clouds hovering over the Middle East. The President immediately rang up the prime minister. "He was delighted by our order to cease fire," Eden recalls, "and commented that we had got what we had set out to do; the fighting was over and had not spread. . . . There seemed no doubt at that moment that friendship between our two countries could be quickly reanimated."[26]

And so, Eisenhower awoke on November 7 to find the morning good. But Eden awoke to face yet another miserable day. Miserable because he was ill. And miserable because he knew that his Suez venture had turned into an ignominious, irretrievable fiasco. Just the day before, British shipowners had been told that it would take three months until the Canal could be cleared and reopened for navigation. Meanwhile, tankers from the Persian Gulf would have to make the long journey to Europe around the Cape of Good Hope. Britain was already facing an oil shortage, and winter was close at hand.

Although there was widespread relief in Britain that a full-scale war in the Middle East had been averted, the prime minister still had to deal with an angry House of Commons. On his own side of the aisle, conservative MPs were aghast that Eden had handed Nasser a major political, if not military victory. And the opposition Labour Party was determined to punish him for getting Britain into the mess in the first place. Moscow's claim that it was Bulganin's threat, not Eden's diplomacy, that deserved credit for stopping the war did little to help the beleaguered prime minister.

In the end, it was General Beaufre who provided the apt, if wry, summing up of the enterprise: "Our mountain was giving birth to a mouse."[27] Eden, reflecting on his government's objectives cited in the House of Commons just a few days before—preventing Nasser from taking over the Arab world, a lasting peace between Israel and its neighbors, and a "just solution" to the Suez Canal problem—must have agreed with Beaufre.

In three bitter wars British forces had met and vanquished formidable enemies near the Nile. Napoleon, Kaiser Wilhelm, Mussolini, and Hitler each tried to gain control over the Isthmus of Suez; each suffered defeat. But the combined forces of Britain and France met with disaster after one short week in their effort to regain control of the Suez Canal from Nasser and his third-rate army.

Why did the Suez enterprise turn out to be such a fiasco once the decision was made by Eden and Mollet to attack Egypt in concert with the Israelis and under the cover of their ultimatum to Israel and Egypt? The British-French-Israeli alliance was, from its outset, an artificial one. It was born in conspiracy, but sired by men who had neither heart for nor gift of conspiracy. In part because of the nature of the alliance, there was little communication or trust between Britain and Israel from the beginning, and between Britain and France toward the end. And from beginning to end, Eden, Mollet, and Ben-Gurion had divergent perceptions of what the operation was supposed to achieve. Even worse, they were not aware until much too late that such differences existed. Add to this a gross miscalculation about international, especially American, reaction. Add, also, for Britain and France, a language problem, individual weapons systems, an excess of prudence by the planners, and a dearth of panache by the commanders. A recipe for disaster certain.

It was Prime Minister Eden's prerogative, of course, to establish

British political objectives, once the military planning started. And Premier Mollet, for his part, had a responsibility to determine what it was the French hoped to achieve. But the Suez venture was a common enterprise, and its success depended upon mutual goals and strategies. Unfortunately, Eden was never able to decide just what British objectives should be—topple Nasser; seize the Canal and then attack Cairo; take Alexandria and then fan out to Cairo and Suez; or simply create a British-French holding operation until the UN could organize some form of international authority over the Canal. Mollet, while sure in his own mind that he wanted the overthrow of Nasser, felt bound by London's wishes; the British, after all, were fielding much the larger force and were providing Malta and Cyprus as staging areas. Ben-Gurion had no such problems. He knew what had to be done for Israel, and he took charge of the operation to assure that it was done.

The British and French commanding officers thought they knew what had gone wrong. General André Beaufre claims the Suez operation was a brilliant military operation, but a political debacle.[28] The view of his British counterpart, General Hugh Stockwell, could be summed up by the sarcastic telegram Stockwell sent to London upon hearing of the cease-fire while troops were still wading ashore: "We've now achieved the impossible. We're going both ways at once."[29] Such querulous notes have, of course, been sounded by generals through the ages—ever since kings first paid someone else to manage their wars. That the refrain is old and tired, however, does not necessarily mean that it is always wrong. And in the case of Suez, the generals were not wrong. Or at least they had sufficient justification to sulk, for the politicians—especially British politicians and, most especially, Anthony Eden himself—wielded a heavy hand in every stage of the military operation, from its early planning to its final execution.

Perhaps subconsciously in emulation of Winston Churchill, his mentor and model, Eden insisted on keeping tabs on every aspect of the military planning. He leaned over the shoulders of his chiefs of staff, kibitzing and second-guessing their deployments, timetables, and tactics. But although Eden was a confident, competent diplomat, he turned out to be an uncertain, amateurish commander-in-chief. And as domestic support for the venture showed signs of wavering and international opposition increased, Eden began first to hesitate and then to vacillate. He was in too deep to pull out, but too worried to press robustly ahead. The planners and the quartermasters were forced to zig and zag to accommodate Eden's changing moods. "By the time the convoys sailed," one of the battalion commanders told me later, "some of the equipment that was needed early on was at the bottom of the holds." In the end, Sir Anthony turned out to be no Sir Winston.

It is astonishing that the actual military operation, when at last its details were settled and it finally got under way, was as successful as it was. Military historians will have to look long and hard to find a better example of soldiers attempting to accomplish their mission in the face of such uncertain and interfering political direction. Yet this should not be taken as absolution for the generals and the admirals from their own sins of omission and commission.

It has been said that high-ranking military officers are prisoners of the strategy and tactics of the last great war they fought. Possibly so, possibly not. But during Suez, it *was* so. World War II, and especially the war in Europe, dominated the experience, the attitudes, and the planning of Eden's military advisers.

Soon after the cease-fire, when the full extent of the British and French military preparations was known, there was a theory floating around London—and I was one of the theorists—that if British and French paratroopers, airborne commandos, and light armor could have been dropped or flown into points along the Canal within twenty-four hours after the expiration of the ultimatum, the outcome might have been very different. Nasser's air force had been either destroyed by the British or withdrawn from battle by the Russians. A large part of Nasser's armies was heavily engaged in the Sinai. The Russians were still politically and militarily preoccupied in Hungary. The UN was still debating. Why did this not happen? Why did it take six days rather than twenty-four hours for landings at the Canal?

I thought at the time (and so misinformed Washington) that the politicians in general, and Eden in particular, had the gung-ho British and French military on a tight leash. Eden's position in the country and in the House of Commons, I reasoned, was so weak that he could not afford heavy casualties, especially among the young National Service conscripts. And so, my explanation went on, he insisted that the RAF bomb every Egyptian airfield, military installation, and naval base in order that the troopships could sail across the Mediterranean and the eventual landings take place with minimum losses.*

I held this view for many years. I was dreadfully wrong. The actual situation was just the reverse, I discovered twenty years later.[30] It was the politicians, chief among them Eden, who were urging a quick and daring

---

*A few days after the ultimatum had expired Eden did, in fact, become worried about casualties among the Egyptians as well as among the British and French forces. But this was in response to the international and domestic outcry against his Suez policy.

air invasion; it was the chiefs of staff who objected.

The British and French generals regarded Egypt as a formidable military power. Perhaps they had some justification for their view: "The sheer weight of their matériel was impressive. . . . The Egyptians even had better rifles than Britain—a good Czech semiautomatic rifle, where Britain had old World War II breech-loading rifles. Britain had no airborne battalion anti-tank gun. No one knew whether the Soviet technicians who were training the Egyptians would be manipulating their matériel."[31]

And so, when plans for their joint attack were first formulated in the summer of 1956, they insisted on assembling a vast armada of warships, mountains of matériel, a hundred thousand troops, and fleets of bombers. After a decade of fighting frustrating insurgencies or mounting nasty "police actions" in Malaya, Kenya, Indochina, and Algeria, the British and French high commands were at last able to fight an old-fashioned war. Here was their first chance since 1945 to use bombers and cruisers, paratroops and landing craft, fighter escorts and infantry. Senior military planners were back on terra cognita. Every service in France and the United Kingdom was stretched to the limit of its thin capability. Emerging out of all this was what military staff college lecturers refer to in awed tones as "combined operations."

The prime minister and the few members of his cabinet who were privy to what was going on were aghast at the scale of the preparations and the strategy that was evolving. Was it really necessary, the chiefs were asked, to think in terms of World War II? Why not a quick thrust involving paratroopers and commandos which would secure the Canal until additional reinforcements arrived to consolidate their positions and then, possibly, push toward Cairo?

Professional soldiers do not relish being advised by amateur strategists—even if the amateurs happen to be their civilian bosses. The British chiefs were not as enthusiastic as he about the Suez venture, Eden discovered immediately following the nationalization of the Canal, but if there were to be an attack on Egypt, they wanted it done their way. And their way would involve a maximum of caution, a minimum of derring-do.

But it would be unfair to lay the chiefs' objections to an immediate airborne landing simply on their desire to relive the air-sea-ground extravaganzas of World War II. There was something else they remembered about that war, and it was this that made them recoil. In mid-September 1944, three paratroop divisions were dropped behind the German lines in Holland. One of the divisions, the British 1st Airborne, was virtually wiped out as it desperately waited at Arnhem for infantry and armored reinforcements due to arrive within forty-eight hours of the air drop, but not able to make contact until ten days had passed. Arnhem was still fresh in the memory of every British professional soldier over the age of thirty.

Eden, too, insisted on having his way; if warships and landing craft left Malta for Egypt before the ultimatum expired it would seem suspicious in the eyes of the world. It would be several days, then, before substantial reinforcements could arrive to relieve the air-dropped units. The chiefs threatened to resign if the prime minister ordered airborne landings before the British and French fleets were within sight of the Egyptian coast. The French commanders, although later frustrated by their ally's inertia, were also reluctant to leave small units exposed on Egyptian soil for more than twenty-four hours.

Adding to the force of the chiefs of staff's argument against early ground combat was the confident claim of the Royal Air Force that its planes might win the war even without an assault by paratroopers, commandos, and infantrymen. (Those were the days when bombing commands, in both Britain and the United States, were flying high—figuratively as well as literally.) Given six days of bombing, the RAF assured the prime minister, the Egyptians would turn on Nasser and victory would be at hand.

Perhaps the RAF did not get a fair chance to prove its point since, under the combined pressure of French impatience and the hot breath of the United Nations, Eden advanced the invasion date from November 6 to November 5. But even that one extra day was not easy to arrange. Much depended on the navy. Lord Louis Mountbatten, then First Lord of the Admiralty, had been opposed to the whole Suez enterprise from the beginning. He seemed content to drag his feet—and, some would say, his fleet, as well—hoping, perhaps, that international pressures would prevent an operation he thought unwise and foolhardy.

When, many years later, I asked General Yehoshofat Harkavi, chief of Israeli military intelligence during Suez, what he thought of the British-French operation, he chuckled at the memory of the time-consuming, grandiose mounting of a typical World War II combined operation. What was needed then was not a great display of military might, but a fast, lean surgical attack on Port Said, Ismailia, and Suez—machismo and daring. "Who did the British [whom he blamed for the operation's failure] think they were invading? The Soviet Union?" General Moshe Dayan also was critical of the British and French generals for overestimating Egypt's military strength and delaying their assault until politics overran the operation.[32]

The British generals' ignorance of the secret alliance with Israel contributed to the problem. Not until October 26, on the very eve of the Israeli invasion, did Eden tell his commanders what had been arranged.

If, as they made their plans, they had known that while they were attacking Egypt from the sea, Israel would be attacking on the west flank, the British command might not have delayed its assault until the last cumbersome landing craft wallowed its way through the Mediterranean from Malta. General Stockwell later claimed that if he had been aware that the Israelis would be close by, he would have recommended, or at least agreed to, a paratroop assault much earlier in the operation.[33] But Eden had taken pains to make sure that he did not know. And so, as my friend the battalion commander said, the British and French used "a sledgehammer to crack a nut."

Why did Eden not share what he knew with those who needed the information? The answer will have to come from someone much closer to Sir Anthony than anyone who has yet tried to divine his motivations that autumn. Perhaps he rationalized that if he jealously guarded the secret of Sèvres, subsequent events would bury or overtake the conspiratorial details of what had transpired in late October. Or perhaps he was reluctant to widen the circle of witting advisers lest he increase the chance of disclosure and thereby jeopardize the credibility of the British-French ultimatum on which he set such great store. In any case, he kept his own counsel, not only before those who did not need to know, but before those who did.

Perhaps only Selwyn Lloyd was kept fully apprised—and even he, as we have seen, was tardily brought into the picture. It was a calculated risk. By keeping the arrangement with the Israelis secret from British military commanders, Eden was endangering the possible success of the operation. By confining the circle of the knowing to only a few key advisers, he insured the enterprise against the risk of inadvertent, premature exposure. And in regard to this, Eden was probably more worried about the effects of a leak to his friends in Washington than to his enemies in Cairo. Eden might have lost however he played his cards, but his excessive secrecy with regard to the Israelis may have cost Britain and France control of the Canal.

Just before the decision to cease fire reached Port Said at sunset on November 6, Generals Stockwell and Beaufre felt that, given forty-eight more hours, British and French troops could fan out along the Canal and consolidate their positions in the towns of Port Said and Ismailia. Politicians and soldiers in London and Paris later were to claim that, if this could have come to pass, Britain and France would have had a major bargaining chip—first, in countering the UN's cease-fire demands and, later, in influencing the withdrawal negotiations. As it was, they claimed, the tiny enclave they had been able to secure had given Eden and Mollet little or no leverage.

According to this theory, two days—three at the most—stood between success and failure of the Suez venture. Thus, if instead of waiting until just before the naval landings on the fifth of November, paratroopers and commandos had been dropped on the Canal as early as the second, or even the third, the British and French forces would have had at least an extra forty-eight hours of operations—even if Eden still had felt compelled to accept the UN's cease-fire demand on the night of November 6.

Suppose Eden had been ready to coordinate British military planning with the Israelis, not in the sense of "coordination" as a euphemism for secret collaboration, but rather of close cooperation? Suppose, as a result, British and French troops had been able to gain control over the entire Canal area instead of just a few square miles? Would this have made any difference? Such questions are academic, of course. But still, even decades later, they gnaw.

The key to the failure lies not only in the hopeless race between fast-moving political developments in London, Washington, New York, and Moscow and the lumbering, elephantine nature of the British and French military effort. It lies also in the eventual goal the attack was to achieve. In the end, the worried Anthony Eden watered down the objective until it bore only a faint resemblance to the original. As early as September, General Sir Kenneth Strong, one of the members of the Joint Intelligence Committee, had predicted that an attack on the Canal without taking Cairo and Alexandria was bound to fail. In the event, even the diluted objective of controlling the Canal was a casualty of poor strategy and timing. "I am not sure," Sir Winston Churchill told Viscount Antony Head some time later, "I should have dared to start, but I am sure I should not have dared to stop."[34]

On Wednesday, November 7, peace returned to the Middle East—if by "peace" is meant silent guns. But a state of tranquillity and harmony was well over the horizon—and still is, more than twenty years later. Only two weeks had passed between the secret meeting outside Paris and the whimpering finale to the grandiose scheme agreed upon there. Only seven days had gone by since Anthony Eden and Guy Mollet had taken their sweet but short-lived revenge on Gamal Abdel Nasser and John Foster Dulles. This was barely a speck of sand in the hourglass of Britain's long history, but for the grudging participant in the Sèvres agreement and the uncertain partner in the military venture, it must have seemed an eternity. The sun was setting at Suez on November 6 when Generals Stockwell and Beaufre first learned of the cease-fire. On that day, the sun was also setting on Britain as a world power—and on Anthony Eden, as well. After more than two centuries of ruling the waves, Britannia had become a vulnerable island. And, at the age of sixty, Eden had seen his world destroyed.

The cease-fire marked a moment of triumph for Gamal Nasser over the two great powers that had long dominated his country. The event enhanced his prestige and power within Egypt, in the Middle East, and throughout the unaligned and Communist world. Port Said was referred to in the Cairo press as "Egypt's Stalingrad." Through the magic of rhetoric it became the scene of victory rather than defeat.

"O brothers in Port Said," one newspaper proclaimed after the cease-fire, "we shall hasten to your side to scuttle and crush the enemy and dump him into the sea. . . . We shall go to you on our pilgrimage, O Port Said. We shall kiss the soil over which you fought. . . . We shall fight courageously and fiercely in the canal, in the delta, and in the countryside. We shall never allow the enemy to stay. If we are not shooting today, it is because we want to preserve peace."[35]

"In the end," wrote Nasser's confidant, Mohamed Heikal, "the Suez affair became a personal business, a duel between two men. It . . . could only end in total victory for one and total defeat for the other. Nasser won and he never felt one speck of pity for Eden."[36]

10

EXODUS

London seemed an eerie place in the days immediately following the cease-fire. The mood music had, at first hearing, a lyrical quality characterized by themes of relief, even of hope. But one did not have to strain very hard to detect another theme in a minor key, echoing a deep sense of resignation, even of despair. And through it all, there were discordant notes of bitterness and anger.

The government—as all governments tend to do when their sun begins to set—was putting up a brave front. Members of Parliament (or, at least, *Conservative* members) were jollying-up their constituencies: "All is well," they said. And inveterate wishful thinkers among the civil servants were assuring each other in their pubs and clubs that, indeed, all was well. But the pound was skittish, the stock market uncertain, and the economic outlook generally grim. Clearly, all was *not* well. A worrisome number of worried British sensed a grim winter ahead—a winter of indeterminate duration.

The lines of young men and women stretching along the north side of Grosvenor Square were first noticeable on Wednesday, the day of the cease-fire. I saw them there on Thursday. And Friday, too. And on every weekday throughout the remainder of the year. Thousands of Britain's most adventurous and most energetic were waiting their turn at the Canadian Immigration Office, and at the immigration offices of Australia and New Zealand. For them, the future now lay across the seas.

For others, the older and more settled ones, it was a time to hedge, if not to pull up stakes. One of these was a member of the Joint Intelligence Committee. A brilliant, if somewhat idiosyncratic intelligence specialist, he had three private preoccupations: the health of the Anglo-American alliance, the health of his investment portfolio, the health of his health. The Suez crisis had ravaged them all. He had had no more inkling than I of what was afoot at the end of October and he was even more outraged than I when it occurred.

My friend did not regard himself as your usual man in the street. The idea of packing up his career in Whitehall in exchange for a job on a sheep ranch would hardly have crossed his mind. Yet his undisguised disgust with Eden's policy and his subsequent decision to transfer most of his savings into American investments provided evidence that a spirit of wariness with respect to Britain's economic future was not confined solely to the young and footloose. By the weekend following the cease-fire, he had somewhat recovered from the trials of the previous two weeks, but he never forgave Eden for the damage done to Anglo-American relations, to his portfolio, and to his digestion.

The second Sunday of November is "Remembrance Sunday" in Britain. Wreaths are laid at the graves and monuments honoring those who died in Britain's wars. In 1956, an accident of the calendar caused Remembrance Sunday and Armistice Day to coincide. November 11, 1956, then, was a time for more than the casual passing thoughts usually given to the issues of war and peace. The short-lived but tragic war in the Middle East seemed as much on British minds that day as the infinitely longer, infinitely bloodier wars that ended in 1918 and 1945. "It is as if we had lost a major battle—without casualties," Sir Oliver Franks, the former British ambassador to Washington, said. "We were disembowelled."[1]

Strident voices were still berating Eden and his government, but many others were raised in defense of the Suez venture. For these, Eden's policy was in the highest tradition of Britain's centuries-old role of the protector of world order. *The Sunday Times* put Suez in historical perspective when it reminded its readers that ". . . our survival depends on the will to act quite as much as the ability to understand the sweep of history in our time. It is now obvious, both from the proof of huge-scale supply of Soviet arms to Egypt and from the still-menacing threat of Soviet intervention, that the Anglo-French action in the Suez Canal area intercepted a danger far greater even than that of a general Middle Eastern war. The dreadful vision emerges of an Arab bloc, armed and backed to the hilt by Soviet Russia engaged in a death struggle with Israel."

The Observer, too, reached back into the past on that day: "It is long since opinion in Britain has been so keenly and deeply divided as it has been throughout the Suez Canal crisis. The strongest feelings—patriotism and the sense of right and wrong—have been aroused. . . . Underlying these feelings there have been two haunting memories—how we failed to deal with Hitler until world war was upon us; and how matters had once been better for the world and for this country, in the 19th century, when there was a Pax Britannica."

Some thoughtful observers took the occasion of Remembrance Sunday to extricate whatever modest treasure could be salvaged from the wreck. "The Government faces bitter criticism for the line it has taken," wrote Nobel Laureate Sir Norman Angell that day. "Yet its policy has produced this magical result . . . that a UN police force has actually come into being."[2]

Eden must have been heartened by these supportive sentiments and by the thousand telegrams of approval received at the Conservative central office, but they hardly compensated for the hard realities he had to confront during the days immediately ahead. On the very evening of the cease-fire he had to break the news to the House of Commons that oil consumption would have to be cut by 10 percent. With the Suez Canal blocked, all but one of the Syrian pipelines blown up, and—a new shock —the refusal of Saudi Arabia to sell to British and French customers, supplies from the Middle East had been sharply cut back. Since this region supplied Britain with 75 percent of its oil and France 90 percent, the prospects were gloomy; a shortfall of 45 percent appeared likely.

The attack on Egypt and the impending oil shortages created other problems. Unemployment, for one: Eight thousand dockers, 11 percent of the country's total dock force, were out of work because of the delays involved in rerouting shipping around the Cape of Good Hope. Financial weakness, for another: The pound was being traded at a worrisome discount, and there were tremendous pressures on Britain's reserves.

Economic difficulties represented only a part of the prime minister's burden in the early post-Suez days. Despite some rallying of support, it was clear that much of the country continued to be dissatisfied with Eden's Middle East venture and with him. On November 13, a British Gallup poll reported that barely a third of the people queried thought "Great Britain was right to take military action in Egypt."* And a few days later, less than half said they were "satisfied with Mr. Eden as Prime Minister." Clearly, he would have to fight for his political life in the weeks ahead.

Anthony Eden's troubles did not stop at the shores of the United Kingdom. Considering the outcome of the Suez war, it was not surprising that there were unpleasant murmurings from across the channel. For the French, the consequences of the debacle were more immediate than for the British. At stake was the battle for Algeria. The consensus, both within the French government and outside it, was that the cease-fire was premature, was implemented against their wishes, and would provide a tremendous psychological uplift for the Algerian nationalists.

Late at night on November 5, Guy Mollet had called his cabinet into session to discuss the possibility of a cease-fire. François Mitterand, now

---

*In late September 1956, 23 percent of the Gallup sample felt that "if England and France decide to use armed force against Egypt" troops and ships (as opposed to warplanes) should be employed.

head of the French Socialist Party and then a cabinet minister, suggested that Mollet publicly order General Beaufre to cease fire, but, privately, indicate that French troops should advance to Cairo. Mitterrand thought this would be a perfect opportunity simultaneously to eliminate Nasser and also Egyptian aid to Algeria. Mollet flirted with this proposition, but then dismissed it; the French would be unable to carry on without British logistics and fire support.[3]

The French laid much of the failure of the Suez attack squarely on the doorstep of Her Majesty's Government, although there was some official understanding of, even sympathy for, the pressures besetting Eden. On November 11, the influential newspaper *Le Figaro* wrote of the "culpable, if excusable, British weakness." And, then, a few days later: "France . . . was the only one in the Suez affair who viewed the situation properly and conducted herself energetically. England, once the decision was made, hesitated. . . . It was up to England, the greatest user of the Canal, to intervene to assure free transit. . . . Why was it that England, after having taken a stand consistent with its traditions, became seized with worry and was so ready to accept the arguments of those who said she was wrong?" Despite an official show of cordiality, the Entente Cordiale was showing signs of strain.*

Meanwhile, the Anglo-American special relationship was still floundering. To be sure, the cease-fire lanced the boil and the President's phone call, immediately after, partly soothed Eden's pain. (Mollet, for his part, was so confident after his conversation with Eden following the President's call that he told the National Assembly on Wednesday night, November 7, that the differences between France and the United States over the Suez invasion had now been repaired.) But the telegrams to London and Paris from Washington that came on the heels of Eden's talk with Eisenhower extinguished the high hopes of both the prime minister and the premier that bygones would be bygones.

Ike's message insisted that the United Nations Emergency Force be dispatched as soon as possible. British and French troops should not only be excluded from the Force but be withdrawn from Egypt as soon as the UN was in place. Both Eden and Mollet felt that Eisenhower was treating Britain and France as aggressors. Washington's position made a mockery of Eden's postattack rationale that British and French forces comprised an advance guard of UN peacekeepers. It all but tore away the last of the prime minister's credibility. The President, unconsciously perhaps, was

---

*In his memoirs, however, Eden continued to believe, or at least to profess, that "there was no recrimination [by the French], political or military, either then or later" (*Full Circle*, p. 645).

treating Britain as Britain had been trying to treat Israel—casting it in the role of the villain. Relations between Washington and London, and Washington and Paris, reverted to the tense, cold state of the past several weeks.

Soon after receiving Eisenhower's message, Mollet and Eden decided that an immediate fence-mending mission to Washington was essential. Eden called his old friend Eisenhower to solicit an invitation and was relieved when the President gave him an encouraging response. But neither Eden nor Eisenhower had reckoned with the mood in Foggy Bottom. In the view of Acting Secretary Hoover and other officials, a visit by the prime minister and the premier to Washington before Britain and France had complied with the United Nations' resolution was bound to be regarded by the Third World as American connivance with the ex-imperial powers; any credit the United States had accumulated in the Middle East, Africa, and Asia during the previous ten days would be dissipated. Hoover phoned Dulles at Walter Reed Hospital to ask him to turn Eisenhower around. The secretary promptly called the White House to urge him to withdraw the invitation. A few hours later Eisenhower informed Eden that the visit was off.[4]

Eisenhower was embarrassed. But Eden was crestfallen. He would have to face difficulties at home and pressures from the United Nations without any assurance that his ties with the United States had been reestablished. Eden had hoped to go before the House of Commons that evening to announce to the honorable members that he and Mollet had been invited to Washington. Adding further to his chagrin, Opposition Leader Gaitskell forced him into a commitment that British forces would not push out of their present tiny enclave near Port Said and would not be reinforced.

"I should feel much more confident," Eden wrote to Eisenhower a few hours after he had received the disappointing news, "about the decisions and actions which we shall have to take in the short term if we had first reached some common understanding . . . on matters such as this. . . . I would feel much happier if we had been able to meet and talk them over soon. . . . I still hope that it may be possible for us to meet within the next few days."[5] It was not possible. Indeed, a meeting between President Eisenhower and Prime Minister Eden on the Middle East or any other subject would never be held again.

The cease-fire did not perceptibly abate the pressures from New York. Now that the fighting was over, the United Nations insisted on the earliest possible withdrawal of French and British troops from Port Said and of Israeli forces from Sinai. But if this were to happen, the Secretariat would first have to organize and dispatch "UNEF," the United Nations Emergency Force.

Eden was later to claim that a United Nations peacekeeping force was his idea. In a speech to the House on the night of November 1, he suggested that the United Nations might "take over the physical task of maintaining the peace" in the Middle East. Early on November 1, however—before Eden's speech in Parliament—the concept conceived by Canada's Minister of External Affairs Lester Pearson was discussed in detail at a Canadian Cabinet meeting.* It was agreed that Pearson should leave immediately for New York and persuade the General Assembly to urge Britain and France to make their forces available to the United Nations. Ottawa surely must have informed London of this idea, and Eden probably took his cue from Pearson when he spoke to the House of Commons several hours later.

In any case, Pearson discovered when he arrived in New York that the majority of the delegates would not entertain the prospect of British and French participation in a UN peacekeeping force. He revised his plan accordingly and then consulted with Secretary Dulles. Dulles agreed to support Pearson's proposition providing it did not delay UN action on the American proposal for an immediate cease-fire. Pearson then discussed the UN force with Secretary-General Hammarskjöld at lunch on November 2. Hammarskjöld was initially wary, but he finally agreed. Later that day Dulles' cease-fire proposal was approved by the General Assembly. Late in the evening on November 3, Pearson proposed the UNEF: "I would like to submit to the Assembly a very short draft resolution: The General Assembly . . . requires, as a matter of priority, the Secretary-General to submit to it within forty-eight hours a plan for setting up . . . an emergency international United Nations force to secure and supervise the cessation of hostilities. . . ." Well before dawn on Sunday, November 4, the resolution was adopted. Twenty-four hours later Hammarskjöld submitted the plan to the General Assembly. UNEF was born.

By November 7, some progress had been made in organizing the Emergency Force. India, Sweden, Denmark, Norway, Colombia, Finland, Indonesia, Brazil, and Canada had agreed to contribute troops. The force would be under the command of General E. L. M. Burns (the Canadian soldier who had headed the UN group established to monitor the truce after the 1948 Arab-Israeli war). The United States agreed to airlift the UNEF troops from their home bases to a staging area in southern Italy. But much more had yet to be done before Pearson's idea was to take

*Pearson later received the Nobel Peace Prize for his UNEF idea.

form. A critical obstacle was Egypt's consent to the indefinite presence of UN troops on its territory.

Nasser had initially agreed in principle to a United Nations force in the area of Port Said that would supervise the British and French withdrawal. A few days later, however, he posed some difficult questions: What nations would be represented in the force? How long would the force remain after the British and French troops left? Where would it exercise its authority? What role did it plan to play in connection with the Canal itself? Would Israel have UN troops stationed on its side of the border?

Hammarskjöld, now that UNEF was actually taking form, was concerned that Nasser's reservations would be seized upon by the Soviet Union as an excuse to renew its proposal to dispatch its own armed forces to the area. Meanwhile, Communist China, not then a member of the UN, was attempting to score a point or two on its own: On November 7, the Egyptian ambassador to Peking disclosed that "280,000 Chinese" had volunteered for military service in Egypt. The secretary-general sent a message to Cairo reminding Nasser that "any wavering from Egypt's side now would undoubtedly isolate Egypt in world opinion which so far has been its best protection. It would further open possibilities . . . which if they were to materialize, would be just as much against what I know to be your hopes as against the interests of us all."[6]

As if to help Nasser read between the lines of Hammarskjöld's message, the Tass News Agency on November 10 reported that

> The Peoples of the USSR are unanimous in the condemnation of those guilty in the aggressive war against the Egyptian people and fully support the resolute measures of the Soviet Government aimed at cutting short aggression in Egypt. . . . The USSR is fully determined to give effect to the statements contained [in Bulganin's letters to Eden, Mollet, and Ben-Gurion] unless an end is put to aggression against Egypt. . . . In leading Soviet circles it has been stated that if Britain, France, and Israel, contrary to the decisions of the UN, do not withdraw all their forces from the territory of Egypt . . . the appropriate authorities of the USSR will not hinder the departure of Soviet citizen volunteers who wish to take part in the struggle of the Egyptian people for their independence.

Nasser may have been impressed by Hammarskjöld's arguments, but not enough to allay his worries about the inclusion of Canadian troops in the UN contingent. The Canadians, he told Hammarskjöld, could not be trusted; they would simply act as surrogates for the British. In a speech to the Egyptian people a few days after the cease-fire, Nasser applied pressure on a sensitive negotiating point: "So long as there is one foreign soldier in Egypt," he told a cheering audience, "we shall not begin clearing the Canal."

The secretary-general regarded Nasser's attempt to influence the composition of UNEF as an unacceptable intrusion on his own authority. In his view, Egypt would have to accept the Canadians or the whole plan would collapse. The Egyptians claimed, in turn, that their sovereignty would be violated by the presence of UN troops, whatever their composition. In exasperation, Hammarskjöld wrote to Foreign Minister Fawzi: "I have done my best to help you. . . . I feel entitled to trust that in the name of our joint interest you will help me by putting the stand I must take on my own rights in the right perspective."[7] The message did the trick. On the fourteenth, Fawzi gave Hammarskjöld's UNEF a green light. The secretary-general immediately left for Naples, where some UN contingents were already waiting to fly to Egypt. On the sixteenth, he flew to Port Said with an advance force of Colombian troops. He then proceeded to Cairo. There, after three days of hard bargaining, the Egyptians insisted that UNEF could remain in Egypt only with their consent, agreed to accept Canadian air and support units, and requested UN help in clearing the Canal.

For the past many weeks the UN had been trying to sandwich consideration of Soviet aggression in Hungary between sessions on the Middle East. But the attack on Egypt had captured most of the attention of delegates and staff. Moreover, there was a noticeable lack of interest among the "unaligned" delegations in Moscow's activities in Eastern Europe.

In Hungary, meanwhile, the new Soviet-controlled regime had tightened its grip, but there was little, if any, news of what was occurring there. Elsewhere in Eastern Europe, the Czech premier had warned that "an iron fist" would be used against anyone creating disorder, and the Poles had demanded that all Soviet advisers be withdrawn from their country. The Soviet-Polish frontier was now teeming with Soviet troops, and border crossing points were closed.

Hammarskjöld had hoped to stop off in Hungary on his way back to New York from Cairo. By the nineteenth, however, he had not received a reply to his request to visit Budapest. He returned directly to New York.

Since the end of October the United States had been finding its position in the United Nations increasingly uncongenial. President Eisenhower, Secretary Dulles, and Ambassador Lodge could hardly have relished the company they found themselves cultivating in their efforts to force Britain, France, and Israel first to cancel their attacks, then to cease fire, and finally to withdraw. While the Soviet Union was simultaneously mocking the Administration's vaunted policy of "liberating" Eastern Europe and getting away with murder in Hungary, Washington allied itself with Moscow, Moscow's satellites, and Moscow's acolytes against America's NATO allies.

Eisenhower, Dulles, and Lodge were forced to imbibe heavy doses of bitter medicine in New York. But after the agreement to comply with the UN's cease-fire resolution, America's participation in the UN's Middle East debates was conducted in a lower key. Away from the United Nations, the Administration was more helpful. As soon as it was clear that Eden had decided to order a cease-fire, Washington approved London's request for assistance to support the pound and waived the interest payment due in December on an outstanding loan. But this, by no means, meant that all was forgiven.

Foreign policy planning rarely takes account of the "what-if?" factor. Elegant policy structures are erected on assumptions based on what planners and decision makers know—or think they know. Because the planners in the Department of State and in many other foreign offices throughout the world are a select group of bright specialists, their explicit or implicit assumptions frequently turn out to be valid. Frequently, but not always. When they guess wrong, the carefully enunciated policy swings and sways, sometimes even collapses. In contrast to military planners, they tend to pay little attention to alternative courses or lines of retreat. The foreign policy process has little time or tolerance for embarrassing questions that start with, "But what if . . ." As a consequence, while there is usually a robust "Plan A," there is rarely a "Plan B."

Eden, Mollet, and Ben-Gurion had a firm "Plan A." It assumed that, despite obvious reservations in Washington concerning use of force to resolve the Canal dispute, Eisenhower and Dulles would support them when the chips were down. If anyone sitting at a conference table in London, Paris, or Jerusalem had asked, "But what if they do not?" he must have been given short shrift.

Eisenhower and Dulles, for their part, had assumed that their friends and allies would recognize the importance the Administration placed on a diplomatic solution to the Suez problem in the autumn of 1956. Apparently no one in Washington had the temerity to ask, "But what if they go ahead?"*

In late October, Eden, Mollet, Ben-Gurion, Eisenhower, and Dulles

---

*Western statesmen are not alone in this tendency toward narrow-angle vision. Probably no one asked Mr. Khrushchev, some years later, "What if the Americans discover the missile sites in Cuba before the sites become operational?"

were all unpleasantly surprised. And there is nothing that great men appreciate less. An unexpected unpleasantness puts them off balance, sends them scurrying back to reexamine sacred premises, and distorts familiar policies beyond recognition.

Mollet, Eden, and Ben-Gurion had treated Washington to a very nasty surprise. It was bad enough that the President and the secretary had not been consulted before the event; they had not even been warned. To add insult to injury, they had been taken unaware at a time when they were counting on preserving an equilibrium in America's relations with its allies and keeping an even keel in foreign policy.

Although Eisenhower had won his election handily, the Republicans failed to gain seats in either the Senate or the House. This meant that the President would have to run the country for at least another two years plagued by an unfriendly Congress. In the offices of the White House and in the cloakrooms of the Capitol there was muttering that the Republicans' poor showing in the congressional elections was, in part at least, a consequence of Eden's and Mollet's unanticipated, embarrassing Suez adventure. The Administration was thus in no mood to let the prime minister and the premier easily off the hook; Britain and France would have to get out of Egypt quickly, without any face-saving shenanigans or cosmetics. And ditto for Israel in the Sinai.

Oil was the big stick to be used against London and Paris, the threat of further curtailment of economic and political support against Jerusalem. Washington made it plain that, despite already-evident shortages, economic dislocations, and the onset of winter, Britain and France could not expect the United States to make oil available from the Western Hemisphere until after their forces had been completely withdrawn from Egypt. To Eden, the United States "seemed to be dominated by one thought only, to harass their allies."[8]

Israel, too, was the recipient of a barely disguised warning. "Statements attributed to your government to the effect that Israel does not intend to withdraw from Egyptian territory . . . have been called to my attention," Eisenhower wrote Ben-Gurion on November 7. "I must say, frankly, Mr. Prime Minister, that the United States views these reports, if true, with deep concern. Any such decision . . . would seriously undermine the urgent efforts being made by the United Nations to restore peace in the Middle East. . . . I need not assure you of the deep interest which the United States has in your country, nor recall the various elements of our policy of support to Israel in so many ways. . . . I urge you to comply with the resolutions of the United Nations General Assembly . . . and to make your decision known immediately. It would be a matter of the greatest regret to all my countrymen if Israeli policy on a matter of such grave concern to the world should in any way impair the friendly cooperation between our two countries."9

The message, with its coy references to continued "support" and "friendly cooperation," was followed by one sent from Acting Secretary Hoover to Foreign Secretary Golda Meir.10 The warning from the State Department was by no means coy; it openly spoke of possible economic sanctions. The Israelis could now be in no doubt about Washington's mood. Hammarskjöld's views were also clear: He told newsmen in New York that Israel was endangering world peace. Within forty-eight hours, Ben-Gurion cabled Eisenhower that "upon the conclusion of satisfactory arrangements with the United Nations in connection with this international force entering the Suez Canal area,"11 they would withdraw. A similar cable was sent to Hammarskjöld. This must have been a difficult step for the Israeli prime minister. Now, when the borders at last seemed secure, there was little inclination in Israel to return to the *status quo ante*. Ben-Gurion confronted an angry Knesset after he made his withdrawal announcement on November 8. The fact that the prime minister's commitment to withdraw Israeli troops was conditioned on the "satisfactory" organization and deployment of UNEF made little difference; sooner or later, his critics felt, the fedayeen terrorists would be back.

Britain and France, too, had qualified their acceptance of the cease-fire and their readiness to bring their troops home from Egypt. They sought assurances that "the international force to be set up will be competent" to supervise the cease-fire and clear the Canal. To complicate Hammarskjöld's problems, Eden and Mollet had sugared the withdrawal pill at home by making oblique, generalized statements to their parliaments and their press to the effect that UNEF would have a role in establishing "international control over the Canal."

Almost two weeks after the cease-fire, British, French, and Israeli forces were still ensconced in the positions they held when the whistle blew. Meanwhile, the situation in the British-French occupation area was becoming increasingly flammable. Soon after the fighting stopped, Nasser's government began to move arms and paramilitary forces into and around the British and French military enclaves. Residents of Port Said suspected of cooperating with the occupiers were harassed or severely punished. Egyptian sniping, sabotage, and terrorism were rampant. Frustrated, angry British and French troops responded, tit for tat.

In mid-November the advance contingent of UN troops arrived in Port Said. Several hundred Cairo policemen came in their wake. Heartened by the presence of the Egyptian police and no doubt encouraged by them, the local population ran wild. Grenades were lobbed at British troopers, and soon there were large-scale attacks on British sentry and command posts. A major of the Royal Scots Regiment was killed in the melee, and that night the troopers of the regiment were given leave and implied permission to avenge the major's death. More than a score of Egyptians were shot. Some time later, Anthony Moorhouse, a lieutenant in the West Yorkshire Regiment, was kidnapped. The cease-fire that had been so tortuously achieved seemed about to melt away.

The Egyptian attacks were by no means unwelcome to the Allied Command. "Happily . . . there still remained some possibility of a resumption of operations," the long-suffering French commander, André Beaufre, recalled. "On 21 November . . . we immediately began to draw up a new plan for an advance to the city of Suez. . . . By the 24th all was ready and everyone was convinced that we should reach Suez by the end of the first day."[12]

Hammarskjöld knew well that, as each day passed, the uneasy truce was becoming more precarious. On his return to New York on November 19, he moved quickly to complete the organization of the United Nations force. On November 28, he was able to tell the UN that the Emergency Force had finally been established with a strength of 4,500 men. Approximately 1,400 UNEF troops were already in Egypt; within a few days another 2,700 would be deployed.

Selwyn Lloyd was then in New York attending the opening sessions of the autumn General Assembly meetings. He spent some harried days consulting with Britain's few sympathetic friends about the terms for withdrawal. Included in Lloyd's package was a phased removal of British and French forces after UNEF was finally in place, the maintenance of a UNEF presence in the Canal area and along the Egyptian-Israeli truce line until the Canal was cleared and pacification was completed, an immediate UN effort to clear the Canal, a continuing effort by the UN to insulate the Canal from national politics, and a major UN effort to resolve Arab-Israeli tensions. In the event, an agreement was reached on only the first three British conditions.

Hardly had the foreign minister left for London when the secretary-general and the British ambassador discussed a target date for British and French withdrawal. Mid-December was settled upon. It was agreed that on the following day, November 29, Lloyd would announce this to the House of Commons. But at the last minute Lloyd backed off. The British, he said in a message to Hammarskjöld, would have to consult with the French before agreeing to the mid-December date. In addition, London and Paris would have to be satisfied that UNEF was big enough for the job, that operations were under way to clear the Canal, and that some progress was being made toward an overall settlement of the Canal dispute. Lloyd told Hammarskjöld that London was also worried by Nasser's claims that "a state of war" still existed and wanted assurance that British and French ships would have free passage through the Canal, once it was cleared. Hammarskjöld received a promise of "free passage" from Foreign Minister Fawzi. He then urged Lloyd to take the rest "on faith."

The next opportunity for Lloyd to announce a withdrawal date came on December 3, when he was scheduled to make a major address to the House of Commons. In his speech, Lloyd reviewed, once again, the background of and the rationale for the government's Suez policy. He warned of the danger of the USSR's growing presence in the Middle East. As a consequence of the large Soviet arms shipments to Egypt, Nasser was "very much under Soviet influence." The British and French intervention "not only rapidly halted local hostilities, but forestalled the development of a general war throughout the Middle East and perhaps far beyond. . . . As soon as the two parties agreed to a cease-fire, we also gave orders to cease our military action." In an effort "to interpose a force to prevent the resumption of fighting . . . we made the request to station detachments in Port Said, Ismailia and Suez for a temporary period. The Prime Minister . . . on November 1st stated we should be glad if the United Nations would take over the physical task of preserving peace. . . . The French and British Governments have come to the conclusion that the withdrawal of their forces in the Port Said area can now be carried out without delay."

Lloyd then moved on to the question of Israel. "Israel should withdraw from Egyptian territory. We have said this repeatedly. With regard to the Gaza strip, it is our view that Israel should withdraw from that also."

And finally: "I claim that we have stopped a local war. We have prevented it spreading. The extent of Soviet penetration has been revealed. We have caused the United Nations to take action by the creation of an international force. We have alerted the whole world to a situation of great peril. We have created conditions under which there can be hope of wider settlements."[13]

It was an astonishing speech, the last gasp of a dying policy. Self-serving, false in detail, and misleading overall, the foreign secretary's remarks were a desperate effort to fiddle the books of a bankrupt venture. Selwyn Lloyd had been kept in the dark when, in mid-October, the foundation for the ill-fated enterprise was first laid. The speech he felt bound to make in Commons on December 3 must have been a painful experience. But he was still Eden's foreign secretary and had to swallow his pride—just one more penance the loyal minister had to pay.

Lloyd himself must have been troubled by this and many other aspects of his post as foreign minister, first under Eden and later under

Macmillan. Years later, when his party was out of power, he had lunch with Richard Crossman, then in the Labour cabinet. Crossman found the ex-foreign minister "amusing and lighthearted." "How you have changed, Selwyn," Crossman said. "Well," Lloyd replied, "there is nothing like being kicked out of your job—especially if you get a job too early, as I did in the Foreign Office—to make a man of you."[14]

Lloyd's dissembling and discomfiture was of little immediate interest to the secretary-general; what concerned him was what was missing from the speech, rather than what was said. And what was missing was an announcement of the date when the British would get out of Egypt. Within hours Hammarskjöld took the initiative. Late in the afternoon of December 3 the secretary-general ordered UNEF to prepare to take over Port Said from the British and French troops "by the middle of December." His orders were released to the press in time for the next morning's edition.

Hammarskjöld now had to firm up arrangements for clearing the Canal as soon as possible after the departure of the British and French. A Dutch and a Danish firm were engaged. Their preliminary survey of the damage found that the job would be even more difficult than earlier suspected. Fifty-one tremendous chunks of stone and steel, including two fallen bridges and more than thirty sunken vessels, had to be removed from the waterway. To expedite the process the British and French agreed that their salvage vessels already in the area could be employed in the clearance effort. Their ships would fly the UN flag and be manned with foreign crews.

Britain and France had had a few difficult weeks since the cease-fire, but by now Israel could not have cared less. When push came to shove, Israel's allies had rushed to wrap themselves in a cloak of righteousness. Eden and Mollet had insisted that Israel should immediately obey the UN resolution, while at the same time they were trying to wriggle their own way out of early compliance. They even had the gall to criticize the Israeli invasion of Sinai. Finally, the British had pressed Hammarskjöld on freedom of navigation, but it was French and British shipping that was specifically mentioned; Israeli shipping was conspicuously ignored. It is not surprising that there was no hue and cry in Israel to "bring the boys home." At the very least, the Israelis expected to maintain troops at Sharm-el-Sheikh to assure freedom of passage through the Gulf of Aqaba and along the Gaza Strip for security on that vulnerable southwest border with Egypt.

On November 7, Anthony Eden discovered that his Suez policy had ended on the worst possible note; he was regarded as an aggressor abroad, but he was no hero at home. For weeks now he had been inhabiting one of Dante's circles in Hell. His doctor, sensing that Eden was on the brink of breakdown, pleaded that he take a respite from the pressures of Downing Street. But the prime minister doggedly pushed himself, hour by hour, through awful days and worse nights. To make matters worse, Eden, the loner, had few people aside from his wife to whom he could turn.

During that autumn, the prime minister, an old Etonian, frequently called Eton's headmaster to discuss his problems. And at the height of the tension, in early November, Eden drove to Eton to sit at the feet of his favorite old teacher, now in his eighties, to bare his soul and to seek approval and reassurance. It was a subconscious quest for the security of his boyhood, a pathetic voyage back to the womb.[15]

Finally, on November 23, the combination of his own exhaustion and a slight lull in the affairs of state persuaded Eden to seek some sun and rest. With his wife, Clarissa, he flew off to Jamaica.

"What made Anthony leave the country?" Lord Moran, Churchill's doctor, asked his patient a few days later. "I am shocked by what he did," Churchill replied. "I should have not done half the work he has been doing; I'd have got others to do it. He let them wake him up at all hours of the night to listen to news from New York."[16]

Eden left his government and the myriad of problems that formed the residue of his benighted Middle East venture in the hands of R. A. ("Rab") Butler, the lord privy seal.

High on Butler's long laundry list were the oil shortages in Britain; the mounting pressures from the UN, the Commonwealth, and the United States; and the need to demonstrate to his countrymen that the British and French position in the UN would stimulate progress in resolving the Canal dispute. For Eden's government this last matter was the heart of the problem.

Eden's absence just at a time when the terms of withdrawal from Port Said were being negotiated worried the Conservative rank and file. Even party moderates were muttering angrily that their government now seemed unwilling or unable to drive any sort of a bargain in exchange for taking its troops out of Egypt. Butler was suspected by the hard-liners of having been, at best, a lukewarm supporter of Eden's Suez policy. The French, too, were wary; word spread quickly around the Quai d'Orsay, when the news of his temporary stewardship was announced, that the lord privy seal had actually opposed the enterprise.[17] Few of his critics seemed to grasp how little leverage Butler could bring to bear in the negotiations for withdrawal.

Perhaps the most difficult task Butler had to face, even more difficult than arranging the graceful extrication of British forces from Egypt, was mending London's mangled relations with Washington and the United Nations. "We cannot repair [the relationship] . . . any more than we are doing," Butler told a *Newsweek* reporter soon after Eden left the country. "At the moment we could not be more coldly treated. . . . We want to work with the UN, but there must be a shift in their position, too. It is not the battalions that matter, it is the spirit of the thing."[18]

It fell to Butler to preside over the withdrawal arrangements on terms significantly less satisfactory than Eden and Butler himself in turn had insisted upon. Even with the boldest face he could put on the agreement, it was clear to all that the Suez Canal would remain under Nasser's sole control.

A seemingly refreshed Eden returned to London on December 14. *The Times* tempered the warmth of its welcome with advice and admonitions: "There are two aspects of affairs to which the Government must now address themselves with all possible speed. The first is that of general policy—restriction or expansion. . . . The second issue is that of efficiency. Leaving on one side whether the recent policy was right or wrong, there is more than one ground for saying that its execution was inefficient. . . . Either Sir Anthony Eden must now show that he can and will lead a vigorous, progressive, efficient Government or the strains that have been set up will demand someone else."

But if Eden had misgivings about what had taken place and what lay ahead, he did not reveal them when he arrived at London Airport. On the contrary: "I am convinced, more convinced than I have been about anything in all my public life, that we were right, my colleagues and I, in the judgments and decisions we took, and that history will prove it so."[19]

The prime minister may well have been the only man in the kingdom who displayed a sense of optimism in mid-December. He was returning to a worried, restive people and a divided, demoralized Conservative Party. Although the country's foreign exchange reserves had been increased by more than $1 billion and the pound had been strengthened in the international market, the economy was beginning to feel the full effect of the oil shortage. In early December the chancellor of the exchequer announced an increase in the tax on oil. This would raise the price of oil one shilling a gallon in addition to the price increases envisioned by wholesalers and retailers. There followed immediately a rise in the cost of a wide range of goods and services, from bus and taxi fares to home heating.

Hardly had Eden removed his homburg and his overcoat at Downing Street when he heard of a new blow to the economy—iron and steel prices would be raised 6 percent. And, then, on December 17, the government was forced to ration gasoline. To compound Eden's woes and to undermine the nation's morale further, Great Britain was hit by the worst storm in decades on Christmas night; roads were impassable in many areas and holiday celebrations were canceled all over the country. Soon after his return to London the prime minister must have begun to long for the peace and warmth—and the distance between him and Her Majesty's Opposition—that Jamaica had provided.

There had been much gossip in Paris and London during Eden's absence that Israel's attack had come as no surprise to the British and French governments, that the events of late October were not quite as the governments had portrayed them. The issue of "collusion" was raised in the press and in Commons. No one mounted the ramparts to accuse Eden and Mollet of lying, but there were deep suspicions—and not only among their opposition parties.

On November 22, Butler was asked in Parliament about the nature of the government's prior knowledge of Israel's intention to invade Sinai. Butler fell back on a statement Eden had earlier made to a similar question: The government, on learning of the Israeli mobilization on October 25, had urged "restraint." Butler then assured the House (to hoots of derision from the Opposition) that "that is the action we took and this is the information we received."[20]

The attack on the government's credibility was pushed by former Labour Prime Minister Attlee, who asked, in a letter to *The Times* on December 15, whether the British and French governments had known in advance of the Israeli invasion of Sinai. "No satisfactory answer has so far been given." With Eden's return, "the country may reasonably ask that he should put an end . . . to an uncertainty which cannot fail to be damaging to the national interest."

Lord Attlee was not alone in his curiosity about this delicate matter. Even members on Eden's side of the aisle challenged the government's official line. A young Conservative MP urged the prime minister on the floor of Commons to tell the nation whether Paris and London had agreed in advance to intervene in Egypt after the Israelis had attacked.

On December 20, Eden was goaded by the Labour front-benchers into addressing the issue: "I wish to make it clear that there was . . . not foreknowledge that Israel would attack Egypt . . . there was not. But . . . there was a risk of it, and in the event of the risk of it, certain discussions and conversations took place. . . ." This was by no means the end of the matter; Eden would be pursued by the collusion charge for years to come.

Premier Mollet and Foreign Minister Pineau had much easier going at home than their British counterparts. On three critical occasions the

Assembly, with little debate, gave Mollet's government overwhelming support: on October 30, when the government announced its intention to occupy Port Said, Ismailia, and Suez in order to guarantee freedom of passage through the Canal; on November 7, when Mollet announced that French "objectives have been realized"; and on December 4, when the government informed the Assembly that it was prepared to withdraw from Port Said and hand the problem over to the United Nations. The Assembly, especially during the turbulent years of the Fourth Republic, was normally not very tolerant of governments in power. Why was it so complaisant with Mollet during the autumn of 1956? The explanation probably lies in the surge of nationalist sentiment sparked by the saga of Indochina and the fighting in Algeria. The attack on Egypt was regarded by most Frenchmen as simply a flanking movement against the Algerian enemy. But when the Suez policy went sour and the story of its shadowy genesis began to leak out, Mollet was given a few rough moments.

In late December the Assembly had its first serious debate on Suez. As one delegate pointed out, the body had thus far been "far more discreet than certain other foreign parliaments" about questioning its government. But now that the Suez affair was winding up, Premier Guy Mollet should do some explaining; he had not been candid with the Assembly. On October 30, after the ultimatum, he told the delegates that the "French and British governments have fully informed the U.S. government of their concerns and their decisions." But, later, on American television, Mollet said, "If your [i.e., the U.S.] government . . . was not informed, and that is true, of the recent events . . . the only reason . . . was our fear that if we had informed it, it would have prevented us from acting."[21]

Foreign Minister Pineau took on the charge of collusion: "There has been a lot of talk, especially in Commons, about collusion among Israel, France, and Great Britain. I really don't see what the practical significance of that term could be. . . . It was normal for France and Great Britain to consult about the danger to Israel."

He then took a swing at his fellow Socialist Aneurin Bevan in Britain, who, early in December, had asked the House of Commons, "What happened? Did Marianne take John Bull to an unknown rendezvous? . . . Did Marianne deceive John Bull or seduce him?" "No, Monsieur Bevan," Pineau responded in his speech to the Assembly, "Marianne did not try to drag John Bull down the road to perdition. She simply searched with him, as is normal for a couple subjected by history to the harshest of ordeals, for a common political solution."

Finally, he acknowledged the pressure that Anthony Eden had suffered in Parliament. "We understood this . . . since we felt, during this same period, all the value of the moral support given to our Government by public opinion and by the French Parliament."[22]

Mollet took the offensive in his summing up. His pro-Israeli anti-UN and anti-American line appealed to the current French mood. "If Israel had done nothing, and if we, on our side, had let Israel be crushed by the coalition raised against it, what kind of reproaches would be heaped on us today? [Applause left, center, right] Did we then have to wait, to continue to wait, to wait for the irreparable, until the United Nations decided to intervene? Certainly, the same people would be asking us today to weep for Israel destroyed, as those with whom we weep together, helpless, for a martyred Hungary."

He reaffirmed the solidity of the French-American alliance and was sure that Eisenhower and the U.S. government also agreed to its importance. "But our allies must realize that there is no such thing as a demi-alliance. . . . The alliance cannot be a one-way street. [Cries of *"Très bien, très bien!"*]

"We were convinced that if we told Americans of our decision they would propose new talks, new delays and that during that time Israel risked disappearing. [Loud prolonged applause from the left, center, and right]"[23]

The session concluded with only a mild censure of Mollet and Pineau; the government won a vote of confidence by a majority of more than three hundred. The delegates were more angry about the shortage of gasoline than they were about being misled by the government.

Any hope that the cease-fire in Egypt would mute the anti-American feeling in Britain was quickly dispelled. Now that the short-lived war was over, the focus of popular attention shifted from the Middle East to emerging problems closer to home. There were two stark facts to face: The aftermath of Suez seriously diminished British international prestige. Even more important, it had sent reeling Britain's already staggering economy. Inevitably resentment heightened against Americans residing in England and the Administration in Washington, especially Secretary Dulles. "Mr. Dulles has lost no time in condemning us for the part which we are playing," Mr. R. G. Nicholson of Sheffield wrote to *The Sunday Times* on November 11. "It is only through his own past intransigence and ineffective mediation that this dangerous situation has arisen."

On Sunday, November 25, we decided to drive to Windsor for dinner, our first family outing in many weeks. Life at school for my daughters had improved somewhat after Miss Humphrey, the headmistress, explained to the more ardent young jingoists that Joan and Susan had little influence on American foreign policy. Although our British friends had remained tried and true, my wife was a convenient target for irate fishmongers and sullen salesgirls. As for me, the pace had eased with the reestablishment of contact between the embassy and the Foreign Office, but official relations were still cool.

We were driving along the Great West Road when I realized that the gas gauge was snuggling cozily between "1 Quarter" and "Empty." Luckily, there was an open service station close by. As I drove in I became aware of the hostile glance the attendant bestowed on our Chevrolet. "We're running short and rationing petrol these days, guv'nor." "How much are you selling?" "Three gallons—except to Americans. They get one." I bought the gallon and drove back to London.

That evening I read an editorial in *The Sunday Times* which added a footnote of documentation to our experience earlier in the day: ". . . the present vigorously anti-British policies of President Eisenhower and his Secretary of State," the writer warned, "are leading to a rapid and dangerous rise of anti-American feeling in Britain. . . . A belief is spreading that American policy is controlled by the oil lobby and that its object is total replacement of British influence and economic interest by America in the Middle East. . . . When we found we had been deceived [by Dulles' SCUA policy] confidence in the American Government's good faith was dealt a disastrous blow."

There were other, and more influential, people worried about the level to which Anglo-American relations had sunk. Sir Winston Churchill, ill as he then was, felt the need to intervene personally with Eisenhower: "Whatever the arguments adduced here and in the United States for or against Anthony's action in Egypt," Churchill wrote in a private letter to the President on November 23, "it will now be an act of folly, on which our whole civilization may founder, to let events in the Middle East come between us."[24]

"Dear Winston," the President replied, "I tried earnestly to keep Anthony informed of public opinion in this country. . . . But so far as Britain and France were concerned, we felt that they had deliberately excluded us from their thinking; we had no choice but to do our best to be prepared for whatever might happen. . . . The first news we had of the attack and of British-French plans was gained from the newspapers and we had no recourse except to assert our readiness to support the United Nations. . . . The Soviets are the real enemy. . . . Nothing would please us more . . . than to see British prestige and strength renewed and rejuvenated in the Mid-East . . . we want to help Britain right now, particularly in its difficult fuel and financial situation. . . . To me it seemed the action of the British Government was not only in violation of the basic principles [of the alliance], but that even by the doctrine of expediency the invasion could not be judged as soundly conceived and skillfully executed. . . . I shall never be happy until our old time closeness has been restored."

Ike was not simply being polite; he was genuinely anxious to close the breach. After he had abruptly turned down Eden's request to visit Washington following the cease-fire, the President told Sherman Adams that "turning down Eden's request for a personal talk did not seem the right thing to do. This was not the right time to be so concerned about appearance and propriety."[25]

A few days later, on November 30, President Eisenhower took a step that cleared away some of the clouds. Discussions between the secretary-general and Sir Pierson Dixon, the British ambassador to the United Nations, and his own talks with Ambassador Caccia convinced the President that the British seriously intended to pull their troops out of Egypt within a few weeks. And so: "The Director of the Office of Defense Mobilization . . . today requested the Secretary of the Interior to authorize fifteen United States oil companies . . . to assist in handling the oil supply problem resulting from the closing of the Suez Canal and some pipelines in the Middle East."[26]

Eisenhower's decision had come none too soon. The western-bound tankers that had sailed through the Canal before the fighting started had, by now, long since discharged their cargoes. In the face of dwindling stockpiles, the Organization for European Economic Cooperation* established an emergency allocation system apportioned on the basis of pre-Suez imports. The system had worked well for several weeks, but without additional supplies Britain and Western Europe would face a cold, difficult winter.

France, with little coal and an economy that was just beginning to recover from World War II, was especially hard hit by the oil shortages: French industry faced slowdowns, de facto rationing for motorists had been put into effect, and train schedules had been cut back. A week before Washington's release of Western Hemisphere oil, Premier Mollet discussed France's difficulties with representatives of the American business community in France. They, in turn, promptly sent a telegram to Washington urging the White House to move ahead quickly, lest impending fuel shortages lead to widespread misery.

---

*A group of industrialized nations, comprising the countries of Western Europe, Britain, Canada, and the United States; the predecessor to the present Organization for Economic Cooperation and Development (OECD).

December 22 marked the end of the British and French operation in Egypt. The Suez war was officially over. But Withdrawal Day 1956 bore little resemblance to Armistice Day 1918 or V-E Day 1945. While the forces of Britain and France were not coming home in defeat, they were certainly not returning crowned with the laurels of victory. It was simply that . . . well, they were just coming home. There were no parades, no galas. Rather, a muted, awkward welcome. Few were so unkind as to mar the mood of the day by saying it had all been a big mistake. But almost everyone felt it had been.

By late November, there were some 13,500 British and 8,500 French troops in Port Said. Five thousand vehicles and ten thousand tons of supplies had been put ashore. The repatriation of such a large force could not wait until the final moment, and so the homeward trek began soon after the date of withdrawal was announced. By December 22 only a few thousand British and French fighting men were still in Port Said, and these were grouped together behind a small perimeter manned by UNEF contingents. The allies' aircraft and warships remained close at hand in case the Egyptians were tempted to mount a last vengeful attack through the thin UN lines.

December 22 was an anticlimax in Britain and France. There had been so much waiting, so much tension in the fifty-four days since the ultimatum that most people in London and Birmingham, in Paris and Lille, were delighted to put the Middle East out of their thoughts and bury themselves in last-minute preparations for Christmas. But to the few thousand men awaiting orders to march to the dockside at Port Said, it was a day of drama and disappointment.

"It is hard to imagine a more thankless task than yours," Eden had telegraphed the commander of the British Expeditionary Force on the eve of withdrawal. "I have greatly admired the patience and the discipline which all ranks . . . have shown throughout this period. . . . I should like to send congratulations and gratitude. I am confident that as history unrolls your efforts will have been shown not to have been in vain."[27]

On the night before their departure a group of British soldiers and another of French set out on separate errands. The British attached a huge Union Jack to the flagpole behind the statue of Ferdinand de Lesseps which towered over Port Said. The French scaled the statue and implanted the tricolor in the hands of de Lesseps. The British and French garrisons, the UNEF contingents, and the Egyptian residents of the town awoke to find the two flags flying defiantly over the Suez Canal.

The Egyptians of Port Said marked Withdrawal Day by burning French and British flags and by joyous, impromptu parades. Thousands marched through the dusty streets of the town bearing pictures of Nasser and waving Egyptian flags. Cries of "Down with Eden and Mollet, long live Nasser!" echoed from building to building, from corner to corner. Throughout the day there was a deafening sound of rifle fire as Egyptian soldiers, policemen, and irregulars shot their weapons skyward as if to speed the enemy on their way.

Perhaps anticipating the sacking of the Suez Canal Company offices by Egyptian mobs, perhaps venting their own spite, the French loaded their ships with the company's furniture and rugs as well as a handsome clock given to de Lesseps by the Empress Eugénie. The British followed suit, packing off with the company's chandeliers and a marble bust of Napoleon.[28]

The French left first. At eleven o'clock in the morning General Beaufre and his aides saluted as the French flag was lowered and the UN flag raised over the French headquarters. "We then crossed the town on foot," General Beaufre recalls. "The balconies were crowded with Egyptians who seemed almost cordial." After the French forces paraded by, the generals and the admirals, the soldiers and sailors left Port Said. "Slowly, all lights burning, the ships glided out of the port. . . . Such was the last scene in a day full of emotion."[29]

The British departed at sunset. Although it had taken nearly a week to mount the landings, the final exit was accomplished in an hour. "As the sun sank behind tumultuous Arab town and coloured the clouds flamingo pink . . . the last tank or two in the final bridgehead rumbled slowly towards the quay . . . the last infantry marched peacefully through the gathering night to the waterfront . . . with a military band blowing blasts of defiance to the Arab town. . . . Left behind for a day or so is Lieutenant Anthony Moorhouse, who was abducted nearly a fortnight ago."[30] (Lieutenant Moorhouse did not come home in "a day or so," but he did eventually, in a coffin—the only hero to emerge from the Suez war.)

As night fell and the British and French fleets disappeared into the darkness, the lights went on in Port Said and in every other town and city in Egypt for the first time since the British air raids of November 2. When the last of the invaders had left the dock, the UNEF units there also withdrew—not to their home countries but westward toward Sinai to follow up the Israeli pullback. Responsibility for maintaining law and order in Port Said was handed over to the Egyptian police. On the twenty-fourth, within hours of UNEF's departure, the Egyptians vented their long-pent-up bitterness against the old Suez Canal Company. The statue of Ferdinand de Lesseps, the last link between the nineteenth century Suez Canal and modern Egypt, was dynamited. Its bits and pieces added to the debris that would have to be cleared from the waterway.

The old year was slipping away in Foggy Bottom. New Year's Eve was cold and damp; snow seemed poised, ready to pounce. The charwomen had already left the State Department building honoring the occasion with an even more than usual slapdash attack on ashtrays, trash baskets, and carpets. Except for a few unlucky duty officers, the great block of glass and stone was dark and empty.

The President and his secretary of state quietly buried 1956 with little sentiment and no nostalgia. To be sure, the Administration had been elected to a second term, full-scale war had been averted in Eastern Europe and the Middle East, and Ngo Dinh Diem, America's protégé, was firmly established in Saigon. But these were the only bright episodes in a year full of crises: Algeria, Jordan, the Aswan Dam, the nationalization of the Canal, the Israeli attack on Sinai, the French-British move against Egypt, Poland, Hungary, the Soviet intervention in Eastern Europe, the Kremlin's rocket threats, Dulles' operation.

The Foreign Office was always gloomy after dark, and on this damp and windy night, Monday, December 31, 1956, it was especially so. After months of frenetic late-hour activity, the big soot-stained building was now virtually deserted. Most of its inhabitants had been away since the weekend before Christmas; many others had left on the previous Friday afternoon, as if to chop off 1956 as early as possible—enough was enough.

Surely, Anthony Eden and Selwyn Lloyd must have been glad to see the last of that terrible year. But even the New Year seemed fraught with trouble. The government was fighting for its life, the economy was shaky, the Commonwealth was bleeding, the Americans were sulking, Cyprus was explosive, Britain's position in the Middle East was shattered, and Eden was desperately ill.

The past several weeks had seen a rash of Little England sentiment. *The Observer* had editorialized that ". . . the Suez crisis has shown that Britain has not got the resources to act as a Great Power, in her own right, even in a traditional sphere of British interest. . . . Where Great Power politics are concerned, we are dependent on America. We cannot assure our vital oil supplies by our own unaided efforts. We cannot defy Russia without full American backing. We cannot, therefore, go it alone."[31] The *Daily Herald* had written that, "stripped of its moral authority, exposed to the mistrust of the world, Great Britain is no longer an enduring Great Power."[32]

In Paris, too, December 31, 1956, offered little except a bridge in time from the known to the unknown. The year Guy Mollet and Christian Pineau had just experienced must have seemed an ominous prelude to dangerous times ahead. Following the debacle at Suez, prospects in Algeria were darker than ever. Mollet would have to deliver a victory there before long or his government, now still popular despite Suez, would go the way of its many predecessors in the Fourth Republic.

For the Israelis, 1956 was a different story with a different ending. Britain and France had been fighting to preserve their past. Israel was fighting to protect its future. The difference was critical. Ben-Gurion must have slept soundly that New Year's Eve behind secure borders and an open path to the sea.

In Moscow that night, the generals and the commissars must have been thanking their lucky stars that they had squeaked through the troubles of the autumn. In Warsaw there was grim satisfaction, and in Budapest there was sullen resignation.

But for some, 1956 had been a good year. In Cairo, Delhi, and Peking, 1956 would be regarded as a time of triumph, the year when the old imperial powers were in retreat.

Harry Truman had published his memoirs the year before. In the first few paragraphs he captured the essence of the mid-fifties: "What we have been living through," he wrote, "is, in fact, a period of nationalistic, social, and economic tensions. These tensions were in part brought about by shattered nations trying to recover from the war and by peoples in many places awakening to their right to freedom."[33]

11

CHANGE

Soon after the first of the year, relations between the London embassy and Whitehall returned to normal—or as normal as they could be, considering what had transpired over the past few months. Ambassador Aldrich had not come back to London, of course. He had been lied to, or at least had been led astray, by the Foreign Office, and that could never be put right. In due course, the new ambassador, John Hay Whitney, would arrive and could start with a clean slate. Until then, Minister Barbour would hold the fort.

As the outline of the events that preceded and followed the ultimatum of October 30 became clearer, both Americans and British became increasingly resentful and angry. Some directed their ire against Dulles, some against Eden, some against both. There was such a sense of muddle about villains and victims that it was difficult to predict whether a particular view would be likely to be held by an American Embassy officer or a British Foreign Office official.

There was a feeling of bafflement, too: Eden was a pragmatic, skilled negotiator; why had he not pursued the encouraging line of discussion Hammarskjöld had initiated with Egypt's Foreign Minister Fawzi in mid-October? Dulles was an artful diplomat; why had he not played out the Aswan negotiation a few more weeks while he discussed the next move with Paris and London? Since Eden put a high value on his relations with Eisenhower, why did he accede to the attack on Egypt on the eve of the presidential election? Since Dulles had a personal stake in the Suez Canal Users Association, why did he continue to sap its strength to the point where it went limp before the eyes of Eden and Mollet? If, as Eden had said, Nasser had to be destroyed, why did he suddenly change the focus of the operation from the overthrow of the government in Cairo to securing a foothold on the Suez Canal? And why did it take so long to mount the attack on Port Said? And why did Eisenhower insist on his pound of British and French flesh once the cease-fire had been honored? Why? Why? Again, one would have been hard-pressed to sort out the nationality of the questioner on the basis of his query. It was too soon after the event for anyone to be clear as to who or what had gone wrong.

As the months went by, my relations with members of the Joint

236

Intelligence Committee and its staff became even closer than they had been before Suez. Those long, awful days between the Israeli invasion and the cease-fire had been a common, terrible experience that had made us brothers in combat. And as old veterans are wont to do, we rehearsed and rehashed the events over beer at the pubs or over brandy after dinner —what had happened, what might have happened, who were the heroes, who the cowards. Some of my colleagues, a few senior ones who really knew, sat quietly by during these postmortems. On occasion, one could catch slight nods or barely perceptible shaking of heads or inadvertent winks among the knowing, but the Official Secrets Act dictated that they remain silent then, a few weeks after it was all over—and for decades to come.

"In the house of Fortune," warns Gracián, the shrewd seventeenth-century Spanish Jesuit, "if you enter by the gate of pleasure you must leave by that of sorrow—Fortune rarely accompanies anyone to the door; warmly as she may welcome the coming, she speeds but coldly the departing guest."

There has been a long procession of ambitious men in history to whom Gracián's admonishment would apply. Anthony Eden was not of this company. He was denied pleasure even when he entered the gate to fame and power; Fortune had kept him standing on the shady side of the threshold for a very long time. When, at long last, Winston Churchill beckoned him across, Eden was tired, sick, burned out. But he did leave by "the gate of sorrow"; Gracián was right in that.

Early in the New Year of 1957, the fever that a few months before had laid the prime minister low assaulted him again. His doctors warned that he would be plagued by such attacks for the rest of his life. "On the morning of 9 January I was working at the Treasury," Harold Macmillan recalls, "when a message was delivered summoning me to Number 10 at 3 o'clock—Eden was in the drawing room. . . . He told me with simple gravity, as a matter decided and not to be discussed, that he had decided to resign his office. . . . There was no way out. The doctors had told him the truth about his health and, though he was not a doomed man, it must be the end of his political life. . . . Throughout our short and painful conversation he was as charming and elegant and as dignified as ever. . . . What seemed so dreadful was that he waited for so long for the premiership, and held it for so short a time."[1]

On January 10, Anthony Eden announced his resignation from the office he had strained and trained for half his life. The matter-of-fact wording of his departure masked the poignancy of Eden's last official act. "I do not feel that it is right to continue in office as the Queen's First

Minister," Sir Anthony had written as his wife looked on, "knowing that I shall be unable to do my full duty by my Sovereign and my country. I have therefore decided, with the utmost regret, that I must tender my resignation to the Queen, which Her Majesty has been graciously pleased to accept."

Now, at sixty, after less than two years at "Number 10," the ex-prime minister was destined to live out his life searching for the warmth of the sun, for relief from pain, for vindication of the one disastrous step he had taken during his thirty years in politics. "Suez" would always remain a dirty four-letter word for Sir Anthony.

Eden had looked upon his campaign against Nasser as a moral crusade. In attempting to achieve his goal, however, he had resorted to arrangements that he would look back upon as personally distasteful. The deal sealed at Sèvres hung over Eden like a black cloud for the rest of his life. His critics referred to the proceedings there as "collusion" but, to the last, Eden insisted on the word "coordination." Whether the events of late October 1956 were described in pejorative or benign terms, the effects for Anthony Eden were the same: He had flown in the face of two fundamental tenets of the Foreign Office "position," a position that he had helped formulate during his years as foreign secretary—the preservation of the Anglo-American special relationship and a pro-Arab policy in the Middle East. And in the end, it was his own downfall, not Nasser's, that Anthony Eden was forced to witness.

Bitter? Yes, Anthony Eden remained bitter—against Nasser and Bulganin, against Hugh Gaitskell and other members of the Opposition, against the British newspapers and the BBC, against the United Nations and, above all, against John Foster Dulles. "The course of the Suez Canal crisis was decided by the American attitude toward it," he wrote in 1960. "If the United States Government had approached this issue in the spirit of an ally, they would have done everything in their power, short of use of force, to support the nation whose economic security depended upon the freedom of passage through the Suez Canal. . . . They would have insisted on restoring international authority in order to insulate the Canal from the politics of any one country. . . . Rather, did they try to gain time, coast along over difficulties as they arose and improvise policies, each following on the failure of its immediate predecessor."[2]

Eden's plaint had merit. Surely, Secretary Dulles provided Britain little help during the critical period. On odd days he advanced. On even, he retreated. Few people in the State Department, let alone the Foreign Office or the Quai d'Orsay, knew the Administration's real position from one moment to the next.

The difficulty may in part, at least, have been rooted in the personali-

ties of two of the principals. Eden and Dulles were both self-confident to
the point of arrogance. They both maintained their own counsel, often
keeping even their senior advisers in the dark. They did not like each
other; indeed, they distrusted each other. Only cruel fortune could have
arranged that this Englishman and this American, of all men, were in
positions of power at that moment in history. And it must have been an
angry god who made sure that everything that either man could do was
done to constrain communication and promote misunderstanding between them and between the governments they served. What could have
possessed the prime minister and the secretary, individually and together, to concoct the poisonous brew of prevarication and dissembling
served up in the autumn of 1956? When all the excuses have been made,
when all the diplomatic rhetoric has been stripped away, two ugly realities
remain: Eden lied to the Americans; Dulles deceived not only the British,
but the French as well.

Shortly before he died, Eden reflected on events in Washington
following the cease-fire. Time may have mellowed him, for he absolved
Dulles of responsibility for some of the indignities Britain and he himself had suffered. The secretary, Sir Anthony recalled, was a stubborn
and uncongenial colleague, but in early November it was White House
adviser Sherman Adams who inspired Eisenhower to make life difficult:
"Poor Foster was in hospital, you know. He may have seen the thing
differently."

Adamant? Yes, Eden was adamant that what he had done was right.
And to the end, he remained convinced that many of the problems besetting the world—including, especially, the growing Soviet influence in the
Middle East—could have been avoided if the British and French had been
able to carry out their objectives.

Philosophical? Yes, philosophical, too, sitting in Florida's sun and
death's shadow in the winter of 1976 as he reviewed the moments of
history he had witnessed or influenced. The world of the fifties was very
different from the one he had known earlier; but he had tried to understand the postwar period and thought he had. More so, in any event, than
many of his old antagonists—Foster Dulles, for one. Well, then, I asked,
what did he now think about his decision to play along with Dulles'
approach toward Suez almost to the very last? He had written in his
memoirs, "The decision whether to endorse the American Users' plan
[SCUA] was one of the most crucial we had to face during the whole Suez
crisis. I now think that this decision on the Users' Club may have been
wrong. The future of the Canal was, among the great powers, primarily
our concern and that of the French; American interest was secondary. We
might have done better to adhere to our own plan."[3] Had he now

changed his mind? With a tired shrug Eden murmured, "I still feel this way."

"And so my war ended," Sir Anthony wrote, ". . . and I emerged tempered by my experience and bereft of many friends, but with my illusions intact, neither shattered nor cynical, to face a changed world."[4] He was telling here of another war—one that had happened long ago. But as he packed his papers and his pictures and walked out of Number 10 into a raw January wind in 1957, Anthony Eden may have been reminded of the feelings he had had on that day in 1919. Only this time, he knew he was being demobilized for the last time.

London awoke on January 11 to read the announcement of Sir Anthony's resignation and his final official statement. Flags on government buildings throughout the city were at half-mast that day. Most Londoners and many of us at the embassy were surprised at this demonstration of sympathy for the broken prime minister. But, as had happened so often during the past year, chance had once again intervened; on the following day the newspapers reported that the official expression of mourning had been in observance of a memorial service held at Westminster Cathedral for the former president of Austria.

The resignation caught Washington by surprise. Although the prime minister had pleaded ill health, there was suspicion among some in the Administration and on Capitol Hill that the failure of his Suez policy and the growing opposition to his leadership were the real reasons behind his decision to abdicate.

Eden's departure was greeted with relief by Eisenhower and Dulles —but it was a dry, joyless sense of relief. Eden had been a difficult, even troublesome partner. Yet he was a sick man and deserved admiration for his courage and compassion for his problems. The President and the secretary had had recent close brushes with danger; there must have been a gnawing feeling in each of them that death would stalk them as it had Eden. And so their relief was mixed with empathy. "Dear Anthony," Eisenhower wrote when he heard the news, "I cannot tell you how deeply I regret that the strains and stresses of these times finally wore you down physically. . . . Now you have retired, I have had a heart attack and a major operation. . . . My admiration and affection for you has [sic] never diminished; I am truly sorry that you have had to quit the office."[5]

In a comment to the press, Dulles, too, was generous. He voiced his "deep regret" and recalled that he had worked with Sir Anthony for many years, during which time they had "always cooperated closely. This friendly association has been a privilege to me and through it I came to admire and respect his ability and effective dedication to the cause of freedom in the world and unity between the free nations."[6]

R. A. Butler, the lord privy seal, was Eden's logical successor. For three weeks, while the prime minister was vacationing in Jamaica, Butler minded the store. When his period of stewardship was over, he left behind a large number of dissatisfied customers. Among Butler's critics were, of course, members of the Opposition who railed against him for being so slow to withdraw British forces from Egypt. But it was not Gaitskell, Bevan, and Company who would influence the selection of Eden's successor. Among those who would were angry men of his own party who felt that he had caved in too soon—and to no purpose.

Butler's early misgivings about Eden's Suez policy were successfully concealed from public view. He dutifully shared the burden of defending the government in the hustings and in Parliament. Shortly before Eden left for Jamaica, Butler had told Commons that Britain would stand fast against blackmail by Nasser "or anyone else"; soon after he took over temporary responsibility for government policy, he warned the United States about pushing Britain too far too hard. But even for many devoid of Butler's genuine or feigned zeal for the Suez enterprise, there was a feeling that, once in, the British should have exacted at least some price for pulling out. Twenty years later, one British politician, still embittered, told me that "Rab had lost his nerve." And a onetime senior Foreign Office official was still decrying "that man Butler."

Some of Butler's critics seemed to have forgotten that, as acting prime minister, he had had a great deal of responsibility but little authority. He was, after all, only the watch officer. Eden was still the captain; it was he who had set the compass by agreeing to accept the cease-fire before the troops had even landed. The small British-French enclave at Port Said hardly could have provided Butler much leverage against formidable pressures to withdraw.

Butler could huff and bluff for a short while, but when it came time for Britain to play for high stakes in early December, rhetoric had to give way to reality. Whether he deserved blame or not, powerful Conservative politicians pointed their fingers at the lord privy seal for "the Suez scuttle." If Butler were chosen to succeed Eden, there was a danger that the Conservative Party, already shaken by recent events, would be badly split.

This was not the only reason why, when Butler's great chance came, it passed him by. There were some front-benchers in the party who thought him a bit too flippant, a bit too cocky about Eden and his plight. "Eden may not be the best prime minister we've had, but he's the best we've got," Butler was reported to have said. And then there was Macmillan—senior in age, the son of an American mother (as was Churchill), acceptable to both the right and moderate wings of the party, and a close, longtime friend of the reelected President of the United States. If the damage to Anglo-American relations could be repaired, Macmillan seemed the obvious person to accomplish it. And so when Eden stepped down, it was Harold Macmillan who was called.

The cabinet met that evening and, by a large majority, endorsed Macmillan as the next prime minister. On the following day, January 10, Macmillan kissed Elizabeth's royal hand. The appointment was now official and the new prime minister set to work to organize his cabinet. Selwyn Lloyd agreed to stay on as foreign secretary. The disappointed Butler accepted the post of home secretary and wished his successful rival "the greatest possible success." And tough, dour Duncan Sandys took on the Ministry of Defence.

Macmillan inherited a splintered party, a battered economy, and a divided country. He had no time to lose in making emergency repairs and in embarking upon longer-term reconstruction. Luckily he had a fortnight of grace; Parliament was in recess and would not reconvene until later in the month. *The Sunday Times* welcomed the new tenant in Downing Street under the flamboyant banner, "A Time for Greatness": "The state of our affairs at home and abroad is far less grievous than it has been depicted by those who have been trying to write us down as a defeated and second class nation. . . . Mr. Macmillan and his new team take up their task in the eye of history at a moment of exacting but enviable opportunity."[7] The new prime minister may well have grimaced when he read *The Times'* final flourish. "Exacting," certainly. "Enviable"—hardly!

Immediately after the announcement of his appointment, Harold Macmillan received a warm congratulatory message from the White House. More important, however, was the private, informal letter from Eisenhower that quickly followed the official communication: "Dear Harold. . . . The purpose of this note is to welcome you to your new headaches. . . . The only real fun you will have is to see just how far you can keep on going with everybody chopping at you with every conceivable kind of weapon. Knowing you so long and well I predict that your journey will be a great one. . . . With warm regards, As ever, D.E."[8] And so, early in the New Year, yet another chapter began in the long history of Anglo-American relations.

During the weeks Dulles was in the hospital and then recuperating in Florida, he had much time to brood, and the Middle East was obviously uppermost in his mind. The Suez debacle had been especially galling. "Suez was Dulles' personal war," Ambassador Ashraf Ghorbal told me years later. "Dulles was determined he would resolve it through his own diplomatic efforts." But he had been misled and made to look a fool by Eden and Mollet. He had a feeling that much of what had happened was a result of his having misjudged and mismanaged the whole affair.

On December 3, to the delight of President Eisenhower and the despair of Senator J. William Fulbright, even then a power on the Senate Foreign Relations Committee, John Foster Dulles bustled into his office and once more took over American foreign policy. Although the ravages wrought by the tension of the summer and autumn and by his bout of sickness added a decade to his appearance, his illness had barely slowed him down. He threw himself, once again, into the thick of fast-moving international events; he seemed to those who saw him to be his same irascible, work-a-holic self.

With Dulles' return to the State Department and with the presidential election and the Suez crisis safely behind him, President Eisenhower found it necessary for his health, or desirable for its own sake, to spend longer and more frequent vacations away from Washington. If the secretary appeared to be de facto "President for Foreign Policy" during the first Eisenhower Administration, he seemed certain to be more so during the second. This was obviously a congenial state of affairs for Dulles. It was he who "wrote most of the Presidential statements," Dulles had told Macmillan in mid-December. "When they had to be tough," he issued them. "When they were idealistic," they came ostensibly from Eisenhower.[9] Now that the President was spending more time on the golf course, the secretary would have an even freer hand.

On December 11, Dulles flew to Paris for a meeting of the NATO Council of Ministers. There, he told his distinguished colleagues that neither the United States nor France and England were blameless in handling the Suez crisis and, consequently, in creating disarray in NATO. But having had the grace to grant this, the secretary proceeded to take much more away. Britain and France had acted immorally, he said, by resorting to force when their own security had not been threatened. Force, he said, could not be used as an instrument of national policy. No member of NATO could be excused for such an action—except possibly the United States, which had global commitments and an acknowledged responsibility for preserving world peace and order.

It was vintage John Foster. Reactions in the press and the chancelleries of Western Europe were predictably outraged: The London *Times* felt that Dulles' views evoked the Monroe Doctrine: ". . . but a vast difference is noted between having said in 1823 'you stay in your part of the world and we'll stay in ours,' and now saying in effect, 'you stay in your part of the world and we won't stay in ours,' because the resources of the Middle East are too vital to do so."[10]

Macmillan, who met with Dulles on December 12, recalled that "it was a rather painful discussion and he [Dulles] was in a querulous and unhappy mood. . . . He went into a long defence of himself and his policies. He was clearly hurt at the criticisms that had been made."[11]

We at the embassy had no inkling of Macmillan's assessment of Dulles' mood. But we had read the secretary's speech to NATO. If there was any possibility of reestablishing close links with Britain, the secretary's excess of morality and dearth of tact had spoiled the chance. Dulles may have been "querulous and unhappy," but we were the ones who now had to pass the collection plate after yet another of the secretary's sermons.

What few then knew was that Dulles was preparing the way for a major new Administration policy on the Middle East—a policy that would be revealed after the turn of the New Year. Senator Fulbright, however, may have had a clue; a day or two after Dulles' NATO speech, he blasted the Administration, and especially the secretary, for an "extremely awkward, maladroit and unwise" foreign policy. Dulles' "preoccupation with pacts" was "misguided" and his "over-optimism and constant shifting of position in the Middle East was [sic] partly responsible for the British and French attack on Egypt."[12]

Rarely is a grandiose concept the product of instant inspiration. A passing thought leads to a notion, which leads to an idea, which leads. . . . More often than not, the process is a result of plural or collective cerebration; one man's musings lead to another's brainstorm. But in the case of John Foster Dulles, this process did not apply; each of his heroic conceptions seemed to emerge whole, if not beautifully formed. Brinkmanship, the liberation of Eastern Europe, the South Asia Treaty Organization, the Middle East Treaty Organization were all born as gleams in Dulles' eye and were soon translated into government pronouncements. There was little, if any, discussion of them in their gestation stage with colleagues or subordinates. The idea of the Suez Canal Users Association, which would keep Britain and France on the track of diplomacy as opposed to military action, was pure Dulles—a notion conceived of in the tranquillity of Duck Island and, within days, announced as solemn policy.

As Dulles brooded about the Suez affair he came to the tardy recognition that much of the difficulty the Administration had had stemmed from the lack of an overarching policy in the Middle East. In truth, except for a special concern for the economic and physical security of the new state of Israel and a commercial stake in Saudi Arabia, Washington had paid the Middle East little mind since the end of World War II. Northeast Asia and Western Europe were the foci of America's political attention, recipients of its economic aid, areas of its military deployments. Although President Truman cast a worried eye on the Middle East in the early postwar years, he confined American involvement to diplomatic pressures when the Soviet Union encroached on Iran in 1946 and to security guarantees for two peripheral nations, Greece and Turkey, in 1947. In 1953, the Central Intelligence Agency assisted in the removal of the bizarre Prime Minister Mossadeq from power in Iran. And two years later, President Eisenhower and Secretary Dulles encouraged the formation of the Baghdad Pact, but they fended off Anthony Eden's repeated requests that the United States join.

America's route to Asia lay not through the Mediterranean Sea and the Isthmus of Suez but across the Pacific Ocean. The Suez Canal had only marginal significance to the American economy; only 15 percent of the nation's total oil imports passed through it. Most Americans, including the President and the secretary of state, regarded Nasser's act as one of expropriation rather than burglary. Few pulses quickened, few blood pressures were elevated on Capitol Hill, Pennsylvania Avenue, or Foggy Bottom on July 26, 1956. Anthony Eden's fury lost much of its force in its transmission across the Atlantic, for when congressmen and Administration officials thought of "the Canal," it was the artificial waterway across Panama they had in mind, not the one across Egypt. (Eden would have enjoyed the fuss and furor in Washington two decades later when the future of the Panama Canal was at issue.)

In the early 1950s Washington gave priority to those areas of the globe where Communism posed a threat. American officials were confident then that the Muslim religion insulated the Arab world from seduction by Moscow. But in late 1956, when the Soviet Union pushed into the area with arms and money, an overall United States policy for the Middle East was more important than ever. And so, in the quiet of his room in Walter Reed Hospital, John Foster Dulles proceeded to develop another grandiose concept. It was delivered in a special message by Eisenhower to Congress on January 5, and it was christened "the Eisenhower Doctrine for the Middle East."

> The Middle East has abruptly reached a new and critical stage in its long and important history. Our country supports without reservation the full sovereignty and independence of each and every nation of the Middle East. . . . Just recently there have been hostilities involving Western European nations that once exercised much influence in the area. Also, the relatively large attack by Israel in October has intensified the basic differences between that nation and its Arab neighbors. All this instability has been heightened and, at times, manipulated by International Communism. . . .
>
> The Soviet Union has nothing whatsoever to fear from the United States in the Middle East, or anywhere else in the world, so

long as its rulers do not, themselves, first resort to aggression.

. . . The reason for Russia's interest in the Middle East is solely that of power politics. Considering her announced purpose of Communizing the world, it is easy to understand her hope of dominating the Middle East. . . . If the nations of that area should lose their independence, if they were dominated by forces hostile to freedom, that would be both a tragedy for the area and for many other free nations whose economic life would be subject to near strangulation. Western Europe would be endangered just as though there had been no Marshall Plan, no North Atlantic Treaty Organization. . . .

Thus we have these simple and indisputable facts:

1. The Middle East, which has always been coveted by Russia, would be today prized more than ever by International Communism.

2. The Soviet rulers continue to show that they do not scruple to use any means to achieve their ends.

3. The free nations of the Middle East need, and for the most part want, added strength to assure their continued independence.

Our thoughts naturally turn to the United Nations as a protector of small nations. . . . The United Nations can always be helpful, but it cannot be a wholly dependable protector of freedom when the ambitions of the Soviet Union are involved.

. . . a greater responsibility now devolves upon the United States.
. . . Our desire is a world environment of freedom, not servitude
. . . the United States must make more evident its willingness to support the independence of the freedom-loving nations of the area. Under these circumstances I deem it necessary to seek the cooperation of the Congress. . . .

The message continued for several more pages, but the bottom line was Eisenhower's request to Congress for a sum of $200 million for special economic aid to countries of the Middle East and approval to meet "overt armed aggression from any nation controlled by International Communism" with "the armed forces of the United States."[13]

All Presidents, and many lesser men, have a burning desire to be remembered as having influenced the course of history. Some—Lincoln, Wilson, Roosevelt—found that great events provided a helping hand. Others, especially in this era of "public relations," have made a conscious effort to apply a glamorous layer of cosmetics to mundane occasions in the hope that they will appear taller among their contemporaries and so catch the notice of future historians. Thus, in 1957, a new—and hastily conceived—presidential statement with regard to the Middle East was not referred to simply as a "policy," but hyped up to be "the Eisenhower Doctrine." (So, also, ten years later, a frail and jerry-built agreement reached by a group of nations fighting in Vietnam was referred to not simply as a "communiqué," but rather as "the Declaration of Honolulu.")

The congressional leadership was not taken by surprise by the President's Middle East initiative; Eisenhower and Dulles had spent several hours on New Year's Day giving them a preview of the message and soliciting their support. Even so, it took two months and much heated discussion for the new policy to pass both Houses.

The Eisenhower Doctrine was greeted abroad with reactions varying from enthusiasm to anger. In Damascus, the government insisted that the maintenance of peace and security in the Middle East was "solely the responsibility of the peoples of this area." But in Beirut, the foreign minister hailed the doctrine as a "good and timely move by the United States." From Moscow, there were predictions that the new American policy was doomed to crumble against the "granite rock" of the Soviet Union. From Turkey came promises of support. Iran was enthusiastic. Israel was wary; its ambassador in Washington was instructed "to seek further details and to obtain clarification." In France, there was cautious approval, despite some disappointment that Washington had left the future of the Canal and the resolution of the Arab-Israeli problem to the United Nations.

The reaction in England was mixed. "Good in parts," *The Times* acknowledged, but crossly criticized the doctrine's preoccupation with Soviet moves in the Middle East and its neglect of intraregional problems. Aneurin Bevan, the Labour Party's old war-horse, thundered that it could "plunge the world into the nightmare of a final war." Official reaction was muted, however: The President is applying to Congress for new powers, and it is therefore inappropriate for the British government to comment at this stage, was the word from Whitehall. But apparently there was a considerable sense of relief among the ministers. "The Eisenhower Doctrine of 1957," wrote Harold Macmillan years later, "would have saved us all in 1956."[14]

On March 9, Eisenhower's "doctrine" became law. More than a year later, in Lebanon, the doctrine was put to test. The government of President Chamoun, a friend of the United States, was being threatened. The matter was taken especially seriously in Washington since the government of Iraq had just been overthrown by a Nasserite group. Although there was no evidence that the Russians were behind the efforts to throw Chamoun out of power, the Administration, as was its habit at the time, saw Moscow's hand writ large. The crisis ebbed and flowed, but finally in mid-July 1958, Eisenhower dispatched an American naval force to put American troops ashore.

I remember that occasion well. We were vacationing in the south of France. On the morning of July 15 I went on an errand to Cannes. The harbor was crowded chockablock with American warships from the Sixth Fleet.

Having completed my business, I dropped in on a nearby bistro. The bar was lined with tanned young Americans in sport shirts and slacks who said they were on liberty from one or another of the ships in the harbor. We were discussing the baseball season at home when four burly armed sailors burst through the door. "Back to your ships and make it fast!" they bellowed. My companions took a final swallow and grudgingly trooped out. "Get that guy!" was the next sound I heard. Two of the gargantuas from the shore patrol prodded and pushed me to the pier where the liberty boats were waiting. I finally freed myself long enough to reach for my wallet and flash my embassy ID. We parted on reasonably friendly terms. And that was the extent of my direct involvement with the Eisenhower Doctrine.

In late January 1957 I received my summons from Washington. Thanks to a friend passing through at Christmas, I knew it was coming and I knew what was wanted. Why, my chiefs were planning to ask me, had I not known what was about to occur on Monday, October 29?

Before leaving I made the rounds of friends in Whitehall to take a private census. Who had been told prior to the "go" decision on Sunday, October 28? Who had not?

Patrick Dean, the chairman of the Joint Intelligence Committee, knew, of course, as did the foreign secretary and the head of the Foreign Office's Middle East Department. The chief of the secret foreign intelligence group knew, as did the chief of the internal intelligence service. The head of the code-breaking service knew, as did, much to my surprise, a senior civil servant in the Commonwealth Relations Office. And, obviously, a few people in the prime minister's office, the chiefs of staff, and the secretary of the cabinet.

But the British ambassadors to Cairo, Tel Aviv, and the UN did not know. And the director of the Joint Intelligence Bureau and the economic and geographic research staffs did not know. Nor did the senior military commanders. Nor did the military intelligence chiefs. Nor did the commanders at Cyprus and Malta. Nor did virtually any senior civil servant in either the Foreign Office or the Ministry of Defence.

All told, I counted fourteen people in London outside the cabinet who had been privy to what was in the wind. "You dumb bastards, if the British military commanders did not know, if the intelligence chiefs did not know, if some of the most senior civil servants in Her Majesty's Government did not know," I asked no one in particular as I strapped on my seat belt, "how the hell should I have known?"

On the following day I met with Allen Dulles and then brother Foster. Allen, warmly, and Foster, coldly, reviewed the events of the preceding several months. "How was it," each asked, that I "did not know?" "Sir," I responded in each session, "if the British military intelligence chiefs did not know, how was I to?" I reminded them of the telegram I had sent on Sunday evening, October 28. Neither could recall seeing it or being told of it. Later that week I attended a meeting of the United States Intelligence Board, which consisted of the heads of all the American intelligence services. "How was it . . .?"; "Gentlemen, if the British military . . ."

It was my first visit home in eighteen months, and aside from the catechism, it was a good week. Except—.Prior to my departure for London I was given an overdue physical examination. Sometime during the past few months, the doctor said, I had had a "cardiac incident—not serious, but be careful." I flew back with the discomforting thought that, so far as I was aware, I was the only American casualty of the Suez war.

However cosmic the Eisenhower Doctrine may have been deemed by its authors, there was an immediate, nasty little problem that it could not handle. This was Israel's determination to stand fast in the Gaza Strip and at Sharm el-Sheikh. The terrorist raids and the strangulation of Israel's seaborne commerce were the primary reasons why Ben-Gurion had agreed to join with Mollet and Eden several months before. Now that the Israelis, at some cost, could count on a secure border and unimpeded shipping, the prime minister was in no mood to restore the unsatisfactory status quo ante.

But Dwight Eisenhower had his own priorities. After all the unpleasant business he had transacted to extricate Britain and France from Egypt, after all the distasteful days and nights he had spent in the uncomfortable political company of the Russians, he was of no mind to see his efforts thwarted by the stubbornness of the Israelis.

On February 3, the President sent a personal message to Ben-Gurion: "It is my earnest hope that this withdrawal [from Gaza and Sharm el-Sheikh] will be completed without further delay. . . . Continued ignoring of . . . the United Nations Resolutions would almost surely lead to the invoking of further United Nations procedures, which could seriously disturb the relations between Israel and other member nations including the United States."[15]

It took a week for the Israeli government to mull this over. And then came the word that Israeli forces would not be withdrawn unless and until Israel could maintain civil control over Gaza and was assured freedom of passage through the Gulf of Aqaba. With regard to Gaza, the State De-

partment replied, "Israeli withdrawal should be prompt and unconditional." Washington promised, however, to "use its best efforts" to see
that UNEF units monitored the border between Gaza and Israel. The
United States agreed that Israel should have free passage in the Gulf and
would try to persuade the United Nations to move UNEF units "into the
Straits area as the Israeli forces are withdrawn."[16]

Ambassador Eban, conscious of the growing impatience of the Administration and the eroding support for Israel in Congress and the
press, tried hard to convince his prime minister that the American position gave Israel much of what it was seeking. "I am afraid," he told his
staff in mid-February, "that our government will not take yes for an
answer."[17]

Despite Eban's urgings, Ben-Gurion paid Washington little notice.
Eisenhower and Dulles saw their shiny new Middle East policy withering
away even before it passed Congress. They brought up the heavy artillery
and aimed it at Israel's most vulnerable target—its economy. In a meeting
with Secretary of the Treasury Humphrey and UN Ambassador Lodge,
it was decided to urge members of the United Nations to stop all government and even private assistance to Israel. Since, in 1956, American Jews
alone had provided more than $100 million to Israel through gifts and
bond purchases, the threat of cutting off nonofficial aid was a serious
matter.

Eisenhower had trouble selling this idea to the pro-Israeli Congress
and decided to make his case in a nationwide radio and television speech
on February 20. Before his broadcast, he sent Ben-Gurion yet another
message: "I would greatly deplore the necessity of the United States
taking positions in the United Nations, and of the United Nations itself
having to adopt measures, which might have far-reaching effects upon
Israel's relations with the rest of the world."[18]

In his speech the President reiterated his position that Israel should
withdraw from Gaza and Sharm el-Sheikh without conditions on the
assurance that the United States would then undertake to see that the
United Nations secured the Gaza border and guaranteed unrestricted
passage for Israeli shipping in the Gulf of Aqaba. Britain and France, he
said, had evacuated Port Said out of "respect for the opinions of man-
kind." Israel was insisting on "firm guarantees" before it withdrew its
forces. But "this raises a basic question of principle. Should a nation
which attacks and occupies foreign territory in the face of United Nations
disapproval be allowed to impose conditions on its own withdrawal?
. . . It would indeed be a sad day if the United States ever felt that it had
to subject Israel to the same type of moral pressure as is being applied
to the Soviet Union." Israel must withdraw immediately or "the United

Nations had no choice but to exert pressure" to assure that this was done.[19]

Ambassador Abba Eban was disappointed that Eisenhower and Dulles would not provide prior American guarantees that Israel's withdrawal would not simply result in a return to the conditions that prevailed before the Israeli invasion in late October. But he was also distraught at Ben-Gurion's adamant stand. If the American assurances were not accepted, the issue would be resolved at the UN, which, for Israel, was hostile territory. He went home for consultation on February 20, the day of Eisenhower's speech. Before leaving, he sought out his old friend ex-Under Secretary of State General Bedell Smith. "Go ahead with what they offered," Smith advised, "and be a little more flexible than Ben-Gurion has been till now."[20]

The future of the Eisenhower Doctrine would hang on Israel's response to the President's private message and public appeal. On February 21, Ben-Gurion made an impassioned speech to his countrymen and to the world. "Is there one law for the Egyptian dictator and another for democratic Israel? . . . In its note to the United States, the Egyptian Government clearly declared that the shipping through the [Tiran] Straits will be free to all nations. . . . Israel, therefore, is entitled to ensure effective guarantees from the United States for freedom of passage. . . . We cannot be asked to permit the return of the Egyptian invaders to the [Gaza] strip. . . . No matter what may happen, Israel will not submit to the restoration of the status quo in the strip."[21]

That was Ben-Gurion's response. He had chosen to ignore the Administration's pressure and General Smith's advice—for the moment, at least.

"Those were terrible months," Golda Meir recalls. "Our phased-out withdrawal . . . was going on . . . but nothing was being said or done to force the Egyptians to agree to enter into negotiations with us, to guarantee the lifting of the blockade of the Strait of Tiran or to solve the problem of the Gaza Strip. . . . I couldn't get through to the Americans —least of all that cold, gray man John Foster Dulles—that our very life depended on adequate guarantees . . . and that we couldn't return to the situation which had existed before the Sinai Campaign."[22]

There were rumors when I was in Washington that the President planned to meet with Macmillan and Mollet as part of his effort to restore pre-Suez relations. Soon after my return to London, the arrangements were fixed. Mollet would come to Washington in late February and Eisenhower would meet Macmillan in Washington or Bermuda on the twenty-first.

Mollet and Pineau had been waiting for this invitation since November. Their relations with the United States were even more strained than those of the British. They were regarded by Eisenhower and Dulles (rightly, as it turned out) as the principal architects of the Suez scheme. Moreover, Mollet did not have the close wartime relations with the President that served Macmillan, and even Eden, in good stead.

Pineau's recollections of Eisenhower are not glowing: "I do not hesitate to say . . . that he was not one of the great Presidents of the United States. If he had not chosen Foster Dulles . . . his opponents could have stated that he possessed neither ideas nor personal policies. He preferred to fall back on the will of God rather than assert his own will. . . . After a long discussion with him you would have the impression that you had found the solution to a lot of problems; actually you would not really have solved any of them. What counted most at this meeting was . . . the impression given by the press to the American people that the difficulties with France had been smoothed out."[23]

The sessions at the summit produced little except an improvement in the atmosphere and some lofty platitudes. Pineau's private meeting with Dulles, however, was a different matter. He found the secretary, "despite the reticence due to the recent past, cordial, almost friendly." If Dulles "had not been able to approve the French position over Suez, he had still understood it." And Dulles "appreciated our efforts to find a solution favorable to Israel."[24]

Then Dulles, after consulting with Hammarskjöld, made a surprising suggestion. Washington, he told his visitor, was handicapped in its ability to resolve the Israeli impasse. If Pineau could work out some arrangement with Hammarskjöld acceptable to all parties, the United States would go along. Would Pineau take on the task? An astonished Pineau agreed. On his arrival in New York, he met with Abba Eban. Eban promised that Israel would accept whatever solution Pineau could work out with the secretary-general.

Pineau then saw Hammarskjöld. They agreed that UNEF should take over Gaza and Sharm el-Sheikh following an Israeli withdrawal. Hammarskjöld suggested that the proposition be discussed privately with Egypt's Fawzi. To Pineau's amazement, Fawzi agreed to meet. At a secret session in Hammarskjöld's apartment they settled on the terms of the UNEF deployment.[25]

Meanwhile, Ben-Gurion had still not replied to Eisenhower's private message of February 20, and the General Assembly was debating military and economic sanctions against Israel. Just before the vote, on March 1, Foreign Minister Golda Meir announced that "the Government of Israel is now in a position to announce its plans for a full and complete withdrawal from the Sharm el-Sheikh area and the Gaza Strip."[26]

Pineau did not take credit for the breakthrough in New York; he was an "agent," he says, rather than the principal.[27] Canada's Lester Pearson probably deserves most of the kudos. His concept of a UN peacekeeping force advanced the previous October gave Israel assurance that a renewal of terrorist raids from Gaza and a blockade at Sharm el-Sheikh would not follow on the heels of its withdrawal. It may have been he, as well, who orchestrated the surprisingly smooth arrangements involving Eden, Dulles, Eban, Hammarskjöld, and Fawzi.

Eisenhower's winter of worry now seemed over. "I believe," he wrote to Ben-Gurion on March 2, "that Israel will have no cause for regret having thus conformed to the strong sentiment of the world community. . . . After the withdrawal there should be a united effort by all of the nations to bring about conditions in the area more stable, more tranquil, and more conducive to the general welfare than existed heretofore. . . . I am, my dear Mr. Prime Minister, Sincerely, Dwight D. Eisenhower."[28]

The arrangement to deploy UN troops instead of Egyptian forces on the border between Gaza and Israel, in Gaza itself, and in Sharm el-Sheikh was not an easy concession for Nasser to make. In particular, lifting Egypt's blockade of the Israeli port of Eilat gave Israel a valuable prize. But Nasser had little choice unless he wanted to sacrifice the goodwill of his newfound friend the American secretary of state and, in the bargain, prolong Israeli occupation of Egyptian territory.

After five months, the Suez war could be said to be officially over. There was still a great deal of litter to clean up and much rebuilding to do, both literally and figuratively, but at least the crisis itself could now be referred to in the past tense.

Offering Prime Minister Macmillan a choice of meeting in Washington or Bermuda was a graceful gesture on the part of Eisenhower. Form becomes more important when pride is injured, and the British were nursing a bad case of injured pride in the winter of 1957. Macmillan naturally chose Bermuda; it was British territory and he could be a gracious host rather than a supplicant guest.

Macmillan was especially anxious to reestablish the close working relationship with Eisenhower he had enjoyed in an earlier, somewhat less exalted wartime incarnation as the British political adviser at the Allied Headquarters in Northwest Africa. But he was interested in more than atmospherics; there were several specific points he wanted to get across to the President.

The prospects for establishing some acceptable form of international control over the Canal were now even more remote than they had been in late July, immediately after nationalization. At that time, at least, Nasser was making some genuflections toward the Constantinople Convention of 1888; now he was maintaining that the British and French invasion relieved him of any past international obligations. Aside from this broad question, thorny problems of compensation for the shares of the Canal Company, shipping tariffs, questions of freedom of passage, standards of maintenance, would all have to be worked out from scratch. And London and Paris were now in a worse bargaining position than they had been in mid-October when negotiations on these issues with Foreign Minister Fawzi had shown some faint promise. Meanwhile, clearance operations in the Canal were moving apace and the waterway would soon be open to traffic, agreement or no agreement. After all that had gone on—nationalization, the twenty-one nation meeting, the eighteen nation meeting, SCUA, the Menzies mission, the debates in New York, the private talks with Fawzi, the fighting at Port Said—the Suez Canal was still a bleeding sore.

The Suez misadventure had served only to increase British anger and scorn toward Nasser. Although this boded ill for any settlement of the outstanding issues, the new prime minister was determined to resolve the problem of the Canal quickly lest he, like Eden, find it an albatross. Macmillan prepared some notes which he would refer to during the meeting with the President:

> I hope you will do everything you possibly can . . . to get a Canal settlement—especially regarding dues—which we can claim as reasonable, if not quite what we'd like!
>
> But if we can't get it—if Nasser is absolutely obdurate . . . if we all have, in the *short* run, to eat dirt, and accept a bad and unjust settlement, I hope you won't say in public or in private that it's a good settlement.
>
> I hope you will denounce Nasser and all his works in the strongest possible terms.
>
> Bring every pressure—political and economic—upon him. . . .
>
> Any other course would I fear cause such a rift between our countries and people as would take much longer to repair than the urgent needs of the world allow.[29]

On his arrival in Bermuda Eisenhower was taken aback by the vitriol that poured forth from Macmillan at any mention of Nasser. "Foster and I at first found it difficult to talk constructively to our British colleagues about Suez. . . . [They] were so obsessed with the possibilities of getting rid of Nasser that they were handicapped in searching objectively for any realistic method of operating the Canal."[30]

Nasser, Suez, and the Middle East dominated the talks, but other touchy items also had to be dealt with. The President urged the British to free Archbishop Makarios and Macmillan promised to do so. (A week later the archbishop was given his freedom from confinement in the Seychelles, but was forbidden to return to Cyprus.) The President agreed to turn over some intermediate ballistic missiles to Great Britain, although the nuclear warheads would remain under American control. Finally, Eisenhower agreed that the United States would try, in private negotiations with Nasser, to work out a satisfactory formula for the Canal.

Following the Bermuda meeting, American Ambassador Raymond Hare, an old Middle East hand, was given the task of breathing new life into the six principles that the British and French, with Egyptian acquiescence, had discussed at the United Nations Security Council the previous October. Discussions in Cairo dragged on for weeks. During this period Americans in London were treated to a half dozen unamusing variations on the theme of the tortoise and the hare that were passing around London dinner tables and Whitehall offices.

Finally, on April 23, an agreement was reached; Foreign Minister Fawzi notified Secretary-General Hammarskjöld that the government of Egypt would "respect the terms and the spirit of the Constantinople Convention of 1888 and the rights and obligations arising therefrom."[31] Egypt also agreed to set aside 25 percent of Canal revenues for maintenance of the Canal. But other arrangements, including those applying to tolls, gave the principal Canal users, including even the Americans, thin satisfaction. "In our view," Ambassador Lodge told the UN Security Council on April 26, "the Egyptian Declaration does not fully meet the six requirements of the Security Council . . . in view of [the] lack of provision for organized and systematic cooperation between Egypt and the users, there is no assurance that the six requirements will in fact be implemented." But, Lodge continued, "perhaps no final judgment can be made regarding the regime proposed by Egypt until it has been tried out in practice."[32]

The tattered Suez Canal Users Association was convened again in London on April 30 to consider the next step. Britain was especially worried that it would find itself isolated if it boycotted the Canal until Nasser agreed to a more satisfactory arrangement. It was clear that, except for France, all SCUA members were planning to permit their shipping to use the Canal. On May 11, British ships, too, were given the green light. A month later, the French followed suit. In the end, of course, Washington, London, and Paris had only two choices: They could take

Nasser's offer, or they could leave it. They took it. SCUA gasped its last pitiful breath and died.

The Canal was now open—officially, as well as in fact. In 1957 a total of 90 million tons of shipping passed through, compared to 116 million in 1955. In the seven months or so of 1957 that British ships used the Canal, 20 percent of that year's total tonnage flew the Union Jack, compared to 30 percent during all of 1955. The hard statistics proved, as no amount of rhetoric could, the Canal's importance to Great Britain.

An outpouring of enthusiasm swept over Egypt following the departure of the French and British forces. Some artificial sweeteners had been injected into Cairo's accounts of the war, but despite the propaganda, the victory was a real one. Beneath the surface of official and public euphoria in Egypt, however, there were disturbing signs of trouble. The country was flat broke. The Egyptian pound had fallen sharply. Cotton exports had fallen off. Foreign tourism had declined to a bare trickle. Only Egypt's national debt and national birthrate showed evidence of impressive growth. A grim picture.

The Canal would not open for traffic again for several months. Aside from the difficulties, originally underestimated, of clearing away the debris, Nasser had insisted that the work be slowed until the Israelis pulled out of Gaza and Sharm el-Sheikh. No tolls were being collected, nor would they be until some time in April, when traffic could once more flow through the Canal. Clearly, Nasser could not make good on his boast to finance the Aswan High Dam from Canal revenues. Adding to Nasser's problem was the cost of the war. Brief as it was, it turned out to be expensive. The cost of replacing captured or destroyed military equipment alone was formidable.

If Nasser was to be able to count on sustained popular support, indeed if Egypt itself was to stay afloat, help from the outside was urgent. Eisenhower's proposal to Congress included funds for countries in the Middle East, but Nasser was not high on Congress' list of would-be recipients; his pro-Soviet, pro-Chinese, and anti-Israeli proclivities saw to that. But he had an alternative: Mr. Bulganin, like Dickens' Mr. Barkis, was willing.

Nasser was a needy and impatient welfare case, but he had to wait his turn. First on the list came the rabid anti-Western, pro-leftist regime in Syria; in 1957 Damascus received $100 million from Moscow. But in 1958 economic assistance to Egypt began. Moscow committed to Nasser $175 million for industrial development and $100 million to fund the first stage of the Aswan High Dam. During the same period the new, pro-Soviet government in Iraq was given $150 million. In 1960 Egypt obtained $225 million for the second stage of the dam and a stream of military equipment, as well. Moscow appeared to be most generous—until Egypt and the other recipients of Soviet largesse learned the hard way the difference between a gift and a loan. All they had received and much more that would follow in the years to come would have to be paid back—with interest. Lady Bountiful turned out to have a bit of Mr. Shylock in her character.

Soon after he became prime minister, Harold Macmillan took some practical, painful steps to adjust Britain's affairs to the stark realities of her current circumstances. As a conscientious chancellor of the exchequer, he had had a good opportunity to evaluate at first hand the country's economic plight. In early 1957 the British had approximately 700,-000 men under arms—a number unnecessarily large for Britain's postwar strategic responsibilities and much too large for its shrunken economy. Meanwhile, the nation had assumed a tremendous burden of social services; National Health, old age pensions, and an expansion of educational facilities and opportunities had been introduced. Clearly, either costly military expenditures or costly civilian benefits would have to be pruned sharply. Even a Conservative government knew where the cuts would have to be made.

Macmillan ordered Defence Minister Duncan Sandys to draw up a comprehensive plan for the reorganization and restructuring of the armed forces with the aim of producing a smaller, more economical military establishment. In mid-April the government published a Defence White Paper detailing its proposals.

The White Paper recommended that the three services be scaled down from 700,000 to 375,000 men. Under this plan British forces committed to NATO in Germany would be reduced gradually from 77,000 to 64,000, the tactical air force cut drastically, several battleships and cruisers scrapped, and all units deployed overseas pared down. National (conscript) Service would be eliminated and, henceforth, the ranks in the army, navy, and air force would be filled by volunteers. All of this, the government maintained, could be done without sacrificing Britain's national security.

As part of the economies, several county regiments were disbanded or merged. Old regimental banners, silver salvers, gold goblets, and artifacts of distant and hard campaigns were sent off to local museums or graced new combined messes. To the extent that the identities of these lost tribes remained, they were preserved in the form of regimental neckties sported by newly mustered-out officers—not a monumental matter, perhaps, but of some poignant consequence, nonetheless, in a country where tradition was the stuff of history.

To compensate for the large cuts in manpower and conventional equipment, Macmillan's government proposed to rely on another deterrent against attack—nuclear weapons. The White Paper proposed that Britain develop a nuclear capability which could be operated and controlled independently of Washington.

Most Britons regarded the government's reorganization of the nation's defense posture as a good thing. The elimination of National Service and the savings implied by the smaller military establishment were obviously popular among those who were tired of so many guns and yearned for more butter. The government made it attractive for many young officers to resign their commissions and many of my friends in the services did so soon after the new defense plan went into effect. Some went into banking or real estate, or found civilian jobs in the government, or emigrated to greener pastures. A few embarked on premature lives of leisure and nothingness.

The new, leaner military posture was not greeted as warmly by Britain's allies as it was by the British themselves. France and Germany, in particular, were worried about the implications of the reduction in the British Army of the Rhine. This was a time when the likelihood of a Soviet thrust into Western Europe was taken seriously, and a time, too, when most NATO members were balancing their own NATO commitments against tight domestic budgets. A reduction of even a few thousand men by one member imposed a strain on the others.

Although there would soon be a much smaller armed establishment, no one in Whitehall was under any illusion that Britain could immediately shuck off its far-flung political responsibilities and the military commitments these implied. The Suez war was over and the British forces had been evacuated from Egypt, but there was no pretending that the nation could now relax. Across the world impatient nationalists and those who would turn nationalist movements to their own, less lofty, ends were making life difficult for those who strained to maintain the comfortable and familiar status quo. Britain, long the center of the international establishment, was now being nibbled and clawed at from one end of the old Empire to the other.

In Cyprus, the situation was deteriorating day by day. EOKA, the Greek-supported terrorist movement, was rampaging all over the island. Archbishop Makarios—none the worse for, and hardly chastened by, his confinement—was castigating the British from political pulpits in friendly countries and complicating the already meager prospects for achieving a solution acceptable to Greece, Turkey, and Great Britain.

In Malaya, the insurgency dragged on, although, as each month passed, the British forces seemed to be gaining the upper hand. But it was a painstaking process and there was no immediate end in sight.

And everywhere in the Middle East where Britain still had a presence, the militants were on the move. From Iraq to Jordan to Oman, leaders friendly to Britain were threatened with removal from office, perhaps removal from this life. In the wings, London was convinced, was the hated Gamal Abdel Nasser, capitalizing on his increased prestige and accelerating his efforts to make Cairo the center of a Pan-Arab world. The soldiers, sailors, and airmen who still remained in Her Majesty's Service would not be likely to while away their time sitting in their barracks and polishing their brass.

Great Britain's decision to "go nuclear" overshadowed every other aspect of the country's new defense policy. Two decades ago the decision of a nation to vote itself into the "nuclear club" was taken even more seriously than today. Up to this point there had been only two nuclear powers, the United States and the Soviet Union. Japan had forsworn any interest in the atom as a weapon. The countries of Eastern Europe had no choice in the matter. The NATO countries had resigned themselves to an uncertain and frightening future in the cold comfort that, in extremis, they could count on the American "nuclear umbrella"; a Soviet nuclear attack on any of them, Washington had promised, would be met by an American retaliatory attack on the USSR. The hideous consequences of such an exchange were then (and are now) regarded by strategic experts and politicians as the most effective deterrent against a general nuclear war.

London's determination to develop its own nuclear weapons capability—at great cost and, admittedly, with only limited effectiveness—seemed both unnecessary and foolhardy. "Why?" I asked colleagues in the Foreign Office and Defence Ministry. The British exchequer was in so parlous a shape, I reminded them, that the government had developed a new global strategic rationale to accommodate smaller, less costly military forces. Why, then, embark on an expensive new nuclear weapons system which, even when it came into being, would be only a tiny fraction of what the Soviet Union could bring to bear on the United Kingdom? Did this make sense in the light of solemn American assurances of nuclear retaliation?

I pressed these questions more from a sense of despair than in the expectation of receiving an answer. But I was given an answer: "Perhaps under different circumstances," a senior Foreign Office official told me one evening over dinner, "it would have been silly for us to develop our own nuclear deterrent, especially in the light of the American umbrella. But since the events of last year we cannot be entirely confident of

America. We are much nearer to the Soviet Union than you, and no responsible British government can now take a chance on the survival of this country." I returned home that night, for the first time in months, under the cold, dark shadow of Suez.

Yet, if the experience of Suez played any role in the ministerial discussions concerning Britain's military future, it could hardly have been definitive. A decision to embark on the one-way street toward a nuclear weapons capability is, after all, too consequential to take overnight—at least in democratic societies. In Britain, the concept of an independent nuclear deterrent had been in the minds of strategic planners since the early 1950s, and a program to produce nuclear bombs had been announced in 1955.[33] The White Paper had merely given the deterrent concept its official blessing. But, as the remark of my Foreign Office friend illustrated, it served as a convincing ex post facto rationale and a reminder of that moment when Washington had let London down and when Moscow had threatened to rocket Britain.

Almost two years later Randolph Churchill boasted to a group of Americans that Britain could reach "twelve cities in the region of Stalingrad and Moscow from bases in Britain and another dozen in the Crimea from bases in Cyprus. We did not have that power at the time of Suez. We are a major power again."[34] And so, if the decision of January 1957 did not necessarily send shudders down the spines of the men in the Kremlin, it did stir the hearts of many in Whitehall who found satisfaction that the nuclear club had been expanded from two to three and that Britain now had "a seat at the table."

Many years later, I heard an echo of the fears and the challenges of the mid-fifties. It was October 1962. I had flown on a U.S. Air Force plane to a military airbase north of London with secret, high-altitude pictures of Soviet nuclear missiles being installed in Cuba. President John Kennedy would soon announce the presence of the missiles and his demands for their removal to the American people, to the Kremlin, and to the world in general. Kennedy wanted America's NATO allies to know that a dangerous confrontation between the United States and the Soviet Union was looming immediately ahead. Ambassador David Bruce and I sat in the prime minister's office and tensely watched him examine the photographs. The handsome office in Downing Street was absolutely still except for the ticking clock and our nervous pipe puffing. Barely audibly, Harold Macmillan finally murmured, "At last Washington can feel what it has been like for us to have been, for years, within seconds of nuclear destruction." And then, looking up apologetically, "I didn't mean that the way it sounded. I shall, of course, give President Kennedy my complete support."

Nothing is ever the same after a great crisis. Sometimes there is only a shift of mood, a revision of expectations. Sometimes there is a great shift in political fortunes. And occasionally even geography is altered.

The convulsion in Hungary in the autumn of 1956 threatened Soviet control. If it had gotten out of hand, a tidal wave of revolution against Moscow's heavy-handed rule would have rolled over the USSR's Eastern European empire. The Kremlin saw to it that it did not get out of control. The threat quickly receded and all that was left by the spring of 1957 were ripples of frustration and despair.

The crisis over Suez, on the other hand, produced changes not only in mood, but in politics and geography as well. The Middle East and the area bordering the Mediterranean Sea will never be the same again.

How to explain the difference between the effects of the two great crises? Why did Hungary cause little more than a ripple, Suez a tidal wave? And why was it that at precisely the same moment, Moscow was able to achieve its objective in an area it considered vital to its national interest, but London and Paris had to abort their effort?

The answer lies in the nature of the governments and personalities involved and in the play of international forces. The Kremlin regarded the revolt in Hungary as an "internal" matter; what took place there was strictly the business of the Soviet Union. The revolt in the streets of Budapest *would* be put down, because if it were not, all of Eastern Europe could go up in flames. Unlike national leaders in the West, Bulganin and Khrushchev had no reason to concern themselves about the views of opposition political parties or domestic public opinion. No Gaitskell, no Stevenson, no Mendès-France could create political difficulties; no London *Observer,* or *New York Times,* or *L'Humanité* could raise awkward questions.

But this is only part of the story; Eden had to buck large British constituencies opposed to the Suez venture, but Mollet had virtually all of France behind him. It was pressure from the outside that made the difference. Here, too, the Kremlin got off scot-free. There are many who would say that if Suez had not diverted attention from Eastern Europe, the Russians would have been constrained from invading Hungary. Possibly so. But probably not. In the context of that time (and, indeed, of the present as well) it is difficult to imagine the UN being able to interpose a UNEF on the border of Hungary—difficult because the UN could not have passed a resolution to this effect, and difficult because, if it had, the Russians would not have permitted UNEF to function. After all, Moscow would not even permit Secretary-General Hammarskjöld to go to Budapest for a firsthand look.

The period that followed World War II was marked by a rise of nationalism throughout Asia, Africa, and Latin America. In many new, poor countries nationalist movements sought not only to establish strong national identities, but also to revenge the past—a past of economic exploitation and political suppression by the rich, white nations of Western Europe—and, by extension, the rich, white United States. The USSR and, later, Communist China were able to exploit this aspect of nationalism to good advantage. The Third World became anti-West and pro-East. Not all of it, of course; some nations genuinely and jealously guarded their neutral stance. Some even maintained close political ties with the West. But, it is fair to say, the years after the war were a time when much of the world went on a double standard; the developed West and any society that professed a pro-Western orientation were expected to adhere to a code of conduct, both within their own societies and in their international dealings, that was considerably more virginal than the behavior of either the Third or Communist world. Thus, India in 1956 could lead the pack against its fellow Commonwealth member, Great Britain, but dismiss Soviet aggression in Hungary with a "no comment."

Soon after the Suez war, Paul-Henri Spaak, a leading European statesman and then the foreign minister of Belgium, expressed the exasperation of many of his colleagues from the West: "Let Israel in desperation send troops into the Sinai peninsula and let Anglo-French forces land at Port Said, and they are sure to be condemned. Meanwhile, those who were looking on impassively at the brutal repression of the revolt in Hungary could not find words harsh enough to damn them. . . . Soviet Russia and the satellite countries . . . [become] passionate defenders of the General Assembly's recommendations every time that Egypt is in question, but they treat all resolutions concerning Hungary like dead letters."[35]

And so, Suez 1956 was not only a watershed for the Middle East, Britain, and France, it also symbolized the beginning of a new era. Henceforth, the have-nots of the world would be able to marshal sufficient political strength to challenge the old great powers.

12

THE NEW REALITIES

It has become chic to attribute much of the social and political ferment of modern societies to something called a generation gap; the old do not "understand" the young, nor do the young share the values of the old. From whichever perspective, the gap is measured not in a dimension of time, but of perception. Thus, in Israel, there is a yawning abyss between those who fought for independence under the British mandate and the children of those veterans or the recent immigrants. In the Soviet Union, the fiery revolutionaries who participated in the uprisings of 1917 were unable to pass the torch on to the less ideological generations who followed them. In the United States, those who lived through the Great Depression still carry emotional scars that separate them from those who did not.

In Europe, the quarter century or so that bracketed Armistice and V-E days represents the Great Divide. Those who experienced the trials of this period at first hand have difficulty conveying their early hopes and later disappointments to a generation too young to bear the marks or carry the pride of those difficult decades. How could the oldsters articulate their feelings as they witnessed their societies cross the threshold from a century of self-confidence into a time of uncertainty?

"Two world wars and their consequences have been too much for us," Sir Arthur Bryant observes. "Like the old cars rattling and wheezing about the streets, the most we can hope to do is keep going until a less-battered generation is ready to supplant us."[1]

Sir Arthur's contemporaries were indeed "battered." And tired—keeping a stiff upper lip can be emotionally exhausting year after year. They had to have been a tough, philosophical lot. Proud, too. For until the outbreak of war in 1939, Britannia still ruled the waves, although, perhaps, not as assuredly as before World War I. Yet the man who sat on the throne was not only a king, he was also an emperor; sheikhs and chiefs, prime ministers and sultans from the four corners of the earth still paid their respects and made their homage to Buckingham Palace. Pink remained the dominant color on the map of the world.

Men of influence in Britain during the 1950s were those whose early lives were fashioned in the knowledge certain that Britain was *Great*

Britain. Everything they had learned and experienced and fought for convinced them that their nation still had a responsibility, indeed a destiny, to play a major role in shaping the course of the twentieth century, just as it had the nineteenth. With the passing of the Empire, it now fell to the Commonwealth, with Britain at its head, to light the way.

When I arrived at Grosvenor Square in the summer of 1955 men such as these led both political parties and populated all but the most junior ranks of key ministries, particularly the Foreign Office and the Treasury. These two great departments had typically attracted the best of those who sought a career in public service. Those chosen were a homogeneous group; they had more in common than perhaps any other collection of civil servants anywhere. Indeed, simply because they *had* been chosen, one could make several significant generalizations about them and about how they perceived themselves, their nation, and the world.

A civil servant in Whitehall was almost certainly male and a graduate of either Oxford or Cambridge (although if he were a Scot, it might have been St. Andrews). But not simply Oxford or Cambridge; he would have attended one of a few select colleges at either university—Balliol at Oxford, for example, or Trinity at Cambridge. There, he would have earned honors in the "Greats," or "Classics," or both. And because he *had* studied at one of these colleges, he almost certainly would have attended one of a few elite schools—Eton or Harrow or Winchester. And this, in turn, meant that he had come from a relatively well-off family and had been exposed to the ministrations of a nanny, perhaps a governess as well.

The young Foreign Office or Treasury careerist knew something about cheese and wine, Georgian silver, first editions, impressionist art. He talked knowingly, if unconvincingly, of classical music, naughty women, and good food. He spoke French and German, possibly Italian and Spanish. He had uncles who had been judges, or colonels, or governors general in India. He had "his" tailor, banker, and club. He had almost certainly served as a combat officer in the 1939–45 war—probably with distinction. Above all, he represented a line of continuity; there was little that distinguished him from his father or his grandfather.

On such men, the fortunes of British foreign policy and the health of the British pound rode for generation after generation.

These men and their counterparts elsewhere in the government, in politics, and in business were not oblivious to the fact that there was something profoundly amiss. Exports and productivity were down, expenditures on social services were mounting. Each year taxes increased, each month another great country house became "open to view."

It would not require a doctorate in economics to realize that the capital Britain had accumulated over the past century as a consequence of profitable overseas investments, innovative technology, and lively foreign trade was now supporting a society that was adding little and taking much. The same pile of chips was being pushed around the economy—some players were getting more, some less, but few new chips were being added.

The symptoms of economic malaise were evident well before Suez 1956—indeed, well before World War II. In the years just before 1939 Britain was piling up deficits amounting to hundreds of millions of pounds in its foreign trade accounts. During the war this trend accelerated, but lend-lease arrangements with the United States masked its significance and gave Britain's fundamentally worsening economic situation the coloration of a temporary, wartime phenomenon. As a consequence, many politicians (and economists, too) on both sides of the Atlantic misjudged the true nature of Britain's postwar difficulties. In 1949, the pound was devalued from $4.03 to $2.80. The strict currency controls that followed the devaluation helped, but were not enough; the chronically troubled pound continued to be shaky despite periodic resuscitation.

But if my generation in Whitehall sensed that the Britain they knew was ill, they sustained themselves on hopes that the illness would soon pass away. They found it hard to grasp, uncongenial to consider that the strength of Old Blighty was in steep decline. To them Britain, with all its postwar problems, should, could, indeed would, continue to exercise a major influence on the course of international events.

Spring 1957 was especially welcome in London. The winter had not been as cold as some in the recent past—luckily, considering the oil shortage. But it certainly had seemed colder, darker, and grayer. The season had particular significance that year. Nature and politicians, both, were stirring after an autumn and winter of stagnation. Prime Minister Macmillan now seemed to have a firm hold on the reins of his party and government, the corrosive Conservative-Labour feud had reverted to a more normal and healthy level of government-Opposition debate. There was, that April, a feeling of rejuvenation and hope.

But few pretended that what happened in the latter half of 1956 was just a nightmare—frightening, but unreal. Even complacent politicians, pukka civil servants, and Colonel Blimps sensed that the period between late October and early November marked a watershed for Britain. There was widespread realization now that British power had eroded during the decade after World War II. In the aftermath of Suez, most British recognized the new reality: The days when their country could play a major, *independent* international role were over. An era had come to a close.

The dividing line between the old and the new was sharply marked by the appearance of a new crop of British writers. By chance, they made their debut in 1956, and it would have been hard to say whether British intellectuals were shaken more by the Suez war or by the New Drama.

John Osborne's play *Look Back in Anger* opened in May 1956. It influenced the style, staging, and content of British theater almost overnight. A new school of playwrights and writers—Arden, Pinter, Amis, Braine, Sillitoe, and a host of others in their late twenties or early thirties —chose the provinces rather than London for their settings. The working classes provided their heroes, antiheroes, and villains. Politics, the welfare state, class struggle, inner conflicts were the basis of their plots. They were anti-Establishment, sometimes even anti–Royal Family. They were searching for new, more relevant values. They were angry.

"We are setting aside a conviction," wrote Malcolm Bradbury, author and teacher, "that . . . we belong to the richest and most developed society the world has ever known. . . . It is perhaps a belated challenge to the genteel tradition that the English are now experiencing."[2]

There was, then, a time lag—a generation gap, so to speak—between the outlook of Whitehall and that of much of the rest of the country. But even there it would come—a readiness to look beyond London and beyond the shores of the United Kingdom from a new, somewhat less Olympian perspective. And Suez would give time a helping hand in this regard.

Although the disaster at Port Said punctuated the end of Britain as an independent international power, it was not a catastrophic event comparable to the defeat of Germany and Japan in 1945. Perhaps an analogy closer to the mark was the American experience in Vietnam—a traumatic national confrontation with the new realities of international power. Of a sudden, assumed strength was transformed into real weakness; old and hallowed preconceptions melted away. Yet the analogy is flawed on two counts: American human losses in Vietnam were infinitely greater than British casualties at Suez. And British strategic losses in the Middle East were infinitely greater than those of the United States in Southeast Asia; Britain had had a long, well-established role in the Middle East and the United States enjoyed only an ephemeral presence in Southeast Asia.

In the last analysis, Suez altered the perceptions rather than the circumstances of British power. The changes that took place in Britain and the Middle East after 1956 were already in train; but Suez accelerated them. The tide of nationalism in the Arab world would have, sooner or later, forced Britain to give up her influence there; an eventual British withdrawal from the Middle East was in the cards. For those who could assess the matter with dispassion, the aftermath of Eden's misadventure in the autumn of 1956 simply gave new impetus to trends already apparent in Great Britain and the Middle East during the two previous decades.

Eden had mounted an old-fashioned war to preserve Britain's position abroad, but by 1956 his countrymen's enthusiasm for overseas adventures and for the outreach of British power had begun to flag. Britain had turned inward. "With the announcement of its impending retreat from Suez," Arthur Bryant laments, ". . . a British Government has put the seal on the process of decline and surrender. Obsessed with 'growth,' profits, wage-claims, gambling, take-over bids, fast air and road transport, sex . . . the people of Britain seem to accept the process much as they do the weather."[3]

The bungled miniwar left an ugly residue of bitterness and acrimony. Much of it was directed toward the United States for its abrupt refusal to go ahead with the Aswan loan, its anti-British stance in the United Nations, its tardy help in relieving Britain's post-Suez economic difficulties. Many British felt that Washington had regarded as a spectator sport Eden's desperate efforts to protect Britain's vital interests in the Middle East; many were convinced that America had gleaned secret satisfaction, even economic advantage, from Britain's disastrous diplomatic defeat.

Prime Minister Macmillan did his best to restore the old relationship, not only because of sentiment and pride, but also because Britain would need the comfort, assurance, and support of the United States as it faced uncertain times to come. In the rigid, polarized world of the late fifties, few nations—large or small, rich or poor, old or newly independent— could avoid choosing sides. Even those countries who stoutly proclaimed to be "unaligned" lost their balance and soon fell off their political tightropes in the direction of either East or West.

The British had no choice, of course. Of their two wartime allies, they were foreordained to cast their lot with the United States, for better or worse. Churchill himself set the course: "Whenever I have to choose between America and Russia," he told de Gaulle during World War II, "it will always be America."

For Dwight Eisenhower and, indeed, for most Americans, the alliance forged during World War II had a deep personal meaning. But this was not the only reason the President was anxious to heal the breach between the two nations. Pragmatism as well as sentiment played a part: Great Britain could still make an important, albeit now lesser, contribution in the continuing great confrontation between East and West. With the Suez matter behind them and a seemingly endless cold war with the Soviet Union ahead, Macmillan and Eisenhower were convinced that the future of both America and Britain lay in close consultation and, when possible, joint action. And so the President did his best to forget the unpleasant and dangerous moments of the recent past.

In London the new ambassador, John Hay Whitney, an energetic, sensible man, was determined to start a fresh, clean chapter. He planned not only to mend the ties with the Conservative government, but also to establish contacts with the Labour Party, from which Ambassador Aldrich had kept very much aloof. Ostensibly he regarded it as infra dig to seek out members of the Opposition, but more likely his patrician personality made him socially uncomfortable with earthy Labour politicians. Whitney felt neither officially constrained nor personally disinclined to associate with the shadow cabinet or Labour back-benchers. And he was ready, even eager, to get out of London—not to the country houses of the rich and the great, but to towns, coal mines, and farming areas.

But, still, the Anglo-American special relationship never quite recovered from the stresses of 1956. The crisscrossing strands of mutual affection, respect, and cooperation between and among politicians, civil servants, military officers, bankers, professors, and artists had been sorely strained; the web would not again have the strength and resiliency it had had during World War II and the decade after. It was not for want of trying; it was just that neither the Americans nor the British could mask or sugarcoat the events preceding, surrounding, and immediately following October and November of 1956.

Perhaps even without the Suez affair, the intimate wartime and early postwar relationships between Washington and London would have settled into a looser, more pragmatic pattern as the years went by. The national interests and international responsibilities of the United States and Britain took on different colorations with the passage of time. The British, for example, soon found it desirable to recognize the government in Peking, while the Americans held steadfastly faithful to Chiang Kai-shek. And while the British were closing out their old commitments east of Suez, the Americans found themselves becoming increasingly involved there. By the end of Eisenhower's second term, Southeast Asia, and in particular tiny Laos, began to preoccupy the vast National Security Council machinery. Kennedy would inherit not only the Laos problem, but would soon discover that his legacy of trouble extended into Vietnam. And soon there would be the Congo and Cuba to divert America's attention further from problems of mutual concern to both London and Washington.

What emerged in the wake of the dark days of Suez was a partnership —of sorts. The Americans, of course, were the senior partners even in areas of the world where there were common interests. In the Middle

East, the Eisenhower Doctrine and, more important, the American Sixth Fleet provided a Pax Americana until 1965, when the United States embroiled itself in Southeast Asia. At that point, and for years after, the Middle East (as well as Western Europe and Latin America) became residual claimants for Washington's time and attention.

Yet the British memory of the autumn of 1956, that ugly residue, would not entirely go away. Ten years after, it was to surface again, even though different political parties now controlled the governments in London and Washington. This time, it was the President's turn to ask and be refused, to berate and curse an inconstant ally. Lyndon Johnson wanted British participation in some form, in any form, in the war against Ho Chi Minh, whom he regarded, just as Eden had once regarded Nasser, as the devil incarnate.

I was then on the White House staff and was charged by President Johnson to bring "more flags" into Vietnam. I urged the British to consider sending at least some medical teams to work in Vietnamese hospitals, or even a handful of social workers to help in the orphanages and refugee camps. The answer from Downing Street was "Sorry. The Prime Minister would have great difficulty in Commons. Most Members of Parliament think Washington is morally in the wrong. And many remember the American reaction to Suez."

The American reaction to the Suez invasion turned out to be more complicated than Anthony Eden and virtually everyone else was able to divine in October and November 1956. What emerged in fact was a secret misunderstanding.

When John Foster Dulles was in Walter Reed Hospital in late November of the year of Suez, he was visited by Selwyn Lloyd, who had come to Washington from the UN meeting in New York, and Harold Caccia, Britain's new ambassador to Washington. "Why did you stop at Suez?" Dulles asked his astonished visitors.[4] A few months later, when the secretary was back at his post, he went even further with Foreign Minister Pineau, who was then visiting Washington. "At Suez we were wrong. You are the ones who were right," he told Pineau at dinner.[5]

In the light of Dulles' remarks to Lloyd and Pineau, my cryptic midnight telephone call from Robert Amory in early November takes on new meaning. "Invade or cease fire," Amory had told me to tell the British. "Either way, it will come out all right." Eden's vacillation, not the possibility of an invasion of Egypt, seemed to have been the problem really troubling Washington at that time.

Dulles may have been making cruel jokes—but the secretary was neither consciously cruel nor inclined toward humor. Amory's call may have been a teaser, an attempt to smoke out British intentions—but there were more effective ways of accomplishing this. The one explanation that does come to mind is incredibly ironic. And yet the autumn of 1956 produced a bumper harvest of ironies.

In Peter Ustinov's comedy *Romanoff and Juliet,* much sport is made of a diplomat who cheerfully acknowledges that his foreign colleague "knows that I know, that he knows, that I know, he knows." In the real world of diplomacy this can sometimes take a different and not altogether amusing turn.

American military strategists had long thought the Suez Canal important to the United States, but when the crunch came their views faded before more immediate political realities. In the end, Washington could not be aroused to support the British and French in their efforts to regain control of the Canal. But Washington did share London and Paris' deep distaste for Gamal Nasser. To be sure, Nasser was not directly threatening American interests in the Middle East; it was the wider international canvas that preoccupied Eisenhower and Dulles. And there, Nasser—the neutralist who sought aid and curried favor from both Moscow and Peking—threw a long, dark shadow over Washington's hopes for a cold war victory on the political and economic battlefield of the "unaligned" world.

But however much the Administration deplored Nasser, the shrill and vituperative hyperbole Eden and Mollet were employing and their bellicose threats of military action to redeem British and French amour propre jarred Eisenhower and Dulles' sense of style and timing. In the back of their minds (and perhaps locked in the vault of the National Security Council) may have been some more graceful and gradual approach toward Nasser's disposal or subvention. If life were to be made difficult for Nasser, the President and the secretary wanted this to be done their way.

Washington lost control of the script in October 1956, when London and Paris decided they could not wait for an elaborate and delicate American plot to unfold—if indeed Washington had anything particular in mind. Eden and Mollet chose a blunter instrument, direct military attack. Eisenhower and Dulles refused to condone, let alone participate in, the carnal act. Instead, they chose a posture of high virtue and then paraded their chastity before the world. But this did not mean that the Administration was not above enjoying the rewards of sin, if they just happened to fall its way.

This, then, may be the clue to understanding those curious, ex post facto hints of secret American support for the course Eden and Mollet had chosen: John Foster Dulles, once his own delaying strategy had fallen apart and the British and French attack was under way, may well have hoped that London and Paris would ignore the stern warnings from Washington and plunge ahead to achieve Nasser's overthrow. But what no one in Washington then knew was that, at the last moment, Eden lost his nerve. The goal would be the occupation of the Canal only. There would be no thrust toward Cairo, no attempt to challenge Nasser head on. The change in objectives, however, did not stem from Eden's fear of Cairo, but rather of Washington. Dulles' warnings were taken at full value. If, in Pliny's words, "Chance is our god," god was not smiling on Anthony Eden in early November 1956.

Her Majesty's Government under its new prime minister, Harold Macmillan, faced a world made even more complicated by the events of 1956. Many a civil servant and minister must have longed for the good old days when far-flung territories did not regard the House of Windsor as an alien anachronism, when India was a subservient, if sullen, member of the Empire, when Cyprus was a colonial winter resort. Harold Macmillan and his cabinet set their course for the high middle ground: They would attend to Britain's relations with Washington, restore its position as the patriarch of a harmonious Commonwealth family, contract the most exposed flanks in the troubled outposts of the old Empire, move cautiously to strengthen bonds with Europe, keep a wary eye on the Soviet Union and China, and reclaim Britain's position as an articulate, influential member of the United Nations.

This would not have been easy, in any case, but the task was complicated by a shrill and insistent chorus from the wings. There were strident voices from the "Suez" group of Conservative back-benchers and the jingoist press insisting on a last-ditch stand at whatever remained of Britain's old Empire. From the other side of the aisle some Labour back-benchers were clamoring for major concessions to Moscow. In counterpoint came strong pleas from business, banking, and military circles to buttress the special relationship with Washington. And—a new voice— earnest arguments from some intellectuals and the Angry Young Men in favor of "Little Britain."

The debate about Britain's proper relationship with Europe waxed stronger than ever in the aftermath of Suez. Pro-Europeans in Parliament, the press, and academe reminded the government that neither the Commonwealth nor the United States had proved a steadfast ally when the United Kingdom's national security interests in the Middle East were at hazard. Now that the British presence and commitments in Asia and Africa were being scaled down, they pointed out, the need to strengthen Britain's ties with friends closer to home was urgent.

But Macmillan, like his Conservative and Labour predecessors, was cautious about turning Britain's back on the Commonwealth and the United States in favor of a hodgepodge of Western European nations. The destiny of Britain seemed to him to lie across the seas rather than across the Channel.

On the day of the Suez cease-fire Germany's Chancellor Adenauer was in Paris, where he told Mollet and Pineau that an integrated Europe would be "your revenge" on the United States.[6] The chancellor's advice probably struck a resonant chord in France, but Prime Minister Macmillan was neither vengeful regarding America nor confident of the value of close British ties to Europe. And so Britain chose to be *of* Europe rather than *in.*

When, in early 1963, London was at last ready to join the Common Market, Paris vetoed Britain's application. President Charles de Gaulle now regarded the Market as a French-run club. British participation, he felt, not only would threaten France's leadership on the Continent, but because of the close British-American relationship, would also dilute the "European" character of the organization. Britain would have to wait another ten years before it could become a full member of what, by then, would be the European Economic Community.

Paris in the spring of 1957 was tense and gloomy. The Suez crisis had, by now, receded, but experts in the Ministry of Finance had begun the tedious business of calculating the claims to be made against Egypt for the property of the old Canal Company. And career officials in the Foreign Ministry were busy trying to repair the damage France had suffered in Washington and at the United Nations.

Algeria continued to dominate the thoughts of every Frenchman. In Algeria itself, the war went on with renewed violence and with ever decreasing prospects for its successful resolution. The humiliation France and Britain had suffered at Port Said the previous November had, as Mollet, his ministers, and generals feared it would, emboldened the Liberation Front. Despite a lethal fence the desperate French had erected along Algeria's eastern border, arms and men from Libya, Tunisia, and Egypt still managed to get through. In the Algerian countryside travel was dangerous by day, suicidal by night. In the cities, no one—civilian or soldier—was safe once the sun had set. A constant stream of new conscripts poured into Algeria to reinforce the French Army, but it was hard —as it would later be hard for Americans in Vietnam—to see light at the end of the tunnel. Paris was facing a losing battle.

Mollet was still in power that April, but uneasily so, and his days were numbered. A new group of hopeful politicians, headed by Mollet's defense minister, Bourgès-Maunoury, would take over in June to make their own fruitless attempt to resolve the Algerian problem.

By 1957, France had become a dispirited nation. In the course of less than two decades, the country had been overrun by the Germans, had lost a long and bloody war in Indochina, had suffered the humiliation of Suez, and was fighting a costly, losing war in Algeria. Adding substantially to the French malaise was a succession of short-lived hapless governments; there were three premiers in the period between Mollet's resignation in June 1957 and Charles de Gaulle's takeover in May 1958.

By the spring of 1958, the situation in Algeria had so deteriorated that the government in Paris had no choice but to enter serious negotiations with the National Liberation Front. The French Army seethed with resentment. Right-wing officers, spurred on by the French *colons* in Algeria and joined by like-minded political figures in France, revolted against the two-week-old government of Premier Pflimlin. On May 13, France teetered on the abyss of a civil war. Enter Charles de Gaulle.

General de Gaulle had been in retirement for years, patiently biding his time and awaiting his cue. His dramatic reappearance on the world stage could not have been better timed. On several earlier occasions he had been urged to reenter politics, but he had judged those moments premature. Now he was confident that he would have a wide base of support. His first official act was a bold one, but boldness was needed. He disbanded the Fourth Republic and took over emergency powers until a new constitution creating the Fifth Republic was approved in January 1959. Under this constitution the president of France would no longer be an ornament but a powerful chief executive. And *le Grand Charles* was It.

De Gaulle was initially of two minds about the war in Algeria. Everything about his background and all his aspirations for the restoration of France's international prestige dictated that the war be fought to a victorious end. Yet his sense of realpolitik and the march of history convinced him that the fighting could be concluded only by negotiations.

In the autumn of 1958, de Gaulle was convinced of the course to be taken. When a member of his cabinet asked, *"Mon général,* what solution do you see for Algeria?"· he replied simply, *"L'indépendance!"*[7]

By 1960, negotiations between heavily guarded representatives of France and the National Liberation Front began in earnest in the resort town of Evian. Soon after the start of these discussions de Gaulle publicly announced his support for Algeria's claim to self-determination. Once again, the Organization de l'Armée Secrète, right-wing French politicians, and the Algerian *colons* encouraged and perpetrated widespread terrorism throughout Algeria and France. Civil war again seemed near.

But de Gaulle stood fast, and in 1962, France recognized Algeria's independence.

The Algerian war had made the succession of feckless French governments a laughingstock internationally and in France, as well. But in Algeria it was no laughing matter; toward the end, the cruelty and violence of both the Liberation Front and the French Army sickened even the jaded world of the postwar period. The people of France were tired of the struggle; their conscripted sons turned into grudging, even mutinous soldiers. The war ended with independence for Algeria—as it was destined to in that period of history in which it was fought.

The end of the fighting brought with it grave problems for France. Nearly a million bitter *colons*—*"pieds noirs"* was their pejorative nickname because of their conspicuous black shoes in the midst of the barefoot Algerians—had to be received and digested into a suspicious French society and an inhospitable economy. The hard-pressed French exchequer spent $3 billion on the resettlement program—half in loans, half in grants. Over and above this, politicians and generals-turned-conspirators had to be brought to justice. Any government faced with these challenges during the years of the Fourth Republic would have fallen. But de Gaulle went from strength to strength.

France under de Gaulle opted to go its own way—in Europe, in the world. The new and powerful president chose to believe that history started with the Fifth Republic—and with him as its personification. He haughtily dismissed both the Entente Cordiale with Britain and the close historic ties with the United States. According to Christian Pineau, France had lost confidence in the worth of American alliances. "The Suez affair," he wrote, "made the French forget the Normandy landing and the Marshall Plan."[8]

When, during the Cuban missile crisis in 1962, ex-Secretary of State Dean Acheson briefed the general on the Soviet nuclear weapons being installed in Cuba and on the speech President Kennedy planned to make, de Gaulle asked Acheson whether he was being "informed or consulted." When Acheson replied that he was being "informed," de Gaulle shrugged. *"Tiens!"* ("Ah, so!") he said, and brushed the aerial photographs aside.

De Gaulle insisted that France be beholden to no one in matters regarding her own defense. He spurred the development of an independent nuclear capability for France (thus enlarging the "nuclear club") and refused to sign the Nuclear Proliferation Treaty of 1963. In 1966 he removed all French forces from the integrated NATO commands, and insisted that any Allied unit not under French orders be pulled out of France. In 1967 NATO Headquarters moved from France to Brussels.

Although in 1956 de Gaulle had little to say about the Suez misadventure, he regarded it as one more reason why France should endeavor to play an independent role in world affairs. And he was determined to remind Frenchmen from time to time of the unfortunate consequences that flowed from relying too heavily on others, even on allies.

In the autumn of 1966 an American diplomat attached to the embassy in Paris traveled to the provinces to take soundings on issues that affected Franco-American relations. The matter that most concerned local French officials, obviously enough, was the war in Vietnam. But much to the diplomat's surprise, the Suez affair was next on the list. One prefect noted that the strain between Paris and Washington was "a logical sequence to what happened at Suez. It was a natural reaction on the part of French officials as they remembered the days when the United States judged them unfairly and made their task impossible." The American expressed surprise at the fact that so many provincial officers still dwelled on Suez after the passage of so much time. "Don't be naive, my friend," the prefect replied. "General de Gaulle believes he can still cause discomfort to certain governments by keeping Suez memories alive. You have heard so much about it because we officials have been instructed to make as much of it as we could on the tenth anniversary."[9]

Le grand Charles proved to be a disconcerting factor on the international scene. The shock waves he produced extended from the Kremlin to the White House and to virtually every center of power in between. But, for the first time in a long time, the French government was taken seriously.

Politicians of more than average force who have unusual popular appeal, who convey a special mystique, have been described as "charismatic." The term has been applied to more men than justly deserve it. But in the case of Charles de Gaulle it was most apt; de Gaulle overflowed with charisma.

According to General Beaufre, the Suez affair was "largely responsible for the events of 13 May 1958."[10] If so, the venture had at least one major positive result. It brought to power the only Frenchman who could have restored the nation's pride and "grandeur."

More than anywhere else, the denouement of the Suez crisis resulted in a sense of relief in Israel. There was some grumbling that Ben-Gurion had given way too soon, that Israel could have exacted an even higher price—passage through the Suez Canal, for example—for withdrawal. But these were the voices of a small right-wing opposition. Most of the country was delighted with what had been achieved. At long last, terrorist raids across the Gaza Strip and the blockade of the Gulf of Aqaba had come to an end with the presence of the UN forces. For a decade, until Egypt ordered the removal of UNEF, there would be no war, even though peace seemed far away.

Israel could now concentrate on its internal economic and social problems. And these were substantial. The Suez war, with all its rewards, was not without cost in money, equipment, and lives. Opening up the Gulf of Aqaba to Israeli ships would require expending large sums to transform the sleepy little fishing village of Eilat into a modern port and to improve the communications between Eilat and the industrial centers of Israel. The harsh Negev would have to be developed to accommodate new immigrants, many of whom had been expelled from Egypt and other Arab lands. And, although its borders were now more secure than ever, Israel's military establishment had to be maintained and constantly improved in the face of continued Arab enmity.

There were pressing external problems as well. Relations with the United Nations continued to be strained and would remain so, for Israel suffered all the disadvantages of being part of the Western world but enjoyed few of the advantages. The withdrawal of Moscow's ambassador in November 1956 was soon followed by the closing of the Soviet Embassy and the onset of a mini–cold war between the USSR and Israel. Meanwhile, Britain kept Israel at a distance following the stresses of its strange, temporary alliance; the Foreign Office's pro-Arab position became once more ascendant, even in the face of Britain's growing problems in the region. France, Israel's old friend and arms supplier, became more "correct," as de Gaulle tried to reestablish the close cultural and economic ties France once had with Algeria, Tunisia, and Morocco, all of whom would have looked askance at a continued French alliance with Israel. To complicate Israel's foreign policy, the prospects for a peace treaty with the Arab world were dimmer than ever.

In the face of doors that were being slammed or that remained tightly shut, Israel's highest priority task was to cope with the damage Suez had wrought to its relations with the United States, its oldest and strongest ally. Yet another urgent step was to win such friends as it could among those nations of the Third World not under Nasser's sway. And so the next decade was devoted to building up its economy within, strengthening its defense forces, mending its fences with Washington, and building bridges to a few "unaligned" nations of Africa. It would need all of this in 1967 when war broke out again.

Heady breezes swept through the Arab world during that spring of 1957. Anthony Eden had thrown down the gauntlet; either London or Cairo would exercise the major influence in the Middle East. Cairo, or

more accurately Nasser, picked up the challenge and won the day. France and Britain had been defeated in Egypt and were on the defensive everywhere else in the Middle East.

The peoples of the Middle East, historically divided by competing royal dynasties, Muslim sects, tribal loyalties, and national jealousies, longed for a unifying spirit. Now, two were at hand—hatred of Israel and idolatry of Gamal Abdel Nasser. Nasser was only too pleased to lead both campaigns. Under the flag of anti-Zionism, Cairo Radio spewed out hourly doses of venom against Israel. And under the flag of Pan-Arabism he could carry on his battle with Britain and France. He lost no time spurring the nationalist, anti-British movements. And he stepped up his support of the National Liberation Front in Algeria.

In every Arab capital that April there was an exhilarating sense of new power; the rich, industrialized nations suddenly seemed very vulnerable. Oil and the political strength of newly independent nations turned out to be a formidable combination, one that promised to influence the global balance of power. The international marketplace for energy and the United Nations General Assembly would be the new settings for the continuing struggle between the lean and hungry Third World and the fat and arrogant West.

But Nasser's "victory" at Port Said was not, without cost—and the bills would soon be coming due. He was causing many sleepless nights in London and Paris, but, he, too, had his share of worries.

Although his post-Suez prestige was high, prestige abroad could not be converted into a solution for serious economic problems at home. Egypt's nationalized economy had been placed under the control of enthusiastic young army officers who may have been competent company or battalion commanders, but who knew little—indeed, less than little, since they did not know that they did not know—about running large agricultural, industrial, or commercial enterprises. What emerged from such arrangements was what almost anyone but a zealous Nasserite would have expected—nothing. Ambitious projects for public housing, hospitals, and schools either remained in the planning stage or, even worse, were abandoned half-finished. Nasser's worthy intentions to improve the plight of the very poor and soak the very rich resulted in the poor remaining poor and many rich becoming poor.

Other Suez-related problems compounded Nasser's economic difficulties. Tourists on whom Egypt had long relied for much of its foreign exchange earnings had been frightened away—the Sphinx had returned to its lonely vigil in the sands outside Cairo. Saudi Arabia, now that the Suez crisis was over and Nasser was throwing his weight against "reactionary" regimes in the Middle East, cut off its financial aid to Egypt.

None of the money authorized for economic aid under the Eisenhower Doctrine was sent Egypt's way; Nasser had even fewer friends on Capitol Hill after Suez than he had had in the spring of 1956 when Senator Knowland warned Secretary Dulles that funds for the Aswan Dam would have rough sledding in Congress. Obviously, no help was forthcoming from such erstwhile sources as France and Great Britain. And although revenues from the Canal were now flowing to Cairo, they hardly made a dent in the mounting deficits.

While Nasser tried to consolidate his gains and assess his losses from the Suez war, arrangements for starting construction on the cherished Aswan Dam had to wait. But in late October 1958 Chairman Khrushchev announced in Moscow that the Soviet Union had approved a loan to Egypt of $100 million as a first installment on the cost of constructing the dam. During the next decade the little backwater town of Aswan became a gigantic building site.

In the face of Moscow's economic and military aid it is no wonder that Nasser shed whatever pretense he had of maintaining an "unaligned" position between the two opposing sides in the Cold War. But in exchange for Communist economic and military assistance, he mortgaged a large part of Egypt's cotton crop, the country's only significant export.

Confronted with serious problems at home, Nasser did what many other desperate leaders have done before and since his time—he turned his own and his countrymen's attention abroad. In early 1958 he arranged a marriage of convenience with Syria. The United Arab Republic was formed with high hopes, extravagant speeches, and Gamal Nasser (naturally) as president. For Nasser it was a satisfying ego trip. But for the Syrians—? The Damascus regime must have agreed to the liaison in a momentary fit of passion or of absentmindedness; it bore the cost of associating itself with Egypt's stagnant economy and growing population and shared little of Nasser's increased prestige.

In February 1960 I happened to be in Cairo and was taken to a huge rally marking the second anniversary of the marriage. Nasser was in Damascus to officiate at the ceremonies there, but his presence was very much felt in the vast, festooned tent. For at least an hour before the formal speeches began, cheerleaders spotted throughout the crowd led fifty thousand voices in the chant NASSER!, NASSER!, while fifty thousand pictures of the great man bobbed up and down to the rhythm of the chant. Armed policemen, hundreds upon hundreds of them, were everywhere.

It was a chilling experience—the massed delegations, the endless rhythmic incantation of The Leader's name, the smell and feel of tyranny.

But the crowd seemed good-natured and the policemen (my friend and guide assured me) had no ammunition for their ancient sidearms. And so I settled down to the interminable, emotional speeches (or, rather, to the whispered translations provided by my companion). I remember nothing about them except constant references to the "perpetual," or "long-lived," or "permanent" association of Egypt and Syria under the banner of the United Arab Republic. Syria seceded eighteen months later.

Despite mounting economic problems and occasional diplomatic setbacks, both Nasser and Egypt were now on the political map of the world. But in 1967 came another war with Israel. This time not even the most clever cosmetician could cover the reality of Egypt's defeat. In six days, Egypt lost almost twelve thousand men, its air force was all but destroyed, its oil installations and air bases in the Sinai were taken over by Israel. The Suez Canal was closed again, not for six months this time, but for eight years.

Between the two Middle East wars of 1956 and 1967 Western Europe and Japan had become increasingly dependent on oil from the region. In 1956, the year of Suez, tankers accounted for two-thirds of the tonnage passing through the Canal. By then, approximately 25 percent of Europe's energy needs was supplied by oil. In the sixties Europe's demand for Middle East oil trebled and Japan's increased seven times. By the end of that decade the United States, too, began to import a significant amount of Middle East oil.

While the Canal was closed in late 1956 and early 1957, Europe made do with oil from the Western Hemisphere and with Middle East supplies that had come by way of the Cape of Good Hope. But Western oil was an emergency, stopgap measure, and oil shipped around the Cape was costly in terms of time and money. For months Europe limped along on about half of its normal oil requirements.

The world's tanker fleet, already tight, was severely strained by the new, longer shipping routes. More tankers were obviously needed to supply the world's insatiable and increasing demand for oil. But changes were on the way that would make a profound difference, not only to the international oil trade but also to the importance of the Suez Canal.

By the end of World War II, the largest oil tankers were 18,000 tons. By 1950, ships of 28,000 to 30,000 tons had been built. But this was just the beginning. Shipbuilding technology and shipping economics soon took over. Larger and larger oil carriers could be constructed, and these required crews of about the same size as those needed to man the smaller ships. By 1957, farsighted experts were predicting tankers of 100,000 tons. By the early sixties, vessels of this size were already in operation. By 1973, shipyards were laying keels for 400,000 tonners, and more than three hundred tankers of at least 200,000 tons, each as long as the Empire State Building, were already in service.[11]

Egypt watched the supertanker with justifiable concern since the Canal could barely accommodate ships of 30,000 tons. Although the number of ships passing through Suez and the annual revenues from tolls increased each year after the Canal reopened in early 1957, it was becoming increasingly evident that the Canal was a convenience rather than a necessity. Soon after the Suez war, much of the world's most vital cargo, except for food, was being carried in vessels that had to ply the route around the Cape of Good Hope, whether the Canal was open or not. When the industrialized nations confronted their next energy crisis in 1973, it was because nations of the Middle East had cut off the supply of oil; the Canal had been blocked six years before.

When the Canal was reopened in 1975, it had been widened and dredged so that ships as large as 60,000 tons could make the journey. Plans are in train to increase the capacity to 150,000 tonners, but this will still be too small to keep up with the trend toward ever larger ships. The problem is economic as well as physical; it now costs twice as much to send oil in a ship small enough to squeeze through the Canal as it does to send it around the Cape in a supertanker.

The Suez Canal is by no means now redundant. But it no longer occupies pride of place among the world's strategic real estate. Nasser's move in 1956 was fortuitous; a decade later, his seizure of the Canal would have given him substantially less leverage among the industrial and maritime powers.

In the spring of 1957, the superships and their implications for global strategy were still in the future. Of greater relevance at that time was the emergence in the Middle East of another kind of giant—a political one: the USSR. Following the British-French withdrawal, Moscow had scored many propaganda points on its claim that Soviet threats to dispatch rockets and "volunteers," rather than the UN's actions, had ended the war and assured a victory for Egypt. The wave of nationalism that swept the region suited Bulganin at least as well as it did Nasser. If the Cairo regime planned to be the force behind anti-Western moves throughout the Middle East, the Kremlin planned to be the force behind Cairo. It would also deal directly with new pro-leftist leaders in Syria and Iraq.

The concern Macmillan and Eisenhower had voiced about Soviet intentions in the Middle East had much more behind it than the tired rhetoric of Cold War speeches might indicate. The Eisenhower Doctrine recognized that, with the virtual departure of the British and with increased Soviet prestige, the Middle East was open to a grave new threat. The United States would now have to assume a role in the region as a whole rather than in just a few countries.

Within a year after Suez there was a perceptible shift in the Middle East from its historic economic and political orientation toward Western Europe. Moscow and Washington, not London and Paris, would now wield major influence in the area.

For the Kremlin, this meant the fulfillment of an cld Russian dream, one that long preceded the Revolution of 1917: Russia would have a presence in the Mediterranean. For the White House, this meant a new policy stance: American commitments to Israel would have to be balanced against the strategic and economic penalties involved in angering the Arabs. For industrialized and developing nations alike, Suez 1956 should have flashed a warning that growing dependence on Middle East oil would place not only their domestic economies but also their international policies in pawn to the whims and aspirations of remote sheikhs and military chieftains. For the world as a whole, and for the countries of the Middle East in particular, it implied a new and dangerous era; the Middle East had become yet another area of push and shove in the great East-West rivalry.

I returned to Washington in the late summer of 1958. New crises in other parts of the world lay ahead. Suez was behind me, but the experience was hard to put out of mind. I had my own Suez residue to grapple with. There were memories of chilling Joint Intelligence Committee meetings, of unpleasant anti-American incidents, of midnight treks to the embassy. There was a still-smoldering resentment directed at two men I scarcely knew, Anthony Eden and John Foster Dulles, who seemed to have done nothing right and everything wrong. And there was a permanent physical souvenir.

It was a curious time, those Suez months. There was high comedy, low conspiracy, and deep tragedy, but mostly tragedy—for individuals and for nations. Enemies found themselves close bedfellows; allies became hostile strangers. Through that terrible period there was an undertone of guilt—a nagging feeling on the part of many in Britain, France, and America that their untimely preoccupation with the Middle East might have cost Hungary its freedom.

When the crisis was over, when the abscess had burst, the world was a different place. But, of all the nations involved, Great Britain was affected most immediately, most dramatically. For although Britain's eco-

nomic and military strength had long been trickling away, Anthony
Eden's Suez policy and its mortifying aftermath made it apparent to
everyone there and to most people everywhere that Britain could no
longer exercise power on a global scale. Sixty years after Queen Victoria's
Jubilee, the lion roared for the last time.

NOTES

Chapter 2

1. Herman Melville, *Moby Dick,* Modern Library, New York, 1950, pp. 232–33.

2. J. E. Nourse, "Ferdinand de Lesseps," *Lippincott's Magazine,* Philadelphia, Vol. XIII, March 1874, pp. 332–37.

3. David McCullough, *The Path Between the Seas,* Simon and Schuster, New York, 1977, p. 49.

4. "Lesseps' Recollections," Review of de Lesseps' *Recollections of Forty Years, The Nation,* New York, Vol. XVI, Jan.–June 1888, pp. 181–82.

5. G. W. Wheatley, "Some Account of the Late Lieut. Waghorn, R.N., The Originator of the Overland Route," *Bentley's Miscellany,* London, Vol. 27, 1850, pp. 350–51.

6. John Bowring, "Recollections of Lord Palmerston," *Fortnightly Review,* London, November 15, 1865 to February 1, 1866, pp. 1–9.

7. Letter of Ferdinand de Lesseps to Count Th. de Lesseps, London, June 25, 1855. From Hugh J. Schonfield, *The Suez Canal in Peace and War, 1869–1969,* University of Miami Press, Coral Gables, Fl., 1969, p. 27.

8. P. H. M., "The Suez Canal—A History," *Appleton's Journal,* New York, April 1880, p. 304.

9. Ferdinand de Lesseps, Letter to the Editor, *Appleton's Journal,* New York, May 1880, p. 466.

10. United States Foreign Relations, 1866, U.S. Department of State.

11. *The Practical Magazine,* The Willmer and Rogers News Company, New York, Vol. 5, No. 6, 1875, p. 163.

12. Letter from President Grant to the viceroy of Egypt, August 31, 1869. Library of Congress, Manuscripts Division, John Bigelow Papers, Washington, D.C.

13. *The Times,* London, November 19, 1869.

14. Edward Frederic Benson, *Queen Victoria,* Longmans, Green and Co., London, 1935, p. 273.

15. "Political Career of Mr. Disraeli," *British Quarterly Review,* Hodder and Stoughton, London, No. CXXVII, July 1, 1876, p. 173.

16. Raphael Patai, *The Arab Mind,* Charles Scribner's Sons, New York, 1973, p. 272.

17. *United States Foreign Relations,* 1880, U.S. Department of State.

18. Edmund Clarence Stedman, *A Victorian Anthology, 1837–1895,* Houghton Mifflin, Cambridge, 1895, p. xi.

19. Henry Morton Stanley, *Through the Dark Continent,* George Newnes, Ltd., London, 1899, vol. 1, pp. 51–52.

20. *Eclectic Magazine,* W. H. Bidwell, New York, Vol. LX, Sept. to Dec., 1863, pp. 125–26.

Chapter 3

1. P. H. M., "The Suez Canal—A History," *Appleton's Journal,* New York, April 1880, p. 303.

2. Humphrey Trevelyan, *The Middle East in Revolution,* Macmillan and Co., Ltd., London, 1970, p. 129.

3. Nathan Appleton, handwritten manuscript, dated Boston, 1890. Library of Congress, Manuscripts Division, Washington, D.C.

4. Winston S. Churchill, *A History of the English Speaking Peoples,* Cassell & Co., Ltd., London, 1958, vol. IV, p. 231.

5. Letter to the Editor of *The Nation,* London, April 24, 1920, pp. 109–10.

6. Winston S. Churchill, *The Second World War,* Vol. II, *Their Finest Hour,* Houghton Mifflin Company, Boston, 1949, pp. 428–29.

7. Ibid., p. 613.

8. Claude Dewhurst, *Limelight for Suez,* R. Schindler, Cairo, 1946, p. 124.

9. Harold Macmillan, *Tides of Fortune, 1945–55,* Harper & Row, New York, 1969, p. 76.

10. George F. Kennan, "United States and the Soviet Union," *Foreign Affairs,* New York, Vol. 54, No. 4, July 1976, p. 683.

Chapter 4

1. Peter Mansfield, *The British in Egypt,* Holt, Rinehart & Winston, New York, 1971, p. 309.

2. Anthony Eden, *Full Circle: The Memoirs of Anthony Eden,* Houghton Mifflin Company, Boston, 1960, p. 124.

3. Harold Macmillan, *Riding the Storm,* Harper & Row, New York, 1971, p. 91.

4. Interviews.

5. Townsend Hoopes, *The Devil and John Foster Dulles,* Little, Brown & Co., Boston, 1973, p. 326.

6. Anthony Eden, op. cit., p. 381.

7. Ibid., pp. 383–84.

8. Humphrey Trevelyan, *The Middle East in Revolution*, Macmillan and Co., Ltd., London, 1970, p. 69.

Chapter 5

1. Sherman Adams, *Firsthand Report*, Harper & Row, New York, 1971, p. 89.

2. Townsend Hoopes, *The Devil and John Foster Dulles*, Little, Brown & Co., Boston, 1973, p. xiv.

3. Robert Murphy, *Diplomat Among Warriors*, Doubleday & Co., Inc., New York, 1964, p. 384.

4. Interview.

5. Lord Charles Moran, *Churchill: Taken from the Diaries of Lord Moran, 1940–1965*, Houghton Mifflin Company, Boston, 1966, p. 591.

6. Ibid., p. 771.

7. Ibid., p. 481.

8. Randolph S. Churchill, *The Rise and Fall of Sir Anthony Eden*, Mac-Gibbon & Kee, London, 1959, p. 19.

9. Robert Murphy, op. cit., p. 382.

10. John Foster Dulles Papers, Princeton University Library, Princeton, New Jersey.

11. Harold Macmillan, *Tides of Fortune, 1945–55*, Harper & Row, New York, 1969, p. 499.

12. Anthony Eden, *Full Circle: The Memoirs of Anthony Eden*, Houghton Mifflin Company, Boston, 1960, pp. 374–75.

13. Harold Macmillan, *Riding the Storm*, Harper & Row, New York, 1971, p. 91.

14. Ibid., p. 92.

15. Sherman Adams, op. cit., p. 247.

16. Anthony Eden, op. cit., p. 374.

17. Gamal Abdel Nasser, "The Egyptian Revolution," *Foreign Affairs*, New York, January 1955, pp. 199–211.

18. Anthony Eden, op. cit., p. 389.

19. Ibid., p. 394.

20. Anthony Nutting, *Nasser*, E. P. Dutton, New York, 1972, p. 136.

21. Anthony Nutting, as recorded by BBC and rebroadcast in *The Suez Affair*, November 8, 1976.

22. Mohamed Heikal, *The Cairo Documents*, Doubleday & Co., Inc., Garden City, N.Y., 1973, pp. 80–81.

23. *The Times*, London, April 27, 1956.

24. Kennett Love, *Suez: The Twice-Fought War*, McGraw-Hill Book Company, New York and Toronto, 1969, p. 134.

25. Paul Johnson, *The Suez War*, MacGibbon & Kee, London, 1957, p. 35.

26. The Secretary's Press Conference, Department of State, May 23, 1956.

27. U.S. Department of State Memorandum, December 2, 1955 (declassified).

28. Mohamed Heikal, op. cit., p. 64.

29. Ibid., p. 65.

30. Washington *Post*, July 18, 1956.

31. See *New York Times*, June 19, 1956.

32. U.S. Department of State Memorandum, June 22, 1956 (declassified).

33. Kennett Love, op. cit., p. 322.

34. Anthony Nutting, *No End of a Lesson*, Clarkson N. Potter, Inc., New York, 1967, p. 44.

35. U.S. Department of State Memorandum, July 19, 1956.

36. Robert Murphy, op. cit., p. 377.

37. Anthony Eden, op. cit., pp. 468–69.

38. Ibid., p. 470.

39. U.S. Department of State Memorandum of Conversation, July 20, 1956 (declassified).

40. *New York Times*, July 25, 1956.

Chapter 6

1. Mohamed Heikal, *The Cairo Documents*, Doubleday & Co., Inc., Garden City, N.Y., 1973, p. 90.

2. *The Suez Canal Problem, July 26–September 22, 1956: A Documentary Publication*, U.S. Department of State, Washington, D.C., 1957, pp. 26–30.

3. U.S. Foreign Broadcast Information Service, Washington, D.C., July 23, 1956.

4. U.S. Department of State, Press Release No. 414, July 28, 1956.

5. Interview with William Clark, then press secretary to the prime minister.

6. Lord Charles Moran, *Churchill: Taken from the Diaries of Lord Moran, 1940–1965*, Houghton Mifflin Company, Boston, 1966, p. 747.

7. Anthony Eden, *Full Circle: The Memoirs of Anthony Eden*, Houghton Mifflin Company, Boston, 1960, pp. 476–77.

8. Robert Murphy, *Diplomat Among Warriors*, Doubleday & Co., Inc., New York, 1964, pp. 382–83.

9. Jacques Baeyens, *Un Coup d'épée dans l'eau du Canal*, Librairie Arthème Fayard, Paris, 1976, p. 16.

10. Robert Murphy, op. cit., p. 382.

11. Terence Robertson, *Crisis: The Inside Story of the Suez Conspiracy*, Hutchinson Press, London, 1964, p. 24.

12. Dwight D. Eisenhower, *The White House Years: Waging Peace, 1956–61*, Doubleday & Co., Inc., Garden City, N.Y., 1965, pp. 664–65.

13. Christian Pineau, *1956/Suez*, Editions Robert Laffont, Paris, 1976, pp. 92, 95.

14. Anthony Eden, op. cit., p. 487.

15. Robert Murphy, op. cit., p. 383.

16. *Hansard*, Parliamentary Debates, August 2, 1956.

17. Anthony Eden, op. cit., pp. 495–96.

18. Sherman Adams, *Firsthand Report*, Harper & Row, New York, 1971, p. 250.

19. Charles E. Bohlen, *Witness to History, 1929–1969*, W. W. Norton & Co., Inc., New York, 1973, p. 425.

20. Ibid., p. 428.

21. *The Suez Canal Problem*, op. cit., p. 102.

22. Mohamed Heikal, op. cit., p. 100.

23. Anthony Eden, op. cit., pp. 504–5.

24. Charles E. Bohlen, op. cit., pp. 429–30.

25. Kennett Love, *Suez: The Twice-Fought War*, McGraw-Hill Book Company, New York and Toronto, 1969, p. 412.

26. Mohamed Heikal, op. cit., p. 103.

27. Robert Murphy, op. cit., p. 384.

28. Dwight D. Eisenhower, op. cit., pp. 666–68.

29. Anthony Eden, op. cit., pp. 519–21.

30. Dwight D. Eisenhower, op. cit., pp. 669–71.

31. Anthony Eden, op. cit., p. 533.

32. Ibid., p. 538.

33. *New York Times*, September 14, 1956.

34. Robert Morse, "After Eight Years, World's Shipping Is Moving Through Suez Canal," *Smithsonian*, Washington, D.C., October 1975, pp. 60–67.

Chapter 7

1. *The Suez Canal Problem, July 26–September 22, 1956: A Documentary Publication*, U.S. Department of State, Washington, D.C., 1957, pp. 358–61.

2. Ibid., p. 356.

3. Interview.

4. *The Suez Canal Problem,* op. cit., p. 357.

5. Ibid., p. 365.

6. Anthony Nutting, *No End of a Lesson,* Clarkson N. Potter, Inc., New York, 1967, p. 70.

7. Anthony Eden, *Full Circle: The Memoirs of Anthony Eden,* Houghton Mifflin Company, Boston, 1960, p. 557.

8. Interviews.

9. *New York Times,* October 9, 1956.

10. Anthony Nutting, op. cit., p. 71.

11. Moshe Dayan, *Story of My Life,* Steimatzky's Agency, Ltd., Jerusalem and Tel Aviv, 1976, p. 160.

12. Anthony Eden, op. cit., pp. 553–54.

13. Abba Eban, *An Autobiography,* Random House, New York, 1977, p. 209.

14. Anthony Eden, op. cit., pp. 563–64.

15. Anthony Nutting, op. cit., p. 96.

16. Robert R. Bowie, *Suez 1956,* Oxford University Press, London, 1974, p. 51.

17. Anthony Nutting, op. cit., p. 91.

18. Ibid., p. 97.

19. U.S. Foreign Broadcast Information Service, Washington, D.C., October 15, 1956.

20. Anthony Eden, op. cit., p. 573.

21. Ibid., p. 574.

22. Ibid., p. 555.

23. Moshe Dayan, op. cit., pp. 174–75.

24. Ibid., p. 182.

25. Ibid., p. 180.

26. Ibid., p. 181.

27. William Clark, interview.

Chapter 8

1. Abba Eban, *An Autobiography,* Random House, New York, 1977, p. 211.

2. Townsend Hoopes, *The Devil and John Foster Dulles,* Little, Brown & Co., Boston, 1973, p. 374.

3. Robert Amory, then deputy director of the Central Intelligence Agency.

4. *Documents on the Suez Crisis, 26 July to 6 November, 1956.* The Royal Institute of International Affairs, Eyre & Spottiswoode, Ltd., London, 1957, pp. 85–86.

5. Abba Eban, op. cit., p. 214.

6. Anthony Eden, *Full Circle: The Memoirs of Anthony Eden,* Houghton Mifflin Company, Boston, 1960, p. 587.

7. Assemblée Nationale, *Débats, Journal Officiel,* December 20, 1956.

8. Dwight D. Eisenhower, *The White House Years: Waging Peace, 1956–61,* Doubleday & Co., Inc., Garden City, N.Y., 1965, pp. 678–79.

9. Interview.

10. Interview.

11. Humphrey Trevelyan, *The Middle East in Revolution,* Macmillan and Co., Ltd., London, 1970, pp. 114–15.

12. United Nations document S/3712, October 30, 1956.

13. Jacques Baeyens, *Un Coup d'épée dans l'eau du Canal,* Librairie Arthème Fayard, Paris, 1976, p. 18.

14. Moshe Dayan, *Diary of the Sinai Campaign,* Schocken Books, New York, 1965, p. 71.

15. U.S. Foreign Broadcast Information Service, Washington, D.C., October 30, 1956.

16. Ibid.

17. Michael Bar-Zohar, *Ben-Gurion: The Armed Prophet,* Prentice-Hall, Inc., Englewood Cliffs, N.J., 1968, pp. 219–20.

18. Townsend Hoopes, op. cit., p. 377, quoting Eisenhower's speech writer Emmet Hughes.

19. Terence Robertson, *Crisis: The Inside Story of the Suez Conspiracy,* Hutchinson Press, London, 1964, p. 170.

20. U.S. Foreign Broadcast Information Service, Washington, D.C., November 1, 1956.

21. *Hansard,* Parliamentary Debates, October 31, 1956.

22. Jacques Baeyens, op. cit., p. 69.

23. Moshe Dayan, op. cit., pp. 114–15.

24. Kennett Love, *Suez: The Twice-Fought War,* McGraw-Hill Book Company, New York and Toronto, 1969, p. 557.

25. Moshe Dayan, op. cit., p. 160.

26. André Beaufre, *The Suez Expedition, 1956,* Frederick A. Praeger, New York, 1969, pp. 88–89.

27. Ibid., p. 97.

28. Anthony Eden, op. cit., p. 611.

29. Hugh Gaitskell, as recorded by BBC and rebroadcast in *The Suez Affair,* November 11, 1976.

30. Lord Charles Moran, *Churchill: Taken from the Diaries of Lord Moran, 1940–1965,* Houghton Mifflin Company, Boston, 1966, p. 755.

31. Peter Calvocoressi, *Suez: Ten Years After,* edited by Anthony Moncrieff, BBC Sound Archives, Pantheon Books, New York, 1967, pp. 15–16.

32. Ibid.

33. Anthony Eden, op. cit., p. 611.

Chapter 9

1. James Eayrs, "Canadian Policy and Opinion During the Suez Crisis," *International Journal,* Canadian Institute of International Affairs, Toronto, Vol. 12, No. 2, 1957, p. 101.

2. Harold Macmillan, *Riding the Storm,* Harper & Row, New York, 1971, p. 164.

3. Peter Calvocoressi, *Suez: Ten Years After,* edited by Anthony Moncrieff, BBC Sound Archives, Pantheon Books, New York, 1967, p. 25.

4. Harold Macmillan, op. cit., p. 164.

5. Richard Crossman, *The Diaries of a Cabinet Minister,* Volume I, Holt, Rinehart & Winston, New York, 1976, p. 141.

6. William Clark, as recorded by BBC and rebroadcast in *The Suez Affair,* November 11, 1976.

7. White House news release, November 5, 1956.

8. United Nations document S/3736, November 5, 1956.

9. *New York Times,* November 6, 1956.

10. Moshe Dayan, *Story of My Life,* Steimatzky's Agency, Ltd., Jerusalem and Tel Aviv, 1976, p. 210.

11. *New York Times,* November 6, 1956.

12. See Townsend Hoopes, *The Devil and John Foster Dulles,* Little, Brown & Co., Boston, 1973, p. 385. Also Terence Robertson, *Crisis: The Inside Story of the Suez Conspiracy,* Hutchinson Press, London, 1964, p. 253.

13. Christian Pineau, as recorded by BBC and rebroadcast in *The Suez Affair,* November 11, 1976.

14. *United States Policy in the Middle East, September 1956–June 1957,* Greenwood Press, New York, 1968, pp. 190–91.

15. Interview.

16. Anthony Howard, "Memoirs of a Suez Warrior," *New Statesman,* London, October 29, 1976.

17. Interview.

18. Keith Kyle, as recorded by BBC and rebroadcast in *The Suez Affair,* November 9, 1976.

19. Interview.

20. Abba Eban, *An Autobiography,* Random House, New York, 1977, p. 228.

21. See also Robert Amory, as recorded by BBC and rebroadcast in *The Suez Affair,* November 11, 1976.

22. Anthony Eden, *Full Circle: The Memoirs of Anthony Eden,* Houghton Mifflin Company, Boston, 1960, pp. 621–22.

23. André Beaufre, *The Suez Expedition, 1956,* Frederick A. Praeger, New York, 1969, p. 117.

24. Kennett Love, *Suez: The Twice-Fought War,* McGraw-Hill Book Company, New York and Toronto, 1969, p. 610.

25. Mohamed Heikal, *The Cairo Documents,* Doubleday & Co., Inc., Garden City, N.Y., 1973, p. 112.

26. Anthony Eden, op. cit., p. 628.

27. André Beaufre, op. cit., p. 122.

28. *The Listener,* London, November 4, 1976, p. 564.

29. Kennett Love, op. cit., p. 630.

30. Much of the following information was obtained through interviews in London in late 1976 with members of Eden's cabinet and with senior civilian and military officials who had been involved at the time.

31. Hugh Thomas, *Suez,* Harper & Row, New York and Evanston, 1966, p. 42.

32. Moshe Dayan, op. cit., p. 203.

33. Hugh Thomas, op. cit., p. 160.

34. Ibid., p. 164.

35. *Al-Jumhuriyan,* Cairo, December 7, 1956.

36. Mohamed Heikal, op. cit., p. 116.

Chapter 10

1. Lord Charles Moran, *Churchill: Taken from the Diaries of Lord Moran, 1940–1965,* Houghton Mifflin Company, Boston, 1966, p. 773.

2. *The Sunday Times,* London, November 11, 1956.

3. Interview.

4. See Townsend Hoopes, *The Devil and John Foster Dulles,* Little, Brown & Co., Boston, 1973, pp. 385–86.

5. Anthony Eden, *Full Circle: The Memoirs of Anthony Eden,* Houghton Mifflin Company, Boston, 1960, pp. 630–31.

6. Brian Urquhart, *Hammarskjöld,* Alfred A. Knopf, New York, 1972, p. 185.

7. Ibid., p. 189.

8. Anthony Eden, op. cit., p. 635.

9. *United States Policy in the Middle East, September 1956–June 1957,* Greenwood Press, New York, 1968, p. 211.

10. Ibid., pp. 212–13.

11. Dwight D. Eisenhower, *The White House Years: Waging Peace, 1956–61,* Doubleday & Co., Inc., Garden City, N.Y., 1965, p. 95.

12. André Beaufre, *The Suez Expedition, 1956,* Frederick A. Praeger, New York, 1969, p. 127.

13. *United States Policy in the Middle East,* op. cit., pp. 240–44.

14. Richard Crossman, *The Diaries of a Cabinet Minister,* Volume II, Holt, Rinehart & Winston, New York, 1977, p. 167.

15. Interview.

16. Lord Moran, op. cit., p. 755.

17. Jacques Baeyens, *Un Coup d'épée dans l'eau du Canal,* Librairie Arthème Fayard, Paris, 1976, p. 149.

18. *Newsweek,* New York, December 3, 1956.

19. Anthony Eden, op. cit., p. 643.

20. *The Times,* London, November 23, 1956.

21. Assemblée Nationale, *Débats, Journal Officiel,* December 18, 1956.

22. Ibid., December 19, 1956.

23. Ibid., December 20, 1956.

24. Harold Macmillan, *Riding the Storm,* Harper & Row, New York, 1971, p. 176.

25. Sherman Adams, *Firsthand Report,* Harper & Row, New York, 1971, p. 260.

26. *United States Policy in the Middle East,* op. cit., p. 358.

27. Anthony Eden, op. cit., p. 645.

28. Jacques Baeyens, op. cit., p. 207.

29. André Beaufre, op. cit., p. 129.

30. *The Times,* London, December 27, 1956.

31. *The Observer,* London, December 9, 1956.

32. *Daily Herald,* London, November 17, 1956.

33. Harry S. Truman, *Memoirs,* Vol. I, *Year of Decisions,* Doubleday & Co., Inc., Garden City, N.Y., 1955, p. x.

Chapter 11

1. Harold Macmillan, *Riding the Storm,* Harper & Row, New York, 1971, pp. 180–82.

2. Anthony Eden, *Full Circle: The Memoirs of Anthony Eden,* Houghton Mifflin Company, Boston, 1960, p. 512.

3. Anthony Eden, op. cit., pp. 536–37.

4. Anthony Eden, *Another World, 1897–1917,* Doubleday & Co., Inc., New York, 1977, p. 168.

5. Dwight D. Eisenhower, *The White House Years: Waging Peace, 1956–61,* Doubleday & Co., Inc., Garden City, N.Y., 1965, p. 120.

6. *New York Times,* January 10, 1957.

7. *The Sunday Times,* London, January 13, 1957.

8. Harold Macmillan, op. cit., p. 195.

9. Ibid., p. 178.

10. *The Times,* London, January 1, 1957.

11. Harold Macmillan, op. cit., p. 178.

12. *New York Times,* December 15, 1956.

13. White House news release, January 5, 1957.

14. Harold Macmillan, op. cit., p. 119.

15. Dwight D. Eisenhower, op. cit., p. 184.

16. Ibid., Appendix J, p. 684.

17. Abba Eban, *An Autobiography,* Random House, New York, 1977, p. 243.

18. Dwight D. Eisenhower, op. cit., p.187.

19. *United States Policy in the Middle East, September 1956–June 1957,* Greenwood Press, New York, 1968, pp. 301–7.

20. Herman Finer, *Dulles over Suez,* Quadrangle Books, Chicago, 1964, p. 480.

21. U.S. Foreign Broadcast Information Service, Washington, D.C., February 22, 1957.

22. Golda Meir, *My Life,* G. P. Putnam's Sons, New York, 1975, pp. 306–7.

23. Christian Pineau, *1956/Suez,* Editions Robert Laffont, Paris, 1976, p. 214.

24. Ibid.

25. Ibid.

26. United Nations provisional document A/PV.666, March 1, 1957.

27. Christian Pineau, op. cit., p. 217.

28. White House news release, Washington, D.C., March 2, 1957.

29. Harold Macmillan, op. cit., p. 253.

30. Dwight D. Eisenhower, op. cit., p. 122.

31. *United States Policy in the Middle East,* op. cit., p. 387.

32. Ibid., p. 391.

33. Andrew J. Pierre, *Nuclear Politics,* Oxford University Press, London, 1972, p. 86.

34. *The Times,* London, November 14, 1958.

35. Paul-Henri Spaak, "The West in Disarray," *Foreign Affairs,* New York, January 1957.

Chapter 12

1. Arthur Bryant, *The Lion and the Unicorn,* Doubleday & Co., Inc., New York, 1970, p. 124.

2. Malcolm Bradbury, "The Taste for Anarchy," *Saturday Review*, New York, June 30, 1962.

3. Arthur Bryant, op. cit., p. 220.

4. Interview.

5. Christian Pineau, *1956/Suez*, Editions Robert Laffont, Paris, 1976, p. 195.

6. Ibid., p. 191.

7. Interview.

8. Christian Pineau, op. cit., p. 191.

9. Interview.

10. André Beaufre, *The Suez Expedition, 1956*, Frederick A. Praeger, New York, 1969, p. 127.

11. See Noël Mostert, *Supership*, Alfred A. Knopf, Inc., New York, 1974, for a dramatic account of the big tankers.

BIBLIOGRAPHY

Books

Acheson, Dean. *Power and Diplomacy.* Cambridge: Harvard University Press, 1958.

Adams, Sherman. *Firsthand Report.* New York: Harper & Row, 1971.

Baeyens, Jacques. *Un Coup d'épée dans l'eau du Canal.* Paris: Librairie Arthème Fayard, 1976.

Bar-Zohar, Michael. *Ben-Gurion: The Armed Prophet.* Englewood Cliffs, N.J.: Prentice-Hall, Inc., 1968.

Beaufre, General André. *The Suez Expedition, 1956.* New York: Frederick A. Praeger, 1969.

Benson, Edward Frederic. *Queen Victoria.* London: Longmans, Green and Co., 1935.

Bohlen, Charles E. *Witness to History, 1929–1969.* New York: W. W. Norton & Co., Inc., 1973.

Bowie, Robert R. *Suez 1956.* London: Oxford University Press, 1974.

Bromberger, Merry and Serge. *The Secrets of Suez.* London: Sidgwick & Jackson, 1957.

Bryant, Sir Arthur. *The Lion and the Unicorn.* New York: Doubleday & Co., Inc., 1970.

Calvocoressi, Peter. *Suez: Ten Years After.* Edited by Anthony Moncrieff. BBC Sound Archives. New York: Pantheon Books, 1967.

Childers, E. B. *The Road to Suez.* London: MacGibbon & Kee, 1962.

Churchill, Randolph S. *The Rise and Fall of Sir Anthony Eden.* London: MacGibbon & Kee, 1959.

Churchill, Winston S. *A History of the English Speaking Peoples.* London: Cassell & Co., Ltd., 1958.

———. *The Second World War.* Volumes I–VI. Boston: Houghton Mifflin Company, 1948–1953.

Copeland, Miles. *The Game of Nations.* New York: Simon and Schuster, 1969.

Crossman, Richard. *The Diaries of a Cabinet Minister.* Volumes I & II. New York: Holt, Rinehart & Winston, 1976–77.

Dayan, Moshe. *Diary of the Sinai Campaign.* New York: Schocken Books, 1965.

————. *Story of My Life.* Jerusalem and Tel Aviv: Steimatzky's Agency, Ltd., 1976.

Dekinjan, R. Hrair. *Egypt Under Nasser.* Albany: State University of New York Press, 1971.

Dewhurst, Claude. *Limelight for Suez.* Cairo: R. Schindler, 1946.

Drummond, Roscoe, and Coblentz, Gaston. *Duel at the Brink.* London: Weidenfeld and Nicolson, 1961.

Eayrs, James, ed. *The Commonwealth and Suez: A Documentary Survey.* London: Oxford University Press, 1964.

Eban, Abba. *An Autobiography.* New York: Random House, 1977.

Eden, Sir Anthony. *Another World, 1897–1917.* New York: Doubleday & Co., Inc., 1977.

————. *Full Circle: The Memoirs of Anthony Eden.* Boston: Houghton Mifflin Company, 1960.

Eisenhower, Dwight D. *The White House Years: Waging Peace. 1956–61.* Garden City, N.Y.: Doubleday & Co., Inc., 1965.

Elgood, P. G. *Egypt and the Army.* London: Oxford University Press, 1924.

Finer, Herman. *Dulles over Suez.* Chicago: Quadrangle Books, 1964.

Franck, Thomas M., and Weisband, Edward, eds. *Secrecy and Foreign Policy.* Chapter 12, "Cabinet Secrecy" by William Clark. London and Toronto: Oxford University Press, 1974.

Georges-Picot, Jacques. *The Real Suez Crisis: The End of a Great Nineteenth Century Work.* New York: Harcourt Brace Jovanovich, 1978.

Glubb, Lieutenant General Sir John Bagot. *Britain and the Arabs.* London: Hodder and Stoughton, 1959.

Hallberg, Charles W. *The Suez Canal: Its History and Diplomatic Importance.* New York: Columbia University Press, 1931.

Harriman, W. Averell, and Abel, Elie. *Special Envoy.* New York: Random House, 1975.

Heikal, Mohamed. *The Cairo Documents.* Garden City, N.Y.: Doubleday & Co., Inc., 1973.

Hoopes, Townsend. *The Devil and John Foster Dulles.* Boston: Little, Brown & Co., 1973.

Horne, Alistair. *A Savage War of Peace: Algeria 1954–1962.* New York: The Viking Press, 1977.

Johnson, Paul. *The Suez War.* London: MacGibbon & Kee, 1957.

Kennan, George F. *Memoirs, 1950–1963.* Boston: Little, Brown & Co., 1972.

Koning, Hans. *A New Yorker in Egypt.* New York and London: Harcourt Brace Jovanovich, 1976.

Laqueur, Walter Z. *The Soviet Union and the Middle East.* New York: Frederick A. Praeger, 1959.

Lenczowski, George. *Oil and State in the Middle East.* Ithaca: Cornell University Press, 1960.

Love, Kennett. *Suez: The Twice-Fought War.* New York and Toronto: McGraw-Hill Book Company, 1969.

McCullough, David. *The Path Between the Seas.* New York: Simon and Schuster, 1977.

Macmillan, Harold. *Riding the Storm.* New York: Harper & Row, 1971.

———. *Tides of Fortune, 1945–55.* New York: Harper & Row, 1969.

Mansfield, Peter. *The British in Egypt.* New York: Holt, Rinehart & Winston, 1971.

Marlowe, John. *Anglo-Egyptian Relations, 1800–1956.* 2d ed. London: Frank Cass & Co., Ltd., 1965.

Mathias, Peter. *The First Industrial Nation: An Economic History of Britain, 1700–1914.* New York: Charles Scribner's Sons, 1969.

Meir, Golda. *My Life.* New York: G. P. Putnam's Sons, 1975.

Melville, Herman. *Moby Dick.* New York: Modern Library, 1950.

Moran, Lord Charles. *Churchill: Taken from the Diaries of Lord Moran, 1940–1965.* Boston: Houghton Mifflin Company, 1966.

Mosky, Leonard. *Dulles.* New York: The Dial Press/James Wade, 1978.

Mostert, Noël. *Supership.* New York: Alfred A. Knopf, Inc., 1974.

Murphy, Robert. *Diplomat Among Warriors.* New York: Doubleday & Co., Inc., 1964.

Nutting, Anthony. *Nasser.* New York: E. P. Dutton, 1972.

———. *No End of a Lesson.* New York: Clarkson N. Potter, Inc., 1967.

Patai, Raphael. *The Arab Mind.* New York: Charles Scribner's Sons, 1973.

Pierre, Andrew J. *Nuclear Politics.* London: Oxford University Press, 1972.

Pineau, Christian. *1956/Suez.* Paris: Editions Robert Laffont, 1976.

Pudney, John. *Suez: De Lesseps' Canal.* New York and Washington: Frederick A. Praeger, 1969.

Roberts, Henry L., and Wilson, Paul A. *Britain and the United States: Problems in Cooperation.* New York: Harper & Row, 1953.

Robertson, Terence. *Crisis: The Inside Story of the Suez Conspiracy.* London: Hutchinson Press, 1964.

St. John, Robert. *Ben-Gurion.* Garden City, N.Y.: Doubleday & Co., Inc., 1959.

———. *The Boss.* New York: McGraw-Hill Book Company, 1960.

———. *Eban.* Garden City, N.Y.: Doubleday & Co., Inc., 1972.

Schonfield, Hugh J. *The Suez Canal in Peace and War, 1869–1969.* Coral Gables, Fl.: University of Miami Press, 1969.

Stanley, Henry Morton. *Through the Dark Continent.* London: George Newnes, Ltd., 1899.

Stedman, Edmund Clarence. *A Victorian Anthology, 1837–1895.* Cambridge, Mass.: Houghton Mifflin, 1895.

Thomas, Hugh. *Suez.* New York and Evanston: Harper & Row, 1966.

Trevelyan, Humphrey. *The Middle East in Revolution.* London: Macmillan and Co., Ltd., 1970.

Truman, Harry S. *Memoirs.* Vol. I. *Year of Decisions.* Garden City, N.Y.: Doubleday & Co., Inc., 1955.

Urquhart, Brian. *Hammarskjöld.* New York: Alfred A. Knopf, 1972.

Documents & Broadcasts

BBC. *Tonight: The Suez Affair.* November 8–11, 1976.

France. Assemblée Nationale. *Débats, Journal Officiel,* 1956.

Great Britain. Parliament. *Hansard,* Parliamentary Debates, 1956–1957.

Princeton, N.J. Princeton University Library. John Foster Dulles Papers.

The Royal Institute of International Affairs. *Documents on the Suez Crisis, 26 July to 6 November, 1956.* London: Eyre & Spottiswoode, Ltd., 1957.

United Nations Documents, October 1956–March 1957.

U.S. Department of State. Memoranda, September 1955–July 1956.

U.S. Department of State. Press Releases, 1956.

U.S. Department of State. *The Suez Canal Problem, July 26–September 22, 1956: A Documentary Publication,* 1957.

U.S. Department of State. *United States Foreign Relations,* 1863, 1866, 1880, 1888.

U.S. Foreign Broadcast Information Service. Middle East. July–November, 1956.

United States Policy in the Middle East, September 1956–June 1957. New York: Greenwood Press, 1968.

Washington, D.C. Library of Congress. Manuscripts Division. Nathan Appleton Papers (1854–1902).

Washington, D.C. Library of Congress. Manuscripts Division. John Bigelow Papers (1854–1936).

White Paper on the Nationalization of the Suez Maritime Canal Company. Cairo: Government Press, 1956.

Articles

Bowring, John. "Recollections of Lord Palmerston." *Fortnightly Review,* London, November 1865–February 1866.

Bradbury, Malcolm. "The Taste for Anarchy." *Saturday Review,* New York, June 30, 1962.

Eayrs, James. "Canadian Policy and Opinion During the Suez Crisis." *International Journal,* Canadian Institute of International Affairs, Toronto, Vol. 12, No. 2, 1957.

Eclectic Magazine, W. H. Bidwell, New York, Vol. LX, 1863.

Howard, Anthony. "Memoirs of a Suez Warrior." *New Statesman,* London, October 29, 1976.

Kennan, George F. "United States and the Soviet Union." *Foreign Affairs,* New York, July 1976.

"Lesseps' Recollections." Review of *Recollections of Forty Years* by Ferdinand de Lesseps, *The Nation,* New York, Vol. XVI, 1888.

The Listener, London, Nov. 4, 1976.

Morse, Robert. "After Eight Years, World's Shipping Is Moving Through Suez Canal." *Smithsonian,* Washington, D.C., October 1975.

Nasser, Gamal Abdel. "The Egyptian Revolution." *Foreign Affairs,* New York, January 1955.

The Nation, London, 1920.

Nourse, J. E. "Ferdinand de Lesseps." *Lippincott's Magazine,* Philadelphia, March 1874.

P. H. M. "The Suez Canal—A History." *Appleton's Journal,* New York, April 1880.

Pearson, Lester B. "Force for U.N." *Foreign Affairs,* New York, April 1957.

"Political Career of Mr. Disraeli." *British Quarterly Review,* Hodder and Stoughton, London, July 1, 1876.

The Practical Magazine, The Willmer and Rogers News Company, New York, Vol. 5, No. 6, 1875.

Spaak, Paul-Henri. "The West in Disarray." *Foreign Affairs,* New York, January 1957.

Wheatley, G. W. "Some Account of the Late Lieut. Waghorn, R.N., The Originator of the Overland Route." *Bentley's Miscellany,* London, Vol. 27, 1850.

INDEX